Commission of the European Communities

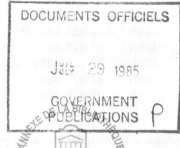

Eighteenth General Report on the Activities of the European Communities 1984

Brussels • Luxembourg • 1985

This publication is also available in the following languages:

DA	ISBN	92-825-4855-4
DE	ISBN	92-825-4856-2
GR	ISBN	92-825-4857-0
FR	ISBN	92-825-4859-7
IT	ISBN	92-825-4860-0
NL	ISBN	92-825-4861-9

Cataloguing data can be found at the end of this publication

Luxembourg: Office for Official Publications of the European Communities, 1985

ISBN 92-825-4858-9

Catalogue number: CB-41-84-814-EN-C

The President and the Members of the Commission of the European Communities to the President of the European Parliament

Sir,

We have the honour to present the General Report on the Activities of the Communities, which the Commission is required to publish by Article 18 of the Treaty establishing a Single Council and a Single Commission of the European Communities.

This report, for 1984, is the eighteenth since the merger of the executives.

In accordance with the procedure described in the Declaration on the System for Fixing Community Farm Prices contained in the Accession Documents of 22 January 1972, the Commission has already sent Parliament the 1984 Report on the Agricultural Situation in the Community.

Under Article 122 of the Treaty establishing the European Economic Community, the Commission is also preparing a Report on Social Developments in the Community in 1984.

And, in accordance with an undertaking given to Parliament on 7 June 1971, the Commission is preparing its fourteenth annual Report on Competition Policy.

Please accept, Sir, the expression of our highest consideration.

Brussels, 5 January 1985

Gaston THORN
President

Wilhelm HAFERKAMP
Vice-President

Lorenzo NATALI
Vice-President

Étienne DAVIGNON
Vice-President

Christopher Samuel TUGENDHAT
Vice-President

Richard BURKE
Vice-President

Antonio GIOLITTI

Giorgios CONTOGEORGIS

Karl-Heinz NARJES

Frans ANDRIESSEN

Ivor RICHARD

Poul DALSAGER

Mr François-Xavier Ortoli, Vice-President, and Mr Edgard Pisani, Vice-President, resigned from the Commission on 26 October and 3 December respectively.

Margin index

Contents

The following currency abbreviations are being used in all language versions of the
General Report and of the other reports published in conjunction with it.

ECU = European currency unit
BFR = Belgische frank/franc belge
DKR = Dansk krone
DM = Deutsche Mark
DR = Greek drachma
FF = Franc français
IRL = Irish pound
LIT = Lira italiana
LFR = Franc luxembourgeois
HFL = Nederlandse gulden (Hollandse florijn)
UKL = Pound sterling
USD = United States dollar

The Community in 1984

General survey

In 1984 the economic climate in the Community was much more favourable than it had been in the previous four years. The recovery that began in the second half of 1983 continued and did much to improve the economic situation. The Community as a whole made significant progress in industrial production and productive investment. Exports expanded, with beneficial effects on the balance of payments, and inflation slowed down. There was also a marked improvement in economic convergence.

External factors, including the vigorous expansion of the US economy and the rise of the dollar (though that has its drawbacks too), sustained and boosted exports.

But despite the revival in economic activity, unemployment, which is now blighting the lives of more than 12 million Europeans, has not been brought under control. Unemployment figures are levelling out in some Member States, but they are still rising in the others. The scale and persistence of unemployment, especially among the young, remains a major cause for concern in all Member States. The question now is whether the Community will succeed in reducing unemployment and stepping up job creation in 1985. This will be one of the priorities—and one of the most difficult tasks—of the incoming Commission.

During the year significant progress was made towards completing the general policy review begun in Stuttgart in June 1983. The Fontainebleau European Council made considerable headway on a number of difficult issues, including reform of the common agricultural policy and the search for an overall compromise in the dispute over financing and the Community budget, thereby giving the green light for reactivation of the accession negotiations.

Notable events in the external relations field included successful completion of the negotiations with the African, Caribbean and Pacific (ACP) countries for the third Lomé Convention, numerous meetings with the US and Japanese authorities, and the San José Conference in Costa Rica.

On the institutional front, a major political development was the adoption by Parliament of the draft Treaty establishing European Union. It has revitalized the debate on the future of the Community and has already provoked ideas and stimulated top-level discussions.

This renewal of the institutional debate prompted the Fontainebleau European Council to set up a Committee on Institutional Affairs, which submitted an interim report to the Dublin European Council. The Committee's full report is to be laid before the European Council in March and will be one of the main items of business at the June meeting. Another decision taken at Fontainebleau was to set up an ad hoc Committee on a People's Europe, which is to prepare measures that will give Europeans a clearer and more positive idea of what the Community is.

Although there was still no uniform electoral system, nearly 120 million Europeans went to the polls for the second time to elect the European Parliament. But the lack of enthusiasm shown by the electorate is a reflection of the deep unease felt by the people of Europe as integration marks time. For the Community's inability to take decisions is becoming more and more obvious. The shortcomings of the Community's cumbersome decision-making procedures are blocking dynamic development, and the practice of making one issue dependent on another tends to hamper any fresh moves.

The Community in the world

The conclusion of the new Convention with the 65 ACP countries was an outstanding event. After laborious negotiations the third Lomé Convention, which boasts many improvements and innovations, was signed in December. The special relationship between the Community and its developing ACP partners was safeguarded. It will continue to be the cornerstone of the Community's policy on development.

Special emphasis was laid on self-sufficiency in food supplies, which has worsened in these countries over the years, by integrating aid in the form of agricultural products more closely into local food strategies. The insecurity of food supplies was dramatically highlighted once again by the famine which assumed tragic proportions in the Sahel and southern Africa. It prompted massive emergency aid from the Community and the Member States. The long-term solution to this problem, which is threatening the lives of millions, is causing concern not only in the Community but throughout the industrialized world.

Turning to the Community's industrialized partners, relations with the United States were dominated by American protectionism. However, thanks to the ongoing dialogue with the US authorities, it proved possible, despite recurring incidents, to prevent tension escalating. The 1982 Steel Arrangement was kept alive and problems involving wine were solved, temporarily at least. But fresh difficulties involving steel pipes and tubes made their appearance towards the end of the year.

Relations with Japan were marked by a growing Japanese awareness of the Community dimension, symbolized by a ministerial meeting with the Commission in the spring. The structural imbalance in trade between the Community and Japan appears to have stabilized. But economic measures designed to open up the Japanese market to Community goods are still relatively limited in range and effect and will not be enough to reverse the present trend. In other areas, notably investment and technology transfer, cooperation with Japan progressed.

Trade, scientific and technical relations with the Community's nearest partners, the EFTA countries, were further strengthened. For the first time ever, a meeting of the Foreign Ministers of all 17 countries was held in Luxembourg. In a Joint Declaration they indicated the areas in which they will pursue and intensify cooperation.

Relations with Latin America moved to a new plane with the organization of a series of bilateral meetings. A new structure for political and economic dialogue with Central America was set up at the San José Conference in Costa Rica. The Community undertook to make a special effort to promote development, advancement and economic integration in the region.

In Asia, the cooperation agreement with China was extended to include the economy, industry and technology, pointing to closer relations and increased trade. The ministerial consultations held in Peking in the autumn were a first expression of this new approach.

Enlargement of the Community

Thanks to many meetings held during the year, considerable progress was made in the accession negotiations with Spain and Portugal. In response to political pressure from certain Member States and the justified impatience of the appli-

cant countries, meeting after meeting was held to define the Community's negotiating position. The Dublin European Council resolved a number of thorny problems, particularly wine, which meant that the negotiations could resume at a brisk pace towards the end of the year. But the Dublin meeting failed to find an acceptable formula for funding the integrated Mediterranean programmes, which are designed to speed up modernization of the Community's southern regions. The link which Greek reservations have established between enlargement and these programmes means that the actual date of accession is somewhat uncertain.

Relations with countries south of the Mediterranean were coloured by the prospect of enlargement and the repercussions this would have on traditional exports to the Community.

The Community's internal development

In March the Council, faced with the need for budgetary restraint, embarked on rationalization of the common agricultural policy in line with the realities of production and consumption. 'Guarantee thresholds' now apply to one third of all agricultural output in terms of value. The milk and milk products sector, where a quota system will operate for five years, provided the model. For cereals, the Community's prices will gradually be brought into line with those of its main competitors to make Community products more competitive on domestic and foreign markets. The Council also decided to dismantle existing monetary compensatory amounts (MCAs) step by step, so as to get back to a single price system, and approved arrangements to prevent the creation of new positive MCAs in the event of a realignment of central rates within the European Monetary System. The Dublin European Council agreed on the broad lines of a reform of the common organization of the market in wine, the aim being to bring production under control prior to enlargement.

The budget dispute, the root cause of the crisis which had dogged the Community since 1979, was resolved at the Fontainebleau European Council in June. A correction mechanism was introduced to provide an annual rebate to the United Kingdom on VAT own resources paid into the Community budget. Agreement was also reached on raising the VAT call-up rate from 1% to 1.4% on 1 January 1986, the target date for enlargement.

However, the respite will be brief. The budget issue will have to be reopened in 1985 since the new VAT own resources made available, which amount to no more than a 0.4% increase, are already mortgaged against the expected cost of enlargement, the 'correction' for the United Kingdom and expenditure postponed until 1986. The problem of the precise budgetary roles of the Council and Parliament remains unresolved, since the two arms of the budgetary authority failed to agree on arrangements for fixing the necessary reference framework for determining annual expenditure. Parliament's rejection of the 1985 draft budget highlights the financial stalemate in which the Community is locked.

In the research and development field, inauguration of the JET (Joint European Torus) project in Culham and agreement on the Esprit programme are shining examples of what can be achieved by joint European action. They point up its crucial importance if the Community is to narrow the technological gap in an area which is vital to Europe's industrial future. The modest progress made in liberalizing public procurement for telecommunications is a further step in the right direction.

There was a renewed awareness in 1984 of the need to consolidate the internal market—an operation which has the singular advantage of escaping the usual budget constraints. The Commission's new approach enabled significant results to be achieved in removing technical barriers to trade, promoting a European standards policy and simplifying administrative formalities by the adoption of a 'single Community customs document'.

The 'internal market' should not be viewed as a purely economic concept. It must be seen to impact upon the everyday lives of the citizens of Europe: easing controls on their movements from one Community country to another is a means to that end.

After three years of negotiations the new European Regional Development Fund Regulation was approved. This will enhance the effectiveness of the Community's structural Funds and help to promote economic convergence by reducing regional disparities. The new Regulation introduces major improvements to provide the Commission with an armoury more adapted to the complexities of its task.

The Council reached agreement on the future relationship between the Community and Greenland, which will enjoy OCT (Overseas Countries and Territories) status but will also benefit from a number of specific arrangements on fisheries.

Although there was political breakthrough on a number of key issues in 1984, decisions on other equally important matters will have to be taken in 1985 if *the action begun is to be brought to fruition. These include the 1985 budget, the whole complex of financial issues (including new own resources and funding of integrated Mediterranean programmes), the development of new policies and completion of the negotiations for Spanish and Portuguese accession. Yet another major issue calling for a decision is the institutional reform envisaged by the Dooge Committee.*

This introduction can do no more than provide a brief review of the main developments on the Community scene in 1984. Details of activities and achievements within the various Community institutions will be found in the body of this Report.

Chapter I

Community institutions and financing

Section 1

Institutions and other bodies

European policy and relations between institutions

European policy

European Union

1.   On 14 February Parliament, by an overwhelming majority, adopted the draft Treaty establishing the European Union put to it by its Committee on Institutional Affairs. [1] This marked the end of the process which began with the formation of the Committee in July 1981 [2] and continued throughout 1982 [3] and 1983. [4]

The draft Treaty has been transmitted to the parliaments and governments of the Community Member States.

Ad hoc Committee on Institutional Affairs

2.   The Fontainebleau European Council decided to set up an *ad hoc* Committee of personal nominees of the Heads of State or Government of the Member States and the President of the Commission to make suggestions 'for the

---

[1] OJ C 77, 19.3.1984; Bull. EC 2-1984, point 1.1.1 *et seq*.
[2] Fifteenth General Report, point 15.
[3] Sixteenth General Report, point 17.
[4] Seventeenth General Report, points 2 and 3.

improvement of the operation of European cooperation in both the Community field and that of political, or any other, cooperation'. [1]

3.   In July Parliament adopted a resolution[2] asking to be associated with the work of this Committee and urging it to use the draft Treaty adopted by Parliament in February as a basis for its discussions. [3]

4.   The Committee has met regularly since September. [4] On two occasions it was addressed by Mr Pflimlin, the President of Parliament, and Mr Spinelli, Chairman of Parliament's Committee on Institutional Affairs and originator of the draft Treaty. [5]

In the interim report which it presented to the European Council in Dublin, the Committee recommended that an intergovernmental conference be held in order to negotiate a draft Treaty of European Union on the basis of existing Community achievements, the report itself, further reports to the European Council and the Stuttgart Solemn Declaration on European Union, in accordance with the spirit and method of the draft Treaty voted by Parliament.

The European Council met in Dublin on 3 and 4 December[6] and asked the Committee to complete its work for the next European Council meeting, in March 1985, and to submit a report which, after preliminary consideration at that meeting, would be the main subject of the following meeting, to be held in June.

In a resolution adopted on 12 December, Parliament recommended that the intergovernmental conference be convened after the European Council meeting in June 1985, that the draft Treaty voted by Parliament be taken as its basis, and that a suitable procedure be set up between Parliament and the conference in order to arrive at an agreement concerning the text to be submitted for ratification by the relevant national procedures. [7]

Ad hoc Committee on a People's Europe

5.   The Fontainebleau European Council also decided to set up an *ad hoc* Committee of representatives of the Heads of State or Government and the President of the Commission to prepare and coordinate action 'to strengthen

---

[1] Bull. EC 6-1984, point 1.1.9 (paragraph 7).
[2] OJ C 239, 10.9.1984; Bull. EC 7/8-1984, point 2.4.16.
[3] Point 1 of this Report; Bull. EC 2-1984, point 1.1.1 *et seq.*
[4] Bull. EC 9-1984, point 2.4.4; Bull. EC 11-1984, point 2.4.7.
[5] OJ C 77, 19.3.1984; Bull. EC 2-1984, point 1.1.1 *et seq.*
[6] Bull. EC 12-1984.
[7] OJ C 12, 14.1.1985; Bull. EC 12-1984.

and promote the identity and image [of the Community] for both its citizens and for the rest of the world'.[1]

The Committee, which has been meeting since November, has concentrated its efforts on practical matters affecting European citizens, such as the crossing of borders, tax reliefs, freedom of movement, mutual recognition of degrees, diplomas, etc. and will postpone until later its consideration of the more symbolic ideas put forward by the European Council (the introduction of a European flag and anthem, the minting of ECUs, etc.).

In November it presented an interim report to the European Council.[2] The European Council meeting in Dublin on 3 and 4 December asked the Committee to make a further report to it for its next meeting in March 1985.[3]

Greek memorandum

6. In a statement issued on 10 April[4] the Council confirmed the Community's resolve to give due consideration to the special problems of the Greek economy on the basis of the analysis made by the Greek authorities in March 1982.[5] Some of Greece's demands have already been met in the Regulations adopted by the Council, which make provision for Community assistance to Greece for agricultural,[6] social[7] and transport[8] projects.

In May the Commission sent the Council further proposals for regulations on agriculture.[9] Parliament gave a favourable opinion on these proposals on 24 May.[10]

Greenland

7. On 20 February the Council approved an agreement, which was signed on 12 March, on future relations between Greenland and the Community.[11] The main elements of the agreement were: OCT status for Greenland, free

---

[1] Bull. EC 6-1984, point 1.1.9 (paragraph 7).
[2] Bull. EC 11-1984, point 2.4.8.
[3] Bull. EC 12-1984.
[4] Bull. EC 4-1984, point 2.4.5.
[5] Sixteenth General Report, point 20.
[6] OJ L 68, 10.3.1984; Bull. EC 3-1984, point 2.4.7.
[7] OJ L 88, 31.3.1984; Bull. EC 3-1984, point 2.4.8; Bull. EC 10-1984, point 2.4.2.
[8] Bull. EC 3-1984, point 2.4.9; Bull. EC 5-1984, point 2.4.6.
[9] Bull. EC 5-1984, point 2.4.7.
[10] OJ C 172, 2.7.1984; Bull. EC 5-1984, point 2.4.14.
[11] Bull. EC 2-1984, point 1.4.1 et seq.

access to the Community for Greenland fishery products, continuing access for Community fishermen to Greenland waters, with a commitment by both parties to conservation and sound management of fish stocks in those waters, and an annual payment of 26 500 000 ECU to Greenland in consideration of these fishing rights.

The Treaty and the attached documents dealing with the future status of Greenland were sent to the 10 Member States for ratification by their parliaments, so that they might come into force on 1 January 1985. As not all of the ratification procedures could be completed in time, the Council has made specific arrangements in the field of fisheries, in line with the provisions of the relevant texts.

Parliament adopted two resolutions on the fisheries aspect of the agreement. [1]

Relations between institutions

8.   The Council informed Parliament [2] that, under the provisions of the Solemn Declaration on European Union, [3] it would consult it prior to the conclusion of 'significant' international agreements by the Community and the accession of new States to the Community.

9.   Parliament passed several resolutions in support of its demand to be given a greater say in the appointment of the new Commission. [4]

10.   On 9 March the Commission asked the Council [5] to begin discussion without delay on the draft Joint Declaration of the Council, Parliament and the Commission on an improved conciliation procedure, which was proposed by the Commission in 1981 [6] and approved by Parliament in December 1983. [7] On 19 June the Council examined a paper from the chair aimed at improving the conciliation procedure. [8] This also formed the subject of a meeting between the enlarged Bureau of Parliament and the Ministers for Foreign Affairs of the Member States, with the President of the Commission also taking part. Because

[1] OJ C 77, 19.3.1984; Bull. EC 2-1984, point 2.4.14; OJ C 172, 2.7.1984.
[2] Bull. EC 3-1984, point 2.4.11.
[3] Supplement 3/82 — Bull. EC; Bull. EC 6-1983, point 1.6.1 (paragraph 2.3.7).
[4] OJ C 117, 30.4.1984; Bull. EC 3-1984, point 2.4.12.
[5] Bull. EC 3-1984, point 2.4.10.
[6] Supplement 3/82 — Bull. EC; Bull. EC 12-1981, point 1.3.1 et seq.
[7] OJ C 10, 16.1.1983.
[8] Bull. EC 6-1984, point 2.4.3.

of the opposition of one of the Member States no progress had been made by the end of the year.

Parliament

11. The second direct elections to the European Parliament took place on 14 and 17 June. [1]

12. Seats in the new Parliament are distributed as follows: [2]

Socialists:	130
European People's Party:	110
European Democratic Group:	50
Communists and Allies:	41
Liberals and Democrats:	31
European Democratic Alliance (formerly the European Progressive Democrats):	29
Rainbow Group:	20
European Right:	16
Non-affiliated:	7

13. At its first part-session Parliament elected Mr Pierre Pflimlin President. [3]

Mrs Maria Luisa Cassanmagnago Cerreti (EPP/I), Mr Siegbert Alber (EPP/D), Lady Diana Elles (ED/UK), Mr Hans Nord (Lib/NL), Mr Patrick Joseph Lalor (EDA/IRL), Mr Horst Seefeld (Soc/D), Mr Mario Didò (Soc/I), Mr Winston Griffiths (Soc/UK), Mr Guidi Fanti (Com/I), Mr Spyridon Plaskovitis (Soc/G), Mrs Nicole Pery (Soc/F) and Mr Poul Møller (ED/DK) were elected Vice-Presidents, and Mr Ernest Glinne (Soc/B), Mr Kurt Wawrzik (EPP/D), Mr Thomas Maher (Lib/IRL), Mr Anthony Simpson (ED/UK) and Mr Angelo Carossino (Com/I) were elected Quaestors.

Parliament decided to set up 18 committees. [4] The Committee of Inquiry into the Treatment of Toxic and Dangerous Substances by the European

---

[1] Bull. EC 6-1984, point 1.2.1 *et seq.*
[2] At 31 December. Bull. EC 7/8-1984, points 1.2.5 and 1.2.6.
[3] Bull. EC 7/8-1984, points 2.4.8 to 2.4.14.
[4] On 31 December the Committees were as follows: Political Affairs (45 members); Agriculture, Fisheries and Food (45); Budgets (42); Economic and Monetary Affairs and Industrial Policy (42); Energy, Research and Technology (30); External Economic Relations (25); Legal Affairs and Citizens' Rights (25); Social Affairs and Employment (30); Regional Policy and Regional Planning (28); Transport (30); Environment, Public Health and Consumer Protection (31); Youth, Culture, Education, Information and Sport (24); Development and Cooperation (42); Budgetary Control (30); Rules of Procedure and Petitions (25); Institutional Affairs (30); Women's Rights (25); Verification of Credentials (9).

Communities and their Member States and the Committee of Inquiry into the Situation of Women in Europe had been of an *ad hoc* nature and now no longer exist; the latter was replaced by a standing committee. A Committee of Inquiry was also set up to investigate the rise of fascism and racism in Europe, in the Community and elsewhere.

14.   Parliament continued its work on the institutional front by adopting the draft Treaty establishing the European Union in February. [1]

During the year Parliament debated the following major issues: budgetary matters, [2] the situation of women, [3] reform of the common agricultural policy, [4] the redefinition of the Community's relations with the United States, [5] the enlargement negotiations, [6] the monetary situation [7] and the famine in Ethiopia and the Sahel; [8] it also adopted a 'plan for European economic recovery'. [9] Parliament adopted a number of resolutions on political cooperation and human rights, particularly with reference to the war between Iran and Iraq, [10] the situation in Lebanon, [11] Afghanistan, [12] Northern Ireland, [13] Iran, [12] continuing violations of human rights in Turkey, [14] the Sakharovs, [15] the arrest of political leaders in Chile[16] and free electoral choice in Nicaragua, [17] the arrest of Mr Jacques Abouchar in Afghanistan[18] and the murder of Father Popieluszko in Poland.[19]

15.   Parliament held 12 part-sessions. It passed 308 resolutions, which included 146 resolutions embodying opinions, 103 resolutions by urgent pro-

---

[1] Bull. EC 2-1984, point 1.1.1 *et seq.*; point 1 of this Report.
[2] OJ C 127, 4.5.1984; Bull. EC 4-1984, point 2.4.9; OJ C 274, 15.10.1984; Bull. EC 9-1984, point 2.4.7; OJ C 300, 12.11.1984; Bull. EC 10-1984, point 2.4.4; OJ C 315, 26.11.1984; Bull. EC 10-1984, point 2.4.9; OJ C 337, 17.12.1984; Bull. EC 11-1984, points 2.4.11 to 2.4.13; OJ C 12, 14.1.1985; Bull. EC 12-1984.
[3] OJ C 46, 20.2.1984; Bull. EC 1-1984, points 2.4.6 and 2.4.7.
[4] OJ C 104, 16.4.1984; Bull. EC 3-1984, point 2.4.14.
[5] OJ C 127, 4.5.1984; Bull. EC 4-1984, point 2.4.7.
[6] OJ C 274, 15.10.1984; Bull. EC 9-1984, point 2.4.7.
[7] OJ C 300, 12.11.1984; Bull. EC 10-1984, point 2.4.5.
[8] OJ C 337, 17.12.1984; Bull. EC 11-1984, point 2.4.11.
[9] OJ C 104, 16.4.1984; Bull. EC 3-1984, points 2.4.19 and 2.4.20.
[10] OJ C 46, 20.2.1984; Bull. EC 1-1984, point 2.4.11; OJ C 172, 2.7.1984; Bull. EC 5-1984, point 2.4.16.
[11] OJ C 77, 19.3.1984; Bull. EC 2-1984, point 2.4.15; OJ C 127, 4.5.1984; Bull. EC 4-1984, point 2.4.11.
[12] OJ C 77, 19.3.1984; Bull. EC 2-1984, point 2.4.15.
[13] OJ C 104, 16.4.1984; Bull. EC 3-1984, point 2.4.23; OJ C 300, 12.11.1984; Bull. EC 10-1984, point 2.4.8.
[14] OJ C 172, 2.7.1984; Bull. EC 5-1984, point 2.4.16.
[15] OJ C 172, 2.7.1984; Bull. EC 5-1984, point 2.4.16; OJ C 239, 10.9.1984; Bull. EC 7/8-1984, point 2.4.17.
[16] OJ C 46, 20.2.1984; Bull. EC 1-1984, point 2.4.11.
[17] OJ C 104, 16.4.1984; Bull. EC 3-1984, point 2.4.18.
[18] OJ C 300, 12.11.1984; Bull. EC 10-1984, point 2.4.8; OJ C 315, 26.11.1984; Bull. EC 10-1984, point 2.4.13.
[19] OJ C 337, 17.12.1984; Bull. EC 11-1984, point 2.4.16.

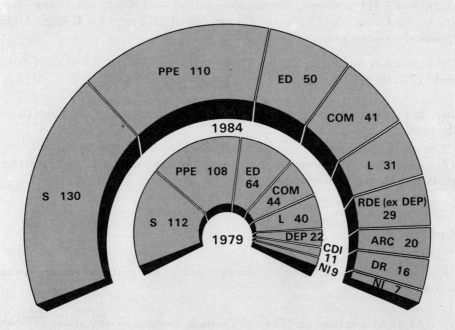

Elections of the European Parliament 1979 and 1984

The minimum number of Members required to form a political group is 21 if all the Members come from a single Member State, 15 if they come from two Member States and 10 if they come from three or more Member States.

1979 : The political groups are indicated by the following abbreviations: S (Socialist), PPE (European People's Party, Christian-Democratic Group), ED (European Democratic Group, formerly European Conservative Group), COM (Communist and Allies), L (Liberal and Democrat), DEP (European Progressive Democrats), CDI (Group for the Technical Coordination and Defence of Independent Groups and Members), NI (Non-attached). Total number of Members 410.

1984 : S (Socialist), PPE (European People's Party), ED (European Democratic Group), COM (Communist and Allies), L (Liberal and Democrat), RDE (European Democratic Alliance), ARC (Rainbow Group), DR (European Right), NI (Non-attached). Total number of Members 434 since Greece's accession.

cedure, 18 resolutions following an early vote, 15 resolutions by written procedure and 172 resolutions on own-initiative reports. It produced 1 700 working documents (224 requests for opinions, 275 reports and 1 122 motions for resolutions).

A total of 2 311 written questions were tabled — 1 976 to the Commission, 262 to the Council and 73 to the Conference of Ministers for Foreign Affairs (political cooperation).

Oral questions numbered 878 — 526 to the Commission, 235 to the Council and 117 to the Conference of Ministers for Foreign Affairs.

16.   In preparation for debates Parliament's committees met 270 times during the year.

17.   The 1984 establishment plan of the Secretariat contained 2 635 permanent posts and 323 temporary ones.

Council

18.   France was in the chair for the first half of the year and Ireland for the second half.

19.   At its 84 meetings in 1984 the Council adopted 53 directives, 351 regulations and 99 decisions.

20.   The European Council met three times — in Brussels in March, in Fontainebleau in June and in Dublin in December. [1]

Intense preparations were made for the Brussels meeting [2] to avoid another failure. [3] Agreement was reached on a large number of issues, but failure to produce a formula for calculating the United Kingdom's refund [4] meant that only the agreement on reform of the common agricultural policy could be finalized. [4] Once the refund issue had been settled at the Fontainebleau European Council, the way was clear for implementation of the agreements reached

---

[1]   Bull. EC 3-1984, point 1.1.1 et seq.; Bull. EC 6-1984, point 1.1.1 et seq.; Bull. EC 12-1984.
[2]   Bull. EC 1-1984, point 2.4.3; Bull. EC 2-1984, point 2.4.9.
[3]   Seventeenth General Report, point 18.
[4]   Bull. EC 3-1984, points 1.1.1 and 1.2.1 et seq.

in Brussels. [1] This meant that an overall solution had finally been found to the budget dispute which had gradually paralysed the Community since 1979. It has three elements: own resources (the call-up rate for VAT will increase to 1.4% from 1 January 1986); budgetary and financial discipline; and the method of calculation and the amount of compensation to be paid to the United Kingdom. [2] The agreements on new policies and the structural Funds reached in March were also confirmed. The European Council reiterated its desire to see the enlargement negotiations concluded rapidly and laid down guidelines for certain aspects of this work. It also decided to set up two *ad hoc* committees, one on institutional affairs and one on the preparation and coordination of action on 'a people's Europe'.

The Dublin European Council [3] reached agreement on reforms in the common organization of the wine market, allowing the resumption of the negotiations with Spain and Portugal, although the agreement was subject to a reservation entered by the Greek Government, linked to the adoption of integrated Mediterranean programmes. The meeting agreed to strengthen the European Monetary System and to expand the role of the ECU. It decided that further food aid should be sent to Ethiopia and the Sahel.

21.   Mr Claude Cheysson and Dr Garret FitzGerald reported to Parliament on the outcome of the European Council meetings. [4]

22.   There were 1 790 permanent posts and 2 temporary posts on the Council establishment plan for 1984.

Commission

23.   The Commission held 44 meetings (composed of 82 sittings). It adopted 5 190 instruments (regulations, decisions, directives, recommendations, opinions), and sent the Council 555 proposals, recommendations or drafts for Council instruments, and 242 communications, memoranda and reports.

24.   Mr François-Xavier Ortoli, Vice-President, having been appointed chairman and managing director of the Compagnie française des pétroles, resigned

---

[1] Bull. EC 3-1984, point 1.1.1 *et seq.*
[2] Points 80 to 82 of this Report.
[3] Bull. EC 12-1984.
[4] Bull. EC 3-1984, point 1.1.3; Bull. EC 7/8-1984, point 2.4.15; Bull. EC 12-1984.

from the Commission with effect from 26 October.[1] On 6 November the Council decided it was not necessary to replace Mr Ortoli as a Member of the Commission before the new Commission was appointed.

On 12 November the Representatives of the Governments of the Member States decided after consulting the Commission to appoint Mr Edgard Pisani Vice-President to replace Mr Ortoli for the remainder of the Commission's term.[2]

Mr Pisani himself resigned from the Commission with effect from 3 December, having been appointed the French Government's delegate in New Caledonia.[3] On 11 December the Council decided not to replace him as Member of the Commission before the new Commission was appointed. On 17 December the Representatives of the Governments of the Member States, after consulting the Commission, appointed Mr Richard Burke Vice-President of the Commission, replacing Mr Pisani until 5 January 1985.[4]

25.   On 4 December the Representatives of the Governments of the Member States, meeting within the European Council, by common accord nominated the Members of the Commission, with Mr Jacques Delors as President, for the period 6 January 1985 to 5 January 1989.[4] The Vice-Presidents are to be nominated later.

Responsibilities will be apportioned among the Members of the new Commission as follows:

Mr Jacques Delors (President): Secretariat-General, Legal Service, Spokesman's Group, Joint Interpreting and Conference Service, Security Office, monetary affairs, coordination of structural Funds;

Mr Lorenzo Natali: cooperation and development, enlargement;

Mr Karl-Heinz Narjes: industrial affairs, information technology, research and science, Joint Research Centre;

Mr Frans H.J.J. Andriessen: agriculture and fisheries;

Lord Cockfield: internal market, Customs Union Service, taxation, financial institutions;

Mr Claude Cheysson: Mediterranean policy and North-South relations;

Mr Alois Pfeiffer: economic affairs, employment, credit and investments, Statistical Office;

---

[1] Bull. EC 10-1984, point 2.4.16.
[2] OJ L 299, 17.11.1984.
[3] Bull. EC 12-1984.
[4] OJ L 341, 29.12.1984.

Mr Grigoris Varfis: regional policy, relations with Parliament;

Mr Willy De Clercq: external relations and commercial policy;

Mr Nicolas Mosar: energy, Euratom Supply Agency, Official Publications Office;

Mr Stanley Clinton Davis: environment, consumer protection, nuclear safety, forestry, transport;

Mr Carlo Ripa di Meana: institutional matters, matters relating to a people's Europe, information policy, culture, tourism;

Mr Henning Christophersen: budget, financial control, personnel and administration;

Mr Peter Sutherland: competition, social affairs, education and training.

Agreement had been reached on the appointment of Mr Delors as President following the Fontainebleau European Council. [1] In the months which followed, Mr Delors held consultations with the governments of the Member States on the composition of the new Commission. In November he met Parliament's Political Affairs Committee.

26.   On the Commission's establishment plan for 1984 there were 9 642 permanent posts (including 1 327 LA (language service) posts) and 395 temporary posts (including 60 LA) paid out of the administrative appropriations; 2 595 permanent and 256 temporary posts paid out of research appropriations; 312 permanent posts in the Office for Official Publications; 43 permanent posts at the European Centre for the Development of Vocational Training and 37 at the European Foundation for the Improvement of Living and Working Conditions.

27.   Under the arrangements between the Commission and Member States' government departments, 24 officials took part in exchange visits for limited periods.

Staff Regulations

28.   The Commission sent the Council a proposal for special and temporary measures for terminating the service of certain scientific and technical staff [2] and a proposal for a Regulation on the five-yearly verification of salary weightings.

---

[1] Bull. EC 7/8-1984, point 2.4.7.
[2] OJ C 176, 5.7.1984.

29. With a view to the accession of Spain and Portugal, the Commission adopted several proposals for regulations to be transmitted to the Council: the first would introduce special and temporary measures applicable to the recruitment of officials; the second would introduce special measures to terminate the service of Community officials; the third would amend Regulation No 260/68 of 29 February 1968 laying down the conditions and procedure for applying the tax for the benefit of the European Communities;[1] the fourth would amend Regulation No 549/69 of 25 March 1969 determining the categories of officials and other servants of the European Communities to whom the provisions of Article 12, the second paragraph of Article 13 and Article 14 of the Protocol on the Privileges and Immunities of the Communities apply.[2]

30. Proposals for amending the conditions of employment of temporary staff to clarify their contracts of employment[3] and for adjustments to their pension and social security scheme[4] are still before the Council.

Data processing

31. In response to the growing demands for machine translation and the need for modern equipment offering satisfactory performance at reasonable cost, the Commission adopted a strategy based on the following principles: a multi-supplier procurement policy, a distributed data-processing architecture, common standards for systems interconnection and maximum portability of applications. The Commission adopted its equipment policy for the period up to 1989 on the basis of two invitations to tender for the selection of suppliers for distributed equipment and the design of the Computer Centre.

32. The data-processing organization introduced in 1982[5] was adapted to the rapid expansion of services offered to users. User support teams were strengthened to provide more assistance to the decentralized data-processing units in the Directorates-General. The software library being set up at present will increase the productivity of applications development and provide users

[1] OJ L 56, 4.3.1968.
[2] OJ L 74, 27.3.1969.
[3] OJ C 213, 9.8.1983.
[4] OJ C 191, 30.7.1979.
[5] Fifteenth General Report, point 51; Sixteenth General Report, point 45; Seventeenth General Report, point 26.

with the data-processing tools they need for electronic offices (e.g. word processing) and personal computers.

33.   Interinstitutional collaboration, coordinated by the Interinstitutional Informatics Committee, has led to the other institutions being given access to the results of invitations to tender issued by the Commission, particularly for equipment and software, and to the coordination of applications development. The interinstitutional documentation centre set up at the end of 1983 is now operational.

The Insis programme for collaboration between the institutions, national government departments (including the telecommunications authorities) and industry was expanded to include the new videotex project for improved transmission of information to Members of the European Parliament.

Language Services

34.   The Commission considered the implications of enlargement for its interpreting and translation services. As regards interpretation, it declared itself in favour of pragmatic arrangements, based on real needs, which would maintain the high quality and efficiency of the interpreting system and which would not result in any language being pushed aside.

An agreement on working conditions and remuneration for freelance interpreters covering the period 1984 to 1988 was concluded between the International Association of Conference Interpreters on the one hand and Parliament, the Commission and the Court of Justice on the other.

The technical assistance provided by the Joint Interpreting and Conference Service (JICS) since 1979 was written into the commercial and economic cooperation agreement between the EEC and China initialled in September. [1]

The JICS continued its effort to recruit and train conference interpreters for the Community languages and Serbo-Croat. A total of 68 tests were organized in Athens, Brussels, Cambridge, Dublin, London, New York and, with an eye to enlargement, Lisbon.

35.   In October the Commission reorganized its Brussels and Luxembourg units to improve the coordination of translation work and bring them into line with translation departments in the other institutions.

---

[1] Point 709 of this Report.

36.   A total of 684 826 pages were translated (509 390 in Brussels and 175 436 in Luxembourg). These figures do not include revision.

Work on software for the incorporation of Greek into the Eurodicautom terminology bank was completed, and Greek terms will be fed in from 1985. The bank now contains 345 331 entries with equivalents in six Community languages and 85 042 abbreviations and acronyms.

37.   A computerized translation system known as Systran has been developed by the Commission departments, and pilot experiments related to specific Directorates-General have been launched using the language couples now available (English-French, French-English and English-Italian).

Other language couples (English-German and French-German) will become operational in 1985, allowing the experiments in progress to be broadened and the value of the system to be tested on a wider scale in the Commission departments.

Court of Justice

38.   On 26 March the Representatives of the Governments of the Member States appointed Mr René Joliet to be a judge in the Court of Justice for the period 10 April 1984 to 6 October 1985.[1] He replaces Mr Josse Mertens de Wilmars, the President of the Court, who had resigned. Following this appointment, the Court elected Lord Mackenzie Stuart as its President until 6 October 1985. Mr Andreas O'Keeffe resigned, and was replaced with effect from 31 December by Mr T.F. O'Higgins.[2]

39.   By decision of 7 February the Representatives of the Governments of the Member States appointed Mr Marco Darmon to serve as Advocate-General from 13 February 1984 to 6 October 1988.[3] He replaces Mrs Simone Rozès, who had resigned.

40.   Until 31 December the composition of the Chambers of the Court was as follows:

---

[1] OJ L 87, 30.3.1984.
[2] OJ L 341, 29.12.1984; Bull. EC 12-1984.
[3] OJ L 40, 11.2.1984.

First Chamber:	President:	Mr Giacinto Bosco
	Judges:	Mr Andreas O'Keeffe
		Mr René Joliet
Second Chamber:	President:	Mr Ole Due
	Judges:	Mr Pierre Pescatore
		Mr Kai Bahlmann
Third Chamber:	President:	Mr Constantinos Kakouris
	Judges:	Mr Ulrich Everling
		Mr Yves Galmot
Fourth Chamber:	President:	Mr Giancinto Bosco
	Judges:	Mr Pierre Pescatore
		Mr Andreas O'Keeffe
		Mr Thijmen Koopmans
		Mr Kai Bahlmann
Fifth Chamber:	President:	Mr Ole Due
	Judges:	Mr Constantinos Kakouris
		Mr Ulrich Everling
		Mr Yves Galmot
		Mr René Joliet

The Advocates-General are: Mr P. VerLoren van Themaat, First Advocate-General, and Sir Gordon Slynn, Mr G.F. Mancini, Mr C.O. Lenz and Mr Darmon.

41. In 1984 312 cases were brought (128 references for preliminary rulings, 41 staff cases and 143 others). Of the 220 judgments or orders issued by the Court, 82 were preliminary rulings, 61 were in staff cases and 77 were in other cases.

42. There were 469 permanent posts and 11 temporary ones on the Court's 1984 establishment plan.

Court of Auditors

43. The Court elected Mr Marcel Mart (Luxembourg) to replace Mr Pierre Lelong as its President with effect from 18 October. [1]

On 31 December the members of the Court were as follows: Mr Marcel Mart, Mr Pierre Lelong, Mr André J. Middelhoek, Mr Aldo Angioi, Mr Keld Brixtofte,

---

[1] Bull. EC 10-1984, point 2.4.35.

Mr Charles John Carey, Mr Paul Gaudy, Mr Lothar Haase, Mr Michael N. Murphy and Mr Stergios Vallas.

44.   During the year, in accordance with the Treaties, the Court delivered a number of opinions, dealing in particular with proposals relating to the Community's budget, [1] the financing of industrial innovation [2] and EMS loans. [3]

It adopted special reports on the management of Community development aid funds by the European Investment Bank, [4] and on application of the Directive of 27 June 1977 [5] concerning scrutiny by Member States of transactions forming part of the system of financing by the Guarantee Section of the EAGGF. [6] It published a special report on the coordination of Community aid to non-member countries, [7] incorporating its recommendations and the Commission's replies. [8] In November it adopted its annual report on the implementation of the General Budget of the Communities in 1983, and European Development Fund operations in the same year. [9]

45.   There were 273 permanent posts and 30 temporary ones on the Court's establishment plan for 1984.

Economic and Social Committee

46.   On 24 October, with Mr François Ceyrac in the chair, the Committee elected Mr Gerd Muhr (workers — Federal Republic of Germany) its new Chairman for a two-year term. Mr Philippus Noordwal (employers — Netherlands) and Mr Umberto Emo Capodilista (various interests — Italy) were elected Vice-Chairmen. [10]

The Committee held 10 plenary sessions, at which social problems, particularly employment, held an important place. It delivered more than 100 opinions, dealing particularly with action against youth unemployment, measures to

---

[1] Bull. EC 3-1984, point 2.4.30; Bull. EC 6-1984, point 2.4.10.
[2] Bull. EC 4-1984, point 2.4.33.
[3] Bull. EC 1-1984, point 2.4.39.
[4] Bull. EC 5-1984, point 2.4.22.
[5] OJ L 172, 12.7.1977.
[6] OJ C 336, 17.12.1984; Bull. EC 10-1984, point 2.4.36.
[7] Bull. EC 7/8-1984, point 2.4.38.
[8] OJ C 224, 25.8.1984.
[9] OJ C 348, 31.12.1984; Bull. EC 11-1984, point 2.4.23.
[10] Bull. EC 10-1984, points 2.4.37 and 2.4.39.

combat poverty, long-term unemployment, and a programme to encourage exchanges of young workers.

It also delivered 9 opinions on its own initiative, on such subjects as industrial medicine, waste management, and relations between the Community and EFTA and Yugoslavia.

On 6 and 7 November it held a conference on 'Europe and the New Technologies', with more than 650 participants. [1]

47.   There were 400 permanent posts on the Committee's establishment plan for 1984.

ECSC Consultative Committee

48.   Mr Alain Audiat (France — coal users) served as Chariman until December. The Vice-Chairmen were Mr Rudolf Nickels (Germany — coal workers) and Mr André Robert (Luxembourg — steel producers).

49.   The Committee held 4 ordinary and 3 extraordinary meetings. It adopted 4 resolutions on ECSC social research, [2] environment policy, [2] energy policy [3] and the social aspects of energy and steel policies [4] and delivered opinions on the Commission's proposals for the coal and steel industries. [5]

---

[1] Bull. EC 11-1984, point 2.4.25.
[2] Bull. EC 3-1984, point 2.4.41.
[3] Bull. EC 5-1984, point 2.4.35.
[4] OJ C 279, 19.10.1984; Bull. EC 10-1984, points 2.4.47 and 2.4.49.
[5] Bull. EC 1-1984, point 2.4.46; Bull. EC 3-1984, points 2.4.38 to 2.4.40; Bull. EC 5-1984, point 2.4.34; Bull. EC 6-1984, points 2.4.11 to 2.4.14; Bull. EC 12-1984.

Section 2

Information for the general public and specific audiences

Information activities

50. As part of the preparations for the second European elections, the Commission stepped up its efforts concerning those sectors of the public which are difficult to reach by the Community's traditional information methods. It concentrated its action on the audiovisual media and sporting events, whose popular appeal makes them particularly suitable for reaching the broadest and youngest sections of the population. In devising the various measures, the Commission made use of the results of surveys on the attitudes and behaviour of Europeans and on socio-cultural development in Europe. [1]

51. At the same time, the Commission continued its policy of decentralizing information in the Member States by setting up suboffices of its Bonn and Paris Information Offices in Munich and Marseilles respectively.

52. During the year the Commission offered 443 paid and 35 unpaid traineeships to young graduates, of whom 376 were nationals of Member States and 102 were from non-member countries.

53. The Commission coordinated the Member States' participation in the international exhibition in New Orleans from 12 May to 11 November in line with the principle laid down by the Council in April 1983. [2] It will do the same for the international exhibitions in Tsukuba, Japan, from 17 March to 16 September 1985 and in Vancouver, Canada, from 2 May to 13 October 1986.

Press, radio and television

54. The number of journalists accredited to the Commission remained at the high level of over 360 from almost 50 countries, of whom around 300 represent newspapers and periodicals and 60 or so radio and television. This total includes some 40 national and international press agencies.

---

[1] Bull. EC 5-1984, point 3.5.1.
[2] Seventeenth General Report, point 50.

The Spokesman's Group held 200 meetings with the press on Commission decisions, proposals and reactions, and Commission meetings were covered by 42 press conferences given by the Spokesman. The President and Members of the Commission gave 25 press conferences on key issues, several of which were given jointly with prominent visitors to the Commission.

The Spokesman's Group also conveyed to the press the Commission's position on the occasion of Council and European Council meetings and at part-sessions of Parliament. Special arrangements were made for international events, such as the London Western Economic Summit, at which the Community was represented.

More than 2 600 information memos and papers were released to the accredited press, while the Information Offices in the Member States and the Delegations in non-member countries received about 720 telexed memos and commentaries, drafted specially for their own use in keeping their press contacts informed.

Office for Official Publications

55. The Office for Official Publications prints and distributes the *Official Journal* and other Community publications on behalf of all the institutions.

In 1984 increased use was made of new computer technologies for producing Community publications; in particular, production of the S series of the *Official Journal* was rationalized as a result.

The systematic introduction of a standard system for text storage on machine-readable media has led to a number of large invitations to tender which have increased access to the market.

From the beginning of the year the Office published notices of Japanese public contracts under the GATT Agreement in both the printed and electronic versions of the S series of the *Official Journal*. This service will be extended to American, Canadian, Scandinavian, Austrian and Swiss notices in early 1985.

Statistical Office of the European Communities

56. The Statistical Office continued to computerize the distribution of statistics in collaboration with the Office for Official Publications and Commission departments.

As regards foreign trade statistics, the Office began to incorporate the Harmonized Commodity Description and Coding System — developed by the Customs Cooperation Council — in its nomenclature of goods. It was also able to supply the Commission Delegation in Geneva with the information needed for the GATT negotiations.

The Office was involved in the Commission's operation to simplify formalities in intra-Community trade by introducing a single administrative document. [1]

In support of development cooperation policy, the Office introduced statistical programmes to improve information on the economic situation in the ACP States. Surveys were conducted into the situation as regards food supply, foreign trade, prices and the national accounts of the countries concerned.

Historical archives

57.   In accordance with its decision to open the Community's historical archives to the public under the 30-year rule, [2] the Commission released the historical archives of the ECSC High Authority for 1952 and 1953 so that they could be consulted by researchers. [3]

At the same time, work continued in preparation for the deposit of the originals of the historical archives at the European University Institute, Florence. On 17 December the Commission, acting on behalf of the institutions which deposit archives, and the European University Institute signed a contract laying down the conditions for the deposit and the rules for keeping the archives at the Institute. [4]

The Commission's relations with workers' and employers' organizations and with the European Youth Forum [5]

58.   In spite of budgetary constraints, the Commission did its utmost in the present difficult times to maintain its contacts with workers' and employers' organizations and ensure that the Community's policies enjoy the widest

---

[1] Point 180 of this Report.
[2] Seventeenth General Report, point 54.
[3] General archives — consultation room and information service, Commission of the European Communities, square de Meeûs 8, 1040 Brussels.
[4] Bull. EC 12-1984.
[5] For more details, see the end of the 'Commission' item each month in the *Bulletin of the European Communities*.

possible support. It arranged many information and consultation meetings for European organizations of workers and employers, thereby involving representatives of the two sides of industry in the preparation and application of Community policy. The workers' and employers' organizations showed their interest by producing a large number of opinions and statements.

The Commission also held preliminary consultation meetings at which the trade union organizations were able to discuss matters such as the economic situation, employment, measures in favour of women, renewal of the Lomé Convention, education and training.

The Youth Forum maintained its position as the main adviser to the Community institutions on youth affairs. It produced statements on Community policies, in particular on equality of opportunity between men and women, the reorganization of working time, Social Fund operations, the renewal of the Lomé Convention and proposals for action by the new Parliament.

Section 3

Financing Community activities

Main developments

59.   For *the first time in the history of the Community, the budget established on the basis of the expenditure forecasts for the year in accordance with the provisions in force (principle of annuality, revenue and expenditure in balance) is to receive its ordinary resources by means of procedures other than those laid down in the Treaty. This was decided by the Heads of State or Government at the Fontainebleau European Council.*

With the own resources available under the existing rules already inadequate in 1984, the 1985 budget will again have to be funded by repayable advances from the Member States, pending the entry into force of the new own resources system.

As revenue and expenditure cannot be balanced with the own resources currently available, the Council sent Parliament a draft budget which did not cover the whole year in respect of certain items of expenditure. On second reading Parliament rejected it as unacceptable. Until the budget procedure for 1985 is completed, expenditure will be covered, as stipulated by the Treaty, under the provisional twelfths arrangements.

Budgets

1984 financial year

General budget

60.   The general budget of the European Communities for 1984, [1] which was adopted by the President of Parliament on 20 December 1983, totalled 27 377.28 million ECU in appropriations for commitments and 25 361.46 million ECU in appropriations for payments.

---

[1] OJ L 12, 16.1.1984.

61.   Supplementary and amending budget No 1/1984 adopted by the President of Parliament increased appropriations by 1 887.17 million ECU to cover additional expenditure, mainly for the agricultural sector. [1] This brought total appropriations for 1984 to 29 264.45 million ECU for commitments and 27 248.63 million ECU for payments.

Following this increase, the share to be covered by VAT own resources exceeded for the first time the resources available under the 1% limit. The overrun of 1 003.4 million ECU was covered by repayable advances made by the Member States under an intergovernmental political agreement. [2]

Implementation of the 1983 and 1984 budgets

62.   A comparison between the rates of utilization of appropriations in 1983 and 1984 is given in Tables 1a and 1b.

1985 financial year

Three-year financial forecasts 1985-86-87

63.   Together with the 1985 preliminary draft budget, the Commission sent the budgetary authority the three-year financial forecasts for 1985, 1986 and 1987, [3] which continue and update the general line of the previous forecasts. [4] The main points are as follows: containment of agricultural expenditure; a significant increase in real terms in expenditure to improve structures; Spanish and Portuguese accession on 1 January 1986; inclusion of the European Development Fund in the budget; assumption of an increase in own resources.

64.   According to the forecasts, the total appropriations for payments required will rise from 28 100 million ECU in 1985 to 33 700 million ECU in 1986 and 37 300 million ECU in 1987, i.e. an annual increase averaging around 10% in real terms.

---

[1] OJ L 329, 17.12.1984; Bull. EC 10-1984, point 1.1.1 et seq.
[2] Bull. EC 4-1984, point 1.1.1 et seq; Bull. EC 6-1984, point 1.1.9 (paragraph 3); Bull. EC 7/8-1984, point 2.3.3; Bull. EC 10-1984, point 1.1.3.
[3] Bull. EC 5-1984, point 2.3.5.
[4] Seventeenth General Report, point 70.

TABLE 1a

Use of appropriations for 1983

million ECU

	Total appropriations[1]		% used		Approps for payments carried over from 1982 to 1983	% used	Appropriations lapsing or available			
							Approps for commitments		Approps for payments	
	For commitments	For payments	Commitments	Payments			Lapsing	Available	Lapsing	Available
COMMISSION										
Operating appropriations										
Agriculture	16 970.1	16 536.5	98.8	98.8	430.4	60.7	82.0	115.1	239.0	144.1
EAGGF Guarantee Section	(15 822.2)	(15 822.2)	(99.8)	(99.8)	(2.6)	(95.4)	(36.4)	—	(36.4)	(0.1)
EAGGF Guidance Section	(985.0)	(612.3)	(87.9)	(79.8)	(391.2)	(59.1)	(20.9)	(98.1)	(159.9)	(123.9)
Fisheries	(105.6)	(56.9)	(83.1)	(56.1)	(30.4)	(75.2)	(1.4)	(16.5)	(8.8)	(12.5)
Social	2 081.2	1 417.1	95.9	56.2	218.4	97.3	11.6	72.9	17.5	608.6
Regional	2 513.4	1 495.4	94.2	92.1	174.4	80.4	2.3	143.2	36.4	115.2
Energy	954.1	885.0	98.1	91.3	31.4	71.2	5.1	12.8	14.1	72.3
Research and investment	538.8	433.7	91.4	86.7	58.0	84.9	5.0	41.2	6.5	60.0
Industry	111.3	62.0	87.5	48.1	31.0	60.6	2.0	12.0	14.1	30.2
Transport	26.5	14.4	42.3	18.2	1.1	99.3	0.3	15.0	0.2	11.6
Environment and consumer protection	13.2	13.6	81.3	29.8	8.3	89.1	0.5	2.0	1.4	9.1
Development cooperation	1 291.6	984.6	82.1	52.6	345.3	84.9	33.6	197.4	56.8	963.1
Food aid	(541.9)	(541.9)	(99.9)	(59.9)	(72.3)	(88.6)	(0.8)	—	(9.1)	(216.6)[2]
Non-associated developing countries	(369.4)	(122.7)	(65.2)	(29.6)	(117.1)	(86.9)	(0.1)	(128.4)	(15.5)	(86.2)
Specific and exceptional measures	(145.6)	(140.0)	(92.6)	(28.5)	(50.6)	(97.8)	(2.7)	(8.1)	(3.4)	(97.4)
Cooperation with Mediterranean countries	(183.2)	(128.5)	(50.4)	(52.1)	(103.8)	(73.6)	(29.9)	(60.9)	(27.4)	(61.6)
Miscellaneous	(51.5)	(51.5)	(100.0)	(97.4)	(1.5)	(92.6)	—	—	(0.1)	(1.3)
Subtotal	24 500.2	21 842.3	96.9	92.7	1 298.3	77.5	142.4	611.6	376.2	1 514.2
Staff and administration	755.7	755.7	98.4	90.9	58.9	83.9	12.4	—	21.9	51.3
Repayment of own resources collection costs	966.9	966.9	96.0	88.1	71.5	97.7	38.4	—	48.1	76.5
Financial compensation to UK and Greece	122.1	122.1	99.6	80.8	44.5	99.4	0.5	—	0.7	23.0
Supplementary measures in favour of UK	887.6	887.6	100.0	100.0	—	—	—	—	—	—
Provisional appropriations	43.7	89.4	—	—	—	—	43.7	—	89.4	—
Contingency reserve	(1.1)	(1.1)	—	—	—	—	(1.1)	—	(1.1)	—
Commission total	27 276.2	24 664.0	96.9	92.3	1 473.2	79.4	237.4	611.6	528.3	1 670.0
Non-diff. appropriations	20 529.6	20 529.6	99.3	96.7	511.0	82.3	146.3	—	236.8	529.6
Differentiated appropriations	6 746.6	4 134.4	89.6	70.5	962.2	77.8	91.1	611.6	291.5	1 140.4
OTHER INSTITUTIONS	404.8	404.8	92.8	82.1	47.8	87.5	28.3	0.8	34.3	44.3
Grand total	27 681.0	25 068.8	96.8	92.2	1 521.0	79.6	265.7	612.4	562.6	1 714.3

[1] Initial budget as amended by transfers of appropriations, plus commitment appropriations remaining from previous financial years and adjustments of commitments from previous years still to be settled.
[2] Including 18 million ECU paid as advances up to 31 December 1983.

TABLE 1b

Use of appropriations for 1984

million ECU

	Total appropriations[1][3]		% used		Approps for payments carried over from 1983 to 1984	% used	Appropriations lapsing or available[2][3]			
	For commitments	For payments	Commitments	Payments			Approps for commitments		Approps for payments	
							Lapsing	Available	Lapsing	Available
COMMISSION										
Operating appropriations										
Agriculture	19 471.8	19 112.2	99.4	99.5	143.9	71.2	1.9	119.2	43.4	91.6
EAGGF Guarantee Section	(18 358.0)	(18 358.0)	(100.0)	(100.0)	(0.1)	79.2	—	—	—	—
EAGGF Guidance Section	(880.7)	(595.6)	(90.7)	(94.4)	(123.7)	(70.2)	—	(82.3)	(36.9)	(33.5)
Fisheries	(154.1)	(87.3)	(94.1)	(71.7)	(7.6)	(65.3)	(1.3)	(32.8)	(3.3)	(38.5)
Miscellaneous	(79.0)	(71.3)	(77.8)	(54.5)	(12.5)	(84.2)	(0.6)	(4.1)	(3.2)	(19.6)
Social	2 437.1	1 622.2	92.9	92.8	608.6	85.5	3.5	170.0	89.8	114.5
Regional	2 511.8	1 462.9	96.0	89.4	115.2	64.2	0.9	99.7	42.1	153.6
Energy	676.0	595.6	98.2	84.9	72.3	58.7	0.1	12.1	30.0	89.9
Research and investment	805.1	515.9	63.1	72.7	60.0	85.9	0.2	297.2	8.6	140.6
Industry	98.6	77.1	59.4	33.0	30.2	88.8	0.4	39.5	3.8	51.2
Transport	567.7	504.7	85.9	84.1	11.6	54.9	—	80.0	5.3	80.4
Environment and consumer protection	21.2	16.0	58.5	20.2	9.1	71.7	0.8	8.0	3.4	11.9
Development cooperation	1 346.6	1 032.3	89.1	74.2	445.6	86.8	0.6	146.8	59.3	265.2
Food aid	(505.0)	(505.0)	(100.0)	(100.0)	(216.6)	(99.5)	(0.1)	—	(1.1)	—
Non-associated developing countries	(366.8)	(131.3)	(73.6)	(83.4)	(69.9)	(63.0)	(0.1)	(96.7)	(26.0)	(21.7)
Specific and exceptional measures	(256.1)	(231.4)	(97.0)	(22.1)	(96.2)	(73.2)	(0.4)	(7.3)	(26.1)	(179.8)
Cooperation with Mediterranean countries	(160.2)	(106.1)	(73.3)	(41.1)	(61.6)	(90.3)	—	(42.8)	(5.9)	(62.4)
Miscellaneous	(58.5)	(58.5)	(99.9)	(99.7)	(1.3)	(90.7)	—	—	(0.2)	(1.3)
Subtotal	27 935.9	24 938.9	96.5	96.0	1 496.5	81.3	8.4	972.5	285.7	998.9
Staff and administration	820.0	820.0	99.3	89.9	56.3	91.6	5.5		10.3	77.5
Repayment of own resources collection costs	1 038.3	1 038.3	99.9	99.5	76.5	100.0	1.3		1.3	3.6
Financial compensation to UK and Greece	44.8	44.8	100.0	90.1	23.0	99.8	—			4.5
Provisional appropriations Contingency reserve	0.1	0.1	—	—			0.1		0.1	
Commission total	29 839.1	26 842.1	96.7	95.9	1 652.3	82.8	15.3	972.5	297.4	1 084.5
Non-diff. appropriations	22 527.5	22 527.5	99.9	98.3	529.6	94.1	13.4		44.4	378.5
Differentiated appropriations	7 311.6	4 314.6	86.7	83.6	1 122.7	77.5	1.9	972.5	253.0	706.0
OTHER INSTITUTIONS	425.6	425.6	96.6	88.6	44.3	85.9	14.6	—	20.8	34.1
Grand total	30 264.7	27 267.7	96.7	95.8	1 696.6	82.9	29.9	972.5	318.2	1 118.6

[1] Initial budget as amended by transfers of appropriations, plus commitment appropriations remaining from previous financial years and adjustments of commitments from previous years still to be settled.
[2] Unused non-differentiated appropriations lapse unless the budgetary authority approves a carryover.
[3] These are provisional figures at 31.12.1984: the EAGGF guarantee and food aid accounts will not be finally closed until 31.3.1985.

General budget

Preliminary draft budget for 1985

65.   On 15 June the Commission sent the budgetary authority the preliminary draft budget for 1985, which it had adopted on 23 May. [1] It totalled 30 228.19 million ECU in appropriations for commitments and 28 103.46 million ECU in appropriations for payments. These amounts were increased by letters of amendment to 30 252.06 million ECU and 28 127.33 million ECU respectively.

Political presentation of the budget

66.   As the Commission had predicted in its preliminary draft budget for 1984, [2] the financing of the existing policies will require more resources than are available within the present limits. In preparing its preliminary draft budget for 1985, the Commission therefore assumed that in 1985 the Communities will be provided with own resources in excess of the current ceiling.

67.   In its preliminary draft, the Commission took account of the general objectives contained in Parliament's resolution of 13 April on the guidelines for the budgetary policy of the Communities for 1985. [3] It shares Parliament's views about what the Community's priorities should be and attempted to reflect these options it went for. However, in some areas of spending, the Commission, and for that matter the budgetary authority too, are bound by unavoidable legal obligations. This is the case, in particular, with agricultural spending and the differentiated appropriations. In 1985 the Commission estimates that 3 200 million ECU in payment appropriations will be needed just for commitments which have still to be met.

Revenue

68.   The Commission estimated that resources of 26 191 million ECU will be available to the Community within the limit of 1% of the VAT base. From its forecasts of expenditure and assuming that the current ceiling on own resources will be raised, it estimated that the proportion to be financed from VAT own resources would require a rate of around 1.12%. However, in view of the obligation to ensure that revenue and expenditure in the budget are in balance,

---

[1] Bull. EC 5-1984, points 1.1.1 *et seq.* and 2.3.1 *et seq.*
[2] Seventeenth General Report, point 72.
[3] OJ C 127, 14.5.1984; Bull. EC 4-1984, point 2.4.9.

the Commission—as a fall-back solution—proposed a Regulation under which Member States would pay advances on own resources to cover the amount of expenditure exceeding available resources. [1] This Regulation would take effect only if the new own resources Decision did not enter into force in time. Parliament gave its opinion on this proposal in October. [2]

Expenditure

69.   The Commission tried to maintain a suitable balance between what is desirable for the development of policies at Community level and what is feasible in view of the general restrictions on public spending in the Community; as regards both agricultural [3] and other spending, it endeavoured at the same time to remain within the guidelines on budgetary discipline set out in its February communication. [4]

70.   The appropriations proposed are based on forecast expenditure of 30 252.06 million ECU in payments. Compared with the initial budget for 1984, this is an increase of 10.50% in commitments and 10.90% in payments. In view of the estimates of own resources (customs duties, agricultural levies, sugar and isoglucose levies) and other miscellaneous revenue, this level of expenditure will require a VAT own resources rate of around 1.12%. [5]

71.   On the basis of the existing agricultural legislation and with no allowance made for possible changes, in particular the 1985 agricultural price decisions, EAGGF Guarantee Section expenditure is estimated at 18 996 million ECU, plus 350 million ECU which the Commission proposes should be allocated to a special programme to run down stocks. This is an increase of 17% over the 16 542.9 million ECU contained in the 1984 budget. However, by reference to the Commission's latest estimates for agricultural spending in 1984 (18 376 million ECU), the rate of increase for 1985 is only 3.7%.

72.   The increase judged necessary for non-compulsory expenditure was 12.75% for both commitments and payments, far higher than the 8.5% set as the maximum rate of increase for these appropriations in 1985. Because of the large volume of commitments entered into before 1 January 1985, the Com-

---

[1] OJ C 126, 12.5.1984; Bull. EC 4-1984, point 1.1.1 et seq.; OJ C 196, 25.7.1984; Bull. EC 7/8-1984, point 2.3.4.
[2] OJ C 300, 12.11.1984; Bull. EC 10-1984, points 2.3.4 and 2.4.10.
[3] Bull. EC 3-1984, point 1.2.1 et seq.
[4] Bull. EC 2-1984, point 1.1.1 et seq.
[5] Point 79 of this Report.

mission argued that a restriction of payment appropriations to a rate not exceeding the maximum rate would leave very little scope for granting new commitment appropriations in 1985, if a normal ratio between payments and commitments was to be maintained.

The Commission proposed increases in commitment appropriations for the Regional Fund and the Social Fund so that, in real terms, the level of activities in 1985 could be the same as in 1984. In line with the conclusions of the European Council [1] and Parliament's budgetary policy guidelines, [2] it also gave special priority in budget terms to research, the Mediterranean programmes and transport.

Budget procedure and establishment of the definitive budget for 1985

73.   On 3 October the Council established the draft general budget for 1985 on first reading. [3] The appropriations approved by the Council reduced the Commission's proposals in its preliminary draft [4] by 7.86% (2 378.98 million ECU) in commitments and 7.74% (2 177.95 million ECU) in payments.

The appropriations entered by the Council reduced the expenditure estimates as compared with the 1984 budget (including supplementary and amending budget No 1/1984) by 4.65% for commitments and 4.76% for payments. Since the draft budget was established within the limit of the own resources currently available, the VAT rate is 0.98%. The volume of unused own resources roughly corresponds to Parliament's margin for manœuvre in non-compulsory expenditure. However, the Council undertook to cover, by 1 October 1985, any additional budgetary requirements arising in 1985 by means of a supplementary and amending budget for which the necessary funds would be provided. [5]

74.   On first reading in November, [6] Parliament departed from the draft budget as established by the Council in two important respects: it returned to the principle of annuality by establishing a budget for 12 months covering all estimated expenditure for the EAGGF Guarantee Section; this increased the estimates of guarantee expenditure by 1 315 million ECU to be covered by repayable advances from the Member States; and it entered as expenditure the compensation to the United Kingdom and the Federal Republic of Germany

---

[1] Bull. EC 3-1984, point 1.1.1 *et seq.*; Bull. EC 6-1984, point 1.1.1 *et seq.*
[2] OJ C 127, 14.5.1984; Bull. EC 4-1984, point 2.4.9.
[3] Bull. EC 10-1984, point 2.3.2.
[4] Bull. EC 5-1984, point 2.3.1 *et seq.*
[5] Bull. EC 10-1984, point 1.1.1 *et seq.*
[6] Bull. EC 11-1984, points 2.3.1 and 2.4.13.

4	
Change (3/	
%	
− 6.81	−
− 6.81	−
− 23.18	−
− 41.57	−
− 14.76	−
− 0.44	−
− 61.71	−
− 71.95	−
	−
− 5.89	−
− 7.92	−
− 29.73	−
− 8.68	−
− 11.99	−
− 13.85	−
− 58.25	−
− 36.32	−
− 15.52	−
− 12.40	−
− 0.31	−
− 15.05	−
− 22.26	−
− 23.55	−
− 33.29	−
− 6.22	−
− 20.99	−
− 4.98	−
+ 1.63	+
− 2.85	−
− 7.79	−

1

amounting to 1 515.9 million ECU; with this amendment, Parliament departed from the conclusions of the Fontainebleau European Council. [1]

Under its own classification for non-compulsory expenditure, Parliament voted increases in payment appropriations within its margin of manœuvre amounting to 373.3 million ECU. According to the classification adopted by the Council and the Commission, these increases amounted to 589 million ECU.

Besides wishing to restore proper budgetary practice, Parliament demonstrated its concern to preserve the priorities it had laid down previously: attacking unemployment by improving employment opportunities, in particular by means of productive investments in new technologies, and assisting developing countries, notably with the campaign against world hunger.

75.   In its second reading, [2] the Council agreed to an increase in expenditure compared with its first draft of 1.45% for commitments and 0.70% for payments, bringing appropriations up to 28 307.04 million ECU and 26 133.10 million ECU respectively. Given the exhaustion of own resources available under the present rules, these expenditure estimates are down on the 1984 figures by 957.41 million ECU for commitments and 1 115.51 million ECU for payments, i.e. 3.27% and 4.09% respectively.

76.   In non-compulsory expenditure, appropriations for commitments were increased by 405.17 million ECU and appropriations for payments by 183.44 million ECU, but the Council did not agree to any increase in compulsory expenditure.

With regard to the financing of the common agricultural policy, the Council referred to the declaration made at its 2 and 3 October meeting [3] and agreed to enter between brackets additional revenue and expenditure of 1 315 million ECU, which is not included in the budget total because of the special characteristics.

In its second reading, Parliament rejected the draft budget, considering that a budget that did not cover 12 months of revenue and expenditure was not acceptable. Parliament asked the Commission to start the procedure for preparing a new draft budget. In accordance with Article 204 of the EEC Treaty and Article 178 of the Euratom Treaty, expenditure will be effected on a monthly basis from 1 January 1985 under the provisional twelfths arrangements. Own

[1] Bull. EC 6-1984, point 1.1.1 *et seq.*
[2] Bull. EC 11-1984, point 2.3.3.
[3] Bull. EC 10-1984, point 2.3.2.

resources from customs duties, agricultural levies and sugar levies are to be paid over every month by the Member States. Own resources accruing from VAT will be paid monthly on the basis of the most recent definitive budget, supplementary and amending budget No 1/1984.

ECSC budget

77.   After consulting Parliament [1] and informing the ECSC Consultative Committee, [2] the Commission decided on 21 December to maintain the levy rate for 1985 at 0.31%. [3] With the addition of other ordinary resources (interest on investments and on loans granted against non-borrowed funds, commitments cancelled, etc.) and extraordinary resources of 122.5 million ECU transferred from the general budget to the ECSC budget to finance measures connected with the restructuring of the coal and steel industries, [4] this provides full cover for the ECSC's requirements of 359.5 million ECU for its operating budget.

The breakdown of requirements is as follows (in million ECU):

Administrative expenditure	5
Redeployment aid	125
Research subsidies	51
Interest subsidies on investment and conversion loans	50
Aid to coking coal	6
Measures in connection with the restructuring of the steel industry	62.5
Measures in connection with the restructuring of the coal industry	60

Own resources

1984 financial year

78.   The original budget of the Communities for 1984 set the VAT rate at 0.99%. A supplementary and amending budget adopted during the year affected revenue as follows:

---

[1] OJ C 12, 14.1.1985.
[2] Bull. EC 12-1984.
[3] OJ L 335, 22.12.1984; Bull. EC 12-1984.
[4] Point 292 of this Report.

(i)   entry of 222 million ECU as the balance of sugar and isoglucose pro-
       duction levies for the 1983/84 marketing year; [1]

(ii)   increase in the estimate for customs duties of 260 million ECU;

(iii) entry of the surplus of revenue over the expenditure outturn in 1983 (307
       million ECU);

(iv)   entry of 266 million ECU as an estimate of the surplus for the current
       year;

(v)   entry of the VAT balance for 1983 ($-$ 198 million ECU);

(vi)   entry of adjustments to VAT balances following the controls of statements
       for 1982 (5 million ECU) and additional adjustments for 1980 and 1981
       ($-$ 14 million ECU);

(vii) replacement of Greece's VAT contribution by a financial contribution
       following the two-year postponement of the introduction of the common
       VAT system; [2]

(viii) increase of the VAT rate to the maximum 1.00%;

(ix)   financing of expenditure (1 003.4 million ECU) exceeding the current
       own-resources ceiling by means of repayable advances made by the
       Member States.

TABLE 3

Budget revenue

million ECU

	1984 outturn	1985 estimates
Agricultural levies	1 260.2	1 387.8
Sugar and isoglucose levies	1 176.4	986.9
Customs duties	7 960.8	8 096.2
VAT own resources	14 372.1	14 377.0
Financial contributions (GNP)	222.5	224.2
Surplus from previous financial year	307.1	token entry
Balance of VAT own resources from previous financial years and adjustments to financial contributions	($-$) 111.7	token entry
Estimated surplus for current financial year	1 001.8	—
Miscellaneous revenue	250.5	226.9
Total	26 439.7	25 299.0

[1] OJ L 254, 22.9.1984; Bull. EC 9-1984, point 2.3.2.
[2] OJ L 360, 23.12.1983; Seventeenth General Report, point 94.

1985 financial year

79.   The resources available to the Community in 1985 in the absence of a definitive budget amount to 25 299 million ECU.

Estimates of revenue for 1985 are given in Table 3.

Future financing of the Community budget

80.   On the basis of the conclusions of the Fontainebleau European Council [1] the Commission sent to the Council and to Parliament on 9 July an amendment [2] to its May 1983 proposal for a Decision on the Community's system of own recources. [3] The proposal now provides for a maximum VAT own resources rate of 1.4% from 1 October 1985 (effective date 1 January 1985) and a budget adjustment system for the United Kingdom in the form of a reduction in the VAT share owed by that Member State to the Community budget. [4] This new Decision will replace the Decision of 21 April 1970 [5] and will include ECSC customs duties and special provisions for research programmes.

The Council was generally in favour of this proposal, apart from the question of the date of entry into force and the effective date. But Parliament, in its opinion of 25 October, [6] attacked it as 'irrevocably abandoning the entire system of own resources introduced on 21 April 1970,' [5] saying that it 'lays aside the principle of a uniform rate of value-added tax' for all Member States. The opinion states that corrective measures should apply on the expenditure side rather than the revenue side and proposes a Community decision, without fresh ratification by national parliaments, for further raising the VAT ceiling to 1.6%. The Commission is concerned to ensure that the Community budget is financed in future in accordance with the conclusions of the Fontainebleau European Council and does not intend to amend its proposal.

---

[1] Bull. EC 6-1984, point 1.1.1 *et seq.*
[2] OJ C 193, 21.7.1984; Bull. EC 7/8-1984, point 2.3.9.
[3] OJ C 145, 3.6.1983; Seventeenth General Report, point 86.
[4] Point 81 of this Report.
[5] OJ L 94, 28.4.1970.
[6] OJ C 315, 26.11.1984; Bull. EC 10-1984, points 2.3.3 and 2.4.10.

Convergence and budgetary matters

81.   This year brought a solution, at least for a few years, to the thorny problem of 'budgetary imbalances'. At the Brussels European Council in March [1] a broad consensus emerged in favour of a corrective mechanism, which was not, however, given final shape because of the lack of agreement on the initial amount of compensation to be granted to the United Kingdom. This compensation was then determined by the Fontainebleau European Council in June [2] as part of the mechanism described in the following terms: 'Expenditure policy is ultimately the essential means of resolving the question of budgetary imbalances.' However, 'any Member State sustaining a budgetary burden which is excessive in relation to its relative prosperity may benefit from a correction at the appropriate time. The basis for the correction is the gap between the share of VAT payments and the share of expenditure.'

On this basis, the European Council decided that the United Kingdom would receive 1 000 million ECU for 1984 and, from 1985, 66% of the difference between its share of VAT payments and its share of expenditure. These corrections will be granted to the United Kingdom in the form of a reduction in the VAT payments for the following year. 'The resulting cost for the other Member States will be shared among them according to their normal VAT share, adjusted to allow the Federal Republic of Germany's share to move to two thirds of its VAT share. The correction formula will be part of the decision to increase the VAT ceiling to 1.4%, their durations being linked.'

The measures agreed upon at Fontainebleau and the commitments to cover the requirements of the 1984 budget have opened the way for payment of the 1 202 million ECU due to the United Kingdom and Germany in respect of 1983. [3] On 26 June the Council adopted the three Regulations for financing special measures relating to energy, employment and transport infrastructures in the United Kingdom and, secondarily, in Germany. [4] After the appropriations needed for these measures had been transferred, [5] the Commission adopted the financing decisions in October. [6]

The Council did not include in its draft budget for 1985 the 1 000 million ECU due to the United Kingdom in respect of 1984 and stated that it would be part

[1]   Bull. EC 3-1984, point 1.1.1 *et seq.*
[2]   Bull. EC 6-1984, point 1.1.1 *et seq.*
[3]   Seventeenth General Report, point 89.
[4]   OJ L 177, 4.7.1984; Bull. EC 6-1984, point 2.3.4.
[5]   Bull. EC 10-1984, point 2.3.5; Bull. EC 7/8-1984, point 2.3.11.
[6]   OJ L 283, 27.10.1984; OJ L 290, 7.11.1984.

of a supplementary and amending budget for which additional funds would be made available. This was one of the main reasons for Parliament's rejection of the draft 1985 budget.

Budget discipline

82.   In the context of work on the future financing of the Community, the Commission sent a communication on budgetary discipline to the Council in February.[1] It proposed certain improvements to the existing budgetary procedures within the framework of the Treaty rules, such as introducing a prior phase of conciliation between the Council, Parliament and the Commission on the structure and volume of the budget and applying specific rules for the various types of expenditure, one of these being the principle that agricultural expenditure should not be allowed to grow faster than own resources.

In March the European Council adopted the principles of this budget discipline,[2] confirming them in June,[3] and after long discussion at the Dublin European Council in December the Council adopted a number of conclusions on the practical implementation of budget discipline.[4]

The Council undertook to lay down a reference framework at the outset of the budgetary procedure which would ensure that agricultural expenditure grew less rapidly than own resources and not to allow the increase in non-compulsory expenditure to exceed the maximum rate determined in accordance with Article 203(9) of the EEC Treaty.

The Council also invited the Commission and Parliament to join it in examining ways of ensuring the cooperation necessary for the three institutions to observe common budget discipline. However, the approach put forward by the Council, in particular as regards non-compulsory expenditure, made agreement with Parliament impossible. At its November part-session Parliament had rejected the unilateral adoption of measures on budget discipline by one arm of the budgetary authority.[5] Consequently, there is no agreement yet on how the reference framework should be drawn up.

---

[1] Bull. EC 2-1984, points 1.2.1 to 1.2.3.
[2] Bull. EC 3-1984, point 1.1.1 *et seq.*
[3] Bull. EC 6-1984, point 1.1.1 *et seq.*
[4] Bull. EC 12-1984.
[5] Bull. EC 11-1984, point 2.3.4.

Budgetary powers

Discharge procedures for 1982 and 1983

83. In a resolution adopted on 10 April Parliament informed the Commission of its reasons for deferring a discharge in respect of the implementation of the general budget for 1982, and requested a reply to its criticisms by 1 September. [1] The Commission replied on 2 August. [2]

Without taking the Commission's replies into consideration, Parliament, in a resolution passed on 14 November, refused to grant a discharge to the Commission for 1982. [3] Parliament presented its refusal as a political judgment of the Commission's management and as a signal to the new Commission that it should pay even greater heed to Parliament's wishes.

The Commission sent its replies to the Court of Auditors' comments on the 1983 financial year to the Court on 29 October. In accordance with Article 84 of the Financial Regulation, [4] the Court then transmitted its annual report to the authorities responsible for giving discharge and to the other institutions on 30 November. [5]

Changes to Financial Regulations

84. Three proposals for amending the 1977 Financial Regulation [4] are still before the Council:

  (i) the proposal made in June 1978 to include all the Community's borrowing and lending operations in the budget; [6]

 (ii) the proposal for a general revision made in December 1980 in accordance with Article 107 of the Financial Regulation, which provides for its periodic review; [7]

 (ii) the proposal made in June 1981 to divide the present Section III of the budget into a Section III for administrative appropriations and a Section VI for operating appropriations. [8]

---

[1] OJ C 127, 14.5.1984; Bull. EC 4-1984, point 2.3.5.
[2] Bull. EC 7/8-1984, point 2.3.13.
[3] OJ C 337, 17.12.1984; Bull. EC 11-1984, point 2.4.13.
[4] OJ L 356, 31.12.1977.
[5] Bull. EC 11-1984, point 2.4.23.
[6] OJ C 160, 6.7.1978.
[7] OJ C 119, 21.5.1981.
[8] OJ C 158, 27.6.1981.

On 15 March, after receiving the opinions of Parliament[1] and the Court of Auditors,[2] the Commission sent the Council an amended proposal for revision of the Financial Regulation incorporating all three above proposals.[3] The amended Financial Regulation cannot be finally adopted until the conciliation procedure with Parliament is completed.

85.   Parliament has made its opinion on other proposals conditional on revision of the Financial Regulation: these other proposals are for updating the 1975 Commission Regulation laying down implementing measures for certain provisions of the Financial Regulation,[4] and for harmonizing the 1975 and 1976 Regulations establishing the Berlin Vocational Training Centre and the Dublin Foundation.[5]

86.   After receiving Parliament's opinion in May,[6] the Commission amended for the third time[7] its proposal[8] amending Regulation No 2891/77[9] implementing the 1970 own resources Decision.

Internal financial control

87.   Financial Control continued its targeted inspections in the Member States, in particular as regards the EAGGF. On the basis of reports to the Commission accompanied by recommendations to the Member States or to Commission departments, improvements were made to administrative practices in the Member States and to Community rules.

88.   Following the report and recommendations from Financial Control, the Commission repealed the 'equity' Regulation,[10] which exempted some operators from MCAs, since it had proved uncontrollable in some cases and had led to speculation at the expense of the Community's finances.

89.   Financial Control prepared a systematic programme of on-the-spot inspections with departments administering Community borrowing and lending oper-

---

[1] OJ C 277, 17.10.1983.
[2] OJ C 232, 11.9.1981; OJ C 122, 13.5.1982.
[3] OJ C 97, 9.4.1984; Bull. EC 3-1984, point 2.3.2.
[4] OJ L 170, 1.7.1975.
[5] OJ C 31, 9.2.1983; Sixteenth General Report, point 94.
[6] OJ C 172, 2.7.1984; Bull. EC 5-1984, point 2.3.10.
[7] OJ C 219, 21.8.1984; Bull. EC 7/8-1984, point 2.3.13.
[8] OJ C 231, 4.9.1982; OJ C 146, 4.6.1983; OJ C 303, 10.11.1983.
[9] OJ L 336, 27.12.1977.
[10] Seventeenth General Report, point 99.

ations; practical improvements to management have been suggested on the basis of the findings.

90. Financial Control continued its leading role in combating fraud and coordinated the regular supply of information to Parliament on this subject.

91. On the basis of a report from Financial Control, the Commission gave priority to the strict administration of assistance for projects under the financial instruments (ERDF, Social Fund, EAGGF Guidance Section, energy, research and so on). The Commission introduced practical measures to ensure that management and control procedures were carried out more satisfactorily in strictest conformity with sound management principles.

Borrowing and lending operations

92. Table 4 shows the loans granted each year from 1982 to 1984.

TABLE 4

Loans granted

million ECU

	1982	1983	1984
New Community Instrument (NCI)[1]	791.1	1 211.8	1 181.8[5]
EEC balance-of-payments loans[1]	—	4 247.3	—
ECSC[2]	740.6[6]	778.1	825.5
Euratom[1]	361.8	366.6	186.0
EIB (from the Bank's own resources)[3]	3 863.4	4 682.9	5 633.8
of which: loans to ACP countries	(122.2)	(90.0)	(79.1)
loans to Mediterranean countries[4]	(288.0)	(337.2)	(541.6)
Total	5 756.9	11 286.7	7 827.1

[1] With guarantee from the general budget.
[2] With guarantee from the ECSC budget.
[3] With guarantee from EIB capital.
[4] With guarantee from the general budget for 75% of the sums lent.
[5] See Table 5.
[6] Including 71.8 million ECU lent outside the Community.

New Community Instrument (NCI) and interest subsidies [1] under the EMS and on loans for the reconstruction of regions struck by earthquake in Italy and Greece

New Community Instrument

93.   Under its Decision of 19 April 1983 to fix the borrowing limit for NCI III at 3 000 million ECU, [2] the Council authorized a second tranche for 1 400 million ECU on 23 July [3] to be on-lent to promote Community investment in energy, infrastructure and the promotion of innovation and new technologies, particularly in small and medium-sized firms.

94.   Loans under NCI I, NCI II and NCI III [4] totalling 1 181.8 million ECU were signed in 1984. Infrastructure accounted for 16.3% of the loans granted, energy for 16.4% and the development of small and medium-sized businesses for 67.3%.

Since 1979, loans totalling 4 199.2 million ECU have been made under this instrument (see Table 5).

TABLE 5

NCI loans, 1984

million ECU

	Operations in 1984			Total NCI 1979-84
	Loans without interest subsidy	Earthquake loans with interest subsidy[1]	Total	
Denmark	134.6	—	134.6	354.2
Greece	69.3	—	69.3	279.6
France	386.3	—	386.3	650.4
Ireland	50.0	—	50.0	348.2
Italy	482.7	14.6	497.3	2 283.2
United Kingdom	44.3	—	44.3	283.6
Total	1 167.2	14.6	1 181.8	4 199.2

[1] Council Decisions of 20 January 1981 (81/19/EEC) and of 14 December 1981 (81/1013/EEC) concerning the earthquakes in Italy and Greece.

---

[1] For the application of interest subsidies, see the annual reports from the Commission to Council and Parliament on borrowing and lending activities. Latest report: 1984 (Bull. EC 7/8-1984, point 2.1.7).
[2] OJ L 112, 28.4.1983; Seventeenth General Report, point 104.
[3] OJ L 208, 3.8.1984.
[4] OJ L 78, 24.3.1982; OJ L 112, 28.4.1983.

Interest subsidies under the EMS on certain NCI and EIB loans

95.   The scheme for allowing interest subsidies under the EMS on certain loans granted to Italy and Ireland as the 'least prosperous Member States fully and effectively participating in the EMS' [1] finished at the end of 1983. The proposal to provide 200 million ECU in interest subsidies on these loans in both 1984 and 1985 [2] has not yet been adopted by the Council.

Interest subsidies on loans for the reconstruction of regions struck by earthquake

96.   Subsidized loans totalling 66.5 million ECU were granted to Italy in 1984 in accordance with the Council Decision of January 1981.   Loans of this type granted since 1981 now total 858.7 million ECU (see Table 6).

The interest subsidies on outstanding loans continued to be paid on the annual due dates. They amounted to 21.69 million ECU for Italy and 2.69 million ECU for Greece.

TABLE 6

Loans with interest subsidies to Italy for the reconstruction of regions affected by earthquakes — 1984

Instrument	Loans signed[1]					Subsidies paid[2]	
	Situation at 1.1.1984 (million ECU)	Loans during 1984 (million ECU)	Situation at 31.12.1984			Amount (million ECU)	%
			Number	Amount (million ECU)	%		
NCI	582.9	14.6	13	597.5	69.6	15.07	69.5
EIB	209.3	51.9	19	261.2	30.4	6.62	30.5
Total	792.2	66.5	32	858.7	100.0	21.69	100.0

[1] Certain loans signed in 1984 will receive subsidies from 1985.
[2] Interest subsidies of 3% per year for up to 12 years. These amounts cover all loans signed since 1981 with the exception of certain loans in 1984 which will receive a subsidy for the first time in 1985.

[1]   OJ L 200, 8.8.1979; amendments in OJ L 295, 21.10.1982; see also Sixteenth General Report, point 103.
[2]   OJ C 163, 22.6.1983; Seventeenth General Report, point 136.
[3]   OJ L 37, 10.2.1981.

EEC balance-of-payments loans

97.   On 29 May the Commission proposed [1] that the Council should raise from 4 000 million to 6 000 million ECU the authorized borrowing limit under the Community facility to support the balance of payments of Member States. [2]

No operations were carried out under this facility in 1984.

Financing ECSC activities

98.   In 1984 the Community continued to support coal and steel industry investment through ECSC financial loans totalling 825.5 million ECU. This amount—higher than the 778.1 million ECU granted the previous year but much lower than the 1980 figure of 1 030.7 million ECU—reflects the Commission's highly selective approach towards the steel sector, where it was concerned to ensure that any investments financed were consonant with its restructuring policy.

Low-interest loans were provided for investments within the priority objectives of job creation, conversion in areas affected by the restructuring of the steel industry and to promote the use of coal. Loans for workers' housing were given at the extremely favourable rate of 1% per year.

Loans granted in 1984 totalled 825.5 million ECU. They break down as follows: 541.3 million ECU for industrial projects (618.4 million ECU in 1983); 247.5 million ECU for conversion programmes (139.6 million ECU in 1983); and 36.7 million ECU for workers' housing (20.1 million ECU in 1983).

99.   The ECSC continued to look to the capital market for funds, raising a total of 863.7 million ECU compared with 749.6 million ECU in 1983.

Financing Euratom activities

100.   In December the Commission sent the Council a proposal for a Decision to increase by 1 000 million ECU the total amount the Commission is empowered to borrow on behalf of Euratom. [3]

---

[1] OJ C 167, 26.7.1984; Bull. EC 5-1984, point 2.1.3.
[2] OJ L 73, 19.3.1981; Fifteenth General Report, point 125.
[3] OJ C 12, 14.1.1985; Bull. EC 12-1984.

101. The Commission continued its lending operations on behalf of Euratom under the 1982 Council Decision, [1] increasing to 2 000 million ECU the total amount which it is authorized to raise to finance investment in nuclear power stations and the enrichment of fissile materials.

102. At 31 December 1984 loans made during the year (at rates obtaining at end of year) totalled 186 million ECU (compared with 366.6 million ECU in 1983). This year's loans went to three firms.

The grand total since such operations began in 1977 is now 1 765.4 million ECU (at the rates obtaining when contracts were signed).

Euratom borrowing in 1984 totalled 214.1 million ECU (compared with 368.8 million ECU in 1983).

European Investment Bank

103. Financing operations by the European Investment Bank [2] amounted to 5 633.8 million ECU from its own resources and 1 269.4 million ECU from resources supplied by the Community, a total of 6 903.2 million ECU in 1984 compared 5 947.8 million ECU in 1983.

The loans granted for projects in the Community totalled 6 194.9 million ECU (89.7% of all financing operations) compared with 5 467.5 million ECU in 1983: 5 013.1 million ECU came from the Bank's own resources and 1 181.8 million ECU (17.1% of the total) from NCI resources. [3]

Loans to Italy continued to account for around half the aid. Greece received less—and Ireland much less—than in 1983. The assistance to these three countries with the most acute structural problems accounted for 57.4% of the Bank's loans in the Community. Loans to the United Kingdom and France increased once again; the remainder went to Denmark, the Federal Republic of Germany, Belgium and Luxembourg.

Loans for regional development projects account for around 53% of all loans in the Community and for 61.5% of the aid from the Bank's own resources. Operations designed to serve the Community's energy objectives totalled 2 247.7

---

[1] OJ L 78, 24.3.1982; Sixteenth General Report, point 111.
[2] The Bank's work in 1984 will be described in detail in its annual report. Copies of the report and of other publications relating to the Bank's work and its operations can be obtained from the main office (100 Boulevard Konrad Adenauer, L-2950 Luxembourg, tel.: 43791) or from its offices in Belgium (rue de la Loi 277, B-1040 Brussels, tel.: 230 98 90), Italy (Via Sardegna 38, I-00187 Rome, tel.: 497941) the United Kingdom (68 Pall Mall, London SW1Y 5ES, tel.: 839 3351) and Greece (Ypsilantou Odos 13-15, Kolonaki, GR-10675 Athens, tel.: 724 98 11/12/13).
[3] Point 93 et seq. of this Report.

million ECU. Loans to infrastructure projects of Community interest remained at a high level (428.2 million ECU).

Aid to industry accounted for more than 34.3% of all financing operations, taking the form of either individual loans (552.2 million ECU, mainly in Italy) or global loans for small and medium-sized ventures involving investment in areas qualifying for regional development aid (675.0 million ECU from own resources) and outside these areas (795.3 million ECU from NCI resources). On-lending totalling 1 403.6 million ECU from current global loans went to 4 624 small and medium-sized firms involved in industry, services and tourism.

The investment projects financed should directly help to create some 44 300 permanent jobs, mainly in industry, quite apart from the considerable spin-off, especially from infrastructure and energy projects, which is more difficult to evaluate.

TABLE 7

EIB loans in 1984

	Amount of loans			Breakdown by sector		
	from own resources	from NCI resources	total %	Industry	Energy	Infra-structure
Belgium	32.5	—	0.5	—	32.5	—
Denmark	190.0	134.6	5.2	41.8	217.5	65.3
FR of Germany	134.3	—	2.2	—	134.3	—
Greece	275.5	69.3	5.6	77.3	123.6	143.9
France	814.0	386.3	19.4	502.9	115.7	581.7
Ireland	124.0	50.0	2.8	83.4	—	90.6
Italy	2 538.2	497.3	49.0	1 368.4	546.6	1 120.5
Luxembourg	16.4	—	0.3	—	—	16.4
United Kingdom	888.2	44.3	15.0	66.1	577.5	288.9
Community	5 013.1	1 181.8	100.0	2 139.9	1 747.8	2 307.2

104. With regard to Euratom operations, the Bank processed and made recommendations to the Commission on various loan applications: it contributed, as agent, to the conclusion of six loan contracts totalling 183 million ECU (these operations are not entered in the balance sheet but in the special section and are not included in the amounts given above).

105. Operations outside the Community totalled 708.3 million ECU, as against 480.3 million ECU in 1983. More than nine tenths of this amount took the form of loans from the Bank's own resources; operations financed out of special resources accounted for 87.6 million ECU.

Assistance to the Mediterranean countries—547.6 million ECU lent almost entirely from the Bank's own resources—went mainly to Spain (140 million ECU), Portugal (80 million ECU) and Yugoslavia (126.3 million ECU); the amounts for the Maghreb and Mashreq countries (175.8 million ECU) and for Israel (20.0 million ECU) were appreciably higher than in the past. Global loans on special terms of 6 million ECU were made from budget resources to Egypt, Tunisia and Jordan.

The operations in the ACP countries under the second Lomé Convention amounted to 79.1 million ECU from the Bank's own resources and 81.6 million ECU in aid in the form of risk capital from budget funds.

106. The Bank obtained the funds it required for lending operations from its own resources by raising a total of 4 361.2 million ECU, largely in the form of public and private issues on the international capital markets or on the national markets of certain member and non-member countries. Of this total, 555 million was raised in ECU.

107. At its annual meeting on 4 June the Bank's Board of Governors appointed Mr Ernst-Günther Bröder EIB President and Mr Alain Prate Vice-President, following the departure of Mr Yves Le Portz and Mr Horst-Otto Steffe.[1] The Board endorsed the recommendations in a report dealing with: the size of loans in the light of any other form of Community aid; financing of industrial projects; environmental protection; international tendering procedures for the supply of goods and services to the projects it finances; and the introduction, for a trial period, of floating-rate borrowing/lending operations.

General budget guarantee for borrowing and lending operations

108. The guarantee by the Community budget can cover both borrowings and lending. For borrowings the Commission provides the budget guarantee to its own lenders when floating an issue under one of its financial instruments—

---

[1] Bull. EC 6-1984, point 2.4.15.

balance of payments facility, Euratom loans, New Community Instrument (NCI). For loans granted, the guarantee is given to the European Investment Bank for the loans it makes from its own resources under the Mediterranean protocols.

In providing this guarantee, the Community gives its lenders or the EIB an undertaking that it will repay capital and pay interest on the due dates and throughout the duration of a borrowing or lending operation in the place of a defaulting debtor.

The likelihood of any permanent default may be regarded as very slight, however, since the operations guaranteed by the Community are either loans to large public promoters or, in the case of private recipients, loans already backed up by usual bank guarantees (security charges on property, etc.). In practice, the budget guarantee would be activated only in odd cases of delay in the repayment of an annual instalment of a loan repayable over several years.

In 1984 authorized borrowing and lending operations guaranteed by the general budget totalled a maximum of 16 400 million ECU; at 31 December the guarantee was in operation for 11 227.6 million ECU of Community borrowings and for outstanding loans of 2 285.0 million ECU granted out of the EIB's own resources. The annual interest corresponding to this capital commitment and covered by the same guarantee amounted at 31 December to 1 183.4 million ECU for 1984 and 1 308.1 million ECU for 1985.

Chapter II

Building the Community

Section 1

Economic and monetary policy

Main developments

109. *The distinct improvement in the international environment in 1984 gave a strong stimulus to growth in the Community as world trade expanded rapidly. At the same time substantial progress was made with stabilization policies and there was greater convergence of economic performances both in the fight against inflation and in current payment balances. In the Community as a whole, however, no progress was made in increasing employment or reducing unemployment, which continued to rise, though at a slower rate.*

Faced with this situation and with the continued uncertainty in the short-term international outlook, the Community endeavoured to create conditions for stronger and more durable growth in the economy and in employment without sacrificing its objective of stabilization, and tried in particular to improve medium-term economic development prospects and measures.

Action was begun, and proposals sent to the Council, aimed at reinforcing the convergence process and establishing a truly competitive market that will encourage both economic efficiency and economic growth in the Community. Study of ways of strengthening the European Monetary System (EMS) was started, likewise examination of a proposal for the minting of a European coinage, the ECU. The Community also played an active part in the work of the international institutions to improve the functioning of the international monetary system.

The economic situation

110. In 1984 the world economy proved distinctly more buoyant than expected, particularly the economy of the United States. The growth of world trade accelerated sharply and could exceed 9% (volume) for the year as a whole. This, together with some increase in internal demand, brought more rapid expansion in the Community's gross domestic product, which will probably have increased by 2.2% in real terms in 1984 as against 0.9% in 1983. For the first time in several years, the economies of all the member countries will have been pointing up, with growth rates ranging between 1.4% and 3.8% for the year as a whole.

111. However, this upturn in activity was not sufficient to prevent a further increase in unemployment in the Community, and the unemployment rate could reach 11% of the labour force, as against 10.4% in 1983.

112. Inflation continued to slow down, and the consumer price deflator for the Community as a whole will probably have fallen from 6.2% in 1983 to 5.1% in 1984. For the year as a whole the inflation rate should be approximately 6.5%, compared with 8.5% in 1983.

113. Since the favourable impact of the growth of world trade was offset by a deterioration in the Community's terms of trade, the improvement in the Community's external position did not continue in 1984. Because of an increase in the deficit on invisibles, the Community's current account is expected to show a deficit of 1 100 million ECU in 1984, compared with a surplus of 2 300 million ECU in 1983.

114. The annual growth rate of the money supply in the Community as a whole is expected to continue to slow down, to stand at 8% by the end of the year compared with 10.1% in 1983. Interest rates in the Community fell slightly: short-term rates declined from 10.7% in November 1983 to 10.1% in November 1984.

Coordination of economic and monetary policies

115. In accordance with the Decision of 18 February 1974 on the attainment of a high degree of economic policy convergence, [1] the Council examined the economic situation in the Community on three occasions: at the first examin-

---

[1] OJ L 63, 5.3.1984.

ation, on 12 March,[1] it concluded that there was no need to adjust the economic policy guidelines for 1984 which it had adopted in December 1983 in the annual report on the economic situation in the Community.[2]

At the second quarterly examination, on 9 July,[3] the Council endorsed the Commission's opinion that it was not necessary at that stage to adjust the economic policy guidelines for 1984.[2] It also took note of the quantitative guidelines for Member States' budgets for 1985.[4]

116. The third examination took place on 10 December. Acting on a proposal from the Commission[5] and in the light of the conclusions of the Dublin European Council,[6] the Council on 19 December formally adopted the annual report on the economic situation in the Community and approved economic policy guidelines for the Member States for 1985.[7]

117. In 1984 the European Council met at Brussels, Fontainebleau and Dublin. At its Fontainebleau meeting, the European Council, confirming the agreement which it had reached in Brussels on 'new policies', set precise objectives for the European economy, notably convergence of economic policies and the financing of investment.[8] It also instructed an *ad hoc* Committee on a People's Europe to examine *inter alia* the suggestion for the minting of a European coinage, the ECU.[9] Lastly, it confirmed the agreement also reached in Brussels on budgetary and financial discipline and instructed the Ministers for Economic and Financial Affairs, in conjunction with the Ministers for Foreign Affairs, to adopt the procedure for implementing the agreement.[10]

At its Dublin meeting,[7] the European Council welcomed the priority given to the problem of unemployment by the Commission in the annual report[5] and approved the balanced package of directives it contained as a coherent economic policy framework for improving the conditions of supply and demand. With a view to their rapid implementation the European Council listed a number of aims for the Council of Ministers, including wider use of the ECU and strengthening of the EMS.

---

[1] Bull. EC 3-1984, point 2.1.1.
[2] OJ L 378, 31.12.1983; Seventeenth General Report, point 128.
[3] Bull. EC 7/8-1984, point 2.1.2.
[4] Bull. EC 6-1984, point 2.1.3.
[5] Bull. EC 10-1984, point 2.1.2.
[6] Point 117 of this Report.
[7] Bull. EC 12-1984.
[8] Bull. EC 6-1984, point 1.1.6.
[9] Bull. EC 6-1984, point 1.1.9.
[10] Point 78 of this Report.

118. At the end of the Western Economic Summit, held in London from 7 to 9 June,[1] the seven Heads of State or Government and the representatives of the Community issued a declaration setting out a full range of steps to be taken for consolidating the recovery that could now be seen to be established.

Medium-term economic development in the Community

119. On 29 June the Commission sent the Council a communication on medium-term economic development in the Community, describing the outlook and practical steps to be taken.[2] In the document, the Commission acknowledged that the experience of an exhaustive medium-term economic policy programme prepared every five years[3] had been disappointing because it had been difficult to obtain a consensus. The Commission advocated a new approach to medium-term economic policy problems, consonant with the spirit of the Council's convergence Decision of 18 February 1974,[4] in the form of measures (identified in conjunction with the Economic Policy Committee) which were more limited in scope but more concrete and effective.

120. In March Parliament adopted two resolutions, one on a programme for European economic recovery[5] and the other on medium and long-term economic prospects in the Community.[6]

European Monetary System

Operation of the EMS

121. The year was marked by greater cohesiveness of the EMS and (despite a period of severe international monetary disturbances) by exchange-rate stability within the system, and this allowed the central rates set on 21 March 1983 to be maintained.[7]

---

1 Bull. EC 6-1984, points 2.1.1 and 3.4.1 et seq.
2 Bull. EC 6-1984, point 2.1.4.
3 The fifth was adopted in July 1982: OJ L 236, 11.8.1982; Sixteenth General Report, point 129.
4 OJ L 63, 5.3.1974.
5 OJ C 117, 30.4.1984; Bull. EC 3-1984, point 2.4.20.
6 OJ C 117, 30.4.1984; Bull. EC 3-1984, point 2.4.22.
7 Seventeenth General Report, point 135.

Five-year review

122. On 12 March the Council made a statement on the results of five years of operation of the EMS[1] on the basis of a communication which the Commission had drawn up after consulting the Monetary Committee. The document studies the contribution of the EMS to the convergence of economic policies required for the creation of a zone of stability in Europe, assessing the degree of convergence brought about by the system and describing the results achieved. It goes on to show how the mechanisms of the system have operated in the interests of orderly exchange-rate management, discussing their adequacy for this purpose and their scope.

Revision of the composition of the ECU

123. On 15 September the Council decided,[2] acting on a proposal from the Commission after consulting the Monetary Committee and the Board of Governors of the European Monetary Cooperation Fund, to revise the composition of the ECU in accordance with the resolution of the European Council of 5 December 1978 on the establishment of the European Monetary System[3] —in particular Section 2.3, which provides for periodic re-examination of the composition of the ECU and, if necessary, its revision.

124. The revision was carried out with due regard for underlying economic criteria and the need to ensure the smooth functioning of the markets. It also complies with the rule in the 1978 resolution that revisions should not, by themselves, modify the external value of the ECU.[3] Nor does it affect the ECU central rates of the currencies participating in the exchange-rate mechanism or bilateral parities within the EMS.

The Greek Government took this opportunity to request the inclusion of the drachma in the ECU, as provided by the Act concerning the Conditions of Accession of the Hellenic Republic.[4] The Council agreed to this.

---

[1] Bull EC 3-1984, point 1.3.1 *et seq.*
[2] OJ L 247, 16.9.1984; Bull. EC 9-1984, point 2.1.4.
[3] OJ L 379, 30.12.1978; Twelfth General Report, point 96.
[4] OJ L 291, 19.11.1979.

Medium-term financial assistance

125. On 10 December the Council extended the period of validity [1] of the Decision setting up machinery for medium-term financial assistance. [2] The Decision will now be valid until 31 December 1986 unless the European Monetary System enters its definitive phase before that date.

Developing the EMS

126. On 10 December the Council, considering that high priority should be given to the further strengthening of the EMS, [3] welcomed the guidelines put forward by the Commission in its communication, accompanied by a draft resolution, proposing a range of measures that would strengthen the system significantly. [4] It accordingly invited the Committee of the Governors of the Central Banks and the Monetary Committee to study the proposals and announce their conclusions expeditiously, taking due account of the legal situation in each Member State.

The Community and the international monetary system

127. The annual meeting of the Board of Governors of the International Monetary Fund, held in Washington in September, [5] was preceded by two preparatory meetings of the Interim Committee. The Community was represented by Mr Alan Dukes, the Irish Minister for Finance and current President of the Council, and by Mr François-Xavier Ortoli, Vice-President of the Commission.

128. On 12 April the Interim Committee of the Board of Governors of the IMF held its 22nd meeting, under the chairmanship of Mr Willy De Clercq, Belgium's Minister for Finance. [6] It analysed the economic situation and welcomed the pace of the economic recovery currently under way in industrial countries. It also noted that growth prospects in the developing countries were improving with the renewed expansion of world trade coupled with some improvement

---

[1] OJ L 341, 29.12.1984; Bull. EC 12-1984.
[2] OJ L 375, 31.12.1980; OJ L 368, 31.12.1982; Bull. EC 11-1984, point 2.1.5.
[3] Bull. EC 12-1984.
[4] Bull. EC 11-1984, point 2.1.4.
[5] Bull. EC 9-1984, point 2.1.1.
[6] Bull. EC 4-1984, point 2.1.2.

in their terms of trade. Most of those taking part, however, expressed great concern about the level of international interest rates and the current account and public finance imbalances in a number of major industrialized countries. But a minority of industrialized countries were not convinced that there was a global international liquidity shortage that required an allocation of SDRs, despite the continuing concern over problems of international indebtedness.

129. The 23rd meeting of the IMF Interim Committee, held in Washington on 22 September, again with Mr Willy De Clercq in the chair, agreed that the temporary enlarged access policy, under which Member States are allowed to borrow from the IMF beyond their normal quotas, would be continued in 1985, though on a reduced basis. [1] However, it was unable to reach agreement on a new allocation—even modest—of SDRs for 1985-86, and it decided to keep the matter under consideration.

Initiatives and measures taken by the Community

New Community Instrument (NCI III)

130. In July the Council decided to open a second and final tranche of 1 400 million ECU under NCI III, [2] to be applied in the same fields of activity as the first tranche. [3] The Council did not approve the allocation of a special 100 million ECU tranche to finance innovation in the Community, having failed to agree on a proposal for a Decision empowering the Commission to assist in the financing. [4]

Borrowing and lending

131. On 29 May the Commission sent the Council a proposal for a Regulation concerning the Community loan mechanism designed to support Member States' payments balances; [5] the proposal was to raise the ceiling on the

---

[1] Bull EC 9-1984, point 2.1.2.
[2] OJ L 208, 3.8.1984; Bull. EC 7/8-1984, point 2.1.5.
[3] OJ L 164, 23.6.1983; Seventeenth General Report, point 143.
[4] OJ C 178, 5.7.1983; Seventeenth General Report, point 144; OJ C 40, 15.2.1984; Bull. EC 1-1984, point 2.1.25.
[5] OJ C 167, 27.6.1984; Bull. EC 5-1984, point 2.1.3.

mechanism to 8 000 million ECU (it now stands at 6 000 million ECU), to restrict any one Member State's entitlement under the instrument to 50% of the total available and to drop the link between balance-of-payments problems serious enough to warrant a loan and increases in oil prices.

132. On 26 July the Commission transmitted to the Council and to Parliament its fourth general report on the Community's borrowing and lending activities, dealing with 1983. [1] The report gives a full description of lending under the Community instruments and examines the link between such lending and the Community's main structural objectives.

[1] Bull. EC 7/8-1984, point 2.1.7.

Section 2

Internal market

Main developments

133. *The Commission has made the strengthening of the internal market one of the main girders of Community policy, considering that the free movement of goods is a necessary condition for the recovery of firms' competitiveness and consequently for the recovery of Community industry. It therefore continued its strategy of placing each individual initiative contributing to the completion of the internal market in an overall political context.*

It was with this aim in mind that the Commission put up to the Council in June a detailed comprehensive programme covering not only the abolition of customs barriers and business law but also the free movement of capital and persons and freedom to provide services, and certain aspects of agricultural, taxation and transport policies.

The European Council at its Fontainebleau meeting said it 'considers it essential that the Community should respond to the expectations of the people of Europe by adopting measures to strengthen and promote its identity and its image both for its citizens and for the rest of the world'; and it set up an ad hoc *committee composed of Representatives of the Heads of State or Government of the Member States to prepare and coordinate this action. It asked the Council to adopt at an early date the single document for the movement of goods (which the Council approved on 18 December),[1] and to consider measures for the abolition at intra-Community frontiers of all police and customs formalities affecting the movement of persons and for a general system of equivalence of university diplomas in order to make a reality of freedom of establishment within the Community.*

The Council reached important decisions concerning technical barriers, company law, simplification of frontier formalities and standardization; and significant progress was achieved in other areas such as trade-mark law. As regards standardization, the Council's 1983 Directive and the policy guidelines it laid down in July signalled the launching of a policy articulated in individual

---

[1] Point 180 of this Report.

measures in the field of new technologies and telecommunications; its purpose is to give European firms the common technical environment they need both to achieve economies of scale and thus secure their competitiveness and to enable them to face on a common basis the competition from large firms outside the Community.

The Commission put forward new proposals to update the right of establishment of general medical practitioners, to integrate the pharmaceuticals Directives into the context of the development of new biotechnology products and to open up merger possibilities for European firms. The Commission also presented major proposals for the protection of the environment against motor-vehicle emissions, which were the subject of important policy debates at the Council, in Parliament and at the Economic and Social Committee.

With a view to establishing a common market in broadcasting, especially broadcasting by satellite and cable, the Commission set out in a Green Paper its considered views on the approximation of certain aspects of national legislation concerning broadcasting and copyright.

Free movement of persons and freedom to provide services

Removal of restrictions

134. The Commission initiated six infringement procedures against Member States to put an end to discrimination affecting freedom of establishment and freedom to provide services.

Mutual recognition of diplomas and access to economic activities

135. On 24 January, in response to the opinions issued by Parliament[1] and the Economic and Social Committee[2] on two 1981 proposals for Directives concerning the free movement of pharmacists in the Community, the Commission amended[3] its proposal on mutual recognition of diplomas and other qualifications in pharmacy.[4] Both proposals are now being considered at

---

[1] OJ C 277, 17.10.1983; Seventeenth General Report, point 168.
[2] OJ C 230, 10.9.1981.
[3] OJ C 40, 15.2.1984; Bull. EC 1-1984, point 2.1.4.
[4] OJ C 35, 18.2.1981; Fifteenth General Report, point 151.

Council level. On 11 December the Commission sent to the Council a proposal for a Directive relating to specific training in general medical practice.[1]

In administering the arrangements for the mutual recognition of diplomas, the Committee of Senior Officials on Public Health and the Advisory Committees on Medical Training,[2] Training in Nursing,[3] the Training of Dental Practitioners[4] and Veterinary Training[5] and the *ad hoc* group of senior officials responsible for the free movement of veterinary surgeons[6] continued their work in circumstances made difficult by the budget crisis. These committees discussed or adopted nine reports, opinions and recommendations aimed at ensuring a comparably high level of training for these professions throughout the Community. The Advisory Committee on the Training of Midwives held its inaugural meeting on 6 and 7 November.[7]

The Commission initiated or continued 57 proceedings for infringement of 16 Directives.

In response to the conclusions of the Presidency on the proceedings of the European Council meeting in Fontainebleau,[8] the Commission embarked upon work to introduce a general system for the equivalence of university diplomas which would enable all Community citizens who so wish to take up employment or to set up on a self-employed basis in any Member State.

136. In response to the wishes of Parliament,[9] on 28 June the Commission presented a Green Paper on the establishment of a common market in broadcasting, especially broadcasting by satellite and cable.[10] New technology has made it possible to broadcast beyond national frontiers, but there are still legal obstacles. To remove these obstacles, the Commission suggests, over and above observance of directly applicable provisions, that certain aspects of national legislation relating to broadcasting (advertising, protection of young people and the right of reply) and copyright should be brought more closely into line. The Commission's suggestions will serve as the basis for wide-ranging public debate before any formal proposals are put before the Council and Parliament. Swift Community action is called for because of the importance of the contri-

---

[1] OJ C 13, 15.1.1985; Bull. EC 12-1984.
[2] Bull. EC 3-1984, point 2.1.13.
[3] Bull. EC 10-1984, point 2.1.10.
[4] Bull. EC 11-1984, point 2.1.8.
[5] Bull. EC 2-1984, point 2.1.12; Bull. EC 10-1984, point 2.1.8.
[6] Bull. EC 3-1984, point 2.1.12; Bull. EC 10-1984, point 2.1.9.
[7] Bull. EC 11-1984, point 2.1.7.
[8] Bull. EC 6-1984, point 1.1.9 (paragraph 6).
[9] OJ C 87, 5.4.1982; OJ C 117, 30.4.1984; Bull. EC 3-1984, point 2.4.22.
[10] Bull. EC 5-1984, point 1.3.1 *et seq.*.

bution that broadcasting—television in particular—can make to European integration, both in the economic field and in the social, cultural and political spheres. Community citizens will benefit from this action.

Special rights of citizens and passport union

137. On 7 June, rather than accept the draft put before it by the Commission in 1982, [1] the Council and the Representatives of the Governments of the Member States meeting within the Council adopted a more limited resolution on the easing of checks on persons at the Community's internal frontiers. [2] The Commission issued a statement pointing out that its draft represented a feasible compromise between the total abolition of checks and security requirements, and intimating that it might make further proposals. At the end of December the Commission adopted a proposal for a Council Directive to ease controls and formalities applying to citizens of Member States crossing intra-Community frontiers.

In response to the President's conclusions at the Fontainebleau meeting of the European Council, [3] the Commission transmitted a communication to the Council on 24 September pointing out ways and means of abolishing police and customs formalities at intra-Community frontiers and securing general recognition of the right to freedom of establishment. [4]

Following up suggestions by the Commission, the Member States issued postage stamps bearing similar designs to mark the second direct elections to the European Parliament in June 1984. [5]

Tourism

138. On 10 April the Council adopted a resolution [6] on a Community policy on tourism, [7] which emphasizes the need for the tourism dimension to be taken more fully into consideration in the Community's decision-making process and invites the Commission to present proposals based on consultations with the Member States.

---

[1] OJ C 197, 31.7.1982; Sixteenth General Report, point 168.
[2] OJ C 159, 19.6.1984; Bull. EC 6-1984, point 1.5.1 et seq.
[3] Bull. EC 6-1984, point 1.1.9 (paragraph 6).
[4] Bull. EC 9-1984, point 1.1.1 et seq.
[5] Bull. EC 6-1984, point 1.2.1 et seq.
[6] OJ C 115, 30.4.1984; Bull. EC 4-1984, point 2.1.9.
[7] Seventeenth General Report, point 173.

On 17 January the Commission put forward a proposal for a recommendation on fire safety in existing hotels. [1] The Economic and Social Committee endorsed the proposal at its July session. [2]

Free movement of goods

139. Major events in this field were the launching of a European standardization policy and renewed progress on the removal of technical barriers to trade.

The Council Directive of 28 March 1983 laying down a procedure for the provision of information in the field of technical standards and regulations [3] became operative in 1984. The Commission signed agreements with the European Committee for Standardization and the European Committee for Electrotechnical Standardization concerning the administration of this procedure.

In the field of technical rules, the procedure laid down in the Directive made it possible to examine rules drafted by the Member States for compatibility with the principles governing the free movement of goods in the Community. As a result, several initial drafts were amended so as to forestall the possible creation of barriers to trade.

At the same time, the Council laid the foundations for a standardization policy in the conclusions which it adopted on 16 July. [4] As regards technical harmonization, the Council stressed the advisability of basing the definition of the technical characteristics of products on a reference to standards wherever possible, indicating that this should be accompanied by a very rapid strengthening of Europe's capacity for standardization. The Commission is currently examining how this general principle can be applied. The Commission also determined broad guidelines for cooperation between itself and the European standardization bodies with a view to achieving the requisite increase in standardization capacity.

140. In the Council, reservations by two Member States to the continuation of work on the removal of technical barriers to trade were withdrawn, and 15 technical Directives were adopted in September. [5]

---

[1] OJ C 49, 21.2.1984; Bull. EC 1-1984, point 2.1.5.
[2] OJ C 248, 17.9.1984.
[3] OJ L 109, 26.4.1983; Bull. EC 4-1984, point 2.1.10.
[4] Bull. EC 7/8-1984, point 2.1.12.
[5] Point 143 of this Report.

Measures having an effect equivalent to quantitative restrictions

141. The Commission continued its efforts to bring about the removal of non-tariff barriers, which are incompatible with Articles 30 to 36 of the EEC Treaty. On 1 January it brought into force new procedures relating to the examination of complaints and the investigation of infringements. These provide for mandatory time limits, periodic checks, more stringent verification and a more systematic recourse to expedited procedures. Notwithstanding the increasingly sophisticated nature of trade barriers, the Commission was able to deal satisfactorily with a very large number of complaints and infringements, mostly through contacting the appropriate authorities of the Member States before taking legal action. In response to a request from Parliament,[1] the Commission submitted its first annual report on the monitoring of the application of Community law.[2]

Safeguard measures

142. At the request of the Greek Government and because of the persistence of economic difficulties in Greece, the Commission adopted Decisions on 11 and 27 January,[3] extending them on 28 November,[4] which partially renewed until the end of 1985 the import restrictions on certain products which had been authorized as safeguard measures in 1983[5] under Article 130 of the Act of Accession. At the same time, it laid down objective criteria with a view to ensuring a fair distribution of the quotas among existing importers, while providing for the participation of new importers in the arrangements.

Removal of technical barriers to trade

143. Efforts to make progress with the removal of technical barriers to trade in industrial products culminated in 15 Directives in this sector being adopted, after lengthy negotiations, on 17 September.[6] These relate to pressure vessels (gas cylinders of seamless steel, seamless unalloyed aluminium and aluminium-alloy and welded unalloyed steel), appliances using gaseous fuels (framework

---

[1] OJ C 68, 14.3.1983.
[2] Bull. EC 4-1984; point 3.3.1.
[3] OJ L 23, 28.1.1984; OJ L 36, 8.2.1984; Bull. EC 1-1984, point 2.1.7.
[4] OJ L 340, 28.12.1984; Bull. EC 11-1984, point 2.1.9.
[5] Seventeenth General Report, point 155.
[6] OJ L 300, 19.11.1984; Bull. EC 9-1984, points 2.1.9 and 2.1.70; Bull. EC 4-1984, point 2.1.11.

Directive and appliances for the instantaneous production of hot water), lifting and mechanical-handling devices (framework Directive, electrically operated lifts), construction plant and equipment (framework Directive, pneumatic concrete-breakers and jackhammers, compressors, tower cranes, current generators for welding and for power supply), electromedical equipment used in human and veterinary medicine, and lawnmowers. The Council also amended its Directive relating to the permissible sound level and the exhaust system of motor vehicles, [1] and its Directive on units of measurement. [2]

This means that the Council has now adopted a total of 177 Directives in this sector. Although, taken together, these can be said to represent progress towards the creation and strengthening of the internal Community market, the fact remains that 39 proposals for Directives have still not been approved owing to lack of agreement among the Member States.

The Commission also adopted a number of Directives in this sector, most of them involving the adaptation to technical progress of existing instruments. They cover electrical equipment for use in potentially explosive atmospheres employing certain types of protection, [3] the labelling of dangerous preparations (pesticides), [4] the permissible sound level and the exhaust system of motor vehicles, [5] clinical mercury-in-glass maximum-reading thermometers, [6] and the classification, packaging and labelling of dangerous substances. [7] This brings the number of Directives adopted by the Commission in this field to 57.

Other proposals made this year relate to restrictions on the marketing and use of certain dangerous substances and preparations (second PCB and PCT Directive), [8] the amendment of Directives concerning the ranges of nominal quantities and nominal capacities permitted for certain prepackaged products, [9] the permissible sound level and the exhaust system of motorcycles, [10] the protection devices of narrow-track wheeled agricultural or forestry tractors, [11] and the amendment of Directives relating to the lead and benzine content of petrol and to motor-vehicle emissions. [12]

---

[1] OJ L 238, 6.9.1984; Bull. EC 9-1984, point 2.1.71.
[2] OJ L 2, 3.1.1985; Bull. EC 12-1984.
[3] OJ L 31, 2.2.1984; Bull. EC 1-1984, point 2.1.9.
[4] OJ L 144, 30.5.1984; Bull. EC 4-1984, point 2.1.84.
[5] OJ L 196, 26.7.1984; Bull. EC 7/8-1984, point 2.1.16.
[6] OJ L 228, 25.8.1984; Bull. EC 7/8-1984, point 2.1.17.
[7] OJ L 251, 19.9.1984; Bull. EC 4-1984, point 2.1.85.
[8] Bull. EC 10-1984, point 2.1.83.
[9] OJ C 18, 25.1.1984; Bull. EC 1-1984, point 2.1.12.
[10] OJ C 263, 2.10.1984; Bull. EC 9-1984, point 2.1.72.
[11] Bull. EC 11-1984, point 2.1.10.
[12] Point 367 of this Report.

144. In the foodstuffs sector, priority was given to the removal of barriers to trade resulting, in particular, from public-health considerations or from other mandatory requirements.

On 15 October the Council adopted the Directive on the approximation of the laws of the Member States relating to ceramic articles intended to come into contact with foodstuffs, [1] which had been proposed by the Commission in 1974. [2] This Directive is designed to protect human health and guarantee the purity of foodstuffs by limiting the amounts of lead and cadmium that may be transferred to food by the articles in question. The Council also amended its Directive on the bulk prepackaging of certain liquids [3] and its Directive on emulsifiers, stabilizers, thickeners and gelling agents for use in foodstuffs. [4]

The Commission sent the Council proposals for Directives relating to: the list of simulants to be used for testing the migration of constituents of plastic materials and articles intended to come into contact with foodstuffs, [5] with a view to ensuring the inertness of these materials to food; quick-frozen foodstuffs for human consumption, [6] in order to assure the consumer of a high-quality finished product through the introduction of rules covering the entire cold chain and incorporating special labelling instructions; modified starches intended for human consumption, [7] so as to establish an approved list of chemically modified starches which are safe for human consumption; and infant preparations and follow-up milk formulae, [8] with a view to defining the essential criteria applicable to the composition of these products. This last proposal was accompanied by a report on baby foods and the application of the (WHO) International Code of Marketing of Breast-Milk Substitutes. The Commission also put forward a proposal relating to methods of sampling and analysis for the monitoring of foodstuffs intended for human consumption. [9]

In its administration of existing legislation, the Commission presented proposals updating instruments in force concerning cocoa and chocolate products,[10] and coffee and chicory extracts.[11]

The early-warning system which has been in existence since 1979 was activated in 15 cases.

---

[1] OJ L 277, 20.10.1984; Bull. EC 10-1984, point 2.1.14.
[2] OJ C 46, 27.2.1975.
[3] OJ L 4, 5.1.1985; Bull. EC 12-1984.
[4] OJ L 2, 3.1.1985; Bull. EC 12-1984.
[5] OJ C 102, 14.4.1984; Bull. EC 4-1984, point 2.1.13.
[6] OJ C 267, 6.10.1984; Bull. EC 9-1984, point 2.1.14.
[7] Bull. EC 12-1984.
[8] OJ C 28, 30.1.1985; Bull. EC 12-1984.
[9] OJ C 53, 24.2.1984; Bull. EC 2-1984, point 2.1.15.
[10] OJ C 32, 7.2.1984; Bull. EC 1-1984, point 2.1.10.
[11] OJ C 90, 31.3.1984; Bull. EC 3-1984, point 2.1.16.

Special attention was paid to international standardization activities, particularly those conducted under the auspices of FAO and WHO (Codex Alimentarius). The Commission acts as the spokesman of the Community in areas of Community responsibility.

145. In the pharmaceuticals sector, the Commission transmitted five proposals to the Council on 3 October with a view to the adoption of urgent measures to facilitate the development and marketing within the Community of medicinal products whose manufacture involves the application of biotechnology and other advanced technologies. [1]

On 13 April Parliament adopted a resolution on the approximation of the laws of the Member States relating to the distribution of veterinary medicines. [2]

Euronorms

146. Working in close collaboration with the Iron and Steel Nomenclature Coordination Committee (Cocor), the Commission initiated discussions with a view to introducing a new procedure for the preparation of Euronorms.

The main aim of this is to transform those Euronorms which now coexist with national steel standards into genuine European standards which would replace the relevant national ones. Although this principle met with broad approval within Cocor, the consultations are still not complete.

Of the eight Euronorms adopted this year, six relate to chemical analysis, one to test methods and one to quality specifications.

Business law

Company law

147. On 10 April the Council adopted the eighth company law Directive (qualifications of persons authorized to carry out statutory audits of annual accounts [3]) on the basis of a proposal presented by the Commission in 1978. [4]

---

[1] OJ C 293, 5.11.1984; Bull. EC 10-1984, point 2.1.16.
[2] OJ C 127, 14.5.1984; Bull. EC 4-1984, point 2.4.9.
[3] OJ L 126, 12.5.1984; Bull. EC 3-1984, points 2.1.17 and 2.1.18.
[4] Supplement 4/78 — Bull. EC; OJ C 112, 13.5.1978; Twelfth General Report, point 108; OJ C 317, 18.12.1979; Thirteenth General Report, point 108.

This Directive supplements the fourth Directive (individual accounts of limited liability companies [1]) and the seventh Directive (consolidated accounts [2]). It guarantees the level of ability of persons responsible for auditing accounts, thus harmonizing the quality of the published accounts of companies and corporate groups. This will be a further safeguard for users of such information. On 27 November the Council, acting on a proposal from the Commission, [3] adopted a Directive amending the amounts expressed in ECU used to define the thresholds of exemption provided for in the abovementioned accountancy Directives for the benefit of small and medium-sized firms. [4] The Commission laid before the Council a proposal for a tenth Directive (cross-frontier mergers of public limited liability companies). [5]

In view of the harmonization effected by these Directives, the Community now acts as a single entity in international organizations (UN, OECD) dealing with accounting standards.

148. In keeping with the priority given by the European Council to cooperation between businesses, [6] the Council continued to study intensively the proposal on the European economic interest grouping [7] and finished its examination of the technical aspects.

Intellectual property

149. On 9 August the Commission amended [8] its proposal for a Regulation on the Community trade mark, [9] taking account of the opinions delivered by Parliament[10] and the Economic and Social Committee. [11] On 9 October the Council took note of what had been accomplished at the first reading and gave instructions for work to proceed at committee level.

150. On 28 February the Council, on the basis of the Commission's proposals, decided that measures needed to be taken to improve the law (including the rules governing intellectual property rights) concerning biotechnology products. [12]

---

[1] OJ L 222, 14.8.1978; Twelfth General Report, point 108.
[2] OJ L 193, 18.7.1983; Seventeenth General Report, point 160.
[3] Bull. EC 7/8-1984, point 2.1.20.
[4] OJ L 314, 4.12.1984; Bull. EC 11-1984, point 2.1.12.
[5] OJ C 23, 25.1.1985.
[6] Bull. EC 6-1984, point 1.1.6.
[7] OJ C 103, 28.4.1978; Seventeenth General Report, point 161.
[8] OJ C 230, 31.8.1984; Bull. EC 7/8-1984, point 2.1.21.
[9] Supplement 5/80 — Bull. EC; OJ C 351, 31.12.1980; Fifteenth General Report, point 142.
[10] OJ C 307, 14.11.1983; Seventeenth General Report, point 164.
[11] OJ C 310, 30.11.1981; Fifteenth General Report, point 142.
[12] Bull. EC 2-1984, point 2.1.30.

151. The fourth session of the Diplomatic Conference for the revision of the Paris Convention for the Protection of Industrial Property was held from 27 February to 24 March. Delegates from the Member States and the Commission met on a number of occasions to prepare common measures on, among other things, the protection of geographical indications.

Civil, commercial and economic law

152. On 10 April the Representatives of the Governments of the Member States signed the Convention on the accession of the Hellenic Republic [1] to the Rome Convention on the Law applicable to Contractual Obligations. [2]

153. The Council's committees continued work on the proposal relating to product liability [3] and on the amended proposal for a Directive to coordinate the laws of the Member States relating to commercial agents. [4] They also proceeded with the examination of the draft agreement designed to amend the Treaties establishing the European Communities with a view to the adoption of criminal law rules to protect the Community's interests.

154. On 29 June the *ad hoc* committee set up to examine the draft Convention on Bankruptcy, Winding-up, Arrangements, Compositions and Similar Proceedings completed the second reading of the draft. [5]

Public contracts

155. As the Council Directives on public works contracts [6] have now been in existence for 13 years, it was felt they should be adapted to current market conditions. The Commission, in close cooperation with the Advisory Committee on Public Contracts, started work on revising the provisions.

156. As regards public supply contracts, the Commission sent to the Council in December a report on the functioning of the Council Directive of December 1976 [7] and on the conclusions to be drawn.

---

[1] OJ L 146, 31.5.1984; Bull. EC 4-1984, point 2.1.16.
[2] OJ L 266, 9.10.1980; Fourteenth General Report, point 135.
[3] OJ C 241, 14.10.1976; OJ C 271, 26.10.1979.
[4] OJ C 13, 18.1.1977; OJ C 56, 2.3.1979; Bull. EC 10-1984, point 2.1.17.
[5] Supplement 2/82 — Bull. EC.
[6] OJ L 185, 1.6.1971.
[7] OJ L 13, 15.1.1977; OJ L 215, 18.8.1980.

Section 3

Customs union

Main developments

157. *In December the Council formally adopted the 'single Community customs document', reflecting its desire to cut red tape at intra-Community frontiers. The adoption of the 'single document' is something of an achievement and can be attributed not only to the hard work put in on the technical problems involved but also to a shift in the political climate in 1984. The blockade of Alpine passes by hauliers protesting at administrative obstacles in the way of the free movement of goods made an impact on politicians as well as the general public. A genuine desire for reforms, among them the introduction of the single document, was manifest at the European Council meeting at Fontainebleau in June.[1] The new customs form, it is now clear, will have a crucial part to play in linking up the various national customs administrations' electronic data-processing systems. The Council agreed on the need for a multiannual programme to tackle this job, and the Commission has put forward the necessary proposals.*

Harmonization of customs rules on trade with non-member countries

Common Customs Tariff

158. An updated version of the Common Customs Tariff (CCT),[2] to come into effect on 1 January 1985, incorporates a sixth round of tariff cuts for most industrial products, as part of the phased reductions agreed by the Community in 1979 in the multilateral trade negotiations.[3] Proposals were made at the Williamsburg Western Economic Summit to bring forward a further round of cuts,[4] but were jettisoned when major OECD countries failed to follow suit.

---

[1] Bull. EC 6-1984, point 1.1.1 *et seq.*
[2] OJ L 320, 10.12.1984; Bull. EC 11-1984, point 2.1.28.
[3] Thirteenth General Report, points 494 and 495.
[4] Bull. EC 5-1983, point 3.4.2; Bull. EC 12-1983, point 2.2.8.

However, in response to a proposal from the Commission the Council agreed to early reductions in duties on some 320 products of particular importance to the trade of developing countries. [1]

159. On 30 January the Council adopted [2] the Commission's proposals for measures designed to cope with wide exchange-rate fluctuations between Community currencies. [3] However, currency movements in 1984 were not in fact marked enough to warrant application of the new measures.

160. The continuing efforts of the Commission and the Member States to ensure correct and uniform application of the CCT nomenclature received a boost when Commission proposals for amendments to the Regulation of 16 January 1969 [4] were adopted by the Council on 16 July. [5] Certain classification measures—classification slips and explanatory notes—can now be adopted by a qualified majority of the CCT Nomenclature Committee, which should make for greater efficiency. The Commission also proposed [6] that the Council should approve on behalf of the Community the International Convention on the Harmonized Commodity Description and Coding System which was adopted by the Customs Cooperation Council on 14 June 1983. Transposition of the new system into the CCT and Nimexe was nearing completion by the end of the year, with the new draft instruments due to be submitted to GATT early in 1985.

Economic tariff matters

161. Normal application of the CCT is waived in many instances by temporary or renewable tariff measures adopted by Council regulation. Such measures, whether required under Agreements or introduced unilaterally, involve reductions in customs duties or zero-rating in respect of some or all imports of a given product. They take the form of Community tariff quotas, tariff ceilings or total or partial suspension of duties.

162. In 1984 10 Community tariff quotas were opened pursuant to commitments entered into by the Community during the GATT multilateral trade

---

[1] Bull. EC 10-1984, point 2.2.25.
[2] OJ L 33, 4.2.1984.
[3] Seventeenth General Report, point 201.
[4] OJ L 14, 21.1.1969.
[5] OJ L 191, 19.7.1984; Bull. EC 7/8-1984, point 2.1.46.
[6] OJ C 120, 4.5.1984; Bull. EC 4-1984, point 2.1.31.

negotiations, while a further 146 Community tariff quotas or ceilings were introduced under bilateral agreements with non-member countries. Another 14 tariff quotas were opened on a unilateral basis in order to improve the Community supply situation for certain products.

163. For the same reason, and also in many cases with the aim of encouraging Community industry to use or introduce new technology, the Council temporarily suspended duties on 922 products or groups of products, mainly chemicals, plastics, medical supplies and products of the electronics or aircraft industries. Tariffs were also suspended on a number of agricultural and fisheries products, to improve the supply of certain types of food.

164. The Regulations giving effect to generalized tariff preferences on imports from developing countries were renewed and updated for 1985 as part of the Community's development aid policy.[1] There are improvements in the arrangements for textiles and provisions designed to enhance the efficiency of the system, allocate preference in such a way as to encourage industrial development in the least-developed countries and streamline GSP management.

Customs valuation

165. Administering the Community rules based on the GATT Customs Valuation Code, the Commission raised the value ceiling above which importers must declare particulars relating to customs valuation with effect from 1 January.[2] Another Commission Regulation adopted on 10 April updated the simplified procedures for determination of the customs value of certain perishable imports.[3]

166. The Customs Valuation Committee set up under the Council Regulation of 28 May 1980[4] continued its consideration of specific valuation issues and adopted a number of conclusions designed to secure uniform practice throughout the Community on points such as the treatment of trade-mark royalties, costing of goods imported from a related firm and sold in the unaltered state, and the valuation of waste imported for destruction.

---

[1] OJ L 338, 27.12.1984.
[2] OJ L 345, 8.12.1983.
[3] OJ L 101, 13.4.1984; Bull. EC 4-1984, point 2.1.33.
[4] OJ L 134, 31.5.1980.

167. The Commission acted as spokesman for the Community at meetings of the Customs Cooperation Council's Committee on Customs Valuation, which was working at technical level to promote uniform implementation of the rules of the GATT Code worldwide. The Commission also contributed to important policy decisions taken by the GATT Committee on Customs Valuation concerning the valuation of imported software (cassettes, disks, etc.) and interest charges payable under financing arrangements.

Customs procedures with economic impact

168. On 13 June the Commission adopted provisions [1] for the implementation of the Regulation of 21 December 1982 on temporary importation arrangements. [2]

169. The Commission also adopted various measures designed to ensure a more uniform application of the inward processing arrangements within the Community. A Directive dated 23 May reformed methods of administrative cooperation between Member States to ensure collection of customs duties when compensating products are released for free circulation in a Member State other than the one in which inward processing was authorized, and to take account of any specific commercial policy measures applying to the imported goods. [3] A Directive of 21 March laid down objective criteria for 'equivalent compensation' to apply to imports and exports of rice under the inward processing arrangements. [4] Commission Directives adopted on 26 July updated standard rates of yield (used in the application of inward processing arrangements to agricultural products) and amended the list of products for which specific methods of taxation exist in the event that they are released for free circulation after processing, rather than re-exported. [5]

Origin

170. The Lomé III negotiations provided further evidence of how important an issue origin rules are in the Community's trade with a considerable number of countries. In 1984, while making no substantive policy changes, the Community did introduce a number of technical reforms.

---

[1] OJ L 171, 29.6.1984, Bull. EC 6-1984, point 2.1.28.
[2] OJ L 376, 31.12.1982.
[3] OJ L 166, 26.6.1984; OJ L 218, 15.8.1984; Bull. EC 6-1984, point 2.1.29.
[4] OJ L 100, 12.4.1984; Bull. EC 3-1984, point 2.1.38.
[5] OJ L 245, 14.9.1984; Bull. EC 9-1984, point 2.1.26.

171. On 3 October the Council adopted a Regulation containing amendments which should provide for greater transparency in the application of Protocol No 3 to the Free Trade Agreements with EFTA countries.[1] The various Joint Committees were also empowered to adopt changes to the rules themselves, which should make for greater flexibility in future. At a more general level, since origin rules, preferential or other, use tariff headings as criteria for the working or processing of goods, the changeover to the harmonized system[2] in 1987 means that the whole corpus of rules will have to be reviewed. This is a major task, and work has already started in collaboration with the Member States and representatives of business and industry.

172. Using recently adopted legislation,[3] the Commission has stepped up efforts to combat fraudulent imports of textile products under false declarations of origin.

General legislation

173. A further measure of harmonization was accomplished with the Council's adoption of a Regulation on the customs territory of the Community[4] to replace that of 29 September 1968.[5] The new Regulation stipulates for the first time that the territorial sea of coastal Member States forms part of the customs territory of the Community.

174. Continuing its work on the harmonization of customs legislation with a view to the eventual drafting of a European customs code, the Commission sent the Council a proposal for a Regulation on customs debt[6] intended to replace the Directive of 25 June 1979[7] — a necessary pendant to the proposed Council Regulation on persons liable for payment of a customs debt,[8] which was amended in June[9] after Parliament had delivered its opinion.[10] In April the Commission also amended[11] its proposal on securities to be given to ensure payment of a customs debt in response to Parliament's opinion.[12]

---

[1] OJ L 323, 11.12.1984; Bull. EC 10-1984, point 2.1.41.
[2] Point 160 of this Report.
[3] Seventeenth General Report, point 214.
[4] OJ L 197, 27.7.1984; Bull. EC 7/8-1984, point 2.1.44.
[5] OJ L 238, 29.8.1968.
[6] OJ C 261, 29.9.1984; Bull. EC 9-1984, point 2.1.24.
[7] OJ L 179, 17.1.1979.
[8] OJ C 340, 28.12.1982.
[9] OJ C 189, 17.7.1984.
[10] OJ C 127, 14.5.1984.
[11] OJ C 113, 27.4.1984; Bull. EC 4-1984, point 2.1.29.
[12] OJ C 77, 19.3.1984.

175. On 14 December the Commission adopted, for transmittal to the Council, a proposal for a Regulation on the entry in the accounts and terms of payment of the amount of the import duties or export duties resulting from a customs debt. [1] The aim is to ensure that the same rules regarding payment facilities, interest etc. apply to businessmen in all Member States.

176. On 15 March the Commission sent the Council a proposal for a Regulation on goods returned to the customs territory of the Community, [2] amending the Council Regulation of 25 March 1976. [3]

177. On 21 November the Commission sent the Council a proposal for a Regulation [4] amending the Council Regulations of 28 March 1983 (on the Community system of reliefs from customs duty) [5] and 28 June 1968 (on the Common Customs Tariff). [6]

178. The Commission also sent the Council a proposal for a Regulation designed to regulate at Community level the action which may be taken by the competent authorities against attempts to import suspected counterfeit goods from non-member countries. [7] This should enable the Community, pending suitable multilateral action in GATT, to protect itself against unfair trading practices.

Simplification of customs checks and formalities in intra-Community trade

179. The new arrangements for movement within the Community of goods sent from one Member State for temporary use in one or more other Member States [8] are due to come into effect on 1 July 1985, and work continued on the preparations. The Council adopted a Regulation [9] on 4 June adding to the list of products annexed to the 19 December 1983 Regulation [10] a further 44 types of commercial sample which will now be able to move within the Community

---

[1] Bull. EC 12-1984.
[2] OJ C 87, 29.3.1984; Bull. EC 3-1984, point 2.1.37.
[3] OJ L 89, 2.4.1976.
[4] OJ C 324, 5.12.1984; Bull. EC 11-1984, point 2.1.35.
[5] OJ L 105, 23.4.1983; Seventeenth General Report, point 217.
[6] OJ L 172, 22.7.1968.
[7] OJ C 20, 22.1.1985; Bull. EC 12-1984.
[8] Seventeenth General Report, point 221.
[9] OJ L 151, 7.6.1984; Bull. EC 6-1984, point 2.1.9.
[10] OJ L 2, 4.1.1984.

under the new Community movement carnet. On 31 July the Commission adopted a set of provisions[1] for the detailed implementation of the 1983 Regulation; the Commission Regulation specifies the form of the Community movement carnet and the procedures to be followed by the holder of the carnet and the various customs offices involved in temporary movement operations.

180. On 18 December the Council approved the Commission's 1982 proposals[2] for a single Community customs document.[3] The 'single document' will replace some hundred forms currently used in trade within the Community, and considerable work aimed at securing agreement on the practicalities went on throughout the year. The list of particulars to be supplied was whittled down still further, representatives of business and industry having unanimously condemned the list adopted on 25 November 1983[4] as too long. Introduction of the new form will mean changes for business and administrations alike, and its entry into force is now scheduled for 1 January 1988 to allow time for the necessary adjustments.

181. On 1 February the Community and its Member States jointly signed the International Convention on the Harmonization of Frontier Controls of Goods[5] which was adopted on 21 October 1982. Under the Convention the Community will be able to work bilaterally with various non-member countries on the streamlining of administrative formalities at their common borders.

182. Following the survey carried out by the Commission with the Member States on the application of the Community transit arrangements, progress was made on a number of issues, including the question of guarantees. Studies are also continuing with a view to computerization of the Community transit system.

Improving the customs union

183. Work on the single Community customs document has highlighted the need for coordinated moves towards the introduction of electronic data-processing techniques in the administration of the customs union. On 15 May the

---

[1] OJ L 222, 20.8.1984; Bull. EC 7/8-1984, point 2.1.43.
[2] Sixteenth General Report, point 211.
[3] Bull. EC 10-1984, point 2.1.33.
[4] Seventeenth General Report, point 220.
[5] OJ L 126, 12.5.1984; Bull. EC 2-1984, point 2.1.35; Bull. EC 4-1984, point 2.1.28.

Council adopted a resolution on the computerization of administrative procedures in intra-Community trade, [1] acknowledging the need for a Community system to facilitate trade and prevent fraud and asking the Commission to put forward the necessary proposals. National computer systems should be linked, as a means of organizing the exchange of information, and administrative systems should be linked with companies' private systems.

184. On 20 November the Commission, as requested, laid before the Council a communication setting out a provisional schedule for this operation. [2] The work covers not only intra-Community trade but — on practical grounds — imports from non-member countries as well, and will form part of the Caddia programme; [3] it will last until 1992. One of the first measures will be the introduction of a new integrated tariff and statistics nomenclature, Taric II; the programming stage is already complete and the first texts have been produced.

185. The Commission continued to take steps to enhance cooperation with and between Member States' customs administrations in order to improve the operation of the customs union. The results of the year's work — under the Directive of 15 March 1976 [4] and the Regulation of 19 May 1981 [5] — were particularly impressive in terms of the recovery of outstanding sums and the detection of major frauds.

---

[1] OJ C 137, 24.5.1984; Bull. EC 5-1984, point 2.1.6.
[2] Bull. EC 11-1984, point 2.1.27.
[3] OJ C 112, 26.4.1984.
[4] OJ L 73, 19.3.1976.
[5] OJ L 144, 2.6.1981.

Section 4

Industrial strategy

Main developments

186. *To help industry redeploy in an atmosphere of gradual growth, the Commission has employed the instruments and constraints of the Treaties to ensure that the common market that represents the framework for the competitiveness of European industry is a unified, open entity.*

In those sectors which are in the process of restructuring, such as steel, textiles and shipbuilding, the market organization and aid control policies have resulted in overcapacities being cut and considerable modernization taking place. This has meant that normal market forces should be restored in the first two sectors in the next few years.

The progress achieved by the standardization and harmonization of regulations in the automobile sector has not yet sufficed to bring about an overall common market. The situation is restricted by national limits on imports from Japan, national aid and by the actions of the companies in the area of distribution. The Commission has set detailed actions in motion in these three areas with the aim of containing the pressure on the common market to become segmented.

In the information technology area, the Commission has launched some important projects, such as Esprit and the work on standardization, and developed a framework for the joint discussion of a European industrial strategy. In the telecommunications sector, 1984 has been significant for the amount of progress made in standardization and the new networks, precompetition research (RACE) and the progressive opening up of public telecommunications equipment contracts.

Overall, by means of the bimonthly meetings of the Directors-General of Industry, Council meetings and the informal meetings of the Industry Ministers, the Commission has helped to bring together points of view and policies with joint examinations and assessments of the results obtained.

Steel

187. The continuing state of manifest crisis in the steel sector led the Commission, after receiving the Council's assent and after consulting the ECSC Consultative Committee, to extend[1] the system of monitoring and production quotas established in 1980[2] until 31 December 1985. This decision gives full effect to the measures adopted by the Commission in December 1983 (minimum prices, guarantees, accompanying document and production certificate)[3] and establishes a link between the anti-crisis measures and the restructuring of the steel industry required as part of the 'aids code' which lapses on 31 December 1985.[4]

During the year the Commission modified the monitoring measures to meet the developments on the market. For instance, it raised certain minimum prices for flat products on several occasions,[5] which should allow companies to improve their resources. These prices, however, are still lower than the guide prices.[6]

The deposit of a guarantee by firms subject to minimum prices and the appointment by them of firms of auditors responsible for observing application of the minimum prices made for better price discipline.[7] Finally, the monitoring of traditional trade patterns by a production certificate and an accompanying document[8] allowed trade to stabilize.

Following an accurate assessment and a certain upswing in consumption, the Commission was able on a number of occasions[9] to adjust production quotas by changing the rates of abatement. The Commission none the less exercised caution to avoid the risk of a price collapse.

To make the measures regarding quantities and prices more effective among producers, the Commission was compelled to accompany them with measures to dissuade firms from trying to circumvent the system. It put an end, for

---

[1] OJ L 29, 1.2.1984; Bull. EC 1-1984, point 1.2.1 *et seq.*
[2] Fourteenth General Report, points 144 and 145; Fifteenth General Report, point 161; Sixteenth General Report, point 171.
[3] OJ L 373, 31.12.1983; Bull. EC 12-1983, points 2.1.12 to 2.1.15.
[4] Point 228 of this Report; OJ L 228, 13.8.1981; Fifteenth General Report, point 217.
[5] OJ L 61, 2.3.1984; Bull. EC 2-1984, point 2.1.19; OJ L 260, 29.9.1984; Bull. EC 9-1984, point 2.1.19.
[6] OJ L 370, 29.12.1982; OJ C 116, 29.4.1983.
[7] Bull. EC 11-1984, point 2.1.17.
[8] Bull. EC 4-1984, point 2.1.20; OJ L 124, 11.5.1984; Bull. EC 5-1984, point 2.1.24; OJ L 332, 20.12.1984; Bull. EC 12-1984.
[9] Bull. EC 1-1984, point 2.1.15; Bull. EC 2-1984, point 2.1.18; Bull. EC 5-1984, points 2.1.22 and 2.1.23; Bull. EC 7/8-1984, point 2.1.30; Bull. EC 9-1984, point 2.1.18; Bull. EC 10-1984, point 2.1.24; Bull. EC 11-1984, point 2.1.14.

example, to the practice whereby certain producers were able to deliver more than their quotas on the common market through the intermediary of other producers that do not have production quotas. While refraining from curtailing producers' freedom to exchange quotas, the Commission now requires firms that do not themselves possess quotas for a type of product to deduct deliveries to their customers from the actual producer's quota.

As in the past, the Commission was obliged to penalize certain firms: 22 such decisions were taken in 1984. [1] The Commission also set up a guarantee system designed to facilitate and accelerate the payment of fines for firms subject to minimum prices.

188. The Commission was aided by a certain revival of activity in the industry. Although the levels of the good years—1974 or even 1979—were not reached, the economic recovery helped to improve the production and consumption of steel products.

In crude steel equivalent, Community production increased from 109.5 million tonnes in 1983 to about 120 million tonnes in 1984, while internal consumption went up from 96.5 million tonnes to about 106 million over the same period. [2]

The rise in consumption stems from growing demand for consumer durables and a recovery in investment. At 10% the rise was much the same as the average for OECD countries (9%) but not as high as the increases recorded in the United States (19%) and Japan (12%). Continued recovery will depend largely on getting a grip on interest rates and the rate of exchange of the dollar.

The situation of steel companies generally improved, several of them achieving financial equilibrium this year. The Commission continued to watch developments in the industry and updated its general objectives beyond 1985. [3]

189. The policy of retraining and redeploying workers was continued. [4] The importance of this is evidenced by the loss of manpower (41% since 1974) that the Community steel industry has had to contend with. For the first five of the last ten years job losses totalled 72 000, 49 000, 35 000, 34 000 and 33 000. At the end of 1984 some 446 000 persons were employed in the industry (excluding Greece).

---

[1] OJ C 34, 9.2.1984; OJ C 269, 9.10.1984.
[2] Quarterly developments in the steel market situation are reported in Bull. EC 4-1984, point 2.1.19; Bull. EC 7/8-1984, points 2.1.22 to 2.1.26; Bull. EC 10-1984, point 2.1.22; Bull. EC 1-1985.
[3] Bull. EC 2-1984, point 2.1.16.
[4] Point 291 of this Report.

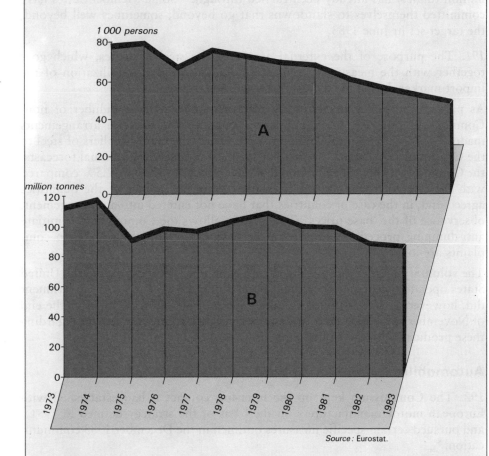

European steel: Output of rolled products and total workforce

Source: Eurostat.

A. Workforce
B. Output

Output of rolled products fell sharply (by 23%) between 1973 and 1983. The fall in the steel industry's workforce over the same period was even sharper (38%). Productivity therefore increased.

190. The restructuring accomplished by Community firms is already well advanced. [1] Although all the plans have not yet been approved, the objective set in 1982 at Elsinore in Denmark has already been attained. [2] Most of the reduction in the production capacity for hot-rolled products called for by the Commission in June 1983 [3] to offset aid granted by Member States (26.7 million tonnes) has already been carried through. [4] Some Member States have committed themselves to shutdowns that go beyond, sometimes well beyond, the target set in June 1983.

191. The purpose of the external aspect of the steel measures, which goes together with the measures taken internally, is a general stabilization of the import market during the delicate restructuring phase.

As part of the policy of voluntary restraint agreed with a number of non-Community countries, the Commission extended the bilateral arrangements made in 1983 with 15 non-Community countries, the main suppliers of steel to the Community. [5] Taking the trend in 1983 as the basis for its annual forecasts, the Commission kept the reduction in likely imports in 1984 at 12.5% compared with the reference year (1980). It ensured strict observance of the quantities agreed and, in the case of countries that have not entered into an arrangement, observance of the 'base prices'. This system allows the Commission to initiate anti-dumping procedures rapidly in the case of underquoting or when complaints are lodged by firms.

The voluntary restraint arrangement on Community steel exports to the United States operated, generally speaking, successfully; the United States Government did, however, feel constrained to take unilateral measures on tubes at the end of November, which led the Community to negotiate an arrangement regarding these products with the United States. [6]

Automobiles

192. The Commission kept up the intensive contact it had established with European motor manufacturers on the basis of the strategy defined in 1981 [7] and pursued certain specific measures outlined in the December 1983 communication. [8]

---

[1] Point 228 of this Report.
[2] Bull. EC 11-1982, point 2.1.15.
[3] Seventeenth General Report, point 177.
[4] Bull. EC 6-1984, point 2.1.13; Bull. EC 11-1984, point 2.1.12.
[5] Point 636 of this Report.
[6] Point 661 of this Report.
[7] Supplement 2/81—Bull. EC; Sixteenth General Report, point 172.
[8] Seventeenth General Report, point 179.

Parliament passed a resolution in March calling on the Commission to develop a coherent approach to help improve the competitiveness and efficiency of the industry. [1]

Shipbuilding

193. The Commission presented to the Council its sixth report on the state of the Community shipbuilding industry, which deteriorated still further during the year. [2] The crisis, which has hit all yards in Western Europe, is the result of an unfavourable internal economic climate and the fierce battle waged by the world's big shipbuilders, Japan and South Korea, to keep their markets.

In the light of this situation, the Commission continued its efforts to put the Community dimension to better use in dealing with the crisis. Internally, it proposed that the Council prolong the fifth Directive on aid to the industry [3] and extend non-quota measures under the European Regional Development Fund to additional areas particularly affected by restructuring. [4] Externally, the Commission endeavoured to spread the load equitably. Japan and South Korea announced certain changes in their policies that are likely to improve load-sharing, but it is too early yet to assess their impact since the decisions were taken in the middle of the year.

Textiles

194. After four consecutive years of falling-off, production in the textile and clothing industries stabilized in the early months of 1984. This was mainly due to technical recovery and improved productivity. None the less, final demand is still falling in some Member States, and the employment situation continues to worsen. The pressure of competition from non-Community countries, especially from parties to the Multifibre Arrangement, was kept up or even increased in some countries. [5]

To find a way out of this situation, the Commission continued its efforts to help the textile industry improve its competitiveness. Internally, it stated its

---

[1] OJ C 117, 30.4.1984; Bull. EC 3-1984, point 2.4.22.
[2] Bull. EC 10-1984, point 2.1.26.
[3] Point 226 of this Report.
[4] Point 349 of this Report.
[5] Points 640 and 641 of this Report.

views on a number of schemes for cutting back production capacities in man-made fibres[1] and focused attention on research in general programmes on energy-saving, development and basic technologies.

Externally, the Commission worked towards mutually acceptable solutions in respect of trade with certain preferential countries and concluded an additional protocol to extend the bilateral agreement with China under the MFA.[2]

New technologies

195. The Council, which had outlined the main points of the Esprit programme in December 1983,[3] approved the appropriations requested for the first five-year phase (750 million ECU from the Community budget, to be matched by industry) and the work programme for 1984 in February.[4] This allowed the Esprit programme to get quickly under way with a call for proposals in March[5] and the despatch of information to more than 7 000 potential participants. Of the 441 proposals received,[6] the Commission selected 90 that fall into Esprit's five main areas of activity (microelectronics, software technology, advanced information processing, office automation and computer-integrated manufacturing). The 29 projects started during the pilot phase[7] of the programme were continued in parallel.[8] In July the Commission published a call for proposals for infrastructure projects.[9]

The Council agreed on a new work programme for 1985 in December and a call for proposals was published on 20 December.[10]

196. As regards telecommunications, the Commission sent the Council a communication in May covering the following lines of action: creation of a Community market for equipment, notably terminals, through the promotion of European standards, mutual recognition of type-approval procedures and gradual opening-up of network operators' invitations to tender; formulation of an R&D cooperation programme; establishment of medium- and long-term aims

---

[1] Point 227 of this Report.
[2] Points 640 and 641 of this Report.
[3] Seventeenth General Report, point 182.
[4] OJ L 67, 9.3.1984; OJ L 81, 24.3.1984; Bull. EC 2-1984, point 1.3.1 et seq.
[5] OJ C 80, 21.3.1984; Bull. EC 3-1984, point 2.1.26.
[6] Bull. EC 5-1984, point 2.1.28; Bull. EC 7/8-1984, point 2.1.35.
[7] OJ L 369, 29.12.1982; Sixteenth General Report, point 179.
[8] Bull. EC 7/8-1984, point 2.1.35.
[9] OJ C 187, 14.7.1984; Bull. EC 7/8-1984, point 2.1.36.
[10] OJ C 340, 20.12.1984; Bull. EC 10-1984, point 2.1.27; Bull. EC 12-1984.

for the development of Community telecommunications services and networks; utilization of modern technologies to support development in less-favoured regions. [1]

On 12 November the Council adopted two recommendations [2]—based on proposals made by the Commission in 1980 [3]—on the harmonization of standards in the field of telecommunications and on the first phase of opening-up of public telecommunications procurement contracts.

197. In technical terms, the year was marked by the conclusion of an agreement between the Community and the European Conference of Postal and Telecommunications Administrations (CEPT) on the harmonization of standards and specifications for type approval of terminals for which the Community intends to speed up installation. [4] Meetings were also organized with the industry and representatives of postal and telecommunications administrations (PTTs) in order to establish a specific R&D cooperation programme in telecommunications. Finally, the third round of in-depth consultations began with PTTs on the development of networks in the Community and on joint projects designed to facilitate developments.

198. In April the Council adopted a Decision to extend the second part of the multiannual data-processing programme (1979-83), which is intended for use mainly in promoting software. [5] On 22 November it prolonged for two years the first part of the programme (public procurement contracts; protection of personal data; research), apart from the standardization work which will come to an end in 1985. [6]

199. The Council held a first exchange of views in February [7] on the Commission communication of 1983 on the development of biotechnology. [8] In May the Commission transmitted a proposal for a decision adopting a research action programme for 1985-89, which the Council approved in December. [9]

200. Work on the establishment of a Community interinstitutional integrated services information system (Insis) [10] proceeded, with the presentation to the

[1] Bull. EC 5-1984, point 1.4.1 et seq.; Bull. EC 12-1984.
[2] OJ L 298, 16.11.1984; Bull. EC 10-1984, point 2.1.30; Bull. EC 11-1984, point 2.1.22.
[3] Fourteenth General Report, point 154.
[4] Bull. EC 3-1984, point 2.1.31.
[5] OJ L 126, 12.5.1984; Bull. EC 4-1984, point 2.1.4.
[6] OJ L 308, 27.11.1984; Bull. EC 10-1984, point 2.1.29.
[7] Bull. EC 2-1984, point 2.1.30.
[8] Seventeenth General Report, point 186.
[9] OJ C 182, 9.7.1984; Bull. EC 4-1984, point 2.1.25; Bull. EC 11-1984, point 2.1.23; Bull. EC 12.1984.
[10] Seventeenth General Report, points 28 and 604.

Council in August of a proposal for several projects in electronic text transmission, electronic message-handling systems, written or vocal (with storage of messages), teleconference systems and access to Community data bases. [1]

201. In August, in response to the opinions given by Parliament and the Economic and Social Committee, [2] the Commission amended [3] the proposal it had made in March [4] for a Decision adopting a long-term programme for the use of computerized telecommunications systems for the processing of data relating to imports/exports and the management and financial control of agricultural market organizations (Caddia). [5]

Other industries

202. In the construction industry, the Commission continued its activities relating to the rational use of energy and to fire safety. In January it transmitted to the Council a proposal for a recommendation on fire safety in existing hotels. [6] In September it organized a symposium in Luxembourg with a view to determining a Community approach in this field. Finally, in December it published two reports on methods of testing and classifying the fire resistance of structural components and on the fire performance of wooden structures and wood-base panels.

203. The Advisory Committee on Community Policy regarding Forestry and Forestry-based Industries [7] met twice during the year. [8] Its work centred on the problems of the supply of raw materials, standards, sawmills and transport.

204. The Committee on Commerce and Distribution delivered two opinions in October on electronic payment in the distributive trades and selective distribution in the automobile industry. [9]

205. The Business Cooperation Centre focused on cooperation between companies in the Member States and in the applicant countries and on the problems of subcontracting. [10]

---

[1] OJ C 247, 15.9.1984; Bull. EC 7/8-1984, point 2.1.37; Bull. EC 12-1984.
[2] OJ C 172, 2.7.1984; OJ C 248, 17.9.1984.
[3] OJ C 215, 16.8.1984; Bull. EC 7/8-1984, point 2.1.38.
[4] OJ C 112, 26.4.1984; Bull. EC 3-1984, point 2.1.28.
[5] Cooperation in automation of data and documentation for imports/exports and management of the agricultural market.
[6] OJ C 49, 21.2.1984; Bull. EC 1-1984, point 2.1.5.
[7] Seventeenth General Report, point 194.
[8] Bull. EC 6-1984, point 2.1.24; Bull. EC 11-1984, point 2.1.24.
[9] Bull. EC 3-1984, point 2.1.20; Bull. EC 10-1984, point 2.1.19.
[10] Bull. EC 4-1984, point 2.1.17; Bull. EC 5-1984, point 2.1.18; Bull. EC 10-1984, point 2.1.19.

206. During the year Parliament adopted resolutions on the problems facing several branches of industry. [1]

Small business

207. On 22 May the Commission sent the Council a communication on the Community policy with regard to small and medium-sized enterprises and the craft industry. [2] This paper, which is a follow-up to '1983 — European year of SMEs and the craft industry', [3] sets out a number of priority measures already taken or to be taken together with national government departments.

208. In conjunction with Parliament, the Commission also followed up its contacts with small business associations to help them find a consensus on the approach and operating methods of a small business centre. In May Parliament adopted a resolution on Community policy in this area. [4]

[1] OJ C 46, 20.2.1984; Bull. EC 1-1984, point 2.4.10; OJ C 77, 19.3.1984; Bull. EC 2-1984, point 2.4.14.
[2] Bull. EC 5-1984, point 2.1.18.
[3] Seventeenth General Report, point 188.
[4] OJ C 172, 2.7.1984; Bull. EC 5-1984, point 2.4.15.

Section 5

Competition [1]

Main developments

209. In the competition area, 1984 was a year of consolidating and strengthening the policy lines previously developed by the Commission. With respect to State aids, the Commission continued to scrutinize in particular detail such sensitive sectors as steel, shipbuilding and textiles, and to develop its general policy on areas such as aids to research and development. In the context of a more effective application of the State-aid rules, action was taken on State holdings in private-sector companies, the recovery of aids granted illegally and steps to simplify administrative procedures. The Court of Justice underlined the importance of the concept 'distortion of competition and effects on trade' in the evaluation of aid proposals.

In the anti-trust area, the Commission maintained a flexible approach, both in individual decisions and in numerous block exemption Regulations, with regard to constructive forms of cooperation between firms. On the other hand, the Commission has taken increasingly severe measures to combat purely anti-competitive behaviour, and there was a striking increase in the number of cases in which horizontal cartels were attacked, several accompanied by very substantial fines.

General rules applying to undertakings

210. On 23 July the Commission adopted a Regulation granting block exemption for patent and know-how licensing agreements which encourage the dissemination of new technology within the Community. [2] Taking account of the conclusions of the Court of Justice in its *Maize seed* judgment, [3] it exempts exclusivity for the licensee from the ban on restrictive practices laid down by Article 85(1) of the EEC Treaty and allows the parties to arrange reciprocal

---

[1] Competition policy activities will be described in greater detail in the *Fourteenth Report on Competition Policy*, to be published in April.
[2] OJ L 219, 16.8.1984; Bull. EC 7/8-1984, point 2.1.50.
[3] Case 258/78 *Nungesser and Eisele v Commission* [1982] ECR 2015; Sixteenth General Report, point 854.

protection against both active and passive competition as long as the patents remain in force. Similar protection is also allowed as between licensees for five years; after this period only protection against active competition is permissible. In view of the complexity and diversity of licensing agreements, the new Regulation introduces an expedited procedure whereby agreements containing clauses not specifically mentioned in the Regulation are exempted, provided they are notified and the Commission does not oppose exemption within six months.

211. The block exemption Regulation on motor-vehicle distribution and servicing agreements [1] was adopted on 12 December and will enter into force on 1 June 1985 for a period of 10 years. [2] It exempts such distribution systems to a greater degree than is generally provided under Community law because of the particular characteristics of this sector, while ensuring competition at all levels of distribution, especially in the interest of European consumers. An accompanying notice explains certain provisions and gives information on the Commission's administrative practice. [3]

212. On 19 December the Commission adopted a block exemption Regulation [4] which, subject to certain conditions, covers agreements providing for joint research and development and joint exploitation of the results. [5] Detailed lists are included of the restrictions covered by the Regulation, and of provisions which may not under any circumstances be included in the agreements. An opposition procedure identical to the one in the patent licensing Regulation is included.

213. On 19 December the Commission also amended the block exemption Regulation on specialization agreements [6] to extend the legal framework of inter-firm cooperation and bring it into line with other Regulations. [7] The total turnover limit is raised from 300 million to 500 million ECU, with the possibility of an opposition procedure where this limit is exceeded, and the market share limit is now 20% instead of 15%.

---

[1] OJ L 15, 18.1.1985; Bull. EC 12-1984.
[2] OJ C 165, 24.6.1983; Seventeenth General Report, point 228.
[3] OJ C 17, 18.1.1985; Bull. EC 12.1984.
[4] Bull. EC 12-1984.
[5] OJ C 16, 21.1.1984; Seventeenth General Report, point 230.
[6] OJ L 376, 31.12.1982; Sixteenth General Report, point 217.
[7] Bull. EC 3-1984, point 2.1.42.

214. On 7 February the Commission amended[1] for the second time[2] its proposal for a merger control Regulation,[3] incorporating certain suggestions made by Parliament[4] and the Economic and Social Committee[5] by widening its scope.

215. In March the Commission presented to the Council a memorandum on civil aviation,[6] together with amendments to its proposal for a Regulation concerning the application of the rules of a competition to air transport,[7] which would restrict the scope of the Regulation to international air transport between Community airports. A second proposal for a Regulation provides for the application of Article 85(3) of the EEC Treaty to certain categories of agreements on capacity sharing, revenue pooling and consultation over tariffs. Parliament delivered an opinion[8] on the proposal for a Regulation on sea transport,[9] endorsing the principle of a Regulation applying the rules of competition to this sector.

216. On 12 October the Commission presented a recommendation[10] for a Council Decision authorizing the opening of negotiations on agreements with non-member countries concerning the protection of legal papers in connection with the application of the rules of competition.[11]

The rules of competition applied to undertakings

217. In 1984 there were 5 decisions applying Articles 65 and 66 of the ECSC Treaty, 20 decisions applying Articles 85 and 86 of the EEC Treaty and decisions rejecting three complaints concerning the same case *(Philip Morris)*. Following publication of the essential contents of agreements in the Official Journal, 3 cases were settled by dispatch of administrative letters.[12] In proceedings under the EEC Treaty 211 cases were settled without a decision being taken because the agreements were brought into line with the competition rules, were termin-

---

[1] OJ C 51, 23.2.1984; Bull. EC 2-1984, point 2.1.42.
[2] OJ C 36, 12.2.1982; Seventeenth General Report, point 231.
[3] OJ C 92, 31.10.1973; Seventh General Report, points 152 and 153.
[4] OJ C 322, 28.11.1983; Seventeenth General Report, point 231.
[5] OJ C 252, 27.9.1982; Sixteenth General Report, point 220.
[6] OJ C 182, 9.7.1984; Bull. EC 2-1984, point 2.1.149.
[7] OJ C 317, 3.12.1982.
[8] OJ C 282, 5.11.1981; Fifteenth General Report, point 206.
[9] OJ C 172, 2.7.1984; Bull. EC 5-1984, point 2.1.172.
[10] Bull. EC 10-1984, point 2.1.43.
[11] Thirteenth Competition Report, points 77 and 78.
[12] Thirteenth Competition Report, point 72.

ated, or expired. On 31 December 1984 there were 4 194 cases pending, of which 3 708 were applications or notifications, 314 complaints by firms and 72 proceedings on the Commission's own initiative. Of the applications and notifications pending before the Commission, some 63% concerned licensing agreements, 24% distribution agreements and 13% horizontal agreements.

218. The Commission took several decisions under Article 85(1) condemning anti-trust violations of the 'classic' type: pricing-fixing, market sharing and quota systems. In the decision against five Community chemical manufacturers producing hydrogen peroxide and derivatives, the fines amounting to 9 million ECU represented the highest ever imposed in an EEC anti-trust case *(Peroxides)*.[1] Several companies in the flat-glass sector received fines totalling 4 million ECU for price alignment and market sharing in the Benelux countries *(Flat glass)*.[2] Fines were also imposed on six zinc producers for violating Article 85(1) *(Zinc producer group)*.[3] The German Milk Promotion Fund was prohibited from giving private aids to promote exports to other Community countries *(Milchförderungsfonds)*.[4] Finally, two important decisions terminated lengthy proceedings. The Commission condemned a restrictive practice engaged in by the main producers and the foreign trade organizations of the Soviet Union, Poland, Hungary, Czechoslovakia and the German Democratic Republic, which had tied up the supply of aluminium from Eastern Europe to the Community at least from 1963 to 1976 *(Aluminium imports from Eastern Europe)*.[5] It also found against a system of concerted prices for bleached sulphate paper pulp sold in the Community. This arrangement, entered into by 40 manufacturers in the United States, Canada, Switzerland, Finland, Norway, Portugal and Spain, lasted from 1973 to 1981. The Commission imposed fines totalling 4 million ECU on the firms involved *(Wood pulp)*.[5]

219. The negative clearance granted to IBM's personal computer distribution system confirmed that selective distribution is justified for certain products, provided the selection criteria are of a qualitative nature, objective and uniformly applied.[6] This policy was also confirmed in two decisons in which exemption was refused to two selective distribution systems in the sanitary ware sector *(Grohe, Ideal Standard)*.[7] With respect to exclusive distribution,

---

1 Decision of 26.11.1984: Bull. EC 11-1984, point 2.1.36.
2 Decision of 23.7.1984: OJ L 212, 8.8.1984; Bull. EC 7/8-1984, point 2.1.53.
3 Decision of 6.8.1984: OJ L 220, 17.8.1984; Bull. EC 7/8-1984, point 2.1.52.
4 Decision of 7.12.1984: Bull. EC 12-1984.
5 Decision of 19.12.1984: Bull. EC 12-1984.
6 Decision of 18.4.1984: OJ L 118, 4.5.1984; Bull. EC 4-1984, point 2.1.47.
7 Decision of 10.12.1984: OJ L 18, 23.1.1985; OJ L 20, 24.1.1985; Bull. EC 12-1984.

an Italian and a French toy manufacturer were fined for giving the latter absolute territorial protection as distributor in France *(Polistil/Arbois).*[1] A decision was taken against an agricultural machinery manufacturer and its independent distributors for segregating the market by means of export bans; a fine was imposed on the manufacturer *(John Deere).*[2] Without formal decisions being necessary, the Commission was able to promote unification of the European automobile market, in the interest of users *(Fiat, Alfa Romeo),*[3] and to eliminate unduly restrictive elements in distribution systems for furniture.[4]

220. For the first time, the competition rules were applied to so-called 'crisis cartels' and in the banking and insurance sectors. Two decisions were taken granting exemption to agreements aimed at reducing structural overcapacities, in the synthetic fibre sector,[5] and a bilateral operation in the petrochemical sector *(BPCL-ICI).*[6] Another operation in this sector aimed at improving capacity utilization was approved by way of administrative letter following publication in the Official Journal *(Rovin).*[7] In the banking sector, the Commission granted exemption to agreements relating to uniform eurocheques,[8] and an exemption was also granted in the industrial insurance sector *(Nuovo Cegam).*[9] A prohibition decision was taken in the fire insurance sector *(Feuerversicherung).*[10]

221. As regards industrial property rights, the Commission exempted a cooperation agreement between two Danish and British brewing groups to ensure optimum utilization of their production facilities in the United Kingdom *(Carlsberg).*[11] The Commission's policy regarding royalty payments was expressed in two cases which could be closed without formal decision *(IGR*[12] and *Uarco*[13]).

222. The Commission dealt with three cases involving the application of the competition rules to asset transfers, in the cigarette sector *(Philip Morris),*[14]

---

[1] Decision of 16.5.1984: OJ L 136, 23.5.1984; Bull. EC 5-1984, point 2.1.48.
[2] Decision of 14.12.1984: Bull. EC 12-1984.
[3] Bull. EC 5-1984, point 2.1.49; Bull. EC 11-1984, point 2.1.48.
[4] Bull. EC 1-1984, point 2.1.33.
[5] Decision of 4.7.1984: OJ L 207, 2.8.1984; Bull. EC 7/8-1984, point 2.1.54.
[6] Decision of 19.7.1984: OJ L 212, 8.8.1984; Bull. EC 7/8-1984, point 2.1.55.
[7] Bull. EC 5-1984, point 2.1.47.
[8] Decision of 10.12.1984: Bull. EC 12-1984.
[9] Decision of 30.3.1984: OJ L 99, 11.4.1984; Bull. EC 3-1984, point 2.1.44.
[10] Decision of 5.12.1984: Bull. EC 12-1984.
[11] Decision of 12.7.1984: OJ L 207, 2.8.1984; Bull. EC 7/8-1984, point 2.1.56.
[12] Bull. EC 7/8-1984, point 2.1.57.
[13] Bull. EC 11-1984, point 2.1.39.
[14] Bull. EC 3-1984, point 2.1.43.

the flat-glass sector *(Mecaniver-PPG)* [1] and the petrochemical sector *(BPCL-ICI)*. [2]

223. As regards the application of Article 86 of the EEC Treaty to abuse of dominant positions, the Commission imposed a fine on British Leyland [3] for having refused to issue type-approval certificates for left-hand-drive Metros, letting the necessary type-approval lapse in order to prevent such vehicles being reimported from other Member States, and for having charged excessive fees. It suspended the proceedings initiated against International Business Machines in 1980 following an undertaking by IBM to change its business practices. [4] IBM will now disclose adequate and timely information to competitors in the Community on its interfaces to enable them to attach their products to its large and medium-sized information systems using its network or systems interconnection system (SNA—systems network architecture). It also undertook to supply its computers in the Community without main memory or with the minimum required for testing.

The rules of competition applied to forms of State intervention

General aids

224. The Commission had to state its views increasingly frequently on State-aid problems arising from the acquisition by public authorities of holdings in company capital. It has therefore spelt out its position on the matter and on Member States' obligations. [5]

As regards the grant of a combination of aids to one and the same firm under aid schemes for different purposes, the Commission, anxious to avoid unduly high aid intensity, decided to introduce a prior notification procedure for individual cases of application meeting certain conditions.

The Commission continued its work on the preparation of draft codes on aids for research and development and energy saving.

---

[1] Decision of 12.12.1984; Bull. EC 12-1984.
[2] Decision of 19.7.1984: 8.8.1984; Bull. EC 7/8-1984, point 2.1.55.
[3] Decision of 2.7.1984: OJ L 207, 2.8.1984; Bull. EC 7/8-1984, point 2.1.59.
[4] Bull. EC 7/8-1984, point 1.1.1 *et seq.*; Bull. EC 10-1984, points 3.4.1 and 3.4.2.
[5] Bull. EC 9-1984, points 2.1.30 and 3.5.1.

Industry aids

225. As it did last year, [1] the Commission had to devote special attention to assistance granted to firms in ailing industries and to rescue aids.

226. Since the situation in the Community's shipbuilding industry worsened in 1983 and 1984, the Council on 18 December extended until 31 December 1986 [2] the aid code for shipbuilding introduced by the Fifth Directive of 28 April 1981. [3] The industry will thus have another two years to complete its restructuring, cut back overcapacity and return to lasting competitiveness. In the course of the year the Commission scrutinized a number of national aid programmes for shipbuilding. In view of the restructuring measures planned by the German yards it approved the introduction of 6% regional production subsidies in Germany. [4] It initiated the procedure of Article 93(2) of the EEC Treaty in respect of proposed aid schemes in Italy [5] and the United Kingdom [6] because the restructuring measures planned by the respective governments did not appear adequate.

227. The Commission tightened up control of assistance to the textile and clothing industry to make sure that it did not have the effect of shifting employment and structural difficulties from one Member State to another. The Commission decided to initiate the Article 93(2) procedure in respect of a new French scheme financed by parafiscal charges [7] and a United Kingdom scheme for the clothing, footwear, knitting and textile industries. [8] It took a final Decision prohibiting the Belgian Government from extending the validity of an aid scheme which had been in force in previous years. [9] Several decisions were also taken on individual cases of application notified by the Italian Government under Act No 675 of 1977. [10] The Commission decided against three schemes of assistance for synthetic fibre producers notified by Belgium, [11] the United Kingdom [12] and Ireland. [13] It was unable to complete the inventory

---

[1] Seventeenth General Report, point 240.
[2] OJ L 2, 3.1.1985; Bull. EC 11-1984, point 2.1.44.
[3] OJ L 137, 23.5.1981; OJ L 371, 30.12.1982.
[4] Bull. EC 3-1984, point 2.1.52.
[5] Bull. EC 10-1984, point 2.1.46.
[6] Bull. EC 7/8-1984, point 2.1.70.
[7] Bull. EC 7/8-1984, point 2.1.77.
[8] Bull. EC 7/8-1984, point 2.1.75.
[9] Bull. EC 9-1984, point 2.1.32.
[10] Bull. EC 4-1984, point 2.1.51; OJ L 186, 13.7.1984; Bull. EC 5-1984, point 2.1.63.
[11] Bull. EC 7/8-1984, point 2.1.78.
[12] Bull. EC 7/8-1984, point 2.1.76.
[13] Bull. EC 7/8-1984, point 2.1.79.

of aids available to the textile industry since certain Member States had still not supplied the information required.

228. The Commission continued applying the steel aids code in the context of the conditional authorizations granted in its Decisions of June 1983.[1] Most Member States submitted their final restructuring plans,[2] a number of which provide for capacity reductions exceeding those required by the Commission.[3] Having looked into their prospects for viability, the Commission approved the plans of many firms and released the aid payable to them.[4]

229. The Commission carried on with its scrutiny of various investment aid schemes notified pursuant to Italy's Act No 675 of 1977,[5] notably concerning the motor industry, mechanical plant and machinery, chemicals and paper.[6] It took a final decision on almost all the schemes, authorizing investment aids only in cases seen to offer adequate compensatory justification in the Community interest and rejecting other assistance.

Regional aids

230. A procedure under Article 93(2) of the EEC Treaty was initiated in respect of German regional aids in Baden-Württemberg, Bavaria, Hesse, Lower Saxony, Rhineland-Palatinate and Schleswig-Holstein on account of the criteria used by these *Länder* to designate assisted areas.[7] A final Decision under Article 93(2) of the EEC Treaty was taken on the investment aids for the improvement of the economic structure of North Rhine-Westphalia, prohibiting assistance for the Borken-Bocholt and Siegen employment areas and approving it for a transitional period in the Gummbersbach employment area.[8]

A final Decision was taken finding against a Belgian scheme to extend the supplementary regional aid granted to counter cyclical difficulties.[9] The Commission approved the substantial changes made to the UK scheme[10] and

---

[1] OJ L 227, 19.8.1983; Seventeenth General Report, point 244.
[2] Bull. EC 2-1984, point 2.1.46.
[3] Bull. EC 2-1984, point 2.1.21; Bull. EC 3-1984, point 2.1.24; Bull. EC 5-1984, point 2.1.26.
[4] Bull. EC 4-1984, point 2.1.51a.
[5] Seventeenth General Report, point 245.
[6] Bull. EC 5-1984, point 2.1.62.
[7] Bull. EC 7/8-1984, point 2.1.66.
[8] Bull. EC 7/8-1984, point 2.1.67.
[9] Bull. EC 5-1984, point 2.1.54.
[10] Bull. EC 12-1984.

accepted the existing Greek scheme except for one operating aid in respect of which the Article 93(2) procedure was initiated. [1]

231. The Commission also decided to raise no objection to two schemes of assistance put forward by the German [2] and French [3] Governments for areas affected by job losses in the steel and shipbuilding industries in the Bremen employment area and in the steel industry in Lorraine.

232. Finally, the Commission took decisions on three individual cases. In the first, it agreed to terminate the Article 93(2) procedure concerning a fork-lift truck manufacturer at Irvine, Scotland. [4] In the other two, it raised objections to French schemes to pay regional development premiums to a textiles and clothing plant [5] and to optics and electronics firms, [1] on account of the relatively healthy socio-economic situation of the areas concerned. The Commission did, however, authorize payment of a lower premium in respect of the optics business on grounds of the situation of the industry.

State monopolies of a commercial character

233. As regards the French alcohol monopoly, the Commission delivered a reasoned opinion on the 'adjustment' *(soulte)* levied on alcohol imported from other Member States and accruing to the Treasury when alcohol sold by the Service des alcools to the various users is subject to a 'price supplement' which goes to finance the domestic alcohol arrangements, [6] these arrangements being considered incompatible with Article 37 of the EEC Treaty.

234. The Commission took the view that the Greek Government, having taken no steps so far to adjust progressively its State monopolies of a commercial character, had failed to fulfil its obligations under Article 40(1) of the Act of Accession and Article 5 of the EEC Treaty. [7] The Commission therefore had to initiate once again the infringement procedure of Article 169 of the EEC Treaty. The arrangements in Greece in respect of pharmaceutical products [8]

---

[1] Bull. EC 12-1984.
[2] Bull. EC 3-1984, point 2.1.48.
[3] Bull. EC 7/8-1984, point 2.1.64.
[4] Bull. EC 1-1984, point 2.1.34.
[5] OJ L 241, 11.9.1984; Bull. EC 6-1984, point 2.1.35.
[6] Bull. EC 2-1984, point 2.1.57.
[7] OJ L 233, 24.8.1983; Seventeenth General Report, point 250.
[8] Seventeenth General Report, point 250.

were found by the Commission to be incompatible with Articles 37, 30 and 95 of the EEC Treaty and with Article 40 of the Act of Accession. As part of the infringement procedure initiated in 1983, the Greek Government was sent a reasoned opinion.

Public undertakings

235.   In applying the Directive on the transparency of financial relations between Member States and public undertakings, [1] the Commission came up against the Italian Government's refusal to supply the information required on AAMS (Amministrazione Autonoma dei Monopoli de Stato) as regards the manufactured tobacco industry. The Italian Government denied that this agency was a 'public undertaking'. The Commission accordingly initiated the infringement procedure of Article 169 of the EEC Treaty and subsequently sent a reasoned opinion. Despite reminders, the Commission received no information from the French Government pursuant to this Directive on the public undertakings operating the industries on which it had requested information [1] and likewise had to initiate the Article 169 infringement procedure followed by the sending of a reasoned opinion.

---

[1]   OJ L 195, 29.7.1980; Seventeenth General Report, point 252.

Section 6

Financial institutions and taxation

Main developments

236. *In the insurance sector, the setting up of a high-level* ad hoc *working party decided by the Council so as to break the logjam in the work to facilitate exercise of the freedom to provide services in the field of non-life insurance has brought the unresolved problems more clearly into focus but has not as yet produced any practical results. Discussions are continuing, and certain matters of basic principle will probably have to be settled before the Court of Justice.*

With regard to banking, progress has been made in coordinating supervisory instruments and procedures in Member States.

On the stock exchange front, there is welcome evidence of genuine headway having been made in strengthening links between stock exchanges in the Community.

237. *In the tax field, the Commission has paid particular attention to the measures needed to revive productive investment, to give a fresh impetus to the process of financial integration, to consolidate the internal market and to foster development of a 'people's Europe'. With these objectives in mind, it has done its utmost to persuade the Council to act on the proposals aimed at promoting cooperation between firms from different Member States and has sent to it a range of proposals on arrangements for the carryover of losses of undertakings, a reduction in or abolition of capital duty, completion of the uniform basis of assessment for VAT, and increases in the tax-free allowances for individuals.*

The Commission has also settled the difficult matter of Greece's infringements of Article 95 of the EEC Treaty. Since 2 July Greece has ended all the existing infringements and, as a temporary measure, has introduced a compensatory tax. This tax, which makes for greater transparency of taxes on importation, has to be phased out over a five-year period.

Financial institutions

Insurance

238. On 10 December the Council adopted[1] the proposal for a Directive[2] bringing certain tourist assistance within the scope of the first Council Directive of 24 July 1973 on insurance other than life assurance,[3] with a view to harmonizing the conditions for the taking up and pursuit of the activity of tourist assistance.

239. On 28 September the Commission sent the Council a communication[4] concerning proposals which it had presented in March 1983 on the conclusion of an Agreement between the Swiss Confederation and the Community concerning direct insurance other than life assurance, and on the implementation of the Agreement.[5] Setting out its position on the opinions delivered by Parliament[6] and the Economic and Social Committee,[7] the Commission indicated that the proposed Agreement was entirely in keeping with the brief given to it by the Council on 23 July 1974 and that there was therefore no need to enter into fresh negotiations with Switzerland.

240. The Commission instituted proceedings before the Court of Justice against Ireland[8] for failure to transpose properly into national law the Directive of 30 May 1978 on Community co-insurance.[9] The Commission's reasons were the same as in the action brought against France and Denmark in 1983.[10] The Commission also instituted proceedings before the Court of Justice against Germany[11] concerning the incorrect implementation of the Directive and the violation of Articles 59 and 60 of the EEC Treaty as regards the general provisions on insurance supervision.[12]

---

[1] OJ L 339, 27.12.1984; Bull. EC 10-1984, point 2.1.49.
[2] OJ C 51, 10.3.1981; Fifteenth General Report, point 232; OJ C 30, 4.2.1983; Seventeenth General Report, point 254.
[3] OJ L 228, 16.8.1973.
[4] Bull. EC 9-1984, point 2.1.37.
[5] OJ C 154, 13.6.1983; Seventeenth General Report, point 255.
[6] OJ C 127, 14.5.1984; Bull. EC 4-1984, point 2.1.52.
[7] OJ C 358, 31.12.1983.
[8] OJ C 236, 6.9.1984; Seventeenth General Report, point 258.
[9] OJ L 151, 7.6.1978; Sixteenth General Report, point 249.
[10] OJ C 327, 1.12.1983; Seventeenth General Report, point 257.
[11] OJ C 233, 4.9.1984.
[12] Seventeenth General Report, point 258.

241. The Court of Justice gave two judgments on 9 February[1] and a third on 21 June[2] on the interpretation of certain Articles of the Directive of 24 April 1972 relating to insurance against civil liability in respect of the use of motor vehicles.[3] The main issue was the definition of the concepts of 'territory in which the vehicle is normally based' and 'provisions of its own national law on compulsory insurance'.

Banks

242. On 18 May the Commission sent the Council a proposal for a Directive[4] amending the Directive of 12 December 1977 on the taking up and pursuit of the business of credit institutions.[5] The aim of this amendment is to enable Greece to continue to make 'economic need' a condition for authorizing the establishment of new banks or the opening of branches by domestic banks or banks from other Member States. Earlier, on 14 March, the Commission had presented the Council with a report[6] drawn up pursuant to the first Directive,[5] which concluded that the Member States which had been authorized to retain this condition in their legislation should be allowed to continue to do so until 15 December 1989.

243. On 12 December the Commission adopted for transmittal to the Council a proposal for a Directive designed to facilitate the activities of mortgage credit institutions across intra-Community frontiers.[7]

244. On 14 March, after receiving the opinions of Parliament[8] and the Economic and Social Committee,[9] the Commission sent the Council an amended proposal[10] for a Directive concerning the annual accounts of banks and other financial institutions.[11]

245. The Banking Advisory Committee, under the chairmanship of Mr H.J. Muller, a member of the Management Committee of the Nederlandsche Bank,

---

[1] OJ C 79, 20.3.1984; OJ C 80, 21.3.1984.
[2] OJ C 186, 13.7.1984.
[3] OJ L 103, 2.5.1972; Sixth General Report, point 114.
[4] OJ C 153, 13.6.1984; Bull. EC 5-1984, point 2.1.64.
[5] OJ L 322, 17.12.1977; Eleventh General Report, point 211.
[6] Bull. EC 3-1984, point 2.1.55.
[7] Bull. EC 12-1984.
[8] OJ C 242, 12.9.1983; Seventeenth General Report, point 262.
[9] OJ C 112, 3.5.1982; Seventeenth General Report, point 262.
[10] OJ C 83, 24.3.1984; Bull. EC 3-1984, point 2.1.54.
[11] OJ C 130, 1.6.1981; Fifteenth General Report, point 236.

devoted part of the two meetings it held during the year to work on observation ratios for monitoring the solvency, profitability and liquidity of credit institutions, [1] and to examination of the draft Directive on the reorganization and the winding up of credit institutions. [2] On the former point, further efforts should bring a solution acceptable to both the Community and the Committee on Banking Regulations and Supervisory Practices (Group of Ten).

246. As provided in the first Directive on the taking up and pursuit of the business of credit institutions, [3] the Commission published the new list of credit institutions authorized to do business in Member States, reflecting the situation at 31 December 1983. [4]

Stock exchanges and other institutions in the securities field

247. The Council Working Party on Economic Questions continued its examination of the proposals for Directives on the prospectus to be published when securities are offered for subscription or sale to the public [5] and on undertakings for collective investment in transferable securities. [6]

248. The work undertaken on the Commission's initiative [7]—in close collaboration with the Committee of Stock Exchanges in the EEC—on stronger links between stock exchanges resulted in a decision to implement the IDIS project (Interbourse Data Information System), which in the first instance will be used for the transmission of equity prices for securities which are officially listed on more than one Community stock exchange. [8]

249. Commission staff continued to examine possible ways in which links could be created or reinforced between national systems for the settlement of securities transactions (security clearing). [9] They also continued their examination of the measures that might need to be taken at Community level to stamp

---

[1] Seventeenth General Report, point 264.
[2] Seventeenth General Report, point 263; Sixteenth General Report, point 256; Fifteenth General Report, point 240.
[3] OJ L 322, 17.12.1977.
[4] OJ C 351, 31.12.1984.
[5] OJ C 355, 31.12.1980; Fourteenth General Report, point 208; OJ C 226, 31.8.1982; Sixteenth General Report, point 261; Seventeenth General Report, point 266.
[6] OJ C 171, 26.7.1976; Sixteenth General Report, point 262; Seventeenth General Report, point 266.
[7] Fourteenth General Report, point 211.
[8] Bull. EC 5-1984, point 2.1.65.
[9] Seventeenth General Report, point 267.

out insider trading on securities markets [1] and started work on a proposal for a Directive on the information to be disclosed in the event of the acquisition or disposal of a large shareholding in a listed company.

Taxation

Indirect taxation

Turnover tax

250. In accordance with the sixth Directive of 17 May 1977—on the harmonization of the laws of the Member States relating to turnover taxes [2]—the Commission on 23 July sent the Council a proposal for a sixteenth Directive designed to eliminate the double taxation which still occurs when goods are acquired by individuals in one Member State and imported into another, [3] and on 17 August a proposal for a seventeenth Directive concerning exemption from value-added tax on the temporary importation of goods other than means of transport. [4]

251. On 20 February the Commission amended [5] its proposal for a twelfth Directive—on expenditure on which value-added tax is not deductible [6]—in order to take account of the amendments proposed by Parliament; [7] in May the Economic and Social Committee delivered a favourable opinion on this new proposal. [8]

252. In accordance with the procedure provided in the sixth Directive of 17 May 1977 [2] the Council on 6 February authorized Italy to derogate until 31 December 1983 from the value-added tax arrangements in the context of aid to earthquake victims. [9] In March the United Kingdom Government introduced a measure—a special tax accounting scheme—derogating from the sixth Direc-

---

[1] Seventeenth General Report, point 270.
[2] OJ L 145, 13.6.1977; Eleventh General Report, point 219.
[3] OJ C 226, 22.8.1984; Bull. EC 7/8-1984, point 2.1.82.
[4] OJ C 244, 13.9.1984; Bull. EC 7/8-1984, point 2.1.84.
[5] OJ C 56, 29.2.1984; Bull. EC 2-1984, point 2.1.60.
[6] OJ C 37, 10.2.1983; Seventeenth General Report, point 272.
[7] OJ C 342, 19.12.1983; Seventeenth General Report, point 272.
[8] OJ C 206, 6.8.1984.
[9] OJ L 40, 11.2.1984; Bull. EC 2-1984, point 2.1.59.

tive with a view to preventing certain types of fraud or tax evasion on supplies of gold between taxable persons. [1]

253. In accordance with the provisions of the sixth Directive, [2] and in response to the Council Decision of 30 June [3] the Commission on 17 July sent the Council a proposal for a twentieth Directive [4]—authorizing the Federal Republic of Germany to grant special aid to its farmers, using VAT as the instrument. [5]

254. On 4 December, the Commission sent the Council a proposal for an eighteenth Directive [6]—providing for the abolition in two stages (on 1 January 1986 and on 1 January 1988) of most of the derogations at present allowed under the Directive of 17 May 1977, [2] in particular those listed in Annexes E (transactions that are normally exempt but that may be taxed during the transitional period) and F (transactions that are normally taxed but that may be exempted from tax during the transitional period) to that Directive.

255. On 5 December the Commission sent the Council a proposal for a nineteenth Directive, [6] clarifying and amending a number of provisions of the Directive of 17 May 1977, [2] notably the principle of territoriality as applied to certain transport operations, the expressions 'fixed establishment' and 'forms of transport', and the definition of the taxable amount on importation.

256. On 31 July the Council adopted [7] a proposal for a tenth Directive — on the application of value-added tax to the hiring out of movable tangible property. [8]

257. In a communication sent to the Council on 13 June [9] Mr Tugendhat, Vice-President of the Commission, underlined the importance of the proposal for a fourteenth Directive [10] in strengthening the internal market; the aim of the fourteenth Directive is to introduce a deferred payment system under which VAT on imports would no longer be collected by the customs authorities but

---

[1] OJ L 264, 5.10.1984; Bull. EC 3-1984, point 2.1.57.
[2] OJ L 145, 13.6.1977; Eleventh General Report, point 219.
[3] OJ L 185, 12.7.1984; Bull., EC 6-1984, point 2.1.88.
[4] OJ C 214, 14.8.1984; Bull. EC 7/8-1984, point 2.1.83.
[5] Bull. EC 7/8-1984, point 2.1.117.
[6] OJ C 347, 29.12.1984; Bull. EC 12-1984.
[7] OJ L 208, 3.8.1984.
[8] OJ C 116, 9.5.1979; Thirteenth General Report, point 190.
[9] Bull. EC 6-1984, point 2.1.38.
[10] OJ C 203, 6.8.1982; Sixteenth General Report, point 270.

would simply be declared in the importer's periodic VAT return to the tax authorities.

Excise duties and other indirect taxes

258. On 10 April the Council extended[1] the second stage of harmonization for excise duties on cigarettes yet again, this time to 31 December 1985.[2]

259. On 20 September the Commission sent the Council a proposal for a Directive[3] amending the Council Directive of 17 July 1969 concerning indirect taxes on the raising of capital (capital duty).[4] This proposal grants Member States the option of exempting the transactions covered by the Directive from capital duty or of taxing them at a single rate of up to 1%, and it abolishes capital duty on transactions which are at present taxable at the reduced rate.

Tax-free allowances

260. On 29 February the Commission amended[5] its proposals for a sixth and a seventh Directive on tax-free allowances for travellers within the Community.[6] These amendments take account of the opinions delivered by Parliament[7] and the Economic and Social Committee.[8]

261. On 20 March the Commission sent the Council two proposals for Directives:[9] the first amends Directive 83/181/EEC of 28 March 1983[10] determining the scope of Article 14(1)(d) of the sixth Directive[11] as regards exemption from value-added tax on the final importation of certain goods; the second amends Directive 83/127/EEC of 28 March 1983[12] on the standardization of provisions regarding the duty-free admission of fuel contained in the fuel tanks of commer-

---

[1]   OJ L 104, 17.4.1984; Bull. EC 4-1984, point 2.1.56.
[2]   OJ C 348, 23.12.1983; Seventeenth General Report, point 278.
[3]   OJ C 267, 6.10.1984; Bull. EC 9-1984, point 2.1.38.
[4]   OJ L 249, 3.10.1969.
[5]   OJ C 81, 22.3.1984, OJ C 72, 13.3.1984; Bull. EC 2-1984, point 2.1.62.
[6]   OJ C 114, 28.4.1983; Seventeenth General Report, points 282 and 283.
[7]   OJ C 10, 16.1.1984.
[8]   OJ C 57, 29.2.1984; Bull. EC 1-1984, point 2.4.42.
[9]   OJ C 95, 6.4.1984; Bull. EC 3-1984, point 2.1.58.
[10] OJ L 105, 23.4.1983; Seventeenth General Report, point 280.
[11] OJ L 145, 13.6.1977; Eleventh General Report, point 219.
[12] OJ L 91, 9.4.1983; Seventeenth General Report, point 504.

cial motor vehicles. Parliament[1] and the Economic and Social Committee[2] have given their opinions on these proposals.

262. On 2 April the Commission sent the Council a proposal for an eighth Directive[3] —increasing tax-free allowances for travellers from outside the Community, on which the Economic and Social Committee delivered an opinion in July.[2]

263. On 30 April the Council adopted[4] the first stage of the multiannual programme of increases in the tax-free allowance for persons travelling within the Community, proposed by the Commission in April 1983.[5]

264. On 3 July the Commission amended[6] its proposal for a fourth Directive[7] introducing a multiannual programme of increases in the relief allowed on the importation of goods in small consignments of a non-commercial character, in order to take account of the opinions of Parliament[8] and the Economic and Social Committee.[9]

265. In its communication to the Council on a people's Europe,[10] the Commission announced its intention of speeding up implementation of its multiannual programme by proposing to the Council as soon as possible that the tax-free allowances for travellers be raised from 280 ECU to 400 ECU, and the relief for small consignments from 70 ECU to 130 ECU, from 1 July 1985.

Direct taxation

266. Following its communication on tax and financial measures to promote investment,[11] the Commission on 11 September sent the Council a proposal for a Directive on the harmonization of the laws of the Member States relating to tax arrangements for the carryover of losses of undertakings.[12]

---

[1] OJ C 172, 2.7.1984; Bull. EC 5-1984, point 2.1.67.
[2] OJ C 248, 17.9.1984.
[3] OJ C 102, 14.4.1984; Bull. EC 3-1984, point 2.1.59.
[4] OJ L 117, 3.5.1984; Bull. EC 4-1984, point 2.1.54.
[5] OJ C 114, 28.4.1983; Seventeenth General Report, point 282.
[6] OJ C 189, 17.7.1984; Bull. EC 7/8-1984, point 2.1.86.
[7] OJ C 3, 6.1.1984; Seventeenth General Report, point 284.
[8] OJ C 127, 14.5.1984; Bull. EC 4-1984, point 2.1.53.
[9] OJ C 103, 16.4.1984.
[10] Bull. EC 9-1984, points 1.1.5 and 1.1.9.
[11] Bull. EC 4-1983, point 1.3.1 et seq.
[12] OJ C 253, 20.9.1984; Bull. EC 9-1984, point 2.1.41.

Tax avoidance

267. Considering that the time was ripe to give a fresh impetus to the fight against international tax evasion and avoidance, the Commission on 29 November sent the Council and Parliament a communication on Community action to be taken in this field. [1]

Supervision of the application of Community provisions

268. In 1984 the Court of Justice delivered four rulings, finding against: Germany, in respect of the exemptions from turnover tax and excise duties applicable to goods in travellers' personal luggage ('butter ships'); [2] Belgium, for retaining the catalogue price as the taxable amount for charging VAT on new cars sold at a discount and ex-demonstration vehicles; [3] and Italy, for failing to adopt within the prescribed period the provisions needed to comply with the Council Directive of 18 December 1978 relating to manufactured tobacco, [4] and with the Directive of 6 December 1979 on mutual assistance for the recovery of claims. [5]

269. Three proceedings were terminated by the Commission, since the Member States concerned had amended their legislation to comply with Community law: the United Kingdom ended the differential levying of excise duty on wines and made-wines; [6] Ireland now permits the remission of tax on exports of goods carried by travellers; and Italy eliminated the State duty on spirits.

270. Several proceedings previously instituted under Article 95 of the EEC Treaty in respect of alcoholic beverages reached an advanced stage. The Commission referred the following cases to the Court of Justice: Italy—excise duties on liqueur wines and VAT on sparkling wines; Denmark—excise duties on fruit wines.

It sent France a reasoned opinion concerning the differential taxation of certain 'liqueur wines' and 'natural sweet wines'.

---

[1] Bull. EC 11-1984, point 2.1.50.
[2] Case 278/82, *Rewe v HZA Flensburg and Others:* OJ C 80, 21.3.1984; Bull. EC 2-1984, point 2.4.26.
[3] Case 324/82 *Commission v Belgium:* OJ C 129, 16.5.1984; Bull. EC 4-1984, point 2.4.32.
[4] Case 280/83 *Commission v Italy:* OJ C 167, 26.6.1984.
[5] OJ L 331, 27.12.1979.
[6] Sixteenth General Report, point 283.

It instituted proceedings against Belgium, which charges a higher rate of VAT on wine than on beer.

271. As to other sectors, the Commission referred two cases to the Court of Justice: France—rules on fees for carrying out health checks on oysters, mussels and shellfish; [1] the United Kingdom—import of perfumes and toilet products containing alcohol.

272. Commission action in response to failure to comply with secondary legislation was as follows:

273. Sixth VAT Directive of 17 May 1977 (uniform basis of assessment): [2]

(i) Institution of new proceedings against: Italy—importation of medical samples; United Kingdom—new scheme for second-hand goods, status of hospitals and private clinics and exemption arrangements for small traders.

(ii) Progress to the reasoned opinion stage in the following cases: Ireland and the United Kingdom—continued zero-rating of certain products; United Kingdom—exemption of supply of services by medical and paramedical professions; France and Ireland—reduction in the taxable amount.

(iii) Reference to the Court of Justice: Ireland and the Netherlands—reduction in the taxable amount where goods are traded in; [3] Germany—exemption for services supplied to the Federal Postal Administration by carriers (in particular railways and airlines). [4]

274. Directives of 19 December 1972 [5] and 19 December 1977 [6] on manufactured tobacco:

(i) Institution of several new proceedings: France—fixing the retail selling price for tobacco at a level other than that set by the manufacturers or the importer; Belgium and the Netherlands—refusal to sell tax bands at a retail price below that charged by the manufacturer or his sole importer.

(ii) Reference to the Court of Justice: Italy—failure to apply the provisions concerning the ratio between the proportional component and the specific component of excise duty on cigarettes.

---

[1] Sixteenth General Report, point 283.
[2] OJ L 145, 13.6.1977; Eleventh General Report, point 219.
[3] Sixteenth General Report, point 280.
[4] Sixteenth General Report, point 279.
[5] OJ L 303, 31.12.1972; Sixth General Report, point 103.
[6] OJ L 338, 28.12.1977; Eleventh General Report, point 228.

Section 7

Employment, education and social policy

Main developments

275. As in previous years, the increase in unemployment continued to be of major concern to the Community. From a figure of 10.8% of the working population at the end of 1983, the percentage unemployed rose to 11.3% at the end of 1984 or some 13.1 million Europeans looking for work. The Community's attention was again concentrated on those hardest hit by unemployment: the Council adopted a number of resolutions which confirmed its determination to improve the situation of women and of the long-term unemployed. The Community intends to fulfil its role as a catalyst by implementing new actions to combat unemployment; thus, on 7 June it adopted a resolution on the contribution of local job creation schemes in the struggle against unemployment.

While problems connected with unemployment are clearly given some priority, they are not the Community's only concern. Looking further into the future, on 22 June the Council adopted conclusions concerning a Community medium-term social action programme[1] *which will provide guidelines for the measures and initiatives in the coming years and see the social policy become an integral part of Community policy. In employment, technological change will, no doubt, be a key factor in Community activity. Another important point is the role of social protection as a major element in social cohesion and a counterpart to the job mobility that is needed in view of technological change and competition; here, particular attention will be paid to demographic trends and migration problems. Finally, the promotion of the social dialogue at Community level will continue to be significant.*

---

[1]   OJ C 175, 4.7.1984; Bull. EC 6-1984, point 2.1.43.

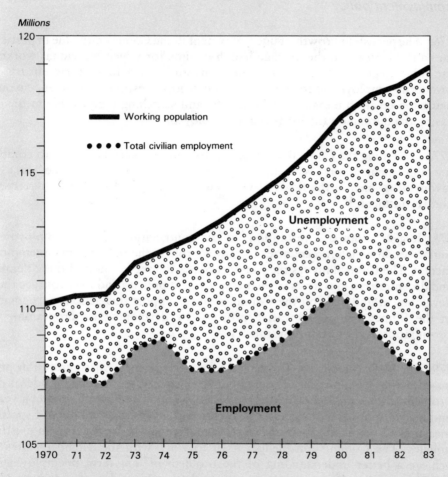

Working population and civilian employment

EUR 10

Source: Eurostat.

The number of jobseekers increased steadily and regularly during the period in question; this increase is related to the entry into the labour market of a larger proportion of women and of the last age groups belonging to the postwar 'baby boom'. Employment, on the other hand, developed irregularly, though with a downward trend. The two downturns in the employment situation are the result of the oil crises of 1973 and 1979, the second having more far-reaching and lasting effects on the overall level of employment.

Employment

Employment policy

276. The persistent growth of unemployment in the Community, due in particular to the increase in the average length of time for which individual workers are jobless, prompted the Community institutions to focus their efforts on promoting employment for the worst-hit categories, especially women, encouraging job-creation measures at local level and searching for possible means of easing the burden on the long-term unemployed.

277. On 7 June the Council adopted a resolution concerning action to combat unemployment among women, which provides for measures to be taken in favour of women in the fields of vocational training and guidance, placement and recruitment. [1]

278. It also adopted a resolution on the contribution of local employment initiatives, in which it recognizes the latter's role in the fight against unemployment. [2] The Council invites the Member States to take account of these flexible and decentralized initiatives in their employment policies and to encourage their development and calls on the Commission to support this action, particularly in the framework of innovative projects, by developing its programme of consultation and information transfer.

279. On 13 December the Council reached agreement [3] on a resolution proposed by the Commission in September [4] which stressed the magnitude of the problem (over 4 million people registered as unemployed for more than a year) and its enormous economic and social cost and suggesting a number of specific measures to be taken at national level to overcome the weaknesses in existing policies. The Commission pledges itself to work with the Member States to achieve a better understanding of the problem of long-term unemployment, encourage their efforts and cooperate with the two sides of industry. This communication was the subject of conclusions reached by the Standing Committee on Employment in October. [5]

---

[1] OJ C 161, 21.6.1984; Bull. EC 6-1984, point 2.1.57.
[2] OJ C 161, 21.6.1984; Bull. EC 6-1984, point 2.1.45.
[3] OJ C 2, 4.1.1985; Bull. EC 12-1984.
[4] Bull. EC 9-1984, point 2.1.43.
[5] Bull. EC 10-1984, point 2.1.52.

280. On the basis of the Commission communication [1] and the conclusions of the Standing Committee on Employment, [2] the Council adopted a set of conclusions on technological change and social adjustment. [3]

Freedom of movement for workers

281. In order to give a European dimension to the employment services, the Commission stepped up its efforts to improve cooperation between employment service officials in frontier areas. Accordingly, it organized 35 exchanges, lasting from one to three months, of placement service officials from eight Member States. [4]

282. The Commission also continued to promote the use of Sedoc, [5] which it views as an effective instrument, in a period of chronic unemployment, for notifying vacancies and applications which cannot be cleared on the national labour markets.

European Social Fund and structural operations

Special measures in favour of certain Member States

283. On 26 March the Council adopted a Regulation on exceptional financial support in favour of Greece in the social field. [6] This measure provides, for the period from 1 January 1984 to 31 December 1988, 120 million ECU for the construction, adaptation and equipment of vocational training centres in the Athens area and the construction, adaptation and equipment of centres for the vocational rehabilitation of the mentally ill and mentally handicapped. The Commission approved the first series of requests on 25 October. [7]

284. Following the overall agreement reached by the European Council at Fontainebleau regarding the Community's financial problems, [8] on 26 June the

---

[1] Bull. EC 1-1984, point 1.3.1 et seq.
[2] Bull. EC 5-1984, point 2.1.69.
[3] OJ C 184, 11.7.1984; Bull. EC 6-1984, point 2.1.47.
[4] Bull. EC 3-1984, point 2.1.64.
[5] European system for the international clearing of vacancies and applications for employment.
[6] OJ L 88, 31.3.1984; Seventeenth General Report, point 317.
[7] OJ L 289, 6.11.1984; Bull. EC 10-1984, point 2.1.56.
[8] Bull. EC 6-1984, point 1.1.1 et seq.

Council was able to adopt a Regulation introducing special measures of Community interest in the field of employment in favour of the United Kingdom.[1] This Regulation provides for financial assistance of 275 million ECU for the implementation of the United Kingdom scheme to create jobs for the unemployed, particularly young people. The Commission adopted the relevant implementing Decision on 19 October.[2]

European Social Fund

285. The new rules governing the tasks of the ESF, adopted by the Council on 17 October 1983,[3] were applied for the first time in 1984.

286. On 27 April the Commission decided that the guidelines for the management of the European Social Fund in 1984-86, originally adopted on 21 December 1983[4] and endorsed by Parliament in March,[5] should continue in effect for the years 1985-87.[6]

287. A breakdown of the appropriations for commitment available in 1984,[7] amounting to 1 902 680 000 ECU is given in Table 8.

TABLE 8

Appropriations for commitment

million ECU

Operations to assist young people under 25:	
Less-favoured regions	501.68
Other regions	914.25
Operations to assist people over 25:	
Less-favoured regions	224.65
Other regions	175.81
Innovative operations	42.68
Total	1 859.06

---

[1] OJ L 177, 4.7.1984; Bull. EC 6-1984, point 2.1.49.
[2] OJ L 290, 7.11.1984; Bull. EC 10-1984, point 2.1.55.
[3] OJ L 289, 22.10.1983; Seventeenth General Report, point 305.
[4] OJ C 5, 10.1.1984; Seventeenth General Report, point 306.
[5] OJ C 117, 30.4.1984; Bull. EC 3-1984, point 2.1.66.
[6] OJ C 126, 12.5.1984; Bull. EC 4-1984, point 2.1.60.
[7] Full information on the Social Fund's activities will be given in its annual report, to be published in July.

288. A breakdown of the assistance approved for each Member State shows that about 32% went to the United Kingdom, 22% to Italy, 12% to Ireland, 11% to France and 5% to Greece.

289. The overall volume of eligible applications corresponded to a sum of 3 270 million ECU, thus exceeding by 72.3% the appropriations available. The difference between the total volume of assistance requested and the total amount actually granted after the application of the weighted reduction went from 476 550 000 ECU in 1983 to 832 720 000 ECU in 1984, the linear reduction being 82 530 000 ECU.

290. The appropriations for payment entered in the 1984 budget amounted to 1 211 900 000 ECU.

Redeployment of workers in ECSC industries

291. Continuing its social measures to assist ECSC workers, the Commission granted non-repayable aid under Article 56(2) (b) of the Treaty to a total of 140 million ECU (conventional aid). Such aid is granted in the form of income support allowances in the event of early retirement, unemployment or reemployment and enables a financial contribution to be made towards expenditure relating to vocational training, mobility and allowances for the reintegration of workers in new jobs. The breakdown by country and industry of ECSC workers granted redeployment aid in 1984 is as follows:

	Coal industry	Steel industry and iron ore mining
Belgium	—	807
Denmark	—	709
FR of Germany	7 146	9 332
France	4 510	—
Italy	—	20
Luxembourg	—	6 087
Netherlands	—	1 084
United Kingdom	12 673	1 770
Total	24 329	19 809

292. As a part of its social support scheme to help workers affected by restructuring measures in the coal and steel industries, the Council adopted decisions authorizing the transfer of exceptional contributions from the general budget of the Communities amounting to 60 million ECU for the coal industry [1] and 62.5 million ECU for the steel industry. [2] These additional resources made it possible to meet the needs of a substantially higher number of beneficiaries in the coal industry and, in the steel industry, to continue and complete the programmes of action authorized under the 1981 social measures scheme. [3]

293. In 1984 the Commission was able to release the following appropriations (broken down according to the origin of the resources) for all the programmes adopted:

TABLE 9

Appropriations committed under Article 56(2)(b) of the ECSC Treaty

million ECU

	Coal industry		Steel industry and iron ore mining		Total	
	Normal resources	Exceptional resources	Normal resources	Exceptional resources	Normal resources	Exceptional resources
Belgium	515.00	1 000	2 089.25	4 160	2 604.25	5 160
Denmark	—	—	1 857.50	280	1 857.50	280
FR of Germany	20 394.00	20 500	15 290.25	19 130	35 684.25	39 630
France	21 129.25	15 400	—	13 170	21 129.25	28 570
Italy	—	—	69.50	15 940	69.50	15 940
Luxembourg	—	—	9 055.50	1 880	9 055.00	1 880
Netherlands	—	—	2 156.25	580	2 156.25	580
United Kingdom	52 998.50	23 100	14 445.00	7 360	67 443.50	30 460
Total	95 036.75	60 000	44 963.25	62 500	140 000.00	122 500

---

[1] OJ L 208, 3.8.1984, Bull. EC 7/8-1984, point 2.1.173.
[2] OJ L 291, 8.11.1984; Bull. EC 7/8-1984, point 2.1.34; Bull. EC 10-1984, point 2.1.25.
[3] Fifteenth General Report, point 272.

Education and vocational training

Cooperation in education

294. On 4 June the Council and the Ministers for Education meeting within the Council adopted two sets of conclusions:[1] the first concerns the primordial role which education and training can and should play in the face of technological change, reinforcing and extending the scope of the June 1983 resolutions relating to the introduction of the new information technologies in education[2] and to vocational training in this respect;[3] the second gives fresh impetus to Community cooperation in education and relates to the teaching of foreign languages, measures to combat illiteracy, the education of migrant workers' children and the integration of handicapped children into ordinary schools.

295. The Commission built up its activities with regard to the transition of young people from school to working life on the basis of a programme comprising 30 pilot projets. It has funded 409 joint study programmes and awarded 136 grants to teachers in higher education and 300 to local administrative staff to enable them to familiarize themselves with other teaching systems. With the aid of the Eurydice network,[4] cooperation as regards the exchange of information was also strengthened.

Specific measures relating to vocational training

296. The implementation of the two Council resolutions of June and July 1983[5] was pursued as part of an overall strategy prepared with the help of the Directors-General for vocational training in the Member States. The demonstration projects of an innovatory and experimental nature referred to in Article 3(2) and certain operations covered by Article 3(1) of the Decision of 17 October 1983 on the tasks of the European Social Fund[6] are an important part of this strategy.

297. Following opinions from Parliament[7] and the Economic and Social Committee,[8] on 13 December the Council adopted[9] a proposal for a Decision

---

[1] Bull. EC 6-1984, point 2.1.41.
[2] OJ C 256, 24.9.1983; Seventeenth General Report, point 314.
[3] OJ C 166, 25.6.1983; Seventeenth General Report, point 313.
[4] Education information network in the European Community.
[5] OJ C 166, 25.6.1983; OJ C 193, 20.7.1983; Seventeenth General Report, point 313.
[6] OJ L 289, 22.10.1983; Seventeenth General Report, point 305.
[7] OJ C 337, 17.12.1984; Bull. EC 11-1984, point 2.1.57.
[8] Bull. EC 11-1984, point 2.4.30.
[9] OJ L 331, 19.12.1984; Bull. EC 12-1984.

relating to the preparation of a third exchange programme for young workers in the Community,[1] designed to improve the flexibility of these schemes by making them accessible to young unemployed persons.

European University Institute in Florence

298. The Commission contributed the sum of 1 280 000 ECU to research and academic activities carried out by the European University Institute in Florence[2] (research projects, library, publications, language department, computer department, study grants for qualified researchers, summer schools, centre for documentation and research on European integration).[3]

European Centre for the Development of Vocational Training

299. The Centre continued to pursue the lines of action adopted by its Management Board for 1983-85 relating to special projects and activities in certain fields.[4] In Berlin in September and November the Board examined the Centre's forthcoming activities for 1985,[5] in close cooperation with the Commission as part of the implementation of the Council resolutions of June and July 1983.[6]

Social security and living and working conditions

Social security and social protection

300. On 13 January the Commission sent to the Council an interim report[7] on the application of the Directive of 19 December 1978 on the progressive implementation of the principle of equal treatment for men and women in matters of social security.[8] This report is a contribution to the effective implementation of the Directive in 1985.

---

[1] OJ C 153, 13.6.1984; Bull. EC 5-1984, point 2.1.78.
[2] The activities of the European University Institute in Florence are described in its annual report and in an information leaflet, both obtainable from the Institute itself (Badia Fiesolana, 5 via dei Roccettini, San Domenico di Fiesole, I-50016 Firenze).
[3] Point 57 of this Report.
[4] Seventeenth General Report, point 320.
[5] Bull. EC 9-1984, point 2.1.49; Bull. EC 11-1984, point 2.1.59.
[6] Seventeenth General Report, point 313.
[7] Bull. EC 1-1984, point 2.1.44.
[8] OJ L 6, 10.1.1979.

301. The Commission sent to the Council a draft recommendation on the social protection of volunteers for development on 12 December. [1]

302. On 13 December the Council reached general agreement [2] on a Decision regarding specific Community action to combat poverty for 1985-89, [3] providing for transnational action/research projects on specific topics, the exchange of information and the transfer of innovatory methods, greater comprehension and perception of the extent of poverty. This action has an appropriation of 25 million ECU.

303. During the 1983/84 academic year the Executive Committee of the Paul Finet Foundation examined 1 145 applications and awarded 918 scholarships, for a total of BFR 14 593 596.

Social security for migrant workers

304. The Administrative Commission and the Advisory Committee on Social Security for Migrant Workers studied various questions relating to the application of the provisions in force. The Court of Justice delivered 11 judgments in cases referred to it for preliminary rulings on the interpretation or validity of the provisions in question.

Equal treatment for women and men

305. In connection with the implementation of its new action programme on the promotion of equal opportunities for women (1982-85), [4] on 15 March the Commission laid before the Council a proposal for a Directive on equal treatment for women in self-employed occupations, including agriculture, and protection during pregnancy and maternity. [5] On 17 April it also presented a draft recommendation on positive action, [6] designed to encourage the generalized development of such action (at the same time, the Commission will promote practical measures, particularly in industry and banking, encouragement of

---

[1] OJ L 6, 10.1.1979; OJ C 16, 17.1.1985; Bull. EC 12-1984.
[2] OJ L 2, 3.1.1985; Bull. EC 12-1984.
[3] OJ C 208, 8.8.1984; Bull. EC 7/8-1984, point 2.1.100.
[4] OJ C 22, 29.1.1982; Supplement 1/82 — Bull. EC.
[5] OJ C 113, 27.4.1984; Bull. EC 3-1984, point 2.1.76.
[6] OJ C 143, 30.5.1984; Bull. EC 4-1984, point 2.1.65.

women's cooperatives). This draft recommendation was adopted by the Council on 13 December. [1]

306. Following opinions by Parliament [2] and the Economic and Social Committee, [3] on 15 November the Commission amended [4] its proposal for a Directive on parental leave and leave for family reasons. [5]

307. Work was begun by expert groups in certain specific fields, including education and training activities, the monitoring of the application of the directives and the analysis of qualitative and quantitative trends in women's employment.

308. On 12 December the Commission sent the Council a memorandum on income tax and equal treatment for men and women. [6]

309. The Commission also continued to monitor the application of the Directive of 9 February 1976 (76/207) on the implementation of the principle of equal treatment for men and women as regards access to employment, vocational training and promotion and working conditions. [7] It brought infringement proceedings before the Court of Justice against Denmark, the Federal Republic of Germany and the Netherlands under Article 169 of the EEC Treaty. [8]

Social integration of handicapped persons

310. The implementation of the action programme to promote the social integration of disabled people [9] was pursued. A Community network of model projects was set up, and the initial phase of a computerized Community data base on the handicapped (Handynet project) was launched.

---

[1] OJ L 331, 19.12.1984; Bull. EC 12-1984.
[2] OJ C 117, 30.4.1983; Bull. EC 3-1984, point 2.1.79.
[3] OJ C 206, 6.8.1984; Bull. EC 5-1984, point 2.4.26.
[4] OJ C 316, 27.11.1984; Bull. EC 11-1984, point 2.1.62.
[5] OJ C 333, 9.12.1983; Seventeenth General Report, point 328.
[6] Bull. EC 12-1984.
[7] OJ L 39, 14.2.1976.
[8] Point 816 of this Report.
[9] OJ C 347, 31.12.1981; Fifteenth General Report, point 296.

Living and working conditions

311. As part of its 1984 work programme, the Dublin-based European Foundation for the Improvement of Living and Working Conditions continued research on shift work, the organization of working time and the transport of dangerous substances. [1]

312. The Commission continued to implement the second instalment of the ninth ECSC subsidized housing scheme. [2] The entire sum of 30 million ECU made available has been committed, and in all Member States the funds are continuing to be paid out or have already been disbursed. Preparatory work for the 10th programme has been begun, as has the operation to redistribute funds not used as intended under the two instalments of the ninth programme.

Wages and incomes

313. On 6 December [3] the Commission sent the Council a report on the application in Greece of the equal pay principle, in accordance with Article 119 of the EEC Treaty and the Directive of 10 February 1975. [4]

Labour law and industrial relations

314. Taking into account the opinions delivered by Parliament [5] and the Economic and Social Committee, [6] in April the Commission sent to the Council an amended proposal for a Directive concerning temporary work and fixed-duration contracts. [7]

315. The established joint committees duly pursued their work in their respective fields: working conditions, health and safety and employment. The first full meeting of the Joint Committee on Inland Navigation was held in June under the new rules extending the Committee's powers by granting both sides of industry a right of initiative and greater independence. [8]

---

[1] Seventeenth General Report, point 330.
[2] OJ C 299, 30.11.1979; Thirteenth General Report, point 232.
[3] Bull. EC 12-1984.
[4] OJ L 45, 19.2.1975.
[5] OJ C 242, 12.9.1983.
[6] OJ C 176, 4.7.1983.
[7] OJ C 133, 21.5.1984; Bull. EC 4-1984, point 2.1.59.
[8] Bull. EC 6-1984, point 2.1.56.

316. In this context it is worth emphasizing that the Council, in its conclusions of 22 June concerning a Community medium-term social action programme, [1] requested the Commission to devise appropriate measures for encouraging the development of joint relations at Community level.

Health and safety

Public health

317. At an informal meeting on 29 November the Health Ministers had detailed discussions on Community cooperation on health-related problems, [2] with particular reference to drug addiction, smoking and infectious diseases, and on the problems of containing health costs.

318. Parliament [3] and the Economic and Social Committee [4] delivered their opinions on the draft Council recommendation concerning the introduction, on a voluntary basis, of a European emergency health card for persons at risk. [5]

319. In May the Commission sent the Council a draft resolution concerning a Community action programme on toxicology for health protection. [6]

Health and safety at work

320. In February the Council adopted a resolution on a second Community action programme on safety and health at work (1983-88). [7]

321. In June the Commission placed before the Council a proposal for a Decision on the ratification of the Torremolinos International Convention for the Safety of Fishing Vessels and application of its provisions by the Member States pending its entry into force internationally. [8]

---

[1] Bull. EC 6-1984, point 2.1.43.
[2] Bull. EC 11-1984.
[3] OJ C 337, 17.12.1984; Bull. EC 11-1984, point 2.1.69.
[4] OJ C 266, 6.8.1984; Bull. EC 5-1984, point 2.1.88.
[5] Seventeenth General Report, point 337.
[6] OJ C 156, 16.6.1984; Bull. EC 5-1984, point 2.1.86.
[7] OJ C 67, 8.3.1984; Bull. EC 2-1984, 2.1.79.
[8] OJ C 183, 10.7.1984; Bull. EC 6-1984, point 2.1.59.

322. In July the Commission transmitted to the Council, [1] in response to the opinion of Parliament, [2] an amended proposal for a Directive on the protection of workers from noise at work. [3]

323. In September it sent the Council a proposal for a Directive on the protection of workers by the proscription of specified agents and/or work activities. [4] This is the fourth individual Directive within the meaning of Article 8 of the framework Directive of 27 November 1980. [5]

324. The Advisory Committee on Safety, Hygiene and Health Protection at Work held two meetings. [6] It approved its eighth annual report and delivered its opinion on the Commission's work plan for the implementation in 1985 of the second programme of action of the European Communities on safety and health at work. [7]

Health and safety (Euratom)

325. In September the Council adopted the Directive on the radiation protection of persons undergoing medical examination or treatment, [8] together with the Directive [8] concerned mainly with the adaptation of Annexes I and III to the Directive of 15 July 1980 laying down basic safety standards for the health protection of the general public and workers against the dangers of ionizing radiation. [9]

326. In March Parliament[10] and the Economic and Social Committee[11] delivered their opinions concerning the draft resolution on transfrontier radiological problems.[12]

327. Pursuant to Article 33 of the Euratom Treaty, the Commission delivered an opinion on two draft nuclear regulations. It also gave an opinion in

---

[1] OJ C 214, 14.8.1984; Bull. EC 7/8-1984, point 2.1.102.
[2] OJ C 117, 30.4.1984; Bull. EC 3-1984, point 2.1.84.
[3] OJ C 289, 5.11.1982; Bull. EC 10-1982, point 2.1.45; Sixteenth General Report, point 322.
[4] OJ C 270, 10.10.1984; Bull. EC 9-1984, point 2.1.51.
[5] OJ L 327, 3.12.1980; Bull. EC 11-1980, point 2.1.38.
[6] Bull. EC 6-1984, point 2.1.60.
[7] Seventeenth General Report, point 341.
[8] OJ L 265, 5.10.1984; Bull. EC 9-1984, point 2.1.55.
[9] OJ L 246, 17.9.1980; Bull. EC 7/8-1980, point 2.1.50.
[10] OJ C 117, 30.4.1984; Bull. EC 3-1984, point 2.1.85.
[11] OJ C 140, 28.5.1984; Bull. EC 3-1984, point 2.4.36.
[12] OJ C 338, 15.12.1983; Seventeenth General Report, point 345.

pursuance of Article 37 in respect of six plans for the disposal of radioactive effluents.[1] In accordance with the recommendation of 3 February 1982,[2] it received initial notification of two such disposal plans.

328. A working party was set up to examine radiological protection criteria for the recycling of materials arising from the dismantling of nuclear installations.

Health and safety (ECSC)

329. The Mines Safety and Health Commission held a plenary meeting from 22 to 24 October,[3] and several meetings of working parties on various aspects of safety and health in the mining, oil and gas industries also took place. During its plenary meeting the Safety and Health Commission approved proposals to the governments on health and safety training for workers in the offshore oil industry and on the protection of workers from the noxious effects of lead. Subjects on which similar studies are still in progress include accident reports, the main facets of fire and explosion prevention and the health and safety aspects of diving.

330. The Steel Industry Safety and Health Commission received the conclusions of five studies on specific safety problems in the steel industry, and arranged exchanges of experience on the hazards of electric-arc steelmaking.

---

[1] Bull. EC 2-1984, point 2.1.80; Bull. EC 4-1984, point 2.1.70; Bull. EC 5-1984, point 2.1.92; Bull. EC 9-1984, point 2.1.56; Bull. EC 10-1984, point 2.1.67.
[2] OJ L 83, 29.3.1982; Sixteenth General Report, point 326.
[3] Bull. EC 10-1984, point 2.1.66.

Section 8

Regional policy

Main developments

331. The outstanding event of the year was the Council's adoption of the new Regional Fund Regulation in June, following a conciliation meeting with Parliament. The Regulation, which will take effect on 1 January 1985, ushers in a fundamental reform not only of the Regional Fund but also of regional policy generally.

332. In January the Council adopted a second series of six specific regional development measures under the Fund's non-quota section. As a follow-up, the Commission sent the Council in December four proposals for regulations which reinforce measures already launched. Most of the proposals are aimed at assisting the conversion of areas suffering from industrial decay. Industrial conversion, now a major task of Community regional policy, is also at the heart of other measures such as the expanded programme of ECSC conversion loans and the fostering of business and innovation centres.

333. In March the Commission adopted the second periodic report on the social and economic situation and development of the regions of the Community. The report examines the situation of the regions in the early 1980s and developments since the first oil shock.

Regional impact assessment of Community policies

334. The regional impact assessment of Community policies is used as the basis for modifying policy courses in response to regional needs or devising back-up measures to counteract any harmful effects they may have in the regions. In the accession negotiations the Communtity is taking account of the problems that enlargement could cause, e.g. for fruit and vegetables in agriculture. The Commission's proposals for the integrated Mediterranean programmes [1] are intended to enable the Community's southern regions to

---

[1]   OJ C 251, 19.9.1983; Seventeenth General Report, point 370.

adapt to the new situation that will be created by enlargement. In 1984 regional impact assessment prompted a strengthening of the specific regional development measures. [1]

335. A number of studies were conducted on the regional effects of new technologies. The Commission proposed a strategy for using modern telecommunication techniques to promote a rapid improvement in infrastructures in the Community's less prosperous regions.

Periodic report on the regions

336. In accordance with the Council resolution of 6 February 1979, [2] the Commission on 7 March adopted [3] the second periodic report on the social and economic situation and development of the regions of the Community. [4] The report, drawn up in close cooperation with the Regional Policy Committee, [5] covers the situation of the regions in the early 1980s and developments since the first oil shock in 1973. It gives an up-to-date and detailed analysis of regional disparities in employment, production, productivity and other factors. It shows that over the past 10 years regional disparities in production have not lessened and are still very wide. Regional labour market disequilibria are characterized by growing differences in unemployment. The future prospects for labour markets in the 1980s suggest a further deepening of regional differences.

Coordination and programmes

337. The regional development programmes provide a frame of reference for Regional Fund assistance and are a necessary instrument for coordinating regional policies. In 1984 the Commission examined the programme for France covering the period 1984-88 and the 1984-86 programme for Friuli-Venezia Giulia submitted by Italy. It also examined the reports updating the programmes for Ireland and Denmark. [6]

1 Point 348 of this Report.
2 OJ C 36, 9.2.1979.
3 Bull. EC 3-1984, point 2.1.89.
4 Fourteenth General Report, point 276.
5 Bull. EC 2-1984, point 2.1.82; Seventeenth General Report, point 355.
6 Bull. EC 9-1984, point 2.1.59.

338. On 19 June the Commission delivered an opinion on the second-generation regional development programmes (covering the period 1981-84) and stated its intention of conducting with each Member State an annual exmination of projects and programmes that could be cofinanced by the Community in line with the priorities drawn up in the light of the regional development programmes. [1]

339. The importance of coordinating regional policies has been further underscored by the inclusion of a section on coordination in the new Fund Regulation. [2]

Regional development studies

340. In view of the extent of industrial decline in the Community and the prominence given to it in the new Fund Regulation, [2] the Commission has undertaken a study of its regional impact.

341. The studies being carried out at the request of Member States include a joint study of cross-frontier cooperation with a view to preparing development programmes for areas straddling the German-Dutch border. Another study, undertaken in association with the Conference of Peripheral Maritime Regions, concerns transport problems for islands in the Community's less-favoured regions.

Regional Policy Committee

342. In 1984 the Regional Policy Committee held four meetings. [3] It advised the Commission [4] in the preparation of the second periodic report on the social and economic situation and development of the regions, [5] and adopted a statement on the report; [6] it examined the regional development programmes for France and Italy (Friuli-Venezia Giulia), and discussed the links between

---

[1] OJ L 211, 8.8.1984; Bull. EC 6-1984, point 2.1.65.
[2] Points 346 and 347 of this Report.
[3] Bull. EC 2-1984, point 2.1.82; Bull. EC 4-1984, point 2.1.75; Bull. EC 6-1984, point 2.1.66; Bull. EC 11-1984, point 2.1.79.
[4] Bull. EC 2-1984, point 2.1.82.
[5] Point 336 of this Report.
[6] Bull. EC 4-1984, point 2.1.75.

the Community's competition policy and national regional aid policies; [1] and it delivered 131 opinions on major infrastructure projects costing more than 10 million ECU, the total investment concerned amounting to 1 059.6 million ECU.

343. The Committee elected a new Chairman, Mr S. Miedema [2] (the outgoing Chairman, Mr Bernard Attali, having been appointed to other duties in his home country) and a new Vice-Chairman, Mrs Andreasen. [3]

Financial instruments

European Regional Development Fund

Fund Regulation

344. On 19 June, following a conciliation meeting with Parliament attended by the Commission, the Council adopted the Regulation reforming the Fund. [4]

345. The Regulation, which will enter into force on 1 January 1985, contains the essentials of the amended version [5] of the Commission's 1981 proposal, [6] taking due account of the proposals in the Commission's report entitled 'Ways of increasing the effectiveness of the Community's structural Funds', drawn up at the request of the European Council at its Stuttgart meeting. [7]

346. The reform, the outcome of three years of negotiation, is an important milestone in the formulation of an overall Community structural policy and significantly strengthens the instruments of Community regional policy. The most important innovations are: provisions on the coordination of Community policies and on coordination between the Community's regional policy and national regional policies, the amalgamation of the Fund's two sections (quota and non-quota) into a single Fund whose resources will be allocated to Member States by reference to ranges setting upper and lower limits to the assistance

---

[1] Bull. EC 6-1984, point 2.1.67.
[2] Bull. EC 11-1984, point 2.1.79.
[3] Bull. EC 2-1984, point 2.1.82; Bull. EC 4-1984, point 2.1.75.
[4] OJ L 169, 28.6.1984; Bull. EC 6-1984, points 1.3.1 to 1.3.11.
[5] OJ C 360, 31.12.1983; Seventeenth General Report, point 362.
[6] OJ C 336, 23.12.1981; Fifteenth General Report, point 324; Sixteenth General Report, point 338.
[7] Supplement 3/83 — Bull. EC; Seventeenth General Report, point 362.

available for each Member State, the gradual changeover from individual project financing to programme financing, and provision for exploiting the potential for internally generated development of regions.

347. The Regulation contains other major innovations, including higher and simplified rates of assistance, a speedier payments procedure through the introduction of a system of advances, and provisions concerning integrated approaches to development, in particular integrated operations.

New non-quota Regulations

348. On 18 January the Council adopted a second series of specific regional development measures under the Fund's non-quota section, for which total assistance from the Fund will amount to 730 million ECU over five years. [1] The measures strengthen non-quota measures already launched to tackle regional problems stemming from the expected enlargement of the Community, restructuring in the steel and shipbuilding industries and energy supply difficulties. Their territorial scope is increased, Greece now being covered by the enlargement and energy supply measures. A new measure was introduced to deal with the regional repercussions of restructuring in the textile industry.

349. The specific Community measure to assist certain areas adversely affected by restructuring in the steel industry [1] is tied in more closely with the Community's policy for the steel industry. In its initial phase, it concerns the areas which have already suffered heavy job losses in the industry. The second phase applies, with increased financial resources, in areas where the Member States' steel industry restructuring programmes, notified under the Commission's decision of August 1981, [2] will have major consequences. Under the second phase, the Commission took a series of decisions concerning areas in Germany, [3] the Netherlands [4] and Belgium. [5]

350. On 21 December the Commission sent the Council four proposals for Regulations extending the territorial coverage of the shipbuilding and textile measures, reinforcing the measures adopted in 1980 to assist the border areas

---

[1] OJ L 27, 31.1.1984; Bull. EC 1-1984, point 2.1.54.
[2] OJ L 228, 13.8.1981; Fifteenth General Report, point 217.
[3] OJ L 249, 18.9.1984; Bull. EC 5-1984, point 2.1.102.
[4] OJ L 249, 18.9.1984; Bull. EC 9-1984, point 2.1.64.
[5] OJ L 275, 18.10.1984; Bull. EC 10-1984, point 2.1.70.

of Ireland and Northern Ireland, and instituting a new measure to assist certain areas adversely affected by the Community fisheries policy. [1]

Fund operations

351. The total 1984 allocation for the Regional Fund in the general budget was 2 140 million ECU, compared with 2 010 million ECU for 1983. Of this amount, 115 million ECU was earmarked for the Fund's non-quota section; part of this sum was transferred to the quota section towards the end of the year.

TABLE 10

Regional Fund grants, by Member State[1]

Quota section

	1975-1984			1984			
	Number of investment projects	Investment involved (million ECU)	Assistance approved[2] (million ECU)	Number of investment projects	Investment involved (million ECU)	Assistance approved (million ECU)	Payments made[2] (million ECU)
Belgium	498	742.75	114.38	151	151.21	33.18	5.63
Denmark	831	583.66	131.76	167	107.60	24.48	28.10
FR of Germany	2 315	8 622.90	544.77	237	1 479.23	109.21	43.92
Greece	1 022	3 956.68	1 093.50	330	775.11	263.21	212.63
France	4 126	12 108.93	1 683.59	539	1 378.65	267.72	190.64
Ireland	938	10 723.68	712.87	139	1 477.91	158.55	101.51
Italy	9 529	21 405.93	4 352.83	1 521	2 464.08	805.85	435.12
Luxembourg	26	56.43	11.97	17	16.76	4.73	2.49
Netherlands	93	857.59	156.16	27	170.94	35.59	14.74
United Kingdom	6 429	20 888.98	2 735.63	1 216	3 209.11	619.68	291.61
Community	25 873	79 947.53	11 537.46	4 394	11 230.60	2 322.20	1 326.39

[1] The amounts in ECU are only approximate figures.
[2] Including studies (Article 12 of the Fund Regulation).

---

[1] Bull. EC 12-1984.

Quota section

352. In 1984 the Commission adopted three series of quota section grant decisions—in May, [1] September [2] and December [3]—after consulting the Fund Committee and, in the case of grants for infrastructure projects costing more than 10 million ECU, the Regional Policy Committee. The number of investment projects receiving grants was 4 394 (3 683 in 1983), and the grants totalled 2 322.22 million ECU.

Industrial and service sector projects accounted for 14% and infrastructure projects 85% of grants. Grants totalling 24.25 million ECU were also made in 1984 to help finance 43 studies under Article 12 of the Fund Regulation. [4] Table 10 summarizes the Fund's activity in 1984 and over the period 1975-84. Nearly all the appropriations available (including carryovers, transfers and adjustments) were committed.

Payments amounted to 1 326 million ECU (as against 1 247 million ECU in 1983), equivalent to 97.4% of the payment appropriations available in 1984. Over the first 10 years of the Fund's operation, from 1975 to 1984, payments totalled 6 372.6 million ECU—55.2% of commitments, compared with 55% at the end of 1983.

Non-quota section

353. Under the first five non-quota Regulations, [5] eight special programmes presented by the Member States were under way in 1984. (A ninth programme —for steel industry areas in Italy—is being drawn up.) The budget allocation for these programmes is 216 million ECU for the period 1981-85. In the first four years 54% of this amount has been committed, of which 37.63 million ECU in 1984.

Conversion loans

354. In the context of its policy for restructuring the Community's steel industry and redeploying steelworkers, the Commission in early April modified the procedures and conditions for granting global loans under Article 56(2)(a) of

---

[1] Bull. EC 5-1984, point 2.1.101.
[2] Bull. EC 9-1984, point 2.1.63.
[3] Bull. EC 12-1984.
[4] Bull. EC 6-1984, point 2.1.69; Bull. EC 7/8-1984, point 2.1.107; Bull. EC 9-1984, point 2.1.62; Bull. EC 11-1984, point 2.1.81.
[5] OJ L 271, 15.10.1980; Fifteenth General Report, point 326.

the ECSC Treaty, with the aim of further improving this financial instrument and deploying it more effectively. It compiled a list—to be updated at intervals—of ECSC employment areas eligible for interest subsidies on global loans. In priority employment areas, the subsidies may be combined with national aid. In addition, they will no longer be calculated by reference to the number of jobs created, but on a flat-rate basis. These changes, coupled with the increase in the interest subsidy on global loans from 3% to 5%,[1] produced a sharp increase in conversion loan applications in 1984.

TABLE 11

Loans granted under Article 56(2)(a) of the ECSC Treaty

million ECU

	B	DK[1]	D	GR[2]	F	IRL[1]	I	L	NL	UK[1]	EC
1961-83	195.87 (22)	11.72 (2)	476.44 (87)	—	371.66 (75)	6.45 (2)	256.78 (27)	14.97 (4)	54.12 (39)	791.55 (78)	2 179.56 (336)
1984	—	—	211.79 (8)	5.00 (1)	—	—	18.04 (1)	10.86 (2)	9.89 (1)	37.37 (4)	292.95 (17)
Total	195.87 (22)	11.72 (2)	688.23 (95)	5.00 (1)	371.66 (75)	6.45 (2)	274.82 (28)	25.84 (6)	64.01 (40)	828.92 (82)	2 472.51 (353)

N.B. The figures in brackets are the number of loans granted.
[1] Since 1973.
[2] Since 1981.

Business and innovation centres

355. Drawing on the pilot projects launched in 1983, the Commission stepped up action to promote the establishment of business and innovation centres that will provide a full range of services for new and innovatory firms in industrial conversion areas. It helped to set up eight new centres and was instrumental in the establishment of a European association of some 40 centres.[2]

Coordinated operations involving more than one financial instrument

Integrated operations

356. In 1984 the Commission continued to monitor and participate in implementation of the integrated operations in Naples and Belfast.[3] For Belfast, the Commission decided to allocate the second tranche of aid, amounting to

---

[1] OJ C 191, 16.7.1983; Seventeenth General Report, point 367.
[2] Bull. EC 11-1984, point 2.1.82.
[3] Sixteenth General Report, point 347; Seventeenth General Report, point 368.

some 33 million ECU,[1] under the Council Regulation of 21 June 1983. A new plan for the integrated operation in Belfast is currently being drawn up by the authorities in Northern Ireland, working in close cooperation with the Commission. No special aid has been granted by the Commission for the Naples integrated operation. However, as a result of continuing close consultations between the local, regional and national authorities and the Commission departments, a number of projects are to be financed under existing Community financial instruments, including the Regional Fund. As in the previous two years, the Commission approved assistance for new feasibility studies for integrated operations (two in France,[3] two in the Federal Republic of Germany,[4] one in Greece,[5] two in Italy[6] and one in Belgium[7]), with total commitments amounting to some 851 000 ECU.

Integrated Mediterranean programmes

357. On 6 September the Commission amended[8] its proposal for a Regulation instituting integrated Mediterranean programmes[9] in response to the opinions expressed by Parliament[10] and the Economic and Social Committee[11] and in the light of certain provisions of the new Fund Regulation.[12]

On the basis of the amended proposal and in view of the agreements reached by the European Council in Brussels[13] and Fontainebleau,[14] the Council resumed its examination of the Regulation in September. Its findings were discussed by the European Council in Dublin.[7]

358. The Commission, with the cooperation of the Member States concerned, also pressed ahead with the pilot projects and studies in preparation for the integrated Mediterranean programmes which it had decided to run in December 1983.[15]

---

[1] Bull. EC 6-1984, point 2.1.70.
[2] OJ L 171, 29.6.1983; Seventeenth General Report, point 371.
[3] Bull. EC 3-1984, point 2.1.93; Bull. EC 12-1984.
[4] Bull. EC 7/8-1984, point 2.1.108.
[5] Bull. EC 2-1984, point 2.1.83.
[6] Bull. EC 11-1984, point 2.1.83; Bull. EC 12-1984.
[7] Bull. EC 12-1984.
[8] OJ C 280, 19.10.1984; Bull. EC 9-1984, point 2.1.58.
[9] OJ C 251, 19.9.1983; Seventeenth General Report, point 370.
[10] OJ C 117, 30.4.1984; Bull. EC 3-1984, point 2.1.90.
[11] OJ C 23, 30.1.1984; Bull. EC 5-1984, point 2.4.25.
[12] Point 344 et seq. of this Report.
[13] Bull. EC 3-1984, point 1.1.1.
[14] Bull. EC 6-1984, point 1.1.7.
[15] Seventeenth General Report, point 370.

Section 9

Environment

Main developments

359. The Commission's first priority was to take due account of the environment in the Community's other policies and to make it an integral part of them, as advocated in the third action programme adopted in 1983. [1]

The next was to implement specific measures called for by the Council and Parliament, notably to monitor hazardous waste consignments shipped to other countries and to combat air pollution, where the Community's principal concerns were to control the lead content in petrol and to deal with acid rain and the resultant problems.

Prevention and reduction of pollution and nuisances

Protection of the aquatic environment

360. Action to combat water pollution remains one of the Community's priorities. On 28 June, acting on the Commission proposal of 3 February, [2] on which Parliament had delivered its opinion, [3] the Council adopted a Decision [4] on the conclusion of an Agreement for Cooperation in Dealing with Pollution of the North Sea by Oil and Other Harmful Substances, which will replace the Agreement signed in Bonn on 9 June 1969.

361. Under the Directive of 4 May 1976, [5] the Council adopted on 8 March a second Directive on discharges of mercury, this time by industrial sectors other than the chloralkali electrolysis industry, [6] and on 9 October a Directive laying down limit values and quality objectives for discharges of hexachlorocyclohex-

---

[1] OJ C 46, 17.2.1983; Seventeenth General Report, point 372.
[2] OJ C 40, 15.2.1984; Bull. EC 1-1984, point 2.1.58.
[3] OJ C 127, 14.5.1984; Bull. EC 4-1984, point 2.4.8.
[4] OJ L 188, 16.7.1984; Bull. EC 6-1984, point 2.1.74.
[5] OJ L 129, 18.5.1976; Tenth General Report, point 277.
[6] OJ L 74, 17.3.1984; Bull. EC 3-1984, point 2.1.101.

ane [1] which had already been endorsed by Parliament [2] and the Economic and Social Committee. [3]

362. As a further measure to implement its action programme on the control and reduction of pollution caused by oil spills at sea, [4] the Commission published an invitation to submit proposals for financial support for pilot projects in this field in the Official Journal on 16 March. [5] Having received Parliament's opinion, [6] it also transmitted to the Council on 2 August an amended proposal for a Directive on the drawing up of contingency plans to combat accidental oil spills at sea. [7]

363. On 10 April the Commission sent to the Council and Parliament a report [8] on the implementation by the Member States of the Council Directive of 20 February 1978 on waste from the titanium dioxide industry. [9]

At Parliament's request, [2] the Commission also sent the Council on 4 June an amended proposal for a Directive on procedures for harmonizing programmes for the reduction of pollution by waste from this industry. [10]

364. In December the Commission sent the Council a proposal for a Decision [11] on a supplement in respect of cadmium to Annex IV to the Convention for the Protection of the Rhine against Chemical Pollution, together with, for the Council's information, a recommendation, by the International Commission for the Protection of the Rhine against Pollution, on the monitoring of cadmium discharges.

Finally, the Commission took part in an international ministerial-level conference on the protection of the North Sea against pollution held in Bremen on 31 October and 1 November at the invitation of the Government of the Federal Republic of Germany. [12] The results of the conference will serve as a basis for the Commission's future work in this field.

---

[1] OJ L 274, 17.10.1984; Bull. EC 6-1984, point 2.1.73.
[2] OJ C 127, 14.5.1984; Bull. EC 4-1984, point 2.4.8.
[3] OJ C 57, 29.2.1984; Bull. EC 1-1984, point 2.4.44.
[4] OJ C 162, 8.7.1978; Twelfth General Report, point 250.
[5] OJ C 75, 16.3.1984.
[6] OJ C 172, 2.7.1984; Bull. EC 5-1984, point 2,4,14.
[7] OJ C 215, 16.8.1984; Bull. EC 7/8-1984, point 2.1.110.
[8] Bull. EC 3-1984, point 2.1.102.
[9] OJ L 54, 25.2.1978; Twelfth General Report, point 252.
[10] OJ C 167, 27.6.1984; Bull. EC 6-1984, point 2.1.75.
[11] OJ C 16, 17.1.1985; Bull. EC 12-1984.
[12] Bull. EC 9-1984, point 2.1.65; Bull. EC 11-1984, point 2.1.86.

Control of air pollution

365. On 28 June the Council formally adopted a Directive on the combating of air pollution from industrial plants. [1]

366. On 6 December, after receiving Parliament's opinion, [2] the Council also reaffirmed [3] the agreement reached in June on the proposal for a Directive laying down air quality standards for nitrogen dioxide. [4]

367. In June the Commission sent to the Council proposals for new Community legislation, [5] which were supplemented in September, [6] and October, [7] with a view to introducing lead-free petrol as far as possible and making a substantial reduction in harmful emissions from motor vehicles. While it was waiting for Parliament's opinion, on 6 December the Council agreed a common position on the proposal on the lead content in petrol. [3]

368. The Commission attended the second meeting of the Executive Body of the Geneva Convention of 1979 on Long-range Transboundary Air Pollution held from 25 to 28 September. [8] At the meeting the Commission signed the Protocol on Long-term Financing of the Cooperative Programme for Monitoring and Evaluation of the Long-range Transmission of Air Pollutants in Europe. [3] On 12 December the Commission decided to recommend that the Council authorize it to take part in negotiations for a second Protocol to the Convention providing for a 30% reduction in all emissions or transfrontier flows of sulphur dioxide by 1993. [3]

369. The Commission proposed preparatory measures to protect forests against fire and acid rain [9] pending the Council's adoption of rules on this issue. [10]

370. Finally, the Commission played an active role in the multilateral conference on the causes and prevention of the damage wrought by air pollution on

---

[1] OJ L 188, 16.7.1984; Bull. EC 3-1984, point 2.1.104.
[2] OJ C 337, 17.12.1984; Bull. EC 11-1984, point 2.1.87.
[3] Bull. EC 12-1984.
[4] OJ C 258, 27.9.1983; Bull. EC 6-1984, point 2.1.77.
[5] OJ C 178, 6.7.1984; Bull. EC 5-1984, point 1.2.1 et seq.
[6] OJ C 291, 31.10.1984; Bull. EC 9-1984, point 2.1.67.
[7] OJ C 318, 29.11.1984; Bull. EC 10-1984, point 2.1.77.
[8] Bull. EC 9-1984, point 2.1.68.
[9] OJ C 208, 8.8.1984; Bull. EC 7/8-1984, point 2.1.112.
[10] OJ C 187, 13.7.1983; Seventeenth General Report, point 381.

forests and water bodies in Europe which was held in Munich from 25 to 27 June. [1]

Noise abatement

371. On 17 September the Council finally adopted 15 harmonizing Directives relating to various industrial sectors [2] which it had approved in April, [3] including a number on the limitation of noise emissions from construction plant and equipment and from lawn mowers.

372. On 3 September the Council again amended [4] its Directive of 6 February 1970 on the permissible sound level of motor vehicles. [5]

373. On 12 September the Commission presented a proposal [6] to the Council amending its Directive of 23 November 1978 on the permissible sound level of motorcycles. [7]

374. On 24 April the Commission sent the Council a communication setting out the Community's response to the Department of State concerning the United States rules on aircraft operating noise limits. [8]

Chemicals in the environment

375. Progress has been made by the Commission in implementing the Council Directive of 18 September 1979 amending for the sixth time [9] the Directive of 27 June 1967 on dangerous substances. [10] The Commission is completing the third phase of its work on the establishment of the inventory of existing chemicals, which involves processing 78 000 declaration forms. The system introduced for processing notifications of new chemicals is also working efficiently and satisfactorily.

---

[1] Bull. EC 6-1984, point 2.1.79.
[2] OJ L 300, 19.11.1984; Bull. EC 9-1984, point 2.1.70.
[3] Bull. EC 4-1984, point 2.1.82.
[4] OJ L 238, 6.9.1984; Bull. EC 9-1984, point 2.1.71.
[5] OJ L 42, 23.2.1970.
[6] OJ C 263, 2.10.1984; Bull. EC 9-1984, point 2.1.72.
[7] OJ L 349, 13.12.1978.
[8] Bull. EC 4-1984, point 2.1.83.
[9] OJ L 259, 15.10.1979; Thirteenth General Report, point 277.
[10] OJ L 196, 16.8.1967.

The Directive of 27 June 1967 on dangerous substances[1] and the Directive of 26 June 1978 on dangerous preparations[2] were both adapted to technical progress by the Commission in April.[3]

376. The Commission continued its work on implementing the Council Directive of 24 June 1982 on the major accident hazards of certain industrial activities (the 'Seveso Directive'),[4] which entered into force on 8 January 1984.

377. In accordance with the Council Decisions of 26 March 1980[5] and 15 November 1982,[6] the Commission prepared three codes of practice seeking to reduce emissions of chlorofluorocarbons in refrigeration and air conditioning systems, in the manufacture of rigid polyurethane foams for the building industry and in cleaning processes which use solvents based on these products.

Protection and optimum use of resources

Recovery and reuse of wastes

378. On 6 December the Council adopted[7] the Commission's proposal for a Directive introducing measures to supervise and control the transfrontier shipment of hazardous wastes inside, entering or leaving the Community, in order to protect human health and the environment.[8]

379. On 26 April, in the light of the opinions given by Parliament[9] and the Economic and Social Committee,[10] the Commission amended[11] its proposal for a Directive on the use of sewage sludge in agriculture.[12]

---

[1] OJ L 196, 16.8.1967.
[2] OJ L 206, 29.7.1978.
[3] OJ L 251, 19.9.1984; Bull. EC 4-1984, point 2.1.85; OJ L 144, 30.5.1984; Bull. EC 4-1984, point 2.1.84.
[4] OJ L 230, 5.8.1982: Sixteenth General Report, point 364.
[5] OJ L 90, 3.4.1980.
[6] OJ L 329, 25.11.1982; Sixteenth General Report, point 368.
[7] OJ L 326, 13.12.1984; Bull. EC 12-1984.
[8] OJ C 53, 25.2.1983; OJ C 186, 12.7.1983; Seventeenth General Report, point 390; Bull. EC 6-1984, point 1.4.1.
[9] OJ C 77, 19.3.1984; Bull. EC 2-1984, point 2.1.91.
[10] OJ C 90, 5.4.1983.
[11] OJ C 154, 14.6.1984; Bull. EC 4-1984, point 2.1.87.
[12] OJ C 264, 8.10.1982; Sixteenth General Report, point 370.

Water management

380. In response to Parliament, the Commission decided to embark on a joint study of water pollution in the French and German stretches of the Saar/Rosselle basin as part of its campaign to combat pollution of the Rhine and other rivers crossing national frontiers. This study should enable the national and Community authorities responsible to adopt a common line of approach and ultimately to improve the situation in the basin.

Conservation of the natural heritage

381. The Commission made three additional amendments[1] to the Council Regulation of 3 December 1982 on the implementation in the Community of the Washington Convention on International Trade in Endangered Species of Wild Fauna and Flora,[2] so as to adapt the Annexes concerning the species covered by the Convention.

General measures

382. On 28 June the Council adopted the legal basis for the funding of action by the Community relating to the environment from the general budget.[3] Under the Regulation in question, which was proposed by the Commission in 1982,[4] 13 million ECU will be available over three years.

383. On 6 December the Council agreed,[5] to adopt a work programme relating to an experimental project concerning the collection, coordination and alignment of information on the state of the environment and natural resources in the Community, starting on 1 January 1985.[6]

384. On 24 April the Commission proposed to the Council a strategy and an action plan for the protection of the environment in the Mediterranean[7]

---

[1] OJ L 64, 6.3.1984; Bull. EC 3-1984, point 2.1.106; OJ L 140, 26.5.1984; Bull. EC 5-1984, point 2.1.112.
[2] OJ L 384, 31.12.1982; Sixteenth General Report, point 374.
[3] OJ L 176, 3.7.1984; Bull. EC 3-1984, point 2.1.95.
[4] OJ C 30, 4.2.1983; OJ C 158, 16.6.1983; Bull. EC 12-1984.
[5] Bull. EC 12-1984.
[6] Seventeenth General Report, point 397.
[7] OJ C 133, 21.5.1984; Bull. EC 4-1984, point 2.1.79.

entailing a package of coordinated measures designed to ensure the harmonious development of socio-economic activities in the region.

International cooperation

385. The Community was extremely active internationally in the field of the environment, notably as regards cooperation with the United Nations Environment Programme, [1] endeavouring to steer existing activities more effectively and achieve common environmental protection objectives.

386. It also made a constructive contribution to the work being conducted under a number of international agreements, [2] particularly in the field of air pollution and the protection of the marine environment and coastal areas.

387. Turning to the question of environment and development, in October the Council and the Representatives of the Governments of the Member States meeting within the Council adopted two resolutions—one on the link between the environment and development, the other on new forms of cooperation with the developing countries on water [3]—followed, in November, by a third on the environmental dimension of the Community's development policy. [4]

388. Bilateral contacts with the United States, [5] Norway, Switzerland, Japan [6] and Austria [7] were consolidated in the talks on improving cooperation with non-Community countries established by the exchanges of letters signed in previous years.

Legal aspects

389. Under the Agreement of 5 March 1973 [8] the Commission received 10 notifications during the year.

390. The Commission redoubled its efforts to check that Community legislation is correctly and fully incorporated into national law.

---

[1] Bull. EC 5-1984, point 2.1.117.
[2] Bull. EC 5-1984, point 2.1.118.
[3] OJ C 272, 12.10.1984; Bull. EC 10-1984, point 2.1.73.
[4] Bull. EC 10-1984, point 2.1.74; Bull. EC 11-1984, point 2.2.34.
[5] Bull. EC 2-1984, point 2.1.92.
[6] Bull. EC 10-1984, point 2.1.80.
[7] Bull. EC 11-1984, point 2.1.88.
[8] OJ C 9, 15.3.1973; Seventh General Report, point 265.

Section 10

Consumers

Main developments

391. *The Council met three times during 1984: on 2 March, 5 June and 17 December. As a result of these meetings a Decision setting up an information system on product safety and a Directive on misleading advertising were both adopted. The Council also discussed two Commission communications on consumer policy. The first of these records the main developments since 1973, relating them to economic and political circumstances, and analyses the progress made in implementing Community consumer policy and the problems encountered, outlining the main objectives for the second programme. The second communication lists the main priority activities proposed for the period from 1985 to 1987.*

Physical protection

392. On 2 March the Council adopted the Decision introducing a Community system for the rapid exchange of information on dangers arising from the use of consumer products.[1] This system — for the exchange of information between the Member States and the Commission — will enable Member States to take appropriate emergency measures when a particular consumer product is found to present an immediate and serious risk for the health or safety of consumers. It will be operational, under Commission management, from March 1985.

393. The pilot experiment under the Council Decision of 23 July 1981 relating to a system of information on accidents involving consumer products[2] was completed on 1 July. The experiment provided preliminary practical experience for setting up such a system at Community level. A report on the results of the pilot experiment and a proposal for a Council Decision on the introduction of

---

[1] OJ L 70, 13.1.1984; Bull. EC 3-1984, point 2.1.111.
[2] OJ L 229, 13.8.1981; Fifteenth General Report, point 364.

the system on a permanent basis were adopted by the Commission, for transmittal to the Council, on 20 December. [1]

394. The Council Directive of 15 July 1980 relating to the exploitation and marketing of natural mineral waters [2] came into force on 17 July. [3]

395. On 15 October the Council adopted a Directive relating to ceramic articles intended to come into contact with foodstuffs. [4]

396. On 24 September the Commission transmitted to the Council a proposal for a Directive on quick-frozen foodstuffs for human consumption. [5]

397. On 3 October the Commission also transmitted to the Council a proposal for a Directive relating to restrictions on the marketing and use of certain dangerous substances and preparations (PCBs and PCTs). [6]

398. On 18 July the Commission adapted to technical progress [7] the Council Directive of 27 July 1976 relating to cosmetic products. [8]

Protection of economic and legal interests

399. A Directive concerning misleading advertising was formally adopted by the Council on 10 September. [9] It aims to protect the consumer, persons carrying on a trade or business or practising a craft or profession and the interests of the public in general against misleading advertising and its unfair consequences. The Directive gives definitions of advertising and misleading advertising for Community purposes; these are particularly useful in an age when developments in communication techniques, especially television, are increasingly making advertising a transnational phenomenon.

400. On 14 February the Commission sent the Council a discussion paper on unfair terms in contracts, [10] which basically outlines the principles governing a

---

[1] Bull. EC 12-1984.
[2] OJ L 229, 30.8.1980.
[3] OJ C 218, 18.8.1984; OJ C 305, 16.11.1984; Bull. EC 7/8-1984, point 2.1.18.
[4] OJ L 277, 20.10.1984; Bull. EC 10-1984, point 2.1.15.
[5] OJ C 267, 6.10.1984; Bull. EC 9-1984, point 2.1.14.
[6] Bull. EC 10-1984, point 2.1.83.
[7] OJ L 228, 25.8.1984; Bull. EC 7/8-1984, point 2.1.115.
[8] OJ L 262, 27.9.1976.
[9] OJ L 250, 19.9.1984; Bull. EC 6-1984, point 1.4.2.
[10] Supplement 1/84 — Bull. EC; Bull. EC 2-1984, point 2.1.94.

satisfactory balance for transactions between the consumer and the vendor, and examines the main abuses found and measures designed to remedy them.

401. On 10 December the Commission decided to send the Council a discussion paper on consumer redress concerning the small claims procedure resulting from the purchase of products and services by the consumer. [1] The Commission is carrying out a number of pilot experiments in this connection with the assistance of the relevant national authorities and, in cooperation with the Belgian Government, has set up an experiment designed to facilitate consumer access to two courts.

402. In response to the views expressed by Parliament, [2] on 22 June the Commission amended [3] its proposal for a Directive on consumer credit. [4] In the new text the Commission specifies, in particular, the factors to be taken into account for the calculation of effective interest rates, the information that must be contained in consumer credit agreements and the specific rules governing doorstep selling and the ownership of goods bought on credit.

Consumer information

403. On 31 January the Commission asked the Council [5] to amend the Directive on the indication of the prices of foodstuffs adopted on 19 June 1979. [6]

Consumer education

404. Following experiments in the network of pilot schools over the last four years, the Commission continued to consider the merits of including consumer education in the curricula of primary and secondary schools, with a view to putting proposals before the Council. It also started work on setting up pilot training schemes for teachers.

---

[1] Supplement 2/85 — Bull. EC (forthcoming); Bull. EC 12-1984.
[2] OJ C 242, 12.9.1983; Seventeenth General Report, point 407.
[3] OJ C 183, 10.7.1984; Bull. EC 6-1984, point 2.1.86.
[4] OJ C 80, 27.3.1979; Thirteenth General Report, point 289.
[5] OJ C 53, 24.2.1984; Bull. EC 1-1984, point 2.1.66.
[6] OJ L 158, 16.6.1979.

Consumer representation

405. The Consumers' Consultative Committee met on 16 May, [1] for the first time with its new membership, [2] and elected Mrs Federspiel to the chair. Over the year it delivered opinions on the common agricultural policy, taxation of certain oils and fats and second-hand vehicles, and the information contained in advertising. It also stated its position on the pilot experiment on accidents in the home and the introduction of a Community system of information on product safety. [3]

International cooperation

406. The cooperation between the Commission and Norway that began in accordance with the terms of an exchange of letters on 21 November 1983 [4] continued and developed.

The Community also took part in the consumer protection work of international bodies such as the Council of Europe and OECD, which are the most active in dealing with consumer protection problems.

---

[1]   Bull. EC 5-1984, point 2.1.120.
[2]   OJ C 88, 30.3.1984.
[3]   Bull. EC 10-1984, point 2.1.86.
[4]   Seventeenth General Report, point 411.

Section 11

Agriculture [1]

Main developments

407. The proposals for adjusting the common agricultural policy to the changed economic situation, which the Commission had presented to the Council in 1983, began to bear fruit in 1984.

When it fixed the agricultural prices for 1984/85 the Council adopted a set of measures for rationalizing the common agricultural policy. These involved a realistic price policy, a return to market unity via the dismantling of monetary compensatory amounts, the control of milk production by means of quotas, extension of the guarantee threshold principle to more products, rationalization of the aids and premiums for various products, and observance of Community preference. Later in the year it adopted some provisions intended to renew the agricultural structures policy and undertook in a resolution to achieve the harmonization of national legislation on agriculture, since this is an essential precondition for the creation of an agricultural common market.

Although these policy decisions were of paramount importance, 1984 also saw a sharp increase in agricultural production. The weather until the summer was particularly favourable, and crop production made a great leap forward, far surpassing its previous records in several sectors. Livestock production showed a more varied development. Beef production continued to grow, partly as a result of the slaughterings brought about by the introduction of milk quotas, while the new curbs on milk production caused a reduction in deliveries which should be more marked in 1985. Production of pigmeat, eggs and poultrymeat was about the same as in 1983.

The disposal of a number of products continued to pose problems, particularly of a budgetary nature. Financing the common agricultural policy became even more difficult as a result of the exhaustion of the Community's own resources. A supplementary and amending budget—made possible in part by additional financing—proved necessary in order to make up the shortfall in appropriations which the Commission had announced in the first quarter.

---

[1] For more details see *The Agricultural Situation in the Community—1984 Report*, published in conjunction with this Report (available from the Office for Official Publications).

Reform of the common agricultural policy

1984/85 price review and the rationalization of the common agricultural policy

408. In its proposals for agricultural prices and related measures for 1984/85, laid before the Council on 17 January, [1] the Commission had stressed the need for overall decisions covering not only the prices but also all the problems which it had raised in its communication of 23 July 1983 on the rationalization of the common agricultural policy. [2] In view of progress made by the Council in a round of meetings [3] and the opinions adopted by Parliament [4] and the Economic and Social Committee, [5] the Commission had amended its original proposals on 22 March in the hope of facilitating an agreement. [6]

409. The overall agreement the Council reached on 30 and 31 March [7] endorses most of the Commission's proposals. It may be summarized as follows:

(i) For the first time, the average level of prices expressed in ECU as adopted by the Council (-0.5%) is lower than the Commission's proposal ($+0.8\%$). However, allowing for the agrimonetary measures (dismantlement of positive and negative monetary compensatory amounts), the average increase in agricultural support prices expressed in national currencies over the previous year is 3.3%; as the general rate of inflation in the Community was put at 5.1% for 1984, these decisions reflect the Council's determination to implement a restrictive policy on agricultural prices.

(ii) A programme for the dismantlement of the positive monetary compensatory amounts in three stages was adopted; they will have been phased out altogether by the beginning of 1987/88 at the latest. The Council also adopted a new system within which future parity alterations under the European Monetary System can no longer entail the creation of positive MCAs. With the abolition or the reduction of the negative MCAs at the beginning of 1984/85, these decisions constitute an important step forward towards the restoration of single prices in the agricultural market. [8]

---

[1] OJ C 62, 5.3.1984; Bull. EC 1-1984, points 1.1.1 to 1.1.17.
[2] Seventeenth General Report, point 413; Supplement 4/83—Bull. EC.
[3] Bull. EC 2-1984, point 2.1.96; Bull. EC 3-1984, point 2.1.113.
[4] OJ C 104, 16.4.1984.
[5] OJ C 103, 16.4.1984; Bull. EC 2-1984, point 2.4.29.
[6] Bull. EC 3-1984, point 2.1.113.
[7] OJ L 90, 1.4.1984; OJ L 103, 16.4.1984; OJ L 107, 19.4.1984; OJ L 113, 28.4.1984; Bull. EC 3-1984, points 1.2.1 to 1.2.8, 2.1.113 to 2.1.119 and 2.1.122 to 2.1.125.
[8] Point 445 of this Report.

(iii) A delivery quota system was introduced for milk for a five-year period. The system, the implementing procedures for which are flexible and realistic in order to allow for the wide variety of situations for dairy farmers in the Community, will help to redress the serious disequilibrium between the supply of and the demand for milk. [1]

(iv) The guarantee thresholds system, already operated for milk, cereals, rape, processed tomatoes and cotton, was extended to sunflower seed, durum wheat and dried grapes. The Council stressed the need to apply it in the market organizations for surplus products or products liable to entail sharp increases in expenditure.

(v) Aids or premiums for milk products, beef/veal, sheepmeat, protein-rich plants and fruit and vegetables were discontinued or adjusted. Without accepting all the Commission's proposals, the Council did acknowledge that much of this expenditure is no longer fully justified at a time of retrenchment.

(vi) Lastly, the Council adopted or undertook to adopt a number of provisions with a view to improving compliance with the Community preference in respect of cereals (as against substitutes), milk products, beef/veal and sheepmeat. It took the view that if the Community required greater discipline on the part of agricultural producers it should be prepared to act in parallel in respect of imports.

The decisions adopted by the Council are the practical outcome of the efforts made for several years by the Commission to adapt the policy to new economic circumstances; they mark a milestone in the development of the policy.

New policy on agricultural structures

410. In the autumn of 1983 the Commission laid before the Council a set of proposals for the renewal of the Community policy on agricultural structures and the establishment of integrated Mediterranean programmes in Greece, Italy and France. [2]

411. On 19 June the Council approved some of these provisions when it adopted a Regulation [3] amending both the Regulation on common measures to improve the conditions under which agricultural products are processed and

---

[1] Point 432 of this Report.
[2] Seventeenth General Report, point 414.
[3] OJ L 180, 7.7.1984; Bull. EC 6-1984, point 2.1.99.

marketed [1] and the Regulation on the stimulation of agricultural development in the less-favoured areas of the west of Ireland. [2]

While retaining the basic elements of the two schemes, the new Regulation, which entered into force on 1 January 1985 for a 10-year period, emphasizes new technologies, the development of new products and by-products, energy savings and recycling of waste, with a view to the creation of additional markets for agricultural products; its scope now also includes the acquisition of equipment for harvesting primary products provided that such investments upstream are beneficial to the farmers involved; again, it makes fuller allowance for certain difficulties with which project organizers may have to contend when raising the funds they need, and strengthens Community financing of projects in regions where the economic situation is particularly difficult or which are more vulnerable than others to problems that will arise when Spain and Portugal join the Community. The new Regulation also stipulated that the Council was to determine the estimated cost of its financing before 1 January 1985. No decision has been taken on this subject, however.

412. Discussion of amendments [3] to the 1972 socio-structural Directives on the modernization of farms, the cessation of farming and occupational skills in agriculture continued. [4] In the meantime, the Directives, due to run out on 31 December 1983, were extended until 30 June and then until 31 December 1984. [5]

413. Partly in the light of Parliament's opinion [6] and of new provisions adopted on the occasion of the reform of the ERDF, [7] the Commission amended its proposal on the integrated Mediterranean programmes. [8] A start was made on implementation of the measures — approved by the Commission at the end of 1983 [9] —preparatory to the implementation of the programmes; these are 13 local operations (six in Greece, four in Italy, three in France) based on a 'multisectoral' approach and involving the Community's various structural Funds.

[1] OJ L 51, 23.2.1977.
[2] OJ L 180, 14.7.1980.
[3] Seventeenth General Report, point 414.
[4] OJ L 96, 23.4.1972.
[5] OJ L 72, 15.3.1984; Bull. EC 2-1984, point 2.1.116; OJ L 285, 30.10.1984; Bull. EC 10-1984, point 2.1.103.
[6] OJ C 117, 30.4.1984; Bull. EC 3-1984, point 2.1.90.
[7] OJ L 169, 28.6.1984; Bull. EC 6-1984, points 1.3.1 to 1.3.11.
[8] OJ C 280, 19.10.1984; Bull. EC 9-1984, point 2.1.58.
[9] OJ L 44, 15.2.1984; Seventeenth General Report, point 370.

414. At the same time, the Community developed its regional or specific structural schemes. On 28 February the Council amended [1] the list of less-favoured agricultural areas [2] in Italy, the United Kingdom and the Netherlands; these areas now cover more than 43% of the Community's utilized agricultural area. In connection with the reply to the Greek memorandum, the Council approved extension of the common measure to accelerate agricultural development in Greece [3] and renewed [4] two Regulations relating to schemes for the development of agricultural advisory services and for the acceleration of collective irrigation operations; [5] the Commission laid before the Council new proposals, on strengthening quality control services for agricultural products and on reducing transport costs in agriculture in Greece. [6]

415. With regard to forestry, the Council continued its examination of the Commission proposal on the protection of woodlands against fire and acid rain. [7] Pending a decision, the Commission proposed that a series of preparatory operations be undertaken. [8]

416. After the adoption in December 1983 of the agricultural research programme for 1984-89 with a smaller budget than the one it had proposed, the Commission was compelled to make a selection among the priorities, scale down certain programmes and consider ways and means of executing certain subprogrammes merely through the coordination of national research work. [9]

Management of the common agricultural policy

EEC market organizations [10]

Crop products

417. At 123.7 million tonnes, the cereals crop for 1983/84 [11] fell short of the 130.8 million tonnes harvested in 1982/83. A special intervention measure was required for wheat of breadmaking quality, confined to 3 million tonnes.

---

[1]   OJ L 82, 26.3.1984; Bull. EC 2-1984, point 2.1.119.
[2]   OJ L 128, 19.5.1975.
[3]   OJ L 68, 10.3.1984; Bull. EC 3-1984, point 2.1.133.
[4]   OJ L 125, 12.5.1984.
[5]   OJ L 293, 25.10.1983.
[6]   Bull. EC 5-1984, point 2.1.137.
[7]   OJ C 187, 13.7.1983; Seventeenth General Report, points 381 and 396.
[8]   OJ C 208, 8.8.1984; Bull. EC 7/8-1984, points 2.1.112 and 2.1.113; Bull. EC 12-1984.
[9]   Seventeenth General Report, points 415 and 592.
[10] For more details see *The situation on the agricultural markets—1984 Report* (forthcoming).
[11] A review of the cereals market is given in Bull. EC 7/8-1984, points 2.1.123 to 2.1.125 and Bull. EC 10-1984, points 2.1.91 and 2.1.92.

Common wheat of breadmaking quality was sold back onto the animal feed market below the buying-in price, and this type of cereals was used more than in the past as feed. Imports of manioc were reduced under the voluntary restraint agreement with Thailand. As a result of the payment-in-kind scheme in the United States and the 1983 drought there, there was an appreciable reduction in maize and soya supplies on the world market.

Despite the restriction of exports of common wheat, in accordance with the Community's international commitments, the combination of these factors enabled the surpluses to be dealt with satisfactorily. By the end of the marketing year, stocks totalled 12.8 million tonnes, i.e. 5 million tonnes less than at the end of 1982/83.

In 1984 cereals production set a new record; the figure is more than 150 million tonnes, the rise being due to a slight increase in areas sown and a sharp improvement in yields.

Under arrangements for the rationalization of the CAP, the Council introduced, [1] from 1984/85 onwards, a guarantee threshold for durum wheat, similar to those already operated for other cereals.

418. Two amendments were made to the basic arrangements concerning rice: the first [2] restricts the subsidy payable on semi-milled rice for the island of Reunion to the level of the levy charged for husked rice; the second [3] introduces a system of increases or reductions adjusting the intervention price depending on the varieties or groups of varieties.

419. World sugar prices had been very low since 1982, and growers cut back areas under beet by 9.2% in 1982 and by as much again in 1983. Yields per hectare having reverted to a normal level, Community production came to 11 million tonnes in 1983/84, i.e. 3 million tonnes less than in 1982/83, but the figure for 1984/85 is estimated at over 12 million tonnes. The breakdown of negotiations for a new International Sugar Agreement [4] was an additional factor depressing world prices in 1983/84; none the less, the Community was able to place most of its exportable supplies.

In June the Council approved [5] a Commission report on the sugar market situation, [6] which concluded that no quota revision was needed during the

---

1   Point 409 of this Report; OJ L 107, 19.4.1984; Bull. EC 3-1984, point 1.2.5.
2   OJ L 21, 26.1.1984.
3   OJ L 107, 19.4.1984.
4   Point 721 of this Report.
5   Bull. EC 6-1984, point 2.1.87.
6   Bull. EC 5-1984, point 2.1.131.

Production and consumption of milk in the Community

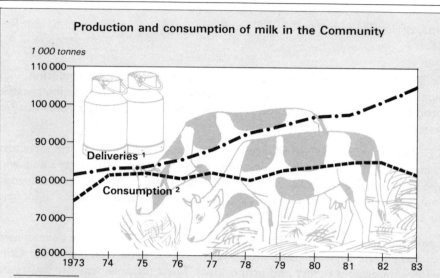

1 000 tonnes

Deliveries [1]

Consumption [2]

[1] Deliveries to dairies, except in the case of Greece (total milk production).
[2] Calculated on the basis of an overall milk balance in terms of milk equivalent (based on buttermilk content).

The sharp increases in milk production over the last 10 years is the result of improved yields per cow. Demand, which had been expanding moderately, fell again in 1983.

Total cereals production — Human and animal consumption Community imports and exports

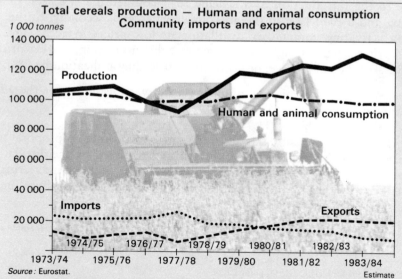

1 000 tonnes

Production

Human and animal consumption

Imports

Exports

Source: Eurostat.

Estimate

Both human and animal consumption of cereals stagnated, or even fell, over the 10-year period. Production (excluding rice), on the other hand, increased sharply, when it was not affected by bad weather, and this posed the problem of how to dispose of cereals on external markets while, paradoxically, the Community continued to import feeding-stuffs.

period of implementation of the production scheme in force until 30 June 1986. [1]

420. Work was carried out on adjusting the basic wine Regulation. The structural disequilibrium of the wine market, the increase in intervention expenditure without a significant impact on prices and repeated crises justified a review of current arrangements.

On 27 April the Council had adopted, [2] after consulting Parliament, [3] structural measures entailing a prohibition of any new planting of table grape and wine grape vines until 1990/91, except for individual authorizations granted under Commission supervision, and altered the intervention arrangements to increase their efficiency.

Because the disequilibria persisted — despite the more favourable development predicted in the forward estimate [4]—a high-level group met and the Commission submitted a report and proposals. [5] Their purpose was the short- and medium-term control of production by reducing areas under vines and through a reduction in the level of support provided by intervention, so as to lessen the incentive to produce wine where there are no commercial outlets. The European Council meeting in Dublin, to which the matter was finally submitted, agreed, firstly, to the introduction of a scheme to encourage the cessation of wine-growing and a reduction in the area under vines and, secondly, to the Commission activating compulsory distillation at low prices in accordance with stricter criteria (stocks higher than four months' utilization, market price less than 82% of the guide price, or production exceeding utilization by 9%). [6]

In December the Commission adopted the forward estimate for the 1984/85 marketing year. [7]

421. Also, the Commission sent to the Council on 14 June [8] a proposal for the organization of the disposal of surplus alcohol obtained by the distillation of wine, for which there is Community responsibility, without interfering with the market for other alcohols and spirituous beverages. The proposal includes use of surplus alcohol as energy products.

---

1 For a review of the sugar market, see also Bull. EC 4-1984, point 2.1.96, Bull. EC 6-1984, points 2.1.96 to 2.1.98 and Bull. EC 11-1984, point 2.1.98.
2 OJ L 115, 1.5.1984; Bull. EC 4-1984, point 2.1.94.
3 OJ C 127, 14.5.1984; Bull. EC 4-1984, point 2.1.95.
4 OJ C 6, 11.1.1984; Bull. EC 1-1984, point 2.1.78.
5 Bull. EC 7/8-1984, point 2.1.130 et seq.; Bull. EC 9-1984, points 2.1.80 to 2.1.82.
6 Point 609 of this Report; Bull. EC 12-1984.
7 Bull. EC 12-1984.
8 Bull. EC 6-1984, point 2.1.92.

422. Acting on a Commission proposal,[1] the Council decided to apply a guarantee threshold to sunflower seeds from 1984/85 onwards.[2]

423. The Council substantially amended the olive oil production aid scheme to ensure better supervision of aid applications;[3] it approved the establishment of special supervisory agencies, notably in Italy and in Greece, tighter control procedures and a penalties scheme. In September and November the Commission adopted detailed rules for applying this scheme.[4]

In addition, in March, in connection with the fixing of agricultural prices, the Council decided to make the aid for olive growers producing less than 100 kg a flat-rate scheme.[5]

424. The Council decided to extend to sweet lupins the special measures laid down for other protein-rich plants but not to renew the aid scheme for dehydrated potatoes.[6]

425. The arrangements supporting use of flax were maintained.[7] Restrictive measures were adopted with regard to hemp to prevent any illegal use.[8] The start of the cotton year was deferred to facilitate management in this secor.[9]

426. The application of the regulations on fresh fruit and vegetables[10] led to withdrawal operations and processing of withdrawn products. Import price movements entailed application of countervailing charges on certain imported products.

427. In connection with the rationalization of the CAP,[11] the Council adapted the scheme for aids to processed fruit and vegetables and set guarantee thresholds for all tomato products and for dried grapes. The Commission decided[12] to renew the safeguard measure concerning certain varieties of dried grapes.[13]

---

[1] Seventeenth General Report, point 439.
[2] Point 409 of this Report; OJ L 113, 28.4.1984.
[3] OJ L 208, 3.8.1984; Bull. EC 7/8-1984, point 2.1.122.
[4] OJ L 258, 27.9.1984; OJ L 288, 1.11.1984; Bull. EC 11-1984, point 2.1.94.
[5] OJ L 113, 28.4.1984.
[6] OJ L 107, 19.4.1984.
[7] OJ L 162, 12.6.1984.
[8] OJ L 191, 19.7.1984; OJ L 199, 28.7.1984.
[9] For a review of the textile sector, see Bull. EC 10-1984, point 2.1.95 et seq.
[10] OJ L 118, 20.5.1972; Bull. EC 12-1984.
[11] Point 408 of this Report.
[12] OJ L 211, 8.8.1984.
[13] A review of this market is given in Bull. EC 2-1984, point 2.1.84.

428. The Commission also sent to the Council, in February, a report with proposals concerning imports of cut flowers (roses and carnations). [1]

429. For leaf tobacco from the 1984 harvest, the Council maintained the intervention price at 85% of the corresponding norm price. [2] Amendments to accelerate the introduction of restrictive measures were made to the regulations when the agricultural prices were fixed for the 1984 crop. [2] The Commission adopted measures for disposal of tobacco outside the Community. [3]

430. For hops, the Council maintained unchanged, for the 1983 harvest, the aid paid on an area basis by variety to support the incomes of growers; most of these were the same as for the 1982 harvest. [4]

431. With regard to seeds, the Commission amended the list of *Lolium perenne L.* varieties, [5] fixed reference prices for hybrid maize for sowing for 1984/85 [6] and determined countervailing charges applicable from 1 July onwards; [6] during 1983/84 the countervailing charges on maize had been adjusted five times.

Livestock products

432. Because of the severe disequilibrium between the supply of and the demand for milk, [7] the Council decided to apply a quota system to milk deliveries from 2 April onwards for five marketing years. [8] At the same time, it maintained unchanged the milk target price for 1984/85, broadened the system of aids for the use of butter and partly-skimmed-milk powder and altered the milkfat/skimmed-milk ratio in the target price, the effect being to reduce the intervention price of butter and step up that of skimmed-milk powder. The reference quantities for 1984/85 being fixed above the level for the subsequent marketing years, the co-responsibility levy for that marketing year was raised from 2% to 3% of the milk target price. [8] Lastly, the Council renewed for two marketing years the aid to small dairy farmers (120 million ECU) [9] and made adjustments to this aid scheme in November. [10]

---

[1] OJ C 54, 25.2.1984; Bull. EC 2-1984, point 2.1.115.
[2] OJ L 107, 19.4.1984.
[3] OJ L 4, 6.1.1984; OJ L 209, 4.8.1984; OJ L 172, 30.6.1984; OJ C 37, 11.2.1984; Bull. EC 12-1984.
[4] OJ L 163, 21.6.1984.
[5] OJ L 160, 16.6.1984.
[6] OJ L 172, 30.6.1984.
[7] Seventeenth General Report, point 447.
[8] OJ L 90, 1.4.1984; Bull. EC 3-1984, point 1.2.4; Bull. EC 4-1984, point 2.1.97 *et seq.*; Bull. EC 9-1983, point 2.1.83; Bull. EC 10-1983, point 2.1.90; Bull. EC 11-1984, point 2.1.95.
[9] OJ L 115, 1.5.1984; Bull. EC 5-1984, point 2.1.125.
[10] OJ L 298, 13.11.1984; Bull. EC 11-1984, point 2.1.100.

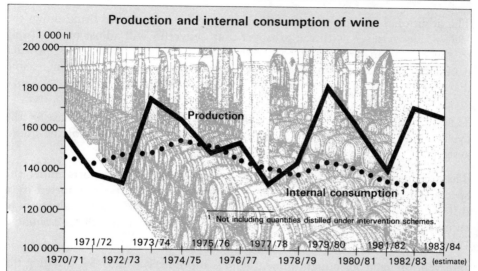

Production and internal consumption of wine

1 000 hl

Production

Internal consumption [1]

[1] Not including quantities distilled under intervention schemes.

| 1971/72 | 1973/74 | 1975/76 | 1977/78 | 1979/80 | 1981/82 | 1983/84 |
| 1970/71 | 1972/73 | 1974/75 | 1976/77 | 1978/79 | 1980/81 | 1982/83 (estimate) |

Source: Supply balance — EUR 10 except for internal consumption in 1970/1971 (EUR 9).

Overproduction of wine is a structural phenomenon: while production continues to grow steadily—despite unfavourable weather conditions in some years—Community wine consumption maintains its downward trend. Since the surpluses are too large for all of them to be exported outside theCommunity, distillation must be resorted to on an ever greater scale.

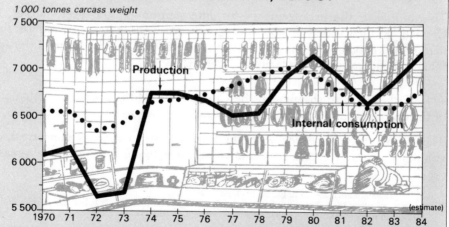

Production and internal consumption of beef/veal in the Community 1970-84

1 000 tonnes carcass weight

Production

Internal consumption

(estimate)

1970 71 72 73 74 75 76 77 78 79 80 81 82 83 84

Beef/veal production follows a five-to-six year cycle influenced by price trends. Starting in 1984, the measures to reduce milk production will lead to increased cow slaughterings. In line with developments in the economic situation, internal consumption began to slacken off after 1973 and again more sharply in 1979. In 1984 there was some upturn in consumption linked with the economic recovery.

The additional levy on quantities exceeding the quota should bring down the 1984/85 deliveries,[1] with the prospect that deliveries will adjust more closely to the quotas in 1985. The reduction in butter and skimmed-milk powder production, the retention of the aid system and recent decisions increasing disposal of butter in store[2] will help to reduce public stocks in 1985.

433. The production of beef/veal, which is now in the upward phase of the cycle,[3] was boosted by culling necessitated by the introduction of the quota system.[4]

The surplus on trade showed a marked increase in 1984. Imports under the special schemes totalled about 700 000 tonnes, but exports—supported by a differentiated refund system—expanded because of the sharp reduction in supplies from the main southern-hemisphere exporters, to reach an estimated record figure of 800 000 tonnes.

Intervention agencies bought in nearly 50% more beef in 1983/84, bringing the total to about 450 000 tonnes. Public stocks of beef were running at about 675 000 tonnes of carcase weight equivalent by the end of 1984.

Market prices had shown little change in 1983/84 and lost ground thereafter; the Commission therefore brought forward to 20 August the buying-in of the carcases and forequarters and hindquarters of adult cattle and activated private storage aids, payment of which could be claimed in advance.[5]

To rationalize the arrangements for intervention on the beef market, the Council decided[6] that from 9 April onwards, for a trial period of three marketing years, beef would be bought in on the basis of the Community scale for the classification of adult bovine animals.[7]

434. With regard to sheepmeat, the Council altered the method of calculation of the ewe premium, the effect of the measure being to cut its cost by 15%.[8]

The Community renewed, with the non-member countries concerned, the voluntary restraint agreements concerning their exports to 'sensitive' areas of

---

[1] Bull. EC 3-1984, point 1.2.4; Bull. EC 11-1984, point 2.1.95.
[2] OJ L 208, 3.8.1984; OJ L 209, 4.8.1984; Bull. EC 7/8-1984, point 2.1.135; OJ L 279, 23.10.1984; Bull. EC 10-1984, point 2.1.99; Bull. EC 11-1984, point 2.1.99; Bull. EC 12-1984.
[3] Bull. EC 7/8-1984, point 2.1.134.
[4] Point 432 of this Report.
[5] OJ L 208, 3.8.1984.
[6] OJ L 90, 1.4.1984.
[7] Seventeenth General Report, point 448.
[8] Bull. EC 3-1984, point 1.2.6.

the Community. The Commission also began exploratory discussions with these countries on a minimum import price system.

435. Very serious difficulties arose on the pigmeat market in the early part of the year: prices fell because of the cyclical increase in production and trade restrictions imposed for health reasons, while at the same time feed prices were rising. However, action to strengthen Community protection,[1] a recovery of exports to Japan and then the United States and the reactivation of private storage aids[1] covering 100 000 tonnes helped to revive quotations, which by March matched the levels of the previous two years and thereafter rose further. Declining production from the middle of the year onwards strengthened this upward movement; at the same time, lower feed prices meant that pig farming was once again very profitable.

On 13 November the Council adopted the Regulation determining the Community scale for grading pig carcases.[2] Its entry into force on 1 January 1985 will mark a new stage in the EEC market organization. Based solely on the carcases' lean meat percentage, the new scale ensures fair payment for producers while helping to make the market and the trade in carcases more transparent.

436. After easing down from April onwards, egg prices stabilized at the end of July, possibly because supply still fell short of 1983 levels. With internal demand marking time and world demand contracting in the medium term, the Community should pursue a cautious policy with regard to production.

437. In the poultrymeat sector, the Community market for chicken was again depressed by the slackening demand for frozen chicken and by keen competition on the world market. Consequently, in most of the Member States, the industry is pursuing a policy of production restraint, while shifting the emphasis of production towards fresh products, cuts and preparations. As in the case of eggs, the world market is taking less poultrymeat from the Community because more and more importing countries are setting up production facilities of their own.

Approximation of laws

438. On the basis of the Commission's 1983 proposal,[3] the Council adopted on 10 May, in the form of a resolution, a programme of work on the harmonization of veterinary, plant health and animal feedingstuffs legislation.[4] The

---

[1] OJ L 11, 14.1.1984; Bull. EC 6-1984, points 2.1.93 to 2.1.95.
[2] OJ L 301, 20.11.1984.
[3] Seventeenth General Report, point 417.
[4] OJ C 134, 22.5.1984; Bull. EC 5-1984, point 2.1.139; Bull. EC 6-1984, point 2.1.101.

programme includes a timetable for proposals to be adopted by various dates reaching up to 1 January 1987.

Legislation on plant health, seeds and propagating material

439. On 28 June the Council adopted provisions to prevent the spread of harmful organisms such as fire blight, San José scale and the leaf miner.[1] It continued its study of the proposals concerning the fixing of the maximum residue levels for pesticides in cereals, livestock products and feedingstuffs,[2] without reaching an agreement.

440. During the year, the Council at first extended temporarily the validity of the system of equivalences applicable to seeds imported from non-member countries[3] and later renewed them.[4]

Animal nutrition

441. On 29 November the Council finally adopted the third amendment of the basic Directive on feed additives.[5] The new rules will make it possible to exercise better control of the identity and distribution of additives, thus strengthening consumer protection.

442. The Commission also laid before the Council a proposal designed to extend the Community arrangements concerning undesirable substances and products in feedingstuffs to the raw materials used for their manufacture.[6] The main purpose of the proposal is to fix a maximum limit for the raw materials' aflatoxin content.

Veterinary legislation

443. On the basis of opinions adopted by Parliament[7] and by the scientific committees attached to the Commission, the Commission laid before the Council on 13 June a proposal for the amendment of the arrangements concern-

---

[1] Bull. EC 6-1984, point 2.1.109.
[2] Seventeenth General Report, points 420 and 421.
[3] OJ L 87, 30.3.1984.
[4] OJ L 2, 3.1.1985.
[5] OJ L 270, 14.12.1970.
[6] OJ C 258, 26.9.1984.
[7] OJ C 128, 16.5.1983.

ing the use of certain hormonal substances in livestock production.[1] The Commission proposes that the use of two substances—trenbolone and zeranol —be prohibited for the time being in the absence of adequate toxicological data and that the use of three natural substances be authorized; it submitted at the same time rules for procedures concerning the authorization of hormonal substances used for fattening, the administration of authorized products and inspection work by the Member States.

Also, the Commission put forward proposals concerning the financing of health inspection and supervision of meat,[2] microbiological controls,[3] medical clearance of staff handling meat[4] and the import of meat-based products.

444. With regard to animal health, on 11 December the Council adopted[5] a number of texts forming part of the work programme it had decided on in May.[6] It amended the rules on intra-Community trade in livestock and meat, as part of efforts to control foot-and-mouth disease, and stepped up the measures to control classical swine fever. It also adjusted the technical measures for combating brucellosis, in the light of new scientific knowledge and the progress achieved in methods of diagnosis. Lastly, it authorized for an unlimited period certain forms of presentation or treatments used for poultrymeat (roped poultry, New York dressed poultry, meat chilled by certain processes).

Agrimonetary measures

445. In 1984 the Community made substantial progress towards the dismantlement of the monetary compensatory amounts.

When the agricultural prices were fixed for 1984/85,[7] the Council approved provisions ensuring that until the beginning of the 1987/88 milk year changes in the central rates within the European Monetary System cannot entail the creation of stable positive MCAs.[8] By the application of a 'correcting coefficient', realignment of the currency parities will normally entail only the creation of negative MCAs or the reduction of positive MCAs, as appropriate.

---

[1] OJ C 170, 29.6.1984; Bull. EC 6-1984, points 1.6.1 to 1.6.5.
[2] OJ C 162, 22.6.1984; OJ C 168, 28.6.1984.
[3] OJ C 255, 22.9.1984.
[4] OJ C 179, 7.7.1984; Bull. EC 6-1984, point 2.1.107.
[5] OJ L 339, 27.12.1984; Bull. EC 12-1984.
[6] Point 438 of this Report.
[7] Point 408 of this Report.
[8] OJ L 90, 1.4.1984; Bull. EC 3-1984, points 2.1.116 to 2.1.120.

The negative MCAs thus created will be dismantled on the basis of Commission proposals framed in the light of the economic situation of the Member States concerned.

At the same time, the Council adopted a programme for dismantling existing positive MCAs in three stages. In the first stage, taking effect at the beginning of 1984/85, three German and Dutch positive MCA points were converted into negative MCAs by means of a correcting coefficient; the negative MCAs thus created were eliminated at the beginning of the marketing year for all the products concerned. In the second stage, taking effect on 1 January 1985, six positive German MCA points and 0.6, 0.7 or 0.8 point (depending on the product) of the Dutch positive MCAs are to be dismantled by revaluation of the 'green' rates for these two Member States. After these operations, four fifths of the positive MCAs will have been dismantled in less than one year; they will have been phased out altogether by 1987/88 at the latest.

In addition, the negative MCAs for Italy and Greece were discontinued at the beginning of 1984/85; a small negative MCA remains for France. The Council also altered certain rules for the calculation and application of the MCAs, in particular with regard to the 'neutral margins' and the basis of calculation for pigmeat. To prevent the alteration in the agricultural prices expressed in marks, due on 1 January 1985, from disrupting market organization, the Commission approved transitional measures concerning sugar and cereals. [1]

Competition

446. In connection with the adoption of the new agricultural prices for 1984/ 85, [2] the Council, acting under Article 93(2) of the Treaty, authorized aids that would otherwise have ranked as incompatible with the common market, as follows:

(i) in Germany, the payment from 1 July [3] of 5% of the price of agricultural products, through the VAT scheme, to take account of the revaluation of the 'green' rate of the mark on 1 January 1985, the compensation not to exceed the effects of the dismantling of the annual monetary compensatory amounts; [4]

---

[1] OJ L 253, 21.9.1984; Bull. EC 9-1984, point 2.1.77.
[2] Point 408 of this Report.
[3] OJ L 185, 12.7.1984; Bull. EC 6-1984, point 2.1.88.
[4] Point 409 of this Report.

(ii) in France, Italy [1] and Greece, [2] aid to short-term private storage of table wines and musts throughout 1984/85, a one-year transitional period having proved necessary before this aid, which came under Community regulations until 1983/84, can be discontinued.

447. In 1984 the Commission received 136 notifications of draft measures introducing or varying national aid schemes. For most of the cases, it decided to raise no objections; it endorsed some schemes, however, only when the national authorities had either provided additional information or undertaken to bring the scheme concerned into line with Community requirements. In 19 cases it initiated the procedure laid down in Article 93 of the Treaty.

448. The Commission also set a countervailing charge of 4 ECU/hl for ethyl alcohol of agricultural origin obtained in France and imported into the other Member States in non-denatured form: [3] it took the view that the French regulations had an effect equivalent to that of a national market organization and affected the markets for these alcohols in the other Member States through their imports.

Other work

Farm Accountancy Data Network

449. The Farm Accountancy Data Network (FADN) musters figures drawn from the accounts of a sample of farms in the Community. Only information obtained in this way can enable a proper assessment to be made of the situation of farms, according to type of production and economic size, in the Community as a whole, in each Member State and in each main region.

The Commission continued its efforts to achieve a further improvement of the FADN not only as a source of information but also as an important instrument for use in the preparation and the management of the CAP and in assessments of the impact and effectiveness of measures adopted.

The FADN sample is being steadily broadened; it was made up of about 42 000 farms in 1984 (the target is 44 000 by 1985). In 1981/82, the last accounting year for which data are available for all the Member States, it represented 3.1

---

[1] OJ L 115, 1.5.1984.
[2] OJ L 124, 11.5.1984.
[3] OJ L 238, 6.9.1984; Bull. EC 9-1984, point 2.1.79.

million farms, which accounted for more than 80% of overall production capacity, covered about 85% of the utilized agricultural area and employed two thirds of farmers and farm workers.

TABLE 12

The agricultural management and regulatory committees

Committee	From 1 January to 31 December 1984			
	Meetings[1]	Favour-able opinion	No opinion	Unfavour-able opinion
Management Committee for Cereals	49	606	87	—
Management Committee for Pigmeat	12	23	1	—
Management Committee for Poultrymeat and Eggs	12	61	—	—
Management Committee for Fruit and Vegetables	9	59	3	—
Management Committee for Wine	36	36	5	—
Management Committee for Milk and Milk Products	36	278	24	—
Management Committee for Beef and Veal	25	96	23	—
Management Committee for Sheep and Goats	10	10	3	—
Management Committee for Oils and Fats	22	73	5	—
Management Committee for Sugar	51	136	30	—
Management Committee for Live Plants	2	2	—	—
Management Committee for Products Processed from Fruit and Vegetables	18	39	1	—
Management Committee for Tobacco	4	6	—	—
Management Committee for Hops	1	1	—	—
Management Committee for Flax and Hemp	2	2	—	—
Management Committee for Seeds	6	6	2	—
Management Committee for Dried Fodder	8	11	—	—
EAGGF Committee	18	7	1	—
Standing Committee on Feedingstuffs	6	5	—	—
Standing Veterinary Committee	28	79	1	—
Standing Committee on Seeds and Propagating Material for Agriculture, Horticulture and Forestry	8	11	—	—
Standing Committee on Agricultural Structures	6	69	3	—
Community Committee on the Farm Accountancy Data Network	5	5	—	—
Standing Committee on Agricultural Research	3	2	—	—
Standing Committee on Plant Health	8	3	—	—
Standing Committee on Zootechnics	1	1	—	—

1 Including joint meetings of management committees, except those on trade mechanisms (12 meetings) and on agrimonetary problems (16 meetings).

Efforts to achieve improved use of FADN data to assist in the decision-making process under the CAP were pressed forward by contributions to the various reports on the situation in agriculture and by many analyses, the main results of which were used in various documents sent to the Council and to Parliament; action has continued with a view to making the data more easily accessible to persons and groups concerned.

Advisory committees and relations with agricultural and other organizations

450. Despite budgetary constraints, the advisory committees met fairly regularly in 1984. The impact of the reduction in the number of meetings was partly offset by separate, restricted consultations with the representatives concerned.

With a view to reducing expenditure on the consultation of non-governmental agricultural organizations, the Commission decided, as part of its policy to achieve management savings, to reduce the number of committee members in 1985. However, it will make every effort to ensure the continuity and effectiveness of this form of consultation.

Financing the common agricultural policy: EAGGF

Guarantee Section

451. The original EAGGF guarantee appropriations entered in the 1984 budget totalled 16 542.9 million ECU, of which 42.9 million ECU covered the fisheries market organization and 350 million ECU were entered in Chapter 100. The Commission had undertaken to make every effort to keep expenditure within these appropriations, since the Community's own resources were approaching their ceiling. Thus, its proposals for the agricultural prices and related measures for 1984/85, [1] presented in January, yielded savings of about 875 million ECU, sufficient to cover the shortfall in appropriations due to the deterioration in the market situation which was already occurring.

452. The Council's decisions of 31 March entailed additional expenditure, estimated at 187 million ECU, instead of the savings proposed. [2] Also, the

---

[1] Point 408 of this Report.
[2] Point 409 of this Report.

shortfall in appropriations due to the market situation widened and an amending and supplementary budget had to be adopted.

The draft amending and supplementary budget adopted by Parliament on 25 October provided an additional 1 833 million ECU, bringing the total appropriations available for 1984 to 18 376 million ECU. [1] The Commission was thus in a position to meet the financial obligations arising under Community regulations *vis-à-vis* farmers and other operators.

453. The EAGGF guarantee appropriations which the Commission had proposed for 1985 totalled 19 346 million ECU (of which 31 million ECU was earmarked for fisheries).

TABLE 13

EAGGF guarantee appropriations, by sector

million ECU

	1983 expenditure	1984 appropriations[1]	1985 appropriations	
			Proposed[2]	Approved[3]
Milk and milk products	4 396	5 811	5 484	5 132
Cereals and rice	2 534	2 030	2 959	2 769
Fruit and vegetables, wine, tobacco	2 527	3 245	2 773	2 595
Meat	2 187	2 772	2 827	2 645
Olive oil and oilseeds	1 621	1 636	2 157	2 018
Sugar	1 316	1 602	1 476	1 381
Other[4]	507	544	1 153	1 000
Refunds on processed products	343	351	390	365
Monetary compensatory amounts	489	410	127	119
Impact of accounts clearance decisions	− 108	− 25	−	−
Total	15 812	18 376	19 346	18 024

[1] Including supplementary and amending budget No 1/1984 and transfers Nos 14 and 21.
[2] Commission's preliminary draft budget, including the 80 million ECU reserve entered at Chapter 100.
[3] Draft budget adopted by the Council on 2 October 1984, the Council having undertaken to cover subsequently any additional needs by supplementary funds.
[4] Including fisheries (26 million ECU in 1983, 43 million ECU in 1984, and 31 million ECU proposed and 24 million ECU approved for 1985).

[1] Point 61 of this Report.

The draft budget established by the Council on 2 October was within the Community resources still available. [1] Without challenging the soundness of the Commission's expenditure estimates, the Council restricted the appropriations to 18 000 million ECU, an amount smaller than that for 1984; but it also undertook to respond by 1 October 1985 to any additional budgetary requirements emerging in 1985, by means of a supplementary budget.

454. In early 1984 the Commission completed its work on clearing the 1978 and 1979 accounts, [2] covering a total of about 18 500 million ECU and releasing 25 million ECU to be credited to the 1984 budget; the work on 1980 and 1981, covering more than 21 000 million ECU, was completed in late December.

Financing food aid

455. The funds available in 1984 for the financing of Community food aid operations — not including the refunds, which rank as guarantee expenditure — totalled 717 million ECU, of which 214.9 million ECU had been carried over from 1983.

The tempo of commitments in 1984 was near to that for 1983. On the other hand, payments were a good deal higher, because the 1984 programme got off to a prompter start and because of the increase in cereals prices on the world market.

456. In 1984 the Commission completed the clearance of food aid expenditure accounts for 1976 to 1979.

Guidance Section

457. The appropriations entered in the 1984 budget, not including carryovers, totalled 792.8 million ECU for commitments and 619.9 million ECU for payments. This was 2.4% less for commitments than for 1983, payments remaining stable.

However, actual payments in 1984 showed an increase, because of the use of appropriations carried over from 1983. At the end of 1984 there were no large amounts available to be carried over, as had been the case in previous years.

---

[1] Bull. EC 10-1984, point 2.3.2; Bull. EC 7/8-1984, point 2.3.4 *et seq.*
[2] OJ L 110, 26.4.1984; Bull. EC 2-1984, point 2.1.126.

In early December the Commission sent the Council a proposal for repealing the provisions of the Regulation of 21 April 1970[1] providing for the fixing of a five-year allocation, and an estimate of expenditure for the period 1985-89.[2]

Common provisions

458. The Commission's staff and the responsible departments in the Member States cooperate to combat irregularities committed to the detriment of the EAGGF. In the period from 1 July 1983 to 30 June 1984 the Member States notified the Commission of 317 cases of irregularities, involving a total of 8.9 million ECU; about three quarters of this sum concerned milk products and beef/veal.

459. Under Article 10 of the Regulation of 21 April 1970,[1] the Commission sent to the Council and Parliament in September the Thirteenth Financial Report on the administration of the EAGGF (1983).[3]

---

[1] OJ L 94, 28.4.1970.
[2] OJ C 13, 15.1.1985; Bull. EC 11-1984, point 2.1.115.
[3] Bull. EC 9-1984, point 2.1.93.

Section 12

Fisheries

Main developments

460. *Two years after the birth of 'Blue Europe', the common fisheries policy has entered into a consolidation phase. For the first time, the TACs of fish in Community waters and the quotas for the current year were fixed by the Council at the start of the year. This allowed fishermen to prepare their fishing year on the basis of precise quotas and the Commission to manage the common fisheries policy in a suitable manner and to help the Member States to carry out their legislative activities in this area. For 1985 the TACs and quotas have already been fixed in advance of the fishing year.*

During the year, the Commission has intensified its control measures and verification of the application of Community rules. It has also improved the functioning of the common organization of the fisheries products market.

Because of the importance of fishing to the Spanish and Portuguese economies, the accession negotiations in this sector have been complex and difficult. [1]

Resources

Internal measures

461. In contrast to previous years, the Council was able to agree as early as 31 January [2] on the total allowable catches (TACs) for 1984, the fishing quotas allocated to the Member States and the conditions on which the TACs may be fished. The Regulation adopted to this effect was amended several times [3] to take account of consultations with non-member countries as and when they were completed and certain scientific opinions made available at a later date.

---

[1] Point 600 of this Report.
[2] OJ L 37, 8.2.1984; Bull. EC 1-1984, points 2.1.84 and 2.1.85.
[3] OJ L 67, 9.3.1984; OJ L 77, 21.3.1984; Bull. EC 3-1984, point 2.1.142; OJ L 156, 13.6.1984; Bull. EC 5-1984, points 2.1.145 and 2.1.146; OJ L 199, 28.7.1984; Bull. EC 7/8-1984, point 2.1.145; OJ L 213, 9.8.1984; OJ L 277, 24.8.1984; Bull. EC 7/8-1984, point 2.1.146; OJ L 253, 21.9.1984; Bull. EC 9-1984, point 2.1.98; OJ L 298, 16.11.1984; Bull. EC 11-1984, point 2.1.116; OJ L 318, 7.12.1984; Bull. EC 12-1984.

The TACs and quotas for 1985 were approved by the Council on 19 December, i.e. before the new fishing year started. [1]

462. To ensure more efficient management of resources, in the light of scientific opinions and biological studies carried out in the Atlantic, various technical measures for the conservation of resources were adopted. For example, the Council made several amendments [2] to Regulation No 171/83 [3] of 25 January 1983 as regards the mesh size of nets, the minimum sizes of certain catches, the duration of certain fishing seasons and by-catches. For its part, the Commission adopted Regulations laying down detailed rules for determining the mesh size of fishing nets, [4] the percentage of by-catches [5] and the attachment of devices to trawls. [6]

463. In 1984 the Member States continued to take national conservation measures to implement the common fisheries policy defined early in 1983. The measures adopted mainly concerned restrictions applicable solely to fishermen of the Member State enacting the legislation, the protection of local stocks and the optimum use of the quotas assigned to each Member State. In 1984, however, no Member State took emergency conservation measures to safeguard a particular stock.

In 1984 the Member States provided notification of 43 national conservation measures, of which 28 have been the subject of comments by the Commission and 15 are still being examined.

The Commission completed its examination of the 512 national measures existing prior to the entry into force of the common fisheries policy, notification of which had been provided by the Member States under Article 19(5) of Regulation (EEC) No 171/83.

464. With a view to more effective arrangements for ensuring compliance with Community rules on the conservation of resources, the Commission took the following action:

(i) it conducted a survey among the Member States on the application of national control procedures and adopted provisions making it possible to

---

[1] OJ L 1, 1.1.1985; Bull. EC 10-1984, point 2.1.112; Bull. EC 12-1984.
[2] OJ L 156, 13.6.1984; Bull. EC 5-1984, point 2.1.148; OJ L 199, 28.7.1984; Bull. EC 7/8-1984, point 2.1.147;
     OJ L 253, 21.9.1983; Bull. EC 9-1984, point 2.1.99; OJ L 335, 22.12.1984; Bull. EC 12-1984.
[3] OJ L 24, 27.1.1983.
[4] OJ L 194, 24.7.1984; Bull. EC 7/8-1984, point 2.1.148.
[5] OJ L 316, 6.12.1984; Bull. EC 12-1984.
[6] OJ L 318, 7.12.1984; Bull. EC 12-1984.

warn Member States of any impending exhaustion of their respective quotas;

(ii) through its inspectors, it verified the application of fisheries control measures at sea and in the majority of ports;

(iii) it took part in administrative investigations into irregularities which it had discovered in the Member States, and decided to institute the Article 169 procedure against Member States which had not correctly applied Community rules on the registering of catches and technical measures of conservation and those which had not kept to their quotas in 1983 and 1984.

The Commission embarked on action to harmonize national inspection methods and procedures. A Community method was devised for measuring, by means of sampling, the rate of by-catches of species for human consumption during fishing for species intended for the fishmeal industry.

The logbooks to be kept by skippers of fishing vessels were made available to the national authorities by the Commission.

Bilateral and multilateral relations

465. In the context of its new relations with Greenland, the Community concluded a 10-year Fisheries Agreement and a five-year Protocol with Denmark and the Home Government of Greenland. [1] The Agreement lays down the principles and rules to be applied to fishing in Greenland waters by vessels flying the flag of a Member State of the Community and provides for financial compensation for Greenland in exchange for access to Greenland waters for Community vessels.

As an interim measure before Greenland's actual withdrawal from the Community, the Council adopted on 19 December a Regulation on the allocation of the catch quotas in Greenland waters for 1985. [2]

466. The Fisheries Agreement with the United States was renewed and signed in October. [3]

---

[1] Bull. EC 2-1984, point 1.4.5.
[2] OJ L 1, 1.1.1985; Bull. EC 12-1984.
[3] OJ L 272, 13.10.1984; Bull. EC 6-1984, point 2.1.118; Bull. EC 7/8-1984, point 2.1.154; Bull. EC 9-1984, point 2.1.102.

The new Fisheries Agreement with Equatorial Guinea was approved by the Council in June [1] and came into force on 3 December.

The Agreement with the Seychelles initialled in January [2] was provisionally applied as from 11 January. [3]

A Fisheries Agreement with Madagascar was initialled on 21 December. [4]

An agreement extending the 1979 Fisheries Agreement with Senegal was initialled in January. [5]

The Commission continued talks with a view to concluding a fisheries agreement with Mauritania. [6]

467. In May the Council adopted the arrangements applicable until December 1984 to non-Community vessels fishing off French Guiana, [7] and in December the arrangements for 1985. [8]

468. Reciprocal fishing rights for 1984 were agreed by the Community and Spain in March and for 1985 in December. [9] Those between the Community and Sweden were fixed in February. [10] In October an exchange of letters between the Community and the Faeroes defined the limit for catches of salmon by the Faeroes in the North Atlantic for the fishing season from 1 October 1984 to 31 May 1985. [11]

469. In 1984 the Community participated as a member or as an observer in the work of several international fisheries organizations, including the North-West Atlantic Fisheries Organization, [12] the North Atlantic Salmon Conservation Organization, [13] the Eastern Central Atlantic Fisheries Organization, [14] the North-East Atlantic Fisheries Organization, [15] the International   Com-

---

[1]   OJ L 188, 16.7.1984; Bull. EC 6-1984, point 2.1.102.
[2]   Bull. EC 1-1984, point 2.1.94.
[3]   OJ L 79, 23.3.1984; Bull. EC 3-1984, point 2.1.151.
[4]   Bull. EC 6-1984, point 2.1.121; Bull. EC 9-1984, point 2.1.104; Bull. EC 12-1984.
[5]   OJ C 48, 21.2.1984; Bull. EC 1-1984, point 2.1.93; Bull. EC 4-1984, point 2.1.112.
[6]   Bull. EC 1-1984, point 2.1.95.
[7]   OJ L 88, 31.3.1984; OJ L 145, 31.5.1984; Bull. EC 5-1984, point 2.1.152.
[8]   OJ L 1, 1.1.1985; Bull. EC 12-1984.
[9]   OJ L 67, 9.3.1984; Bull. EC 2-1984, point 2.1.132; Bull. EC 3-1984, point 2.1.148; Bull. EC 12-1984.
[10] OJ L 61, 2.3.1984; Bull. EC 2-1984, point 2.1.134.
[11] OJ L 264, 5.10.1984; Bull. EC 7/8-1984, point 2.1.158; Bull. EC 10-1984, point 2.1.111.
[12] Bull. EC 9-1984, point 2.1.105.
[13] Bull. EC 1-1984, point 2.1.97; Bull. EC 5-1984, point 2.1.158.
[14] Bull. EC 10-1984, point 2.1.119.
[15] Bull. EC 11-1984, point 2.1.123.

mission for the South-East Atlantic Fisheries, [1] the Convention on Fishing and Conservation of the Living Resources in the Baltic Sea and the Belts, [2] and the Convention on the Conservation of Antarctic Marine Living Resources. [2]

Now that the International Convention for the Conservation of Atlantic Tunas has been amended, [3] the Community can become a contracting party.

470. The Commission represented the Community at the World Conference on Fisheries Management and Development held in Rome from 27 June to 6 July. [4]

Market organization

471. The trend towards greater stability on the white fish market, first observed in 1982 and confirmed in 1983, continued for the first half of 1984. In overall terms, production and withdrawals showed a slight fall, whereas the average prices for products placed on the market increased moderately, with the exception of saithe and hake.

As regards pelagic species, the situation showed certain similarities with that of white fish. In the first half of the year production was down (except for herring), while prices rose slightly (except for mackerel and Mediterranean sardines). Withdrawals, particularly of Mediterranean sardines and anchovies, though falling substantially, were still excessive.

In two additional reports submitted to the Council on 18 May [5] and 15 November, [6] the Commission examined in detail how the foreseeable increase in available quantities of North Sea herring would affect the Community market. After analysing the market situation, the report outlines the development prospects for herring production and defines the requirements of the processing sector.

472. To prevent serious disturbance of the market as a result of imports at prices substantially lower than those applied in the Community, a minimum free-at-frontier price was agreed for Bulgarian exports of frozen trout [7] to

---

[1] Bull. EC 12-1984.
[2] Bull. EC 9-1984, point 2.1.105.
[3] Bull. EC 7/8-1984, point 2.1.160; Bull. EC 11-1984, point 2.1.124.
[4] Bull. EC 7/8-1984, point 2.1.159.
[5] Bull. EC 5-1984, point 2.1.159.
[6] Bull. EC 11-1984, point 2.1.125.
[7] Bull. EC 2-1984, point 2.1.138.

France and protective measures were applied to imports into the Community of frozen squid originating in Poland. [1]

Furthermore, the Council agreed on 19 December that with effect from 1 July 1985 dried cod, salted cod and cod in brine should be removed from the list of products qualifying for total suspension of Common Customs Tariff duties. [2]

473. To improve the operation of the new common organization of the market in fisheries products, [3] the Commission adopted Regulations concerning:

(i) tighter supervision of the activities of producers' organizations in combination with application for the financing of aids; [4]

(ii) certain changes to the procedure for granting and withdrawing recognition of producers' organizations; [5]

(iii) certain detailed rules for the granting of financial compensation; [6]

(iv) conversion factors for frozen squid. [7]

On 18 December the Council extended [8] for 1985 the exemption accorded to Greece under the rules for the granting of a special carryover premium for Mediterranean sardines and anchovies with regard to the provision for the conclusion of contracts between processors and individual producers. [9]

474. On a proposal from the Commission, on 4 December the Council raised the guide prices for fishery products for the 1985 fishing year by an average of 3.2% over 1984, keeping the producer price of tuna intended for the canning industry at the 1984 level.[10] On 19 and 20 December the Commission adopted a number of technical regulations in this field.[11]

---

[1] OJ L 261, 2.10.1984; Bull. EC 10-1984, point 2.1.220.
[2] OJ L 267, 6.10.1984; Bull. EC 12-1984.
[3] OJ L 379, 31.12.1981.
[4] OJ L 73, 16.3.1984; Bull. EC 3-1984, point 2.1.152.
[5] OJ L 186, 13.7.1984; Bull. EC 7/8-1984, point 2.1.161.
[6] OJ L 297, 14.11.1984.
[7] OJ L 333, 21.12.1984; Bull. EC 12-1984.
[8] OJ L 335, 22.12.1984; Bull. EC 12-1984.
[9] OJ L 235, 10.8.1982.
[10] OJ L 318, 7.12.1984; Bull. EC 12-1984.
[11] OJ L 332, 20.12.1984; OJ L 335, 22.12.1984; Bull. EC 12-1984.

Structures

475. 1984 was taken up mainly with the implementation of the structures policy adopted by the Council on 4 October 1983. [1]

476. Acting under Regulation (EEC) No 2908/83 on a common measure to restructure, modernize and develop the fisheries sector and develop aquaculture, [1] the Commission on 13 February laid down detailed rules for the execution of decisions concerning the granting and payment of aid. [2] Under the appropriation for 1983 and the first instalment of the appropriation for 1984, the Commission decided to finance 338 projects for the construction of vessels, 439 for the modernization of vessels, 50 for aquaculture units, and 6 for artificial reefs. The total aid granted amounted to some 64 million ECU.

The Commission also cooperated with the Member States on the preparation of multiannual guidance programmes.

477. Pursuant to Regulation (EEC) No 2909/83 on measures to encourage exploratory fishing and cooperation through joint ventures in the fisheries sector, [1] the Commission defined the special and the Community waters where fishing operations may be undertaken in the course of exploratory voyages. [3]

478. As regards the adjustment of capacities in the fisheries sector (Directive 83/515/EEC) [1] the Commission approved the measures planned by the United Kingdom, [4] Denmark, [5] Belgium, [6] the Federal Republic of Germany [7] and Greece. [8]

479. Under Regulation (EEC) No 355/77 on common measures to improve the conditions under which agricultural products are processed and marketed, [9] the Commission decided to grant approximately 11.9 million ECU in aid from the EAGGF Guidance Section to 77 investment projects in the fisheries sector. A specific programme presented by Greece was approved on 30 November. [8]

---

[1] OJ L 290, 22.10.1983; Seventeenth General Report, point 485.
[2] OJ L 46, 16.2.1984; Bull. EC 2-1984, point 2.1.139.
[3] OJ L 120, 5.5.1984.
[4] OJ L 18, 21.1.1984.
[5] OJ L 64, 6.3.1984.
[6] OJ L 131, 17.5.1984.
[7] OJ L 196, 26.7.1984.
[8] OJ L 322, 11.12.1984.
[9] OJ L 51, 23.2.1977.

480. Lastly, the Commission monitored for the fisheries sector in December 1983, [1] in preparation for the integrated Mediterranean programmes.

481. As required by Articles 92 and 93 of the EEC Treaty, Member States notified the Commission of 18 draft measures whereby national aids would be granted to the fisheries and aquaculture sector. Most of the drafts concerned did not meet with any objections, but in four cases (measures notified by the Federal Republic of Germany, [2] the United Kingdom, [2] France [3] and Italy [4]), the Commission initiated the procedure laid down in Article 93(2) of the Treaty. The Article 93(2) procedure was terminated in respect of four schemes which had been notified by France, [5] Greece [6] and Germany. [7]

---

[1] OJ L 44, 15.2.1984; Bull. EC 12-1983, point 2.1.184.
[2] Bull. EC 6-1984, point 2.1.125.
[3] Bull. EC 7/8-1984, point 2.1.164.
[4] Bull. EC 10-1984, point 2.1.122.
[5] Bull. EC 4-1984, point 2.1.114.
[6] Bull. EC 7/8-1984, point 2.1.165.
[7] Bull. EC 2-1984, point 2.1.142; Bull. EC 11-1984, point 2.1.132.

Section 13

Transport

Main developments

482. *Considerable progress was achieved this year towards the creation of a common transport policy. In the field of inland transport, for instance, the Council at the end of the year adopted Directives governing the weights and dimensions of commercial road vehicles and the use of vehicles leased for the shipment of goods by road, together with a Regulation on the Community quota and a recommendation concerning commercial cooperation between railway undertakings.*

In the field of infrastructures, it did not succeed in approving the general criteria for selecting projects which may receive financial support from the Community but it adopted the projects to be financed on the 1983 and 1984 budgets.

483. *For its part, the Commission has continued its work in accordance with the guidelines and the timetable set out in the 1983 communication concerning inland transport.[1] In particular, it put forward proposals designed to place railways on a sound financial footing and to introduce social legislation in the field of road transport. On the whole, it tried to put forward pragmatic proposals, due account being taken of the specific nature of the transport sector, especially of the problems linked to achieving a balance between the different modes of transport. It has also attempted to further the process of harmonization and liberalization of inland transport advocated by the European Council in March and June and reiterated in December.*

In the course of the year the Commission also sent the Council two communications on the future development of the common transport policy, concerning the sea[2] and air[3] transport sectors respectively. In each of them the Commission mapped out a general plan of action, set the main guidelines and put forward the basic proposals which it feels are necessary for a modicum of progress to be achieved. These two communications and that on inland trans-

---

[1] OJ C 154, 13.6.1983; Seventeenth General Report, point 492.
[2] Bull. EC 12-1984.
[3] OJ C 182, 9.7.1984.

port of 1983[1] together spell out a Community policy which covers all modes of transport and meets Parliament's call for an overall approach.

The Court of Justice examined the action for failure to act brought against the Council by Parliament in 1983.[2] Its judgment is expected in 1985.

Infrastructure

484. On 19 December the Council adopted a Regulation on a specific measure in the field of transport infrastructure,[3] which grants a total of 95 million ECU towards the infrastructure projects to be funded from the 1983 and 1984 budgets, including several specifically designed to improve the traffic flow at frontier-crossing points.[4]

485. To provide the Council with the medium-term policy framework which it had requested for future measures, on 18 December the Commission sent the Council a report aiming at establishing a programme of major transport infrastructure projects of benefit to the Community as a whole, complete with a set of objective criteria to be applied and arrangements for combining Community funding with national aid.[5]

To fill the gap until the programme is set up, on 10 September the Commission also sent the Council a proposal for a Regulation concerning special measures for 1985.[6]

Special measures of Community interest

486. On 26 June the Council adopted a Regulation[7] introducing special measures of Community interest relating to transport infrastructure in the United Kingdom and in the Federal Republic of Germany in 1983.[8] On 17 October, as a result of the decision to transfer funds taken by Parliament in

---

[1] OJ C 154, 13.6.1983; Seventeenth General Report, point 492.
[2] Seventeenth General Report, point 490.
[3] OJ L 333, 21.12.1984; Bull. EC 12-1984.
[4] Bull. EC 3-1984, point 2.1.157.
[5] Bull. EC 5-1984, point 2.1.163; Bull. EC 12-1984.
[6] OJ C 263, 2.10.1984; Bull. EC 9-1984, point 2.1.107.
[7] OJ L 177, 4.7.1984; Bull. EC 6-1984, point 2.1.126.
[8] Point 81 of this Report; Bull. EC 6-1984, point 1.1.1 *et seq.*

October, the Commission adopted the decisions concerning financial aid to be granted under these measures. [1]

Inland transport

Functioning of the market

Access to the market

487. On 19 December the Council adopted a Regulation authorizing a substantial increase in the Community road haulage authorization quota over the next five years. [2] However, it has yet to act on the Commission proposal to liberalize road freight services between the Member States completely once the five-year period is over.

On 14 March, as part of its proposals concerning the 'single document', [3] the Commission sent the Council proposed amendments [4] to the 1976 Regulation on the Community quota [5] and the 1965 Directive on bilateral authorizations [6] with the aim of abolishing the journey record sheet accompanying transport authorizations issued under the quota system once the 'single document' has been introduced.

488. On 19 December the Council adopted a Directive on the use of vehicles hired for the carriage of goods by road. [7] In April the Commission had amended [8] its original 1983 proposal [9] in order to take account of Parliament's opinion. [10]

489. On 13 December the Commission sent to the Council two proposals for directives and a draft regulation intended to harmonize the competition situations existing in the traffic between the Community's seaports and their

---

[1] OJ L 290, 7.11.1984; Bull. EC 10-1984, point 2.1.125.
[2] OJ L 333, 21.12.1984; Bull. EC 12-1984; Bull. EC 5-1984, point 2.1.168.
[3] Point 180 of this Report.
[4] OJ C 86, 28.3.1984; Bull. EC 3-1984, point 2.1.9.
[5] OJ L 257, 29.12.1976; OJ L 369, 20.12.1982.
[6] OJ 88, 24.5.1965.
[7] OJ L 335, 22.12.1984; Bull. EC 12-1984.
[8] OJ C 111, 26.4.1984; Bull. EC 4-1984, point 2.1.118.
[9] OJ C 155, 14.6.1983; Seventeenth General Report, point 496.
[10] OJ C 10, 16.1.1984.

hinterlands by organizing on a standard basis the market in inland transport from and to these ports. [1]

490. In the light of Parliament's opinion, [2] on 19 July the Commission amended [3] its proposal for a Directive on access to the occupation of carrier of goods by inland waterway and on the mutual recognition of diplomas, certificates and other evidence of formal qualifications for this occupation. [4]

491. On 8 November the Council took a decision on joint action by the Member States party to the Revised Convention for the Navigation of the Rhine. [5] This enabled the Central Commission for the Navigation of the Rhine to adopt a resolution concerning the conditions for issuing the certificate that a vessel belongs to the Rhine navigation fleet.

Rates and conditions of carriage

492. On 19 December the Council adopted a proposal for a recommendation calling on the Member States' railways to expand their present cooperation into a dynamic, effective commercial policy for international goods and passenger services between Member States. [6]

Approximation of structures

493. On 19 December the Council adopted a Directive on the weight and size of commercial road vehicles, [7] laying down certain standards such as vehicle dimensions, the total loaded weights for five- or six-axle units (40 tonnes) and the weight on each axle (apart from the drive axle). Exemptions are to be granted to the United Kingdom and Ireland.

494. On 12 December the Council adopted a third Directive on summer time arrangements for 1986, 1987 and 1988. [8]

---

[1] OJ C 14, 16.1.1985; Bull. EC 12-1984.
[2] OJ C 248, 17.9,1984; Bull. EC 7/8-1984, point 2.4.47.
[3] OJ C 214, 14.8.1984; Bull. EC 7/8-1984, point 2.1.170.
[4] OJ C 351, 24.12.1983; Seventeenth General Report, point 500.
[5] Bull. EC 11-1984, point 2.1.134.
[6] OJ L 333, 21.12.1984; Bull. EC 12-1984; OJ C 187, 13.7.1983; Bull. EC 6-1983, point 2.1.220; OJ C 191, 16.7.1983; Bull. EC 6-1983, point 2.1.217; OJ C 254, 22.9.1983; Bull. EC 9-1983, point 2.1.131.
[7] OJ L 2, 3.1.1985; Bull. 12-1984.
[8] OJ L 331, 19.12.1984; Bull. EC 12-1984.

495. On 19 December the Council and the Representatives of the Governments of the Member States meeting in the Council adopted a resolution on the implementation of a Community programme on road safety, [1] on which Parliament [2] and the Economic and Social Committee [3] had given their opinion in May. They also agreed that 1986 should be designated 'Road Safety Year' in the Community.

496. The Commission sent the Council on 17 January two proposals on the financial balance of railway undertakings, one relating to the improvement of their finances and the harmonization of the rules governing the financial relations between the railways and their governments, the other concerning aid to rail transport. [4]

On 20 March the Commission proposed that the Council should lift all restrictions on the duty-free admission of fuel contained in the normal fuel tanks of commercial motor vehicles, with effect from 1 July 1985. [5]

The same day the Commission proposed that the Council should amend [6] the Regulation of 25 March 1969 on the harmonization of certain social legislation relating to road transport [7] and the Regulation of 20 July 1970 concerning the introduction of recording equipment in road transport. [8] The Council acknowledged the urgency of the need to reach a decision in this matter.

Multimodal transport

497. On 14 December the Community signed an agreement with Spain concerning the international combined road/rail carriage of goods that frees the final road stretch of a journey from the system of quotas and authorizations. [9]

---

[1] OJ C 341, 21.12.1984; Bull. EC 12-1984; OJ C 95, 6.4.1984.
[2] OJ C 172, 2.7.1984.
[3] OJ C 206, 6.8.1984.
[4] OJ C 36, 10.2.1984; Bull. EC 1-1984, point 2.1.100.
[5] Point 261 of this Report.
[6] OJ C 100, 12.4.1984; Bull. EC 3-1984, point 2.1.168.
[7] OJ L 77, 29.3.1969; OJ L 73, 17.3.1979.
[8] OJ L 164, 27.7.1970; OJ L 181, 4.7.1973; OJ L 334, 24.12.1977.
[9] OJ C 49, 21.2.1984; Bull. EC 1-1984, point 2.1.103; Bull. EC 12-1984.

Sea transport

498. On 24 May Parliament delivered an interim opinion[1] on the Commission proposal for a Regulation laying down detailed rules for the application of Articles 85 and 86 of the Treaty to maritime transport.[2]

Air transport

499. The Commission sent the Council a communication proposing a general framework for a common air transport policy on 20 March.[3] After an initial exchange of views, the Council acknowledged that a number of changes needed to be made to the current system and set up a working party, which reported on 12 December.[4] The Council endorsed the findings of the report and asked that proposals be made before the end of 1985.

500. Parliament adopted a number of resolutions on air transport, including one on airport charges on 30 March,[5] one on the safety of air transport on 13 April[6] and one on airport planning in the Community on 21 May.[7]

Frontier crossings

501. Following incidents at a number of frontier-crossing points in the Alps in February,[8] on 22 March the Council considered ways of bringing forward the adoption of national measures to give effect to the Council Directive of 1 December 1983 on the facilitation of physical inspections and administrative formalities in respect of the carriage of goods between Member States.[9]

International cooperation

502. On several occasions the Council examined the problems connected with charges imposed on road vehicles in certain non-member countries, in particular Switzerland, Austria and Yugoslavia.[10] The Commission pressed the Swiss

---

[1] OJ C 172, 2.7.1984.
[2] OJ C 282, 5.11.1981; Fifteenth General Report, point 206.
[3] OJ C 182, 9.7.1984; Bull. EC 2-1984, point 2.1.149.
[4] Bull. EC 5-1984, point 2.1.70; Bull. EC 12-1984.
[5] OJ C 117, 30.4.1984; Bull. EC 3-1984, point 2.4.22.
[6] OJ C 127, 14.5.1984; Bull. EC 4-1984, point 2.4.9.
[7] OJ C 172, 2.7.1984; Bull. EC 5-1984, point 2.4.15.
[8] Bull. EC 2-1984, points 2.1.8 to 2.1.11.
[9] OJ L 359, 22.12.1983; Seventeenth General Report, point 514; Bull. EC 3-1984, point 2.1.6.
[10] Bull. EC 3-1984, point 2.1.173; Bull. EC 12-1984.

authorities to ensure that no discrimination against Community vehicles would result from the new charges being levied. In December Parliament adopted a resolution on the imposition of road taxes by Switzerland. [1]

503. On 16 December the Commission sent the Council a second report on the negotiations with Austria in the field of inland transport. [2] At its 11 and 12 December meeting the Council asked that the examination of the balance of traffic between Austria and the Community be expedited and the possibility of concluding a cooperation agreement with Austria investigated, without excluding appropriate arrangements for Community participation in the infrastructure costs incurred by Austria should this prove to be justified. [3]

504. On 15 October the Commission sent the Council a proposal that the Community and the Member States should make a joint declaration accepting, subject to certain reservations, the resolution on the facilitation of road transport adopted by the UN Economic Commission for Europe. [4]

Transport and energy

505. After Parliament [5] and the Economic and Social Committee [6] had given their opinions, the Commission amended [7] its proposal for a Directive on fuel rationing for commercial transport between the Member States in the event of an energy crisis. [8]

---

[1] OJ C 12, 14.1.1985; Bull. EC 12-1984.
[2] Bull. EC 10-1984, point 2.1.129; Bull. EC 11-1984, point 2.1.135.
[3] Bull. EC 12-1984.
[4] Bull. EC 10-1984, point 2.1.124.
[5] OJ C 77, 19.3.1984; Bull. EC 2-1984, point 2.1.148.
[6] OJ C 140, 28.5.1984; Bull. EC 3-1984, point 2.4.36.
[7] Bull. EC 6-1984; point 2.1.132.
[8] OJ C 195, 22.7.1983; Seventeenth General Report, point 518.

Section 14

Energy

Main developments

506. The world energy situation was once again marked by excess supply, at least in the short term. However, despite prices which, in national currencies, remained high because of the fresh rise in the rate of exchange of the dollar, demand was high in the Community, higher than in previous years owing to a certain degree of economic recovery. This trend is an important factor which, if it continues, should be watched closely.

At all events, the energy situation in the Community has improved appreciably since 1973. Internal energy demand has fallen by more than 6%, while GDP has increased in real terms by almost 20%. Internal demand for oil is down by almost a third, and dependence on imported oil has halved. Security of supply has also shown a marked improvement, owing both to the increase in the internal production of energy and to the diversification of Community suppliers.

However, these advances must not hide the fact that the Community is still faced with a number of problems, in particular the size of the oil bills, the investment needed for the medium and long term, energy dependence that is unlikely to decrease to any great extent in the medium term, and the implications of environmental protection. The Commission has therefore focused a great deal of attention on the results and prospects of the energy policies pursued by the Member States and has initiated a general study designed to produce, in 1985, new guidelines for the next 10 years.

Community energy strategy

507. In a communication to the Council reviewing the Member States' energy policies, [1] the Commission provided a complete analysis of those policies (with more detail than in the past), assessing their consistency with the Community's objectives and examining the main problems for the future. It also highlighted the significant progress that had been made towards achieving the Community's

---

[1] Bull. EC 2-1984, point 2.1.152.

objectives for 1990 [1] and stressed the risk that, in the years ahead, the differences between Member States, with regard to their dependence on imported oil might become more acute.

508. In another communication analysing progress in the structural changes made in the context of these policies, [2] the Commission highlighted a number of priority tasks which the Community and the Member States would have to take on if the objectives set by the Council [1] were to be met. These tasks were: the continued implementation of a rational energy-pricing policy; improved energy efficiency, especially through the use of new technologies; promotion of oil and gas exploration; strengthened links with the oil-exporting countries; improved measures for dealing with oil-crisis situations; encouraging the consumption of solid fuel through the use of better combustion technologies; modernizing the Community's coal industry; developing a genuine common energy-supply market through greater integration of the electricity and gas transmission networks; encouraging the replacement of oil by electricity, ensuring an adequate, secure supply of gas for the 1990s; and continuing efforts to develop and market new and renewable forms of energy. The Council held detailed discussions in May [3] and November [4] on these communications. As requested at the Energy Ministers' meeting in November, [4] the Commission sent the Council a working paper [5] analysing energy supply and demand in the Community in the year 2000; this is essential to the preparation of proposals on the new long-term objectives. The illustrative nuclear programme, approved by the Commission for transmittal to Parliament and the Economic and Social Committee will be officially published in due course. It is an important factor in the definition of long-term objectives. [6]

509. The Commission sent the Council a detailed report on the application of Community energy-pricing principles, especially as regards gas and electricity prices, [7] in which it drew attention to a number of complex problems arising from the application of these principles and called for more detailed analysis and close cooperation between the Commission and the Member States. At its November meeting the Council held a wide-ranging policy discussion on the basis of this paper. [8]

---

[1] OJ C 149, 18.6.1980; Fourteenth General Report, point 440.
[2] Bull. EC 2-1984, point 2.1.152.
[3] Bull. EC 5-1984, point 2.1.175.
[4] Bull. EC 11-1984, point 2.1.137.
[5] Bull. EC 12-1984.
[6] Bull. EC 11-1984, point 2.1.144.
[7] Bull. EC 9-1984, point 2.1.111.
[8] Bull. EC 11-1984, point 2.1.139.

510. In October the Commission took the Decisions associated with the special measures of Community interest relating to energy strategy and laying down the conditions—adopted in June by the Council[1]—attaching to the financial assistance granted by the Community to programmes, measures or projects carried out in the United Kingdom (255 million ECU) and the Federal Republic of Germany (201 million ECU).[2]

511. The Commission also continued to support studies designed to analyse the energy demand of a region or municipalities and what possibilities are available for meeting that demand with local resources. The measures involved regions in France, Germany, Belgium, Italy and the Netherlands.

Relations with countries producing or importing energy

512. Relations with the industrialized countries continued to develop within OECD's International Energy Agency and the Economic Commission for Europe, and through regular bilateral contacts with the main countries in question.[3]

513. The Commission and the International Atomic Energy Agency held several meetings to improve the implementation of the cooperation agreement between the Community and the Agency in areas other than safeguards.[4]

514. Cooperation continued with the developing countries in the field of energy programming. With some 50 projects, at a total cost of 6 million ECU, the Community contributed—by training specialist managers, sending out experts and carrying out studies and analyses in conjunction with the countries concerned—to the systematic collection of energy data and to the processing and use of the data collected.

The Commission also provided technical assistance to energy planning institutions and helped to finance seminars organized jointly with several developing countries and regional organizations. These activities were centred on Brazil, Mexico, Venezuela, Ecuador, the People's Republic of China and—in a seminar on energy data organized jointly with OAPEC in October, the conclusions of which were formally adopted at the OAPEC-Commission meeting held in

[1] OJ L 177, 4.7.1984; Bull. EC 6-1984, point 2.1.134.
[2] OJ L 283, 27.10.1984; Bull. EC 10-1984, point 2.1.130.
[3] Point 782 of this Report.
[4] Point 770 of this Report.

Kuwait in December—on the Arab countries. At the same time the Commission continued its work on the analysis, methodology and evaluation of energy supply and demand. Through a network of 10 energy institutes in Europe and the Third World, some 40 researchers were associated with this programme. A jointly developed methodology was presented at an international seminar in Brussels in December.

Energy savings and rational use — New energy sources

515. With an overall budget of 265 million ECU for 1983-85 [1] the Council renewed, [2] for 1984 and 1985, the Regulations on the granting of Community financial support for programmes of demonstration projects relating to the development of energy saving, renewable energy sources, alternatives to oil and gas, and liquefaction and gasification. [3]

The Commission meanwhile continued its evaluative work in order to provide the information required for drawing up a proposal on renewing these programmes for a further period. The impact of these programmes and the interest shown in them by industries and organizations in the Community were considerable.

Further to its call for submission of projects published in February, [4] in response to which 775 proposals were received, the Commission adopted:

(i) one decision on 68 energy-saving projects, granting support worth 26.2 million ECU; [5]

(ii) four decisions on 131 projects in the field of alternative energy sources, granting support worth 30.4 million ECU; [5]

   (a) 8.59 million ECU for 36 wind power projects,

   (b) 11.14 million ECU for 30 projects relating to biomass and energy from waste,

   (c) 5.57 million ECU for 39 projects relating to the use of solar energy, and

   (d) 5.1 million ECU for projects on the use of hydroelectricity;

(iii) two decisions in the field of oil and gas substitution: [5]

---

[1] Bull. EC 3-1984, point 2.1.182.
[2] OJ L 196, 26.7.1984; Bull. EC 7/8-1984, point 2.1.176.
[3] OJ L 195, 19.7.1983; Seventeenth General Report, point 531; Thirteenth General Report, point 394.
[4] OJ C 42, 15.2.1984; Bull. EC 2-1984, point 2.1.155.
[5] Bull. EC 11-1984, point 2.1.147.

(a) 5.57 million ECU for 9 projects relating to the use of electricity and heat, and

(b) 12.81 million ECU for 11 projects on the use of solid fuels;

(iv) and finally one decision worth 20.29 million ECU for 9 projects on the liquefaction and gasification of solid fuels. [1]

516. Referring to the framework programme on energy saving adopted by the Council in 1980, [2] the Commission sent the Council on 2 February a comparative review of the Member States' energy-saving programmes. [3] The Commission concuded that many improvements were possible, often at little or no extra cost, even in Member States which had already drawn up fairly complete programmes.

Having examined this communication, [4] the Council adopted a resolution stressing the importance of an integrated energy-saving policy.

517. Acting upon the general conclusions in its communication of 2 February, [5] the Commission sent the Council on 20 December a programme for the rational use of energy in the building industry, [6] defining several courses of action and in particular stressing the need for thermal auditing as an essential prerequisite to the upgrading of the energy efficiency of existing buildings.

Sectoral aspects

Oil and gas

518. Increased tension in the Gulf and the resulting dangers for world oil supplies led the Commission to step up its contacts with the industrialized consumer countries [7] and the main oil producers. In its relations with OAPEC the Commission pursued several cooperation ventures. The Commission and OAPEC organized and financed a seminar for the first time on a joint basis. [8]

---

[1] Bull. EC 11-1984, point 2.1.146.
[2] OJ C 149, 18.6.1980; Fourteenth General Report, point 441.
[3] Bull. EC 2-1984, point 2.1.153.
[4] Bull. EC 5-1984, point 2.1.176.
[5] Bull. EC 2-1984, point 2.1.153.
[6] Bull. EC 11-1984, point 2.1.145.
[7] Point 782 of this Report.
[8] Point 514 of this Report.

519. Concerned to improve the transparency of the oil market, the Commission, in conjunction with the industry, decided to try out a rapid data collection system for oil stocks (Eurostock).

520. After 10 years of applying the Council Regulation of 1973,[1] the Commission carried out an overall evaluation of the results of the Community programme of support for the development of new technologies in the hydrocarbons sector,[2] which it is proposing to continue after some improvements have been made. The most outstanding results of the programme were presented at Luxembourg from 5 to 7 December at a symposium organized by the Commission.

521. The Commission sent the Council a communication on natural gas,[3] in which it continued its analysis of the long-term security of supplies. The Council held a policy discussion on this document on 22 May,[4] following which it asked the Commission to prepare a further communication taking into account the Council's suggestions.[5]

Solid fuels [6]

522. Demand for coal went up — partly offsetting the fall in 1983[7] — as a result of the increase in energy demand that accompanied the improvement in the general economic situation. Imports rose, and producers' stocks declined. Community production went down slightly in Belgium, France and the Federal Republic of Germany, and — as a result of strikes — considerably in the United Kingdom. By contrast, the demand for and production of lignite and peat remained stable.

523. Further to the Council's review,[8] after Parliament[9] and the Economic and Social Committee[10] had given their opinions, of the proposal for a Regulation on Community financial support for industries producing solid fuels (moderniza-

---

[1] OJ L 312, 13.11.1973.
[2] Bull. EC 5-1984, point 2.1.179.
[3] Bull. EC 4-1984, point 2.1.121.
[4] Bull. EC 5-1984, point 2.1.181.
[5] Bull. EC 10-1984, point 2.1.131.
[6] For coal research see point 57 of this Report; for demonstration projects see point 515.
[7] Seventeenth General Report, point 538.
[8] Bull. EC 5-1984, point 2.1.177.
[9] OJ C 104, 1.6.1984; Bull. EC 3-1984, point 2.1.177.
[10] OJ C 35, 9.2.1984.

tion and restructuring of the coal industry and the development of brown coal and peat production),[1] the Commission amended its proposal,[2] in particular by tightening up the eligibility criteria for projects and limiting the budget appropriations to 200 million ECU. Despite these changes the proposal was not approved by the Council in November.

524. The Council decided[3] on 23 July to authorize the transfer of 60 million ECU in respect of 1984 from the general budget to the ECSC budget,[1] to help resolve the social consequences of restructuring and modernizing the coal industry. Agreement was also reached on how to divide this sum among the Member States concerned, taking into account the number of jobs shed and the level of support afforded by each Member State in connection with each job affected.[4]

525. On 23 March the Commission, having received the Council's assent, extended[5] for the period 1984-86, with some alterations compared with the original proposal,[6] its Decision of 25 July 1973 on measures designed to facilitate the production and sale of coking coal and coke for the steel and metallurgical industries.[7] The Community's financial contribution amounts to 36 million ECU a year, of which 6 million ECU are provided by the ECSC budget.

Heat and power

526. Having stagnated somewhat over the last few years, electricity demand rose in 1984.[8] Accordingly, the Commission drew the Council's attention to the need to continue to try and meet 70-75% of primary energy requirements from nuclear-based and solid-fuel-based electricity generation and use more of the electricity thus generated as a substitute for petroleum products.[9]

527. The Commission, with a view to presenting proposals to the Council, carried out further studies[10] on combined heat and power production (CHP)

---

[1] OJ C 232, 30.8.1983, Seventeenth General Report, point 539.
[2] OJ C 264, 3.10.1984; Bull. EC 9-1984, point 2.1.112.
[3] OJ L 208, 3.8.1984; Bull. EC 7/8-1984, point 2.1.173.
[4] Bull. EC 5-1984, point 2.1.178.
[5] OJ L 80, 24.3.1984; Bull. EC 3-1984, point 2.1.179.
[6] OJ C 132, 19.5.1983; Seventeenth General Report, point 540.
[7] OJ L 259, 15.9.1973.
[8] Seventeenth General Report, point 543.
[9] Bull. EC 2-1984, point 2.1.152.
[10] Seventeenth General Report, point 544.

and on the potential for strengthening international electricity interlinking, the aim being to promote CHP in industry and district heating networks and to ensure greater integration of electricity grids in the Community, especially as regards those countries which are not interconnected at present.

Nuclear energy

528. The Commission completed preparation of the Community's third illustrative nuclear programme,[1] having informed the Council of its intention of drawing up such a programme, in accordance with Article 40 of the Euratom Treaty, in a communication on the nuclear part of the Community's energy strategy.[2] The purpose of the programme, which deals with the industrial and economic aspects of the future development of nuclear energy in the Community, is to set out the Commission's perspective on nuclear energy between now and the end of the century, for the benefit not only of governments and economic operators in the Member States but also of any other interested bodies.

529. Following lengthy discussions with the parties concerned, on 14 November the Commission transmitted to the Council an amended version[3] of its proposed amendment of Chapter VI of Title Two of the Euratom Treaty (the capter concerning supplies),[4] account being taken of the developments that had occurred in the context of political cooperation. The Member States having reached a consensus on the transfer of nuclear materials in the political cooperation context, the Commission also transmitted two proposals for Regulations to implement the new provisions of Chapter VI.[5]

530. On 2 May the Commission transmitted to the Council a communication on the transport of radioactive materials in which it discusses all aspects (regulatory, technical, administrative and radiological) of this type of transport.[6]

---

[1] Bull. EC 11-1984, point 2.1.144.
[2] Sixteenth General Report, point 523.
[3] Bull. EC 11-1984, point 1.3.1 et seq.
[4] OJ C 330, 16.12.1982; Sixteenth General Report, point 525.
[5] Bull. EC 12-1984.
[6] Bull. EC 5-1984, point 2.1.186.

Supply Agency

531. The general downturn which, since 1981, has been affecting activities on the primary markets for both natural uranium and enrichment services persisted in 1984 as a result of the unexpectedly sharp cutbacks in the nuclear programmes. However, the high cost of financing stocks led numerous undertakings to reduce them, thus maintaining activities in the secondary market (resales and miscellaneous arrangements).

Consequently, only one long-term contract for the supply of natural uranium and four long-term enrichment contracts were concluded out of a total of around 130 contracts signed by the Supply Agency in 1984 (50 for the supply of uranium and 80 for the provision of enrichment services and special fissile materials).

532. There were no serious problems as regards the supply of nuclear fuels and related services, a situation likely to remain unchanged in the short and medium term. In the longer term, however, investments will be necessary to offset the gradual exhausting of mines currently in operation. With regard to natural uranium, the Community depended on imports for over 75% of its supplies in 1984. Of the seven external supplier countries, no one country accounted for more than 25% of the total supplies. Since the market continued to be oversupplied the downward trend in prices expressed in US dollars persisted: the average price paid by electricity utilities for natural uranium under medium and long-term contracts should be less than USD 31 per pound of U_3O_8, the average price of 1983. Spot-market prices again fell sharply from USD 24 in December 1983 to USD 16.5 in October 1984.

533. The market for special fissile materials continued to reflect the existence of stockpiles and transactions on the secondary market for toll enrichment services, enrichment plants having a surplus capacity at world level. The largest supplier of enrichment services, the US Department of Energy, proposed a new type of contract (the 'Utility Services Contract') with interesting conditions for the conversion of current contracts; nevertheless, only a small number of Community clients took advantage of this, the majority obtaining supplies from plants within the Community.

Section 15

Safeguards

534. In 1984 the Euratom Safeguards Directorate conducted physical and accounting checks on average stocks of over 77 tonnes of plutonium, 13 tonnes of high-enriched uranium, 17 000 tonnes of low-enriched uranium and 98 000 tonnes of natural uranium, depleted uranium, thorium and heavy water. These stocks were held in more than 540 nuclear installations in the Community and gave rise to over 325 000 entry lines. The checks carried out gave no reason to suspect that any diversion had taken place.

535. The inspections carried out by the Safeguards Directorate [1] accounted for almost 6 200 man-days, plus travelling time. The increase over the previous year was made possible by the rationalization of inspection procedures brought about by the new arrangements for the allocation of tasks and responsibilities within the Directorate. [2]

536. Relations with the International Atomic Energy Agency continue to develop satisfactorily. The Liaison Committees referred to in Article 25 of the Protocol to the Agreement of 5 April 1973 [3] met twice at high level and twice at a lower level. The high-level Liaison Committee referred to in Article 25 of the Protocol to the Agreement of 27 July 1978 (France) [4] met for the first time in September.

537. The Euratom/IAEA working party [5] set up by the high-level Liaison Committee with the task of clarifying certain points relating to inspection goals met several times in 1984. A paper on the Euratom inspection goals was given at the European Safeguards Research and Development Association symposium held in Venice in May.

Over the years, the Commission has endeavoured to implement gradually the Community's obligations under the verification agreements with the IAEA. It has concentrated mainly on the agreement concerning those Member States

---

[1] Seventeenth General Report, point 554.
[2] Seventeenth General Report, point 559.
[3] OJ L 51, 22.2.1978; Bull. EC 2-1977, point 2.2.26.
[4] Twelfth General Report, point 394.
[5] Seventeenth General Report, point 557.

which do not have nuclear weapons, the agreements concerning the nuclear-weapon Member States being more recent.

538. All nuclear installations in the non-nuclear-weapon Member States are subject to IAEA inspection. A 'facility attachment', which defines inspection procedures, has to be negotiated with the IAEA in respect of each one of these installations. The negotiation process is complicated and inevitably takes a considerable amount of time, given, among other things the large number of installations concerned.

539. The Commission is able to report, however, that considerable progress has been made over the past year with measures being agreed with the Agency to simplify and accelerate negotiation. It therefore expects that almost all of the facility attachments still pending will be able to take effect in the near future, the only exceptions being particularly complicated individual cases or new installations.

A general approach designed to simplify the preparation of facility attachments for those installations (around 180) holding only small quantities of nuclear material has been agreed with the IAEA. Efforts have also been made to negotiate facility attachments for Community uranium-enrichment plants of the gas-centrifuge type, one of which is in the Netherlands, the other in the United Kingdom. In the case of the latter, this constitutes part of the implementation of the agreement concerning the United Kingdom. The documents will take account of the agreement reached at international level during the Hexapartite Safeguards Project. [1] The negotiations are now well advanced and the facility attachments concerned are likely to enter into force in 1985.

---

[1] Seventeenth General Report, point 558.

Section 16

Nuclear safety

Main developments

540. *The Commission continued its activities under the programme described in its communication to the Council concerning the Community's role as regards the safety of nuclear installations and the protection of public health.* [1]

Radiation protection

541. On 3 September the Council again amended the basic safety standards for the health protection of the general public and workers against the dangers of ionizing radiation, [2] updating Annexes I and III to the Directive of 15 July 1980 [3] in the light of the most recently available scientific data.

542. On 26 October the Commission sent Parliament its second Report on the application of Article 37 of the Euratom Treaty, covering the last half of 1982 and the whole of 1983. This Report was drawn up at the request of Parliament. [4]

543. On 19 December the Council approved, [5] Parliament having delivered its opinion, [6] the multiannual research and training programme in the field of radiation protection (1985-89), which the Commission had proposed in June 1983. [7]

Plant safety

544. On 19 December the Council agreed to entrust to the Joint Research Centre the execution of the multiannual research programme on reactor safety (1984-87) [8] proposed by the Commission in June 1983. [9]

---

[1] Seventeenth General Report, point 560.
[2] OJ L 265, 5.10.1984; Bull. EC 9-1984, point 2.1.55.
[3] OJ L 246, 17.9.1980.
[4] OJ C 27, 15.12.1980; Resolution of 20.11.1980 on the siting of nuclear power stations in frontier regions.
[5] Point 579 of this Report.
[6] OJ C 46, 20.2.1984; Bull. EC 1-1984, point 2.1.105.
[7] OJ C 179, 6.7.1983; Seventeenth General Report, points 562 and 596.
[8] Point 566 of this Report.
[9] OJ C 250, 19.9.1983; Seventeenth General Report, point 563.

Radioactive waste

545. On 31 January the Council took a formal decision adopting a research programme on the decommissioning of nuclear installations. [1]

546. On 19 December the Council approved the implementation of a new multiannual research programme on the management and storage of radioactive waste (1985-89), [2] which the Commission had laid before it in May. [3]

547. On 14 March Parliament adopted a resolution on the dumping of chemical and radioactive waste at sea. [4]

Transport of radioactive materials

548. On 2 May the Commission sent the Council and Parliament a report on the transport of radioactive materials within the Community, describing the present situation and indicating the approach it intended to adopt in the future. [5]

549. Referring to the collision which occurred in the North Sea in August and resulted in the sinking of a cargo vessel carrying radioactive material, Parliament adopted a resolution on 13 September relating *inter alia* to the transport of radioactive materials and waste. [6]

International action

550. A cooperation agreement between the European Atomic Energy Community and Switzerland's Société Coopérative Nationale pour l'Entreposage des Déchets Radioactifs concerning R&D relating to the management of radioactive waste was signed in Brussels on 21 June. [7]

On 20 September the European Atomic Energy Community and the United States Nuclear Regulatory Commission signed an agreement in Brussels concerning research on nuclear safety (particularly reactor safety) to replace an earlier agreement signed in 1979 which had expired on 18 March 1984. [8]

---

[1] OJ L 36, 8.2.1984; Bull. EC 1-1984, point 2.1.110.
[2] Point 563 of this Report.
[3] OJ C 166, 26.6.1984; Bull. EC 4-1984, point 2.1.129.
[4] OJ C 104, 16.4.1984; Bull. EC 3-1984, point 2.4.17.
[5] Bull. EC 5-1984, point 2.1.186.
[6] OJ C 274, 15.10.1984; Bull. EC 9-1984, point 2.4.9.
[7] Bull. EC 6-1984, point 2.2.30.
[8] Bull. EC 9-1984, point 2.1.116.

Section 17

Research and development

Main developments

551. *Despite the budgetary difficulties affecting the Community, the year has been notable for a desire to pursue and apply the guidelines and goals of the 1984-87 framework programme for Community research, development and demonstration activities, and, in particular, to point them more firmly in the direction of the new technologies.*

Although research policy is recognized as having a prime role in the construction of Europe, the Council was unable to see its way to adopting the programmes and financial indicators initially proposed by the Commission. However, given the current economic situation and despite the indecision which had prevailed up to then, on 19 December the Council did approve (subject to Parliament's views on some of them) the programmes on fusion, radiation protection, radioactive waste, biotechnology, stimulation, Brite, and non-nuclear energy, and concluded that the appropriations necessary for their implementation should amount to a total of 1 255 million ECU.

The boost given to research, to development, and to increased expertise in new technologies of the future was most clearly seen in the following areas: Esprit, the European strategic programme for research and development in information technology, which, over the period 1984-88, will involve the Community in any outlay of 750 million ECU, a sum to be matched by industry; and the Brite and biotechnology programmes, the latter promising to have a favourable effect on a number of Community sectors, such as industry and agriculture, and to promote the gradual provision of the infrastructure needed for expansion.

The start of the JRC multiannual research programme (1984-87) has enabled previous research projects to be continued and an increasing number of processes, experimental methods and new materials to be developed.

In the field of nuclear fusion, JET, the largest tokamak in the world, has produced excellent results, including several absolute records for obtaining high-temperature plasma.

However, the picture would not be complete if no mention were made of the constant efforts undertaken to prevent research being dispersed, to promote

*collaboration by increased concertation and coordination, and the harmoniz-
ation required before the industrial markets can be opened up.*

*It is with the same desire to support the 'sectoral' Community research pro-
grammes that the stimulation programme exists to facilitate exchanges of
experience and information, desirable measures of interpenetration and the
mobility of research workers. The experimental phase of this programme was
successfully completed in 1984. On 19 December the Council, by deciding on
a four-year stimulation plan, demonstrated its interest in this new form of
action being pursued.*

*The general agreement reached by the Council in December, which links the
horizontal stimulation action to a number of specialized research programmes,
thus ends the year on a note of hope commensurate with the financial commitments entered into.*

Community R&D policy

Framework programme for 1984-87

552. At the Fontainebleau European Council [1] and at the Council meetings of
29 June and 6 November, the need to increase the proportion of Community
resources devoted to financing priority Community research and development
activities was emphasized, in particular the activities broadly described in the
1984-87 framework programme adopted in 1983 [2] (but without mention of the
financial requirement originally estimated overall at 3 750 million ECU).

However, because of budgetary constraints and despite the efforts of the
Commission to establish a hierarchy of priorities for the programme proposals, [3] which would enable the most urgent actions or those with appropriations already included in the 1984 budget to get under way, it was only on 19
December that the Council approved implementation of the programme and
agreed on the sums to be allocated to each action, which were, in fact, less
than those originally proposed by the Commission.

The Council's approval respects the spirit, the selection criteria and the scientific
and technical aims of the framework programme. In addition, the Council

---

[1] Bull. EC 6-1984, point 1.1.6.
[2] OJ C 208, 4.8.1983; Seventeenth General Report, point 568.
[3] Bull. EC 5-1984, point 2.1.187.

undertook to re-examine and, if necessary, revise these programmes, taking account of its previous commitment to a progressive increase in the expenditure for Community R&D activities.

On 19 January Parliament adopted a resolution on efficiency and choice in Community financing of research and industry. [1]

Structures and procedures

553. In an attempt to make the present system more efficient and rational, the Council, acting on a proposal from the Commission, [2] decided on 29 June to alter the structures and procedures for the management and coordination of the Community's research, development and demonstration activities. [3] Under this Decision, Management and Coordination Advisory Committees (CGCs) under the aegis of the Commission were established to replace the Crest subcommittees, most of the Advisory Committees on Programme Management (ACPMs) and the Concerted Action Committees (Comac).

554. On 24 May the Commission decided to amend [4] its 1971 Decision on the reorganization of the JRC [5] with a view to setting up a Board of Governors and a Scientific Council to assist and advise it.

Stimulation of European scientific and technical cooperation and interchange

555. In the light of the results of the two-year Community experimental project set up in June 1983, [6] on which the Council expressed its satisfaction in February, [7] the Commission sent the Council on 16 April a plan to stimulate European scientific and technical cooperation and interchange for the period 1985-88, [8] which was endorsed by Parliament [9] and the Economic and Social

---

[1] OJ C 46, 20.2.1984.
[2] OJ C 113, 27.4.1983; Seventeenth General Report, point 570.
[3] OJ L 177, 4.7.1984; Bull. EC 6-1984, point 2.1.138.
[4] OJ L 177, 4.7.1984; Bull. EC 5-1984, point 2.1.189.
[5] OJ L 16, 20.1.1971; OJ L 319, 16.11.1982.
[6] OJ L 181, 6.7.1983; Seventeenth General Report, point 569.
[7] Bull. EC 2-1984, point 2.1.164.
[8] OJ C 142, 29.5.1984; Bull. EC 4-1984, point 2.1.132.
[9] OJ C 315, 26.11.1984; Bull. EC 10-1984, point 2.1.140.

Committee [1] in October. On 19 December the Council agreed to the implementation of this programme within an appropriation estimated at 60 million ECU.

556. The Commission made a second call for proposals concerning the experimental project [2] in February. [3] While 5 000 research teams showed an interest, 620 requests for Community support were made and 86 accepted. These will benefit from the types of support provided for (research grants, subsidies, twinning of laboratories in different countries).

Horizontal activities

557. As called for in the 'Plan of action relating to the evaluation of Community research and development programmes' adopted by the Council in June 1983, [4] the Commission embarked upon further retrospective evaluations of the results of Community R&D programmes by teams of independent outside experts. The first wholly financed programme to be subjected to outside evaluation was the JRC Ispra establishment's programme on remote sensing from space.

The Commission also evaluated various R&D activities, namely the environment programme (comprising an 'own research' project, a shared-cost project and several concerted-action projects), the COST 50 project on materials for gas turbines and the COST 501 project on high-temperature materials for fossil energy conversion, the medicine and public health programme and the raw materials programme.

Internal and external R&D evaluation methods have been improved, and exchanges of information have been made easier through frequent contact with experts.

558. Under the second research programme on forecasting and assessment in science and technology (FAST II) (1983-87) [5] work on research with good prospects was started in areas laid down by the Council (relationships between technology, employment and work, changes in services and technological development, new industrial systems in communications and food, integrated development of renewable natural resources). [6]

---

[1] OJ C 343; 24.12.1984; Bull. EC 10-1984; point 2.1.140.
[2] OJ L 181, 6.7.1983; Seventeenth General Report, point 569.
[3] OJ C 29, 4.2.1984.
[4] OJ C 213, 9.8.1983; Seventeenth General Report, point 571.
[5] OJ L 293, 25.10.1983; Seventeenth General Report, point 572.
[6] See FAST: Aims and work programme, doc. XII/201-84.

Following a call for proposals in March, [1] study contracts were concluded with 50 European research centres. At the same time, a network of 10 national research units was set up to strengthen the links between FAST and the Member States.

International cooperation

559. European cooperation in the field of scientific and technical research (COST) was strengthened by the conclusion of agreements relating to five concerted-action projects on the environment. [2]

The Council also adopted two decisions on concerted-action projects: one on food [3] and the other on the use of lignocellulose-containing by-products and other plant residues for animal feeding. [4]

In addition, the Commission has requested the Council to give it a remit to negotiate two framework agreements for scientific and technological cooperation between the Community and Sweden and between the Community and Switzerland. [5]

The Community's main R&D objectives

Energy

Nuclear energy from fusion

560. One of the most remarkable European achievements in research on the peaceful uses of atomic energy, the JET (Joint European Torus) project, was inaugurated at Culham, Oxfordshire, in the United Kingdom, on 9 April. [6]

561. On 22 May the Commission sent the Council a proposal for a Decision on a research and training programme (1985-89) on controlled thermonuclear

---

[1] OJ C 66, 7.3.1984.
[2] OJ l 339, 10.12.1984; Bull. EC 12-1984.
[3] OJ L 151, 7.6.1984; Bull. EC 5-1984, point 2.1.191.
[4] OJ L 103, 16.4.1984; Bull. EC 4-1984, point 2.1.123.
[5] Bull. EC 11-1984, point 2.1.149.
[6] Bull. EC 4-1984, point 1.4.1 et seq.

fusion.[1] This proposal revises the fusion programme for 1982-86, adopted in May 1982,[2] with a view to obtaining the necessary funds for extending the performance of JET and preparing the technological basis for NET (Next European Torus) and its conceptual design. The new programme includes: extending the performance of JET through the use of powerful heating systems and continuing the experiments in progress; further work on the complementary programme of plasma physics by associated laboratories, with the completion of five devices to tackle the particular problems of plasma confinement that cannot be studied in JET; research in NET to demonstrate the technological feasibility of fusion. On 19 December the Council agreed to the implementation of this programme, though it limited the appropriations considered necessary to 690 million ECU.

The Commission also sent the Council a proposal on the setting-up of a tritium-handling laboratory at Ispra.[3] The staff complement and appropriations considered necessary (12.5 million ECU) have already been provided for in the JRC's multiannual programme for 1984-87.[4]

In 1984 JET induced currents of up to 3.7 megamperes in hydrogen or deuterium and produced plasmas at temperatures as high as 40 million degrees. The maximum confinement time (a measure of the effectiveness of the confinement of the magnetic field) was 0.6 of a second, which in itself is a record and represents a third of that needed in a fusion reactor. Density and temperature will have to be increased in roughly the same proportions. These results were obtained with an ohmic heating power of only 3 megawatts.

The studies conducted on the Euratom-IPP association's Asdex tokamak improved understanding of discharge phenomena both under conditions of intense heating and great density and in the boundary layer. The detailed studies carried out on the Euratom-CEA association's TFR tokamak enabled particle and energy diffusion to be analysed in a plasma subjected to high-power auxiliary heating. Finally, the continuing work on plasma heating by radio frequencies, mainly at the associated laboratories in Culham, Frascati and Grenoble, led to a better understanding of the physical processes underlying this method of heating.

562.   Under its new (1984-87) programme[4] the JRC continued to study reactor materials technology and safety in the following areas—irradiation of austenitic

---

[1]   OJ C 198, 27.7.1984; Bull. EC 5-1984, points 2.1.194 to 2.1.196.
[2]   OJ L 157, 8.6.1982; Sixteenth General Report, point 555.
[3]   OJ C 198, 27.7.1984; Bull. EC 6-1984, point 2.1.196.
[4]   OJ L 3, 5.1.1984.

steels (especially in the Ispra cyclotron), experiments on materials for the breeding blanket, involvement in the work on NET (preliminary project and safety aspects).

Nuclear energy from fission

563. The second shared-cost research programme on the management and storage of radioactive waste (1980-84) [1] has now ended. More than 130 different research activities have yielded results on, for example, the conditioning, identification and storage of waste in stable geological formations underground. The joint studies on the safety of geological storage in particular (the Pagis project) are dealt with in a first report intended to provide a methodological approach for the Community. On 3 May the Commission sent the Council a proposal for a third shared-cost research programme (1985-89). [2] On 19 December the Council approved the implementation of this five-year programme and assessed the appropriations necessary at 120 million ECU, including those allocated to the radiation protection programme.

The JRC began work in the same area in close coordination with the activities under the shared-cost programme. A budget of 49 million ECU has been allocated for the period 1984-87.

Internationally, there was further cooperation with the International Atomic Energy Agency and the Nuclear Energy Agency. A joint NEA-Commission report entitled 'Geological storage of radioactive waste' has been published. Cooperation continued with Atomic Energy of Canada Ltd and the US Department of Energy, while an agreement was concluded with Cedra (the Swiss national intermediate waste storage cooperative). [3]

On 19 January Parliament adopted a resolution on the need for Community measures for the final storage of radioactive waste and the reprocessing of irradiated nuclear fuel. [4]

564. On 31 January the Council formally adopted the second research programme concerning the decommissioning of nuclear installations (1984-88). [5] The 12 million ECU allocated to the programme will permit the full-scale

---

[1] OJ L 78, 25.3.1980; Fourteenth General Report, point 494.
[2] OJ C 166, 26.6.1984; Bull. EC 4-1984, point 2.1.129.
[3] Bull. EC 6-1984, point 2.2.30.
[4] OJ C 46, 20.2.1984.
[5] OJ L 36, 8.2.1984; Bull. EC 1-1984, point 2.1.110.

testing of certain of the techniques used in decommissioning obsolete nuclear equipment which has been removed from service in the Member States.

565. The experiments on the characteristics and behaviour of transuranium elements such as plutonium and americium were stepped up at the JRC's Karlsruhe establishment. They comprise the preparation, irradiation inside a reactor and laboratory analysis of specific targets. Progress was made in the analysis of in-pile behaviour and in the large-scale experiments on the dispersion—in the event of fire—of actinide aerosols within a leak-tight plutonium-handling containment.

In the field of the guarantee and monitoring of fissile materials, in addition to the setting-up of a data-processing system linking various laboratories, new non-destructive testing equipment is being installed at Ispra to enable the fissile content of materials to be determined (Perla project).

566. As part of its research into nuclear reactor safety, the JRC's Ispra establishment brought a data bank on line to act as a clearing house for information on abnormal events within nuclear installations. The strength of large steel plates incorporating certain faults was tested (PISC II), and the programme of tests on the structural integrity of reactor pressure vessels (one-fifth scale) entered its experimental stage. The large test loop for simulating loss-of-coolant accidents in water-cooled reactors (LOBI-MOD 2) has now been fully developed at Ispra, and the first tests on small breaks have been carried out.

The work on fast reactors has concentrated on an analysis of the consequences of a lack of sodium flow in a reactor core and the removal of residual heat from a destroyed fuel bed (FARO test installation, PAHR project). The programme of tests carried out jointly in this area by NCR (USA), PNC (Japan) and the JRC ended in December. Preparations have been made for the experimental study of equipment structures subjected to dynamic and seismic forces.

In addition, after about 20 years of intensive operation, the high-flux reactor vessel at Petten was replaced this year by an improved model and the reactor was operating normally again in December.

Finally, the shared-cost research on reactor safety was hampered by the absence of any decision on the Commission's proposal for a new multiannual programme (1984-87).[1] On 19 December the Council agreed to entrust the execution of this programme to the Joint Research Centre.

---

[1] OJ C 250, 19.9.1983; Seventeenth General Report, point 581.

Non-nuclear energy

567. A good number of research projects under the second non-nuclear energy R&D programme [1] were completed while a decision adopting a new programme for 1983-87 [2] was awaited from the Council; at the same time the absence of a decision curtailed some projects which ought to have been extended in view of the progress that had been made by them and the promise they offered. On 19 December, however, the Council approved the four-year programme, limiting the sum considered necessary to 175 million ECU.

In the mean time it was felt to be appropriate to widen the range of fields covered by the programme proposed in 1983 to include hydrocarbons research. The Commission therefore sent the Council, on 24 May, a proposal for a Decision on a shared-cost R&D programme (1984-87) in the field of optimization of production and utilization of hydrocarbons [3] as a complement to the R&D programme in the field of non-nuclear energy.

In the solar energy field, a dozen conferences and symposia were held and almost 40 publications issued on photovoltaic conversion, biomass, wind power, solar architecture and solar heating. Fifteen photovoltaic pilots plants, with outputs ranging from 30 to 300 kW, have been completed and are now operational. These plants cater for needs as diverse as the desalination and disinfection of drinking water in the Mediterranean area, rural electricity supplies, powering a television transmitter and various items of electronic equipment in an airport control tower, the production of hydrogen for industrial purposes, the supply of electricity to a public recreation centre and swimming pool, and even the laying-on of electricity for a village in the tropics.

Six conferences and symposia and numerous publications on energy saving have dealt with specific subjects such as the saving to be made in industry and buildings, building materials and electric-storage batteries. Significant results have also been obtained from advanced technologies such as heat pumps for household and industrial use, high-capacity batteries for electric vehicles, internal combustion engines and fluidized-bed combustion.

Substantial progress has been made on geothermal energy by exploring new low- and high-enthalpy geothermal fields, developing bottom-drilling equipment, generating electricity by unconventional means and experimenting with the mechanics of hot, dry rocks.

---

[1] OJ L 231, 13.9.1979; Thirteenth General Report, point 416.
[2] OJ C 218, 13.8.1983; Seventeenth General Report, point 582.
[3] OJ C 154, 14.6.1984; Bull. EC 5-1984, point 2.1.197.

The models developed from energy-system analysis have been fully developed and perfected so that they can be used better on a Community scale. Specific studies have mainly concentrated on energy consumption up to the year 2000.

The JRC has been active in two main areas. The tests on solar energy systems have resulted in new specifications for the qualification tests on photovoltaic conversion systems and the development of new measuring methods for heat collectors. And management of energy in the habitat is being developed in close cooperation with the International Energy Agency.

Raw materials

568. The main results obtained in 1984 from the 1982-85 Community R&D programme [1] in the raw materials sector, and more particularly from the subprogramme dealing with metals and mineral substances, are as follows: in exploration, the discovery of important signs of scheelite (tungsten ore) in Sicily and tantalum in Greenland, and the identification of highly favourable lead-zinc sectors in Ireland; great progress in developing methods of identifying and analysing metals in the platinum group; and in ore processing, the development of advanced technologies for complex ores and for synthesizing new reagents for use in the flotation of oxidized lead-zinc ores.

Information-exchange symposia on oxidized and complex-ore processing techniques were attended by representatives both of the Commission and of two North American public bodies—the US Bureau of Mines and Canmet. Preliminary contact was also established with the People's Republic of China with a view to cooperation on ore processing and prospecting.

Of the 77 contracts under way since 1981 under the recycling of urban and industrial waste subprogramme, 21 had given rise to industrial applications and 18 to patents.

The emergence of a new family of permanently magnetic Nd-Fe-B materials has caused the initial subprogramme on substitution and materials technology to take on a new bias towards this sector. These materials open up new industrial horizons, particularly for the manufacture of permanent-magnet motors or power generators.

Industrial ceramics are being studied intensively in order to optimize powder technology and the reliability and reproducibility of the finished products.

---

[1] OJ L 174, 21.6.1982.

In the subprogramme on wood, seven contracts were concluded with Swedish bodies under the 1983 cooperation agreement. Several promising results have already been obtained, especially in one of the crucial sectors of the industry: small sawn wood.

Industry

569. In a Decision adopted on 29 February the Commission set up an Industrial Research and Development Advisory Committee (Irdac) to advise on the preparation and implementation of Community policy on industrial R&D (including its industrial and social repercussions).[1] This Committee replaces the Advisory Committee on Industrial Research and Development, which was set up in 1978.[2]

Industrial technologies

570. In anticipation of a Council Decision on an action programme concerning basic research in industrial technologies for Europe (Brite),[3] Commission departments assisted in setting up multinational groups comprising at least one industrial partner and R&D teams from at least two Member States. When the time comes, these groups may submit project proposals. Information briefs of a non-confidential nature on other similar or related projects were sent to all those who had shown interest (more than 3 000, over half of them firms). On 19 December the Council approved the implementation of the Brite programme (1985-88) with an overall budget limited to 125 million ECU).

The high-temperature materials (HTM) programme at the JRC's Petten establishment this year commenced a new four-year period with activities in the three areas of steels and alloys, industrial components and, recently, engineering ceramics. At the same time two other projects are being developed: the HTM Data Bank, which is now in operation, and the HTM Information Centre, which provides the necessary links and exchanges, especially with industry.

In the field of applied metrology and reference materials,[4] the programme covered 70 applied metrology projects relating to such aspects as the calibration of gas and water meters, the plotting of electrical units, the measurements

---

[1] OJ L 66, 8.3.1984; Bull. EC 2-1984, point 2.1.159.
[2] OJ L 203, 27.7.1978.
[3] OJ C 230, 27.8.1983; Seventeenth General Report, point 585.
[4] OJ L 26, 28.1.1983.

required in microelectronics and the properties of double glazing. The programme also enabled 23 reference materials to be developed and certified, which brings the number now offered by the Community Bureau of References to 134. [1]

In this area, the JRC's Geel establishment has started to operate as a storage and distribution centre for some of the reference materials under the relevant programme. This establishment is also developing 'biological reference materials'. In the nuclear reference materials sector, the establishment is about to certify a new reference material, uranium oxide U_3O_8, with the aim of standardizing, in conjunction with the US National Bureau of Standards, isotopes analyses using the non-destructive γ-spectroscopy method.

571. Steel research and pilot and demonstration projects under Article 55 of the ECSC Treaty continued this year. On the criteria defined in the guidelines for aid to steel research for 1981-85, [2] 74 projects were selected from the 200 proposals received. [3] The financial assistance granted totalled 17.5 million ECU, shared virtually equally between production and product research. As provided in the pilot and demonstration project programme, [4] the Commission decided to grant financial support (of the order of 6.4 million ECU) to seven projects relating mainly to the continuous casting and working of steel. [2]

572. In the field of technical research on coal, the Commission granted 19 million ECU under Article 55 to 46 research projects relating to mining techniques, the use and upgrading of coal and the dissemination of knowledge. [5]

Under the two stages of the biomolecular engineering programme (1982-86), [6] 52 new contracts were selected, for a budget of 4.5 million ECU. [7] These contracts were divided between six priority sectors, and the first European 'centres of excellence' were set up for work aimed at promoting new applications in agriculture and the food processing industries. At the same time 52 contracts were signed for post-doctoral training, covering wider areas of biotechnology.

---

[1] The full catalogue of reference materials available can be obtained free of charge from the Community Bureau of Reference, rue de la Loi 200, 1049 Brussels (DG XII/C/3).

[2] OJ C 99, 2.5.1981.

[3] Bull. EC 6-1984, point 2.1.142; Bull. EC 10-1984.

[4] OJ C 81, 24.3.1983.

[5] Bull. EC 3-1984, point 2.1.191; Bull. EC 9-1984, point 2.1.119.

[6] OJ L 375, 30.12.1981; Fifteenth General Report, point 594; OJ L 305, 8.11.1983; Seventeenth General Report, point 587.

[7] Research and training programme in biomolecular engineering, Catalogue of contracts, August 1984 (Office for Official Publications, Luxembourg, of DG XII/F/2, Commission of the European Communities, Brussels).

573. Since the biomolecular engineering programme clearly demonstrated the potential and usefulness of Community action aimed at promoting the use of modern biology in agriculture and industry, on 11 May the Commission sent the Council a proposal for a Decision concerning a Community research action programme in the field of biotechnology (1985-89). On 19 December the Council approved this proposal, for which it considered an appropriation of 55 million ECU necessary.

574. On 12 November the Council adopted two recommendations on telecommunications. [1]

Esprit

575. On 28 February the Council adopted the Esprit programme (European strategic programme for R&D in information technology). [2]

Agriculture

576. The Commission has been responsible for implementing [3] the joint research programmes and the programmes for coordinating agricultural research (1984-88) adopted by the Council in December 1983. [4] The financing considered necessary for the full duration of the programme amounts to 30 million ECU (rather than the 65 million proposed by the Commission), which meant that the Commission had to make a choice of priorities and scale down various programmes, some of which will have to be reduced to no more than coordination of national efforts.

In accordance with Parliament's wishes, [5] the Commission studied the possibility of carrying out a research programme aimed at reducing agricultural surpluses. This showed the need for a preparatory phase to investigate the situation in the various sectors concerned (milk, sugar, starch, etc.) and determine the state of the art concerning the processing of plant products upstream of their various potential outlets (food, energy, fine chemicals, etc.). An appropriation of one million ECU was allotted to this initial phase, which it is estimated will last one year.

---

[1] Point 196 of this Report.
[2] Point 195 of this Report.
[3] Bull. EC 3-1984, point 2.1.188.
[4] OJ L 358, 22.12.1983, Seventeenth General Report, point 592.
[5] OJ C 242, 12.9.1983.

Environment

577. On 1 March, after receiving Parliament's endorsement,[1] the Council adopted[2] the Commission's proposal[3] — prompted by the need to boost research on acid rain and toxic waste — for a Decision to revise the 1981-85 environment R&D programme[4] and to proceed with COST projects in this field. The 1981-85 programme consists of two subprogrammes: environmental protection and climatology. Environmental protection projects were launched in the following areas: effects of pollutants on human health and the environment; ways of reducing and preventing pollution, nuisances and waste; and the protection, conservation and management of the natural environment.

About 50 new contracts have been concluded since the invitation to submit proposals for the climatology subprogramme[5] — in the two research areas 'understanding climate' and 'man-climate interactions'. Research is continuing on possible changes to the climate as a result of the growing accumulation of CO in the atmosphere caused by the use of fossil fuels, which could affect our agricultural and water resources.

Research into acid rain, in which the JRC is involved, was intensified, and close cooperation established with the new European Centre for the Prevention of Air Pollution, Karlsruhe, with special reference to the study of pollutant migration.

578. The programme of action on environmental research being conducted as part of the JRC's multiannual programme for 1984-87[6] is more particularly concerned with the protection of the environment, the use of aerospace remote-sensing techniques and industrial hazards. The remote sensing from space programme is targeted on agriculture, ground-use and the protection of the sea. The industrial hazards programme has this year included the definition of experimental projects on the analysis of risks, structural reliability and industrial waste.

---

[1] OJ C 77, 19.3.1984.
[2] OJ L 71, 14.3.1984; Bull. EC 2-1984, point 2.1.162.
[3] OJ C 274, 13.10.1983; Seventeenth General Report, point 594.
[4] OJ L 101, 11.4.1981; Fifteenth General Report, point 589.
[5] OJ C 4, 6.1.1983.
[6] OJ L 3, 5.1.1984.

Health and safety

579. The multiannual research and training programme in the field of radiation protection (1980-84) [1] entered its final stage. About 300 contracts covering more than 400 individual research projects were concluded during its lifetime, dealing in particular this year with neutron dosimetry, the behaviour of radio-nuclides in estuaries, 'models' of lungs to simulate the inhalation of radioactive substances, biochemistry and the genetics of DNA repair, and quality mainten-ance in medical diagnosis. On 19 December the Council approved the pro-gramme for 1985-89, [2] which was endorsed by Parliament in January; [3] the appropriations required, together with those for the radioactive waste pro-gramme, were put at 120 million ECU.

580. Community coordination of research on a national level as part of the R&D programme in the field of medicine and public health (1982-86) [4] reached both budgetary and management saturation point.

Parliament asked the Commission to put forward an emergency Community programme of research into the measures to combat AIDS (acquired immune deficiency syndrome) in a resolution adopted on 20 January. [3] Upon investi-gation it proved that Community coordination should be possible under the 1982-86 programme.

The Commission and the Canadian Government signed an agreement in December to promote cooperation in medicine and public health research.

581. The sum allocated this year to ECSC social research amounted to 8 million ECU. The first financial aid was granted to the fifth research programme on industrial hygiene in mines. [5] The fourth programmes on ergonomics [6] and technical control of nuisances and pollution at the place of work in the environment of iron and steel works [7] are reaching their final stages; a proposal for a new ergonomics programme has been submitted for consultation.

---

[1] OJ L 78, 25.3.1980; Fourteenth General Report, point 494.
[2] OJ C 179, 6.7.1983; Seventeenth General Report, point 596.
[3] OJ C 46, 20.2.1984.
[4] OJ L 248, 24.8.1982; Sixteenth General Report, point 588.
[5] OJ C 332, 8.12.1983.
[6] OJ C 161, 1.7.1980.
[7] OJ C 147, 13.6.1979.

Development aid

582. The programme of research and development in the field of science and technology for development (1983-86) [1] entered is operational phase. Following three calls for proposals, [2] 136 projects were selected, requiring Community financing of the order of 18 million ECU.

583. The new heading — covering 2 million ECU — entered in the 1984 budget to finance scientific cooperation projects, especially with developing countries linked to the Community by cooperation agreements but not benefiting from a financial protocol, enabled a number of projects to be financed in Brazil, the People's Republic of China, India, Israel and the Asean countries, for instance. Exploratory contacts were made with other countries (including Mexico, Yugoslavia and Pakistan) to identify needs and areas suitable for scientific cooperation.

---

[1] OJ L 352, 14.12.1982; Sixteenth General Report, point 554.
[2] Seventeenth General Report, point 599; OJ C 21, 28.1.1984; Bull. EC 1-1984, point 2.1.114.

Section 18

Industrial innovation and the information market

Main developments

584. The three-year plan for the transnational development of the support infrastructure for innovation, adopted at the end of 1983, and the five-year programme for the development of the specialized information market in Europe, adopted on 27 November, provide the Commission with a general framework in which to continue to take positive steps designed to equip the Community with mechanisms and new structures for cooperation in these two closely linked sectors.

Two Commission proposals to the Council, concerning respectively the establishment of a European loan system for financing innovation in small and medium-sized undertakings and more effective use of the results of Community research, have not yet been adopted. The first failed to win the unanimous approval of the Council, while the second is still the subject of discussions and negotiations as regards both its financial and its technical aspects.

The Commission will continue its efforts to ensure that these dossiers and those concerning the parameters directly affecting the capacity for innovation are brought to a successful conclusion, and to establish a genuine Community information policy.

Transnational supporting infrastructure for innovation and technology transfer

585. The Consultative Committee on Innovation and Technology Transfer set up as part of the three-year plan for the transnational development of the supporting infrastructure for innovation and technology transfer[1] took up its duties in early 1984. It met five times[2] and delivered favourable opinions on specific projects, some of which will receive Community aid. These include the

---

[1] OJ L 353, 15.12.1983; Seventeenth General Report, point 609.
[2] Bull. EC 2-1984, point 2.1.32; Bull. EC 5-1984, point 2.1.30; Bull. EC 6-1984, point 2.1.25; Bull. EC 9-1984, point 2.1.22; Bull. EC 12-1984.

founding of a European Association for the Transfer of Technology, Innovation and Industrial Information [1] and cooperation between organizations promoting technology transfer between small and medium-sized businesses. [2] A European inventors' federation was constituted in July. These activities are in line with the priorities set by the Commission in April, after they had been endorsed by the Committee. [3]

Financing of innovation

586. No agreement was reached in the Council [4] on the proposal concerning a European loan for the financing of innovation. [5] The European Venture Capital Association (EVCA) [6] expanded its activities, helping to organize the fifth symposium on the financing of innovation. [7] The study of the impact of taxation measures on innovation was continued. [8]

Promoting the utilization of research results

587. The work on harmonizing the system of contracts governing the dissemination, protection and exploitation of the results of jointly funded Community research has continued in accordance with the principles and aims of the communication on promoting the utilization of the results of Community-sponsored research and development, sent to the Council in 1983. [9] Almost 3 500 topics were processed in 1984, 25 patent applications were filed, two exploitation contracts signed, 40 exploitation files opened and 403 new abstracts incorporated into the Euro-Abstracts database (EABS). Forty or so inventions arising from Community research were presented at specialist exhibitions held in Birmingham and Düsseldorf.[10]

Finally, the method of desulphurizing the flue gases of fossil-fuel power stations devised at the JRC Ispra establishment resulted in a call for proposals on the

---

[1] Bull. EC 5-1984, points 2.1.31 and 2.1.32; Bull. EC 10-1984, point 2.1.31.
[2] OJ C 210, 10.8.1984.
[3] Bull. EC 4-1984, point 2.1.26.
[4] Bull. EC 1-1984, point 2.1.25; Bull. EC 6-1984, point 2.1.27.
[5] OJ C 178, 5.7.1983; OJ C 40, 15.2.1984; Seventeenth General Report, point 611.
[6] Seventeenth General Report, point 610; Bull. EC 5-1984, point 2.1.35.
[7] Bull. EC 10-1984, point 2.1.32.
[8] Seventeenth General Report, point 612.
[9] OJ C 99, 13.4.1983; Seventeenth General Report, point 608.
[10] Bull. EC 2-1984, point 2.1.34; Bull. EC 4-1984, point 2.1.7; Bull. EC 6-1984, point 2.1.26; Bull. EC 9-1984, point 2.1.23.

construction of a pilot plant intended experimentally to determine the technical and economic value of this process. [1]

Information market

588. Once Parliament[2] and the Economic and Social Committee[3] had delivered their opinions, the Council adopted the five-year programme (1984-88) for the development of the specialized information market in Europe on 27 November. [4] The priority areas for this programme were identified, and the measures to give effect to it are being worked out. [5]

589. The Commission continued to work on the setting up of an interinstitutional network of integrated services (Insis). [6] It launched pilot projects intended to spur the Community's high-technology computerized telecommunications industry and to promote the use of new technologies, particularly in the fields of electronic mail and videoconferencing.

590. On the basis of calls for proposals made in 1983[7] the Commission has concluded contracts with almost 25 European public and private bodies to set up new information services dealing with various specialist aspects of the energy sector. It has also helped to finance the setting up of new systems in the biotechnology, biomedicine, agriculture, energy and environment fields.

591. The Commission has launched an electronic document delivery programme (Docdel) to stimulate the use of state-of-the-art electronics in the publishing business. [8] The contracts governing the financing of 10 experiments were signed between January and August. Parallel to this the Commission has begun to prepare the digital communication system using the Apollo satellite[9] with the collaboration of the European Space Agency and the national posts and telecommunications administrations. This system would enable the cost of full-text documentation transmission to be reduced.

---

[1] OJ C 317, 28.11.1984; Bull. EC 11-1984, points 2.1.26 and 2.1.151.
[2] OJ C 117, 30.4.1984.
[3] OJ C 140, 28.5.1984.
[4] OJ L 314, 4.12.1984; Bull. EC 11-1984, point 2.1.25.
[5] Bull. EC 3-1984, point 2.1.33; Bull. EC 12-1984.
[6] Point 200 of this Report; OJ L 368, 28.12.1982; Seventeenth General Report, point 604.
[7] Seventeenth General Report, point 601.
[8] Bull. EC 1-1984, point 2.1.24.
[9] Apollo: Article procurement with on-line ordering; Bull. EC 5-1984, point 2.1.34; Bull. EC 7/8-1984, point 2.1.40.

Specialized information and the Euronet-Diane network [1]

592. The extension and development of the Euronet-Diane network was pursued in several directions:

(i) negotiations were conducted with Austria [2] and Norway [3] with a view to improving cooperation agreements; preliminary discussions were started with Yugoslavia; Spain and Portugal will join Euronet-Diane on accession to the Community;

(ii) at technical level the Euronet telecommunications network will be replaced by the end of 1985 by the interconnection of the networks set up by the national posts and telecommunications networks;

(iii) finally, the number of databases and banks available was increased to about 600; in 1984 50 Diane host computers served 5 000 users for a total of more than 100 000 hours.

In June the Commission signed further contracts enabling its work on Euronet-Diane to continue and its ECHO host computer to be made available. [4]

Removal of language barriers

593. As part of its third plan of action (1983-85) for the improvement of the transfer of information between Community languages [5] the Commission is continuing to extend the Systran (computer assisted translation) system by adding English/German and French/German versions. The system is undergoing operational testing in several departments.

594. The Eurotra research programme (advanced-design translation system) [6] has reached the end of its first two-year phase. The second phase of the programme (1985-86) will begin on 1 January 1985 as originally scheduled.

595. Two standardized multilingual dictionaries were completed in 1984: the Eudised thesaurus on education, compiled in nine languages (including Spanish and Portuguese) with the collaboration of the Council of Europe, and the Eurovoc thesaurus, providing a comprehensive Community vocabulary in seven languages, which is already in use.

---

1   Direct information access network for Europe.
2   Bull. EC 2-1984, point 2.1.33.
3   An agreement was signed with Norway on 19 December.
4   Bull. EC 3-1984, point 2.1.34.
5   Sixteenth General Report, point 598; OJ C 57, 2.3.1983; Seventeenth General Report, point 605.
6   OJ L 317, 13.11.1982; Sixteenth General Report, point 598; Seventeenth General Report, point 606.

Section 19

Culture

596. On 22 June the first meeting of the Council and the Ministers for Cultural Affairs meeting within the Council was held in Luxembourg.[1] A second meeting was held on 22 November.[2]

597. In June Ministers endorsed three resolutions on audio-visual piracy, the rational distribution of films through all the audio-visual communication media and measures to ensure an appropriate place for audio-visual programmes of European origin. These resolutions were formally adopted in July.[3] Ministers also reached agreement on implementation of cultural cooperation in the context of the Solemn Declaration on European Union.[4]

598. In November Ministers reached agreement on a resolution, which was adopted in December, on increased use of the European Social Fund to assist cultural workers.[5] Parliament had also passed a resolution on the position of such workers in May.[6]

Although they were unable to adopt a resolution on increased cultural cooperation as provided for by the Solemn Declaration on European Union,[7] Ministers agreed on a work programme for the specific projects referred to in the draft resolution.[8]

599. In April the Commission published a notice calling for proposals for pilot projects under its scheme to protect and conserve the Community's architectural heritage.[9]

---

[1] Bull. EC 6-1984, points 2.1.61 to 2.1.64.
[2] Bull. EC 11-1984, point 2.1.73.
[3] OJ C 204, 3.8.1984; Bull. EC 6-1984, point 2.1.62.
[4] Bull. EC 6-1984, point 2.1.63.
[5] OJ C 2, 4.1.1985; Bull. EC 11-1984, point 2.1.74.
[6] OJ C 172, 2.7.1984; Bull. EC 5-1984, point 2.4.15.
[7] Bull. EC 6-1983, point 1.6.1 (paragraph 3.3).
[8] Bull. EC 11-1984, point 2.1.75.
[9] OJ C 145, 1.6.1984; Bull. EC 4-1984, point 2.1.73.

Chapter III

Enlargement and external relations

Section 1

Main developments

600. *The Community and the countries which have applied to join it made special efforts throughout the year to complete the accession negotiations in 1984. The meeting of the European Council at Fontainebleau on 25 and 26 June reaffirmed that the negotiations should be completed by 30 September. Although the complexity of the matters being negotiated and their importance for a 12-member Community meant that this date could not be met, at a meeting in Luxembourg in October the Community and Spain and Portugal confirmed the irreversibility of the two applicant countries' integration into the Community and set 1 January 1986 as a firm deadline for this further enlargement of the Community. The political and economic significance of this was fully recognized.*

In the negotiations themselves, 1984 saw work intensify on agriculture, while genuine negotiations on all aspects of fisheries got under way. The Community also put to Spain and Portugal its views on the institutional aspects of a Community of Twelve, agreement on which was reached with Spain in December.

The accession negotiations should be completed in early 1985.

601. *As regards relations with the developing world, a new ACP/EEC Convention was signed in Lomé on 8 December 1984, incorporating significant innovations and improvements on the previous convention. For the first time the preamble refers to basic human rights, and there is a joint declaration on respect for human dignity. The provisions on trade have been reinforced as against the previous convention; as regards financial and technical cooperation,*

the new convention stresses the need to seek self-reliance in foodstuffs through action concerning the ACP States' production, environment and foreign trade. Lomé III also makes specific provision for emergency aid to refugees.

The fact that the convention was concluded on time and that despite its own economic difficulties the Community substantially incresased the total amount of finance available (8 500 million ECU) is to be seen as an encouraging achievement. The Commission hopes that it may serve to help the continuation of the North-South dialogue, which is currently deadlocked at world level.

Development work under the previous conventions continued in 1984, as did the programmes affecting the southern and eastern Mediterranean countries and the non-associated developing countries, financed from the Community budget.

The special programme to combat hunger in the world was put into effect in 1984, and specific projects to prevent desertification and erosion were adopted by the Commission.

In order to help deal with the famine caused by the widespread drought in Africa, especially in the Sahel countries and Ethiopia, the Commission decided in the early autumn on an emergency plan for these countries. Meeting on 3 and 4 December, the European Council stressed the need for concerted international action. By the next harvest, the Community and its Member States are to supply 1.2 million tonnes of cereals to the countries affected.

602. As regards multilateral relations, particular attention was devoted to maintaining and strengthening trade and to the consequences for the international trade system of some developing countries' indebtedness. Through certain initiatives on trade, the Community was able to take a leading role in the debate.

The Community also became a contracting party to the Convention on the Law of the Sea, the first United Nations convention making express provision for signature by international organizations.

603. There was major progress in the Community's bilateral relations. At the first EEC/EFTA ministerial meeting, in Luxembourg, important decisions were taken concerning future cooperation between the Community and the EFTA countries.

At a meeting of Community and Central American Foreign Ministers in San José, Costa Rica, the Community side stressed its political and economic commitment to the region.

For the first time since diplomatic relations were established between the Community and China, a Chinese Prime Minister paid an official visit to the Commission.

Relations with the United States were again disturbed by a number of disputes, though close and regular bilateral contact prevented them breaking out into open conflict. The Community continued to broaden and strengthen its relationship with Japan, but the measures taken to open the Japanese market to Community products remained limited in scope and the Community's trade deficit with Japan is still worrying.

604. *The Community's commercial policy was reinforced by the adoption of a 'new instrument' setting up clearly defined procedures for the exercise by the Community of its international rights. In the matter of export credit, the Community and its main trading partners among the industrialized countries reached a new, more permanent agreement within OECD.*

605. *The number of diplomatic missions from non-member countries accredited to the European Communities increased from 124 in 1983 to 127 in 1984.*

Section 2

Enlargement and bilateral relations with applicant countries

Portugal

606. Negotiations were stepped up with a total of nine ministerial meetings and two meetings at deputy level in the course of the year. [1]

607. The main emphasis was on the important matters of agriculture and fisheries. The negotiations on agriculture gathered momentum, and agreement was reached on many of the issues concerned. The negotiations on fisheries, which had largely remained in abeyance till this year, led to agreement on a number of points. A broad measure of agreement was also reached on institutional questions and the European Investment Bank, which were discussed in July.

608. Negotiations continued throughout the year on customs union, external relations, taxation, right of establishment, economic and financial matters, social affairs and patents. Broad or full agreement was reached on everything but social affairs and patents.

609. Following the agreement reached in Luxembourg on 22 October, Portugal and the Community signed a joint statement in Dublin on 24 October in which they acknowledged the irreversibility of the process of Portugal's entry into the Comunity, declared their determination to reach agreement shortly on the issues still outstanding, and indicated their firm objective of achieving accession on 1 January 1986. [2]

610. Futher discussions were held between the Commission and the Portuguese delegation on secondary Community legislation.

---

[1] Bull. EC 1-1984, point 2.2.1; Bull. EC 2-1984, point 2.2.2; Bull. EC 3-1984, point 2.2.3; Bull. EC 4-1984, point 2.2.1; Bull. EC 5-1984, point 2.2.2; Bull. EC 6-1984, point 2.2.4; Bull. EC 7/8-1984, point 2.2.1; Bull. EC 9-1984, point 2.2.3; Bull. EC 10-1984, point 2.2.2; Bull. EC 11-1984, point 2.2.2; Bull. EC 12-1984.
[2] Bull. EC 10-1984, point 1.2.1.

611. At bilateral level, in response to requests by the Portuguese Government, the Commission sent to the Council in September a communication on the import arrangements to be applied by Portugal *vis-à-vis* the Community in 1985 under the 1972 EEC-Portugal Agreement. Negotiations were concluded early in December: Portuguese residual customs duties will continue to be applied to the Community in 1985 and some aspects of the current protocol on motor vehicles will be extended for three years.

612. Implementation of the December 1980 Agreement on pre-accession aid to Portugal [1] continued with the approval by the Commission of grants totalling some 19.26 million ECU for agriculture, regional infrastructure and vocational training projects. [2] Some 79.43 million ECU of grant aid has been allocated since the Agreement entered into force in 1981.

Under the second section of the 1980 Agreement, which provides for subsidized loans from the EIB's own resources, the second 75 million ECU instalment (1 July 1983 to 30 June 1984) [3] was committed in full to small business and energy projects. [4]

In September the Community approved a further loan package of 150 million ECU for the period 1 July 1984 to 31 December 1985. [5]

In December special grants totalling 50 million ECU were voted for the improvement of farming and fisheries structures in Portugal. [6]

613. In July Mr Thorn visited Lisbon, where he discussed the progress of the accession negotiations and how they could be speeded up with President Ramalho Eanes, Prime Minister Mário Soares and members of the Portuguese Government. On 25 October Mr Thorn and Mr Natali met Mr Soares for an exchange of views on the prospects for completing the negotiations. [7] The European Parliament/Portuguese Parliament Joint Committee met in February and November.

---

[1] OJ L 349, 23.12.1980; Sixteenth General Report, point 612; Seventeenth General Report, point 624.
[2] Bull. EC 5-1984, point 2.2.3; Bull. EC 6-1984, point 2.2.6.
[3] Seventeenth General Report, point 624.
[4] Bull. EC 4-1984, point 2.4.41; Bull. EC 6-1984, point 2.4.23.
[5] Bull. EC 9-1984, point 2.2.2; Bull. EC 5-1984, point 2.2.1.
[6] OJ L 333, 21.12.1984; Bull. EC 12-1984.
[7] Bull. EC 10-1984, point 1.2.1 *et seq.*

Spain

614. Considerable progress with the accession negotiations was made at the nine ministerial meetings and three meetings at deputy level,[1] at which the two sides exchanged statements on social affairs, customs union and free movement of goods, external relations, agriculture, fisheries, patents, secondary legislation, Euratom, ECSC, institutional matters, the EIB and economic and financial matters.

Negotiations on patents were completed, enabling Spain to withdraw its final reservations on the right of establishment. A major step was taken towards completion of the external relations chapter with the conclusion of negotiations on the adoption by Spain of the preferential trade agreements linking the Community with Mediterranean countries and the ACP States and overseas countries and territories, and the unilateral scheme of generalized tariff preferences.

As far as Euratom is concerned, agreement was reached on the introduction of exchange of information on nuclear energy and Spain's nuclear external relations with non-Community countries or international organizations.

As regards customs union in the industrial sector, agreement was reached in December on the length of transitional tariff measures. These will run for seven years and be phased out in eight annual instalments. On the date of accession Spain will also introduce, for a three-year period, a tariff quota at a reduced rate of duty for imports of motor vehicles from the Member States of the present Community.

Agreement was also reached in December in negotiations on steel products on the conditions of post-accession integration of the Spanish steel industry. It was agreed that the Spanish Government will be able to grant aid to its industry over a period of three years from the date of accession and the volume of Spanish supplies to the present Community market was laid down. During this period Spain may make use of exceptional aid arrangements for the restructuring of its industry.

Customs union negotiations regarding EEC and ECSC industries were for the most part completed towards the end of the year.

---

[1] Bull. EC 1-1984, point 2.2.2; Bull. EC 2-1984, point 2.2.4; Bull. EC 3-1984, point2.2.5; Bull. EC 4-1984, point 2.2.2; Bull. EC 5-1984, point 2.2.4; Bull. EC 6-1984, point 2.2.6; Bull. EC 7/8-1984, point 2.2.3; Bull. EC 9-1984, point 2.2.4; Bull. EC 10-1984, point 2.2.3; Bull. EC 12-1984.

The two sides moved significantly nearer agreement on the various aspects of the social affairs chapter. Spain expressed willingness to agree to a seven-year transitional period on immigration and right to take up employment, provided the situation is reviewed at the end of five years, while the Communiuty was prepared to accept a standstill clause guaranteeing that Spanish migrant workers would not be in a worse position after the signing of the Act of Accession, with the right to full equality of treatment applying from accession itself. The Community put forward its proposal for a seven-year transitional period on family allowances for those members of a worker's family who have remained in the country of origin, whereas Spain wants these provisions to apply in full from the date of accession.

The negotiations on agriculture were primarily concerned with general transitional arrangements. Intensive discussions with Spain and efforts within the Community itself to define a Community position in this key sector mean that it sould be possible shortly to reach agreement on the broad outlines of such arrangements. The Community has to a large extent been able to define its negotiating position on wine, having amended existing Community provisions to attain a better balance on this market in an enlarged Community. [1] The Community has also worked out its negotiating position on vegetable oils.

Efforts were made to define the Community's negotiating position on the various aspects of fisheries.

615. At the ministerial meeting on 23 October the Community made a statement affirming its political commitment to Spanish accession and confirmed the target date of 1 January 1986. [2]

616. Under the arrangements for financial cooperation between the Community and Spain established in 1981 [3] the EIB granted Spain loans totalling 50 million ECU in 1984 for small businesses, regional infrastructure and energy projects; [4] this accounts for the last of the 100 million ECU package approved in 1983 for the period 1 July 1983 to 30 June 1984.

617. The Community voted in September to continue financial cooperation in the form of a further 250 million ECU loan package for the period 1 July 1984

---

[1] Point 420 of this Report.
[2] Bull. EC 10-1984, point 1.2.1 *et seq.*
[3] Fifteenth General Report, point 630; Sixteenth General Report, point 619; Seventeenth General Report, point 629.
[4] Bull. EC 6-1984, point 2.4.22.

to 31 December 1985.[1] Loans totalling 70 million ECU were granted in November.[2]

In October the Commission proposed to the Council that Spain be given a 28.5 million ECU grant to help restructure its fishing fleet.[3]

618. Further discussions were held between the Commission and the Spanish delegation on secondary Community legislation.

619. Mr Thorn visited Madrid in March for talks with King Juan Carlos, the Prime Minister, Mr Felipe Gonzalez, and Foreign Minister Fernando Morán. In May Mr Natali was received in Madrid by Mr Morán and Mr Manuel Marín, State Secretary for Relations with the Community, and in September Mr Gonzalez and Mr Marín paid an official visit to Belgium, in the course of which they had talks with the Commission. The joint committee composed of members of the European Parliament and the Spanish Cortes met in May and November.[4]

---

[1] Bull. EC 9-1984, point 2.2.2; Bull. EC 5-1984, point 2.2.1.
[2] Bull. EC 11-1984, point 2.4.36.
[3] Bull. EC 10-1984, point 2.2.4.
[4] Bull. EC 11-1984, point 2.2.5.

Section 3

Commercial policy

Implementing the common commercial policy

Commercial policy instruments and import arrangements

620. On 17 September the Council formally adopted a Regulation [1]—which it had approved in April [2]—on the strengthening of the common commercial policy, with particular reference to protection against illicit commercial practices. The aim of this new commercial policy instrument is twofold. First, it is designed to enable the Community to react more effectively if a non-member country engages in any international commercial practice which is incompatible with international law or the generally accepted rules, so that the injury caused to Community producers can be removed. Secondly, it is intended to ensure full exercise of the Community's rights with regard to the commercial practices of other countries.

The Regulation supplements the Community's other commercial policy instruments with transparent and effective Community procedures that will allow action to be taken against a range of illicit practices by non-member countries, notably restraints on commodity exports or import controls. it is expressly stated that any action taken along these lines to remove injury to Community industry on the Community market or on other markets must be in accordance with the spirit and letter of the Community's obligations under international law.

621. The Community's basic instruments for protection against dumped or subsidized imports were clarified and consolidated by a Council Regulation of 23 July (for EEC products) and a Commission Decision of 27 July (for ECSC products). [3]

---

[1] OJ L 252, 20.9.1984; Bull. EC 9-1984, point 2.2.5.
[2] Bull. EC 4-1984, points 2.2.3 and 2.2.4; for details of the Commission proposal, see Seventeenth General Report, point 630.
[3] OJ L 201, 30.7.1984; Bull. EC 7/8-1984, point 2.2.7.

622. Anti-dumping duties were levied on imports of vinyl acetate monomer from Canada, ball bearings from Japan and Singapore and concrete reinforcing bars from Spain. A countervailing duty was also levied on imports of tube and pipe fittings of malleable cast iron from Spain. In other cases the inquiry was closed after the exporting firms had agreed to raise their prices. The products involved here were caustic-burned natural magnesite from China, hand-knitting yarn from Turkey, cold-rolled steel sections from the German Democratic Republic and Romania, choline chloride from the German Democratic Republic and Romania, horticultural glass from Czechoslovakia, the German Democratic Republic, Hungary, Poland, Romania and the USSR, pentaerythritol from Spain and Sweden, propyl alcohol from the United States, sensitized paper for colour photographs from Japan, kraftliner paper from Spain, asbestos-cement corrugated sheets from Czechoslovakia and the German Democratic Republic, oxalic acid from the German Democratic Republic and Brazil, copper sulphate from Bulgaria and Hungary, paraformaldehyde from Spain, shovels from Brasil and artificial corundum from China and Czechoslovakia.

623. On 18 April the Commission adopted safeguard measures in respect of imports into France of quartz watches with digital display. [1]

624. On 17 December the Council laid down, as it does each year, the quotas to be opened by the Member States in 1985 for imports from State-trading countries. [2]

625. For 1984 the Commission adopted 45 decisions covering mainly the opening of additional import quotas over and above those adopted by the Council at the end of 1983. [3]

Trade agreements

626. The Council authorized the extension for a further year of a number of trade agreements concluded by Member States with non-member countries where such agreements did not hinder the implementation of the common commercial policy. [4]

---

[1] OJ L 106, 19.4.1984.
[2] OJ L 344, 31.12.1984.
[3] OJ L 381, 31.12.1983.
[4] OJ L 40, 11.2.1984; OJ L 150, 6.6.1984; OJ L 274, 17.10.1984; OJ L 308, 27.11.1984.

627. It also authorized the automatic renewal or continuance in force of certain friendship, trade and navigation treaties and the like between Member States and other countries. [1]

Export credits

OECD Understanding on Export Credits for Ships

628. On 23 January the Council prolonged, for the first time without setting a terminal date, the period of application in the Community of its Decision of 28 April 1981 on the conclusion of the OECD Understanding on Export Credits for Ships. [2]

Guidelines for Officially Supported Export Credits ('Consensus')

629. The OECD Arrangement on Guidelines for Officially Supported Export Credits ('Consensus'), which entered into force in October 1983, [3] provides for the introduction of a permanent system for the automatic adjustment of minimum interest rates every six months on the basis of the average of rates of interest of the currencies which constitute the International Monetary Fund's special drawing rights. For the first half of 1984 the average was such that on 15 July interest rates were raised for the first time for all categories of buyer countries.

On 22 October the Arrangement was extended until 15 April 1985.

630. In July the Council adopted a Decision on the application of a sectoral agreement on export credits for nuclear power stations, [4] which entered into force at OECD level on 10 August. This agreement contains guidelines which complement those of the general 'Consensus'; it provides for longer repayment periods (15 years instead of 10) and higher minimum interest rates.

631. On 10 December the Council adopted a Community position in preparation for the opening of negotiations with the other participants in the Export

---

[1] OJ L 339, 27.12.1984.
[2] Fifteenth General Report, point 643.
[3] Seventeenth General Report, point 637.
[4] Bull. EC 7/8-1984, point 2.2.9.

Credits Arrangement on a sectoral agreement covering aircraft and on linked aid credits.

Credit insurance

632. On 27 November the Council adopted a Directive governing reciprocal obligations on the part of Member States' export credit insurance bodies acting on behalf of or with the support of the State, or on the part of the authorities acting in place of such bodies, in the case of joint guarantee for a contract involving one or more subcontractors in one or more Member States of the Community. [1]

Export promotion

633. Representatives of the Member States' export promotion bodies attended a meeting in Rome in June, at which Mr Haferkamp was present, to look at the scope for closer cooperation at Community level and identify joint measures to promote exports. Under the 1984 Community budget the Commission was able for the first time to make a financial contribution to these export promotion efforts.

634. In 1984 two trade missions visited countries with a high rate of economic growth, namely, the Asean countries and the Gulf States.

Individual products

Steel [2]

External element of the 1984 steel plan

635. Since 1978 imports of steel products into the Community have been subject to either arrangements or basic prices. Imports this year totalled 9.2 million tonnes, some 400 000 tonnes lower than in 1983.

---

[1] OJ L 314, 4.12.1984.
[2] See also points 187 *et seq.* and 661 of this Report.

636. In accordance with the directives given by the Council in November 1983, arrangements were concluded for 1984 with 15 supplier countries which together provide three quarters of the Community's supplies. [1] Under the system established for 1984 certain rules were tightened up after failure to observe them had created management difficulties in 1983, particularly as regards the phasing of deliveries, geographical distribution and breakdown by product category. Frequent consultations were held to ensure that the rules were being observed, with the result that few serious difficulties were encountered this year. Some of the penalties imposed on certain partners in 1983 were not lifted in 1984, and entitlement to the penetration margin for heavy plate was withdrawn from one State-trading country.

637. As regards imports of steel products subject to basic prices, only limited interest was shown in marketing these products—which are largely supplied by the less-industrialized or developing countries—in the Community, partly as a result of the high level of the dollar. Failure to observe the basic price may trigger off anti-dumping measures, but the Community had no occasion to apply this type of trade protection measure in 1984.

External element of the 1985 steel plan

638. In October, on the basis of a Commission communication sent to the Council in September, [2] the latter confirmed the main body of the 1984 provisions. Quantities were raised slightly in view of a probable improvement in apparent consumption from 1984 to 1985. Given the generally satisfactory operation of the arrangements in 1984, the Commission relaxed certain rules such as the strict timetable for the phasing of deliveries.

Autonomous arrangements

639. The five Member States which had maintained autonomous quotas in respect of State-trading countries extended them in May by a unanimous Decision of the Representatives of the Governments of the Member States of the ECSC, keeping the quantities at the same level as for the preceding year since the total volume under the 1984 arrangements was unchanged from the 1983 level.

---

[1] Bull. EC 4-1984, point 2.2.8.
[2] Bull. EC 9-1984, point 2.2.8.

Textiles

Bilateral agreements with non-member countries

640. The bilateral agreements on textiles concluded between the Community and various supplier countries under the Multifibre Arrangement (MFA), which entered into force on a *de facto* basis on 1 January 1983,[1] functioned satisfactorily. The problems encountered in the administration of these agreements were dealt with by the Textile Committee, which met at regular intervals throughout the year.

641. An Additional Protocol to the Textile Agreement between the Community and China was initialled in Peking on 29 March and approved by the Council in June.[2] This Protocol specifies the quantitative limits applicable in 1984-88 and makes a number of changes to the initial Agreement to bring it into line with the other bilateral MFA agreements.

642. The GATT Textiles Committee met in Geneva in October to make a full examination of the MFA on the basis of a report prepared by the Textiles Surveillance Body. The Community representative described the situation in the Community's textiles and clothing industries, stating that it still gave cause for concern.

643. The GATT Textiles Committee also held two special sessions in January and September to examine various new measures taken by the United States on trade in textiles. At the September session the Community expressed particular concern over the new United States regulations on rules of origin and import procedures.[3]

644. Commission representatives attended a number of meetings of the GATT Working Party on Textiles and Clothing which examined new opportunities for liberalizing trade in textiles and clothing. An interim report on this subject was put before the parties to the General Agreement in November.

645. The Community also took part in the meetings of the Textiles Surveillance Body, which are held regularly in Geneva to monitor the implementation of the MFA.

---

[1] Seventeenth General Report, point 642.
[2] OJ L 198, 27.7.1984; Bull. EC 3-1983, point 2.2.13.
[3] Bull. EC 9-1984, point 2.2.11.

Arrangements with preferential countries

646. A new textile arrangement between the Community and Spain covering a two-year period was initialled on 24 January. The administrative cooperation agreement with Malta was extended on 29 February for two years (1984-85), and on 16 March the agreement with Turkey on exports of cotton yarn was also renewed for the same period.

647. Talks were held on the renewal of the administrative cooperation agreements with Morocco and Tunisia.

648. In the continued absence of any comprehensive arrangement with Turkey, the Community was obliged to take safeguard action against imports of a number of textile products from Turkey. [1]

649. A number of negotiating meetings were held with Portugal in order to resolve certain problems involving the application of the pre-accession agreement. A definitive agreement was drawn up in Lisbon on 10 October.

Non-ferrous metals

650. The export arrangements applied in 1984 [2] for waste and scrap of certain non-ferrous metals were continued for 1985; [3] these arrangements comprise quotas for exports of copper ash and waste and the monitoring of exports of aluminium and lead waste.

---

[1] OJ L 187, 14.7.1984; Bull. EC 7/8-1984, point 2.2.14; OJ L 335, 22.12.1984.
[2] Seventeenth General Report, point 648.
[3] OJ L 335, 22.12.1984; Bull. EC 12-1984.

Section 4

Relations with industrialized countries

Multilateral aspects

651. The basic problems dominating the Community's relations with its main industrialized partners were the need to strengthen world economic recovery, the problem of the indebtedness of the least-developed countries and the undertaking to resist the continuing protectionist trends. These concerns were expressed in the declaration on economic policy adopted at the London Western Economic Summit meeting from 7 to 9 June,[1] at which the Commission was represented by Mr Thorn and Mr Ortoli.

The problems caused for the international trading system by the continuing protectionist trend, the problems of the indebtedness of certain developing countries and the proposal for a new round of multilateral negotiations were also examined during a number of informal meetings which Trade Ministers held during the year; the Commission was represented at these meetings by Mr Haferkamp.[2]

In order to help reverse the trend of protectionism, the Community and its partners among the industrialized countries agreed last May, at a ministerial meeting of the OECD Council,[3] following the Council's Decision of December 1983,[4] and subject to completion of the necessary internal procedures, to bring forward by one year, to 1 January 1985, the tariff reductions proposed for 1986 under the Tokyo Round multilateral trade negotiations.

In fact, although a number of OECD's member States have applied this agreement, the United States authorities failed to obtain the necessary powers from Congress. Consequently, it has not been possible for the United States to introduce the proposed tariff reductions; Canada has also not done so for the same reasons.

In view of this situation, the Council decided on 8 November to bring forward the tariff reductions planned for 1 January 1986 to 1 July 1985, provided the main trading partners, including the United States, took similar measures as

[1] Bull. EC 6-1984, point 3.4.1 *et seq.*
[2] Bull. EC 2-1984, point 2.2.16 and Bull. EC 6-1984, point 2.2.20.
[3] Bull. EC 5-1984, point 2.2.65.
[4] Bull. EC 12-1983, point 2.2.8.

agreed in OECD. Tariff reductions for products of particular interest to the developing countries will in any case be brought forward to 1 January 1985.

International cooperation in the fields of science and technology has been improving constantly. In addition to the cooperation which is continuing, following the Versailles and Williamsburg Western Economic Summits,[1] the Community signed several agreements this year with the United States (exchange of information in the field of mining technology, research into nuclear safety), Canada (medical research) and Switzerland (management of radioactive waste). The mutual will of the Community and Japan to cooperate in the scientific and technical field was expressed in an exchange of letters signed in December.

Bilateral relations

Countries of the European Free Trade Association [2]

652. The Foreign Ministers of the 10 Community Member States and the seven member countries of the European Free Trade Association met in Luxembourg on 9 April — the first such meeting since the free trade agreements between the Community and the EFTA countries were signed in 1972. The Ministers assessed the functioning of the free trade agreements, in particular since the removal by both sides in January of the last tariff barriers and quantitative restrictions in trade between them in industrial goods, and discussed a number of international economic issues. They also drew up guidelines on how cooperation both under the existing agreements and further afield should be continued and consolidated, and indicated in a final Joint Declaration [3] the areas in which they agreed to cooperate.

Among the meetings held to follow up the Luxembourg Declaration were the May meeting in Sweden of the Heads of Government and other ministers from the EFTA countries [4] and the meeting in Geneva in November when Mr Thorn and Mr Haferkamp discussed with ministers from the EFTA countries Community and EFTA priority measures. [5]

---

[1] Bull. EC 6-1982, point 3.4.1; Bull. EC 5-1983, point 3.4.1.
[2] Austria, Finland, Iceland, Norway, Portugal, Sweden and Switzerland.
[3] Bull. EC 4-1984, point 12.1. *et seq*.
[4] Bull. EC 5-1984, point 2.2.17.
[5] Bull. EC 11-1984, point 2.2.24.

653. In April Parliament adopted resolutions on relations with Scandinavian countries and on economic and trade relations with the EFTA countries. [1] In March the Economic and Social Committee adopted an own -initiative opinion on relations between the Community and the EFTA countries. [2]

654. In June a five-year cooperation agreement on research and development in high-level radioactive waste management was signed between Euratom and Switzerland's Société coopérative nationale pour l'entreposage des déchets radioactifs. [3]

655. Problems connected with the taxing of road vehicles in Switzerland and Austria were discussed by the Council in March and December. [4]

656. As in previous years, numerous meetings were held throughout the year between the Commission and the EFTA countries on matters such as economic and monetary policy, environment, health and safety at the workplace, consumer protection, transport, cooperation on development aid, energy, standards and industrial policy. A meeting between the EFTA Secretariat and the Commission took place in Brussels in March, and representatives of the Economic and Social Committee and the EFTA Advisory Committee met in Berne in October. [5]

657. The joint committees set up under the free trade agreements met in June, July, November and December. [6] In addition, ministerial-level talks were held in Brussels in June with Sweden and Norway. [7]

658. The steel arrangements with certain EFTA countries were renewed for 1984. [8] The ECSC-EFTA joint committees discussed the market situation and the operation of the agreements.

659. The Austrian Vice-Chancellor, Mr Norbert Steger, [9] the Finnish Minister for Trade, Mr Jermu Laine, [10] and the Finnish Minister for Industry, Mr Seppo

---

[1] OJ C 127, 14.5.1984; Bull. EC 4-1984, point 2.4.9.
[2] OJ C 140, 28.5.1984; Bull. EC 3-1984, point 2.4.32.
[3] Bull. EC 6-1984, point 2.2.30.
[4] Bull. EC 3-1984, point 2.1.173; Bull. EC 12-1984.
[5] Bull. EC 10-1984, point 2.2.23.
[6] Bull. EC 6-1984, point 2.2.28; Bull. EC 7/8-1984, point 2.2.21; Bull. EC 11-1984, point 2.2.25; Bull. EC 12-1984.
[7] Bull. EC 6-1984, point 2.2.29.
[8] Point 636 of this Report.
[9] Bull. EC 2-1984, point 2.2.21.
[10] Bull. EC 5-1984, point 2.2.20.

Community — EFTA trade

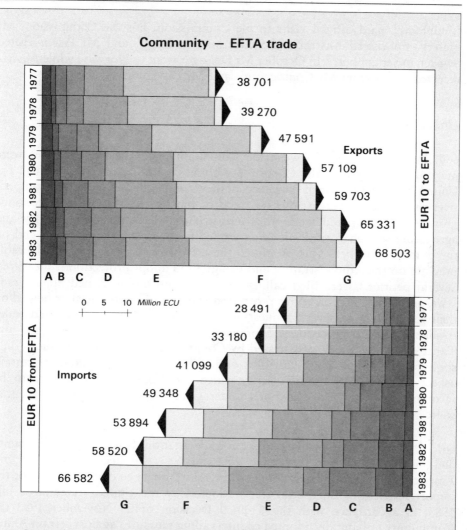

A Food and live animals chiefly for food, beverages, tobacco
B Crude materials, inedible, except fuels
C Mineral fuels, lubricants; animal and vegetable oils and fats
D Chemicals and related products
E Manufactured goods classified chiefly by raw material
F Machinery and transport equipment, miscellaneous manufactured articles
G Miscellaneous articles and transactions

There was a steady and balanced increase in trade between the Community and the EFTA countries during the period 1977-83, in part because tariff barriers were eliminated on 1 July 1977. The switch to a surplus for EFTA on its trade in mineral fuels in 1980 is due to the increase in exports of energy products by Norway to the Community.

Source: Bulletin mensuel du commerce extérieur 1958-1983, p.107.

Lindblom, [1] paid official visits to the Commission. For the Commission, Mr Haferkamp visited Austria and Switzerland in May [2] and Mr Pisani visited Sweden in September. [3] In October Mr Dalsager went to Norway, while Austria received a visit from Mr Contogeorgis and Mr Davignon. [1]

United States

660. In 1984 relations between the Community and the United States were marked by concern in the Community about mounting protectionism in the United States. [4] Because of the effects of the strong dollar on American competitiveness and the repercussions on trade of the United States' high economic growth rate compared with other industrialized countries, US industry and agriculture saw their position being eroded both on external markets and on the domestic market. This prompted these two sectors to apply considerable pressure on the Administration and Congress to adopt protectionist measures. Several petitions were filed calling for protection under United States trade laws, and in Congress, various protectionist bills were introduced or helped on their way. However, several requests for import restrictions were rejected under regular American procedures. Moreover, the final version of the Trade and Tariff Act 1984, which was passed by Congress on 10 October, includes only some of the protectionist measures originally proposed, for example certain aspects of the Wine Equity Act, [5] which the Community considers to be incompatible with US obligations under GATT and which are a potential source of conflict.

661. One of the main problem areas in trade relations between the Community and the United States in 1984, as in 1982 and 1983, was steel. [6] No satisfactory American offer having been submitted by mid-January in compensation for the import restrictions on special steels adopted by the United States on 5 July 1983, in accordance with the Council Decision of 23 November 1983 the Community unilaterally adopted countervailing measures against certain American exports, with effect from 1 March. [7] The Arrangement of October 1982

---

[1] Bull. EC 10-1984, point 2.2.21.
[2] Bull. EC 5-1984, points 2.2.18, 2.2.19 and 2.2.22.
[3] Bull. EC 9-1984, point 2.2.20.
[4] See Bull. EC 2-1984, point 2.2.17; Bull. EC 10-1984, point 2.2.17; OJ C 127, 4.5.1984; Bull. EC 4-1984, point 2.4.7.
[5] Bull. EC 10-1984, point 2.2.17.
[6] Sixteenth General Report, point 655; Seventeenth General Report, points 656 and 657.
[7] Bull. EC 1-1984, point 2.2.16; Bull. EC 2-1984, point 2.2.18; Bull. EC 3-1984, point 2.2.18; Bull. EC 5-1984, point 2.2.13.

with the United States on exports of carbon steel from the Community was threatened by a petition for safeguard measures filed by Bethlehem Steel at the beginning of the year. [1] The US International Trade Commission (ITC) found that there was serious injury caused by the increase in imports of a certain number of carbon and alloy steel products [2] and recommended a package of restrictions made up of tariff and quota measures. [3] The Commission and the Council deplored this finding in statements to the press. [4] For certain other products, particularly pipes and tubes, no injury was found and no measures were proposed by the ITC. On 18 September the US President rejected the ITC's recommended remedy and announced an overall programme for stabilizing trade in steel, designed to limit imports to about 18.5% of the US market. [5] This meant that the 1982 Steel Arrangement would be maintained, but the measures would create difficulties for Community countries which export pipes and tubes. For together with the Steel Arrangement the US and the Community signed an exchange of letters on pipes and tubes providing that there should be consultations if Community exports to the US exceeded the 1979-81 average of 5.9% of US consumption. Taking the view that this had in fact happened, the US Government asked for consultations on 6 April, calling on the Community to reduce its exports to the agreed level.

Following lengthy discussions the Community made an offer on 17 and 18 November—accepted *ad referendum* by the US—to limit exports to a market share of 7.6% (rather than 5.9%), subject to certain exceptions. [6] However, the US rejected the offer on 27 November and ordered a complete embargo on imports of pipes and tubes from the Community until 31 December and a restriction of imports in 1985 to 5.9% of apparent consumption. The US Government based its action on the new Trade and Tariff Act, which authorizes it to enforce quantitative restrictions agreed under bilateral arrangements. The Community felt that these measures were not consistent with the exchange of letters, according to which the 5.9% figure was not a mandatory ceiling on Community exports but simply the level beyond which consultations were required. On 28 November the Council, having been informed of the US decision, decided to terminate the exchange of letters and reserve all its rights under GATT rules. It called for a special meeting of the GATT Council, which met on 17 December. Negotiations between the Commission and the US were

---

[1] Bull. EC 1-1984, point 2.2.17.
[2] Bull. EC 6-1984, point 2.2.21.
[3] Bull. EC 7/8-1984, point 2.2.15.
[4] Bull. EC 6-1984, point 2.2.21; Bull. EC 7/8-1984, point 2.2.16.
[5] Bull. EC 9-1984, points 2.2.15 and 2.2.16.
[6] Bull. EC 11-1984, point 2.2.19.

later resumed, and agreement was reached on 5 January 1985 along the lines of what had been agreed *ad referendum* in November: a market share of 7.6% for Community products, excluding products the American industry cannot supply; a 10% subceiling for oil country tubular goods; and a partially satisfactory arrangement for tubes unloaded but not cleared through customs during the embargo (29 November to 31 December).

662. Another area in which difficulties arose regularly in the course of the year was agriculture. Wine exports from the Community were the main target of grape growers and the wine industry in the United States. A petition from the American Grape Growers Alliance for Free Trade seeking an investigation with a view to imposing countervailing and anti-dumping duties on French and Italian ordinary table wines was nevertheless rejected by the ITC on 6 March. [1] In a press release issued on 17 February the Commission had said it was seriously concerned about this petition. [2]

663. The Community was also concerned about the 1984 Wine Equity and Export Expansion Act, which Congress had been considering since August 1983. The original bill contained various provisions which the Community considered to be incompatible with US obligations under GATT and a potential threat to Community wine exports to the United States. As a result of persistent pressure by the Community both on the US Government and Congress and on the opposition groups, the original wording of the bill was made a little more flexible. Nevertheless, the measure adopted by Congress on 10 October as a part of the Trade and Tariff Act 1984 contains a provision enabling grape producers to file anti-dumping suits and request countervailing duties again on Community wine imports to the American market. This provision is incompatible with GATT rules, and its application might spark off a major trade dispute, given that the Community would have no choice but to react forcefully, making full use of its rights within GATT. [3] At the traditional ministerial meeting on 14 December between an American delegation chaired by Secretary of State George Shultz and a Commission delegation led by Mr Thorn, the Commission clearly expressed its concern about all these protectionist developments. [4]

664. Two decisions facilitating imports of American wine were adopted by the Community in 1984. First, the minimum reference price system for wines

---

[1] Bull. EC 1-1984, point 2.2.21; Bull. EC 3-1984, point 2.2.19.
[2] Bull. EC 2-1984, point 2.2.19.
[3] Bull. EC 9-1984, point 2.2.17; Bull. EC 10-1984, point 2.2.17.
[4] Bull. EC 12-1984.

imported from the United States was dropped on 16 March; [1] and, second, on 20 June the Council adjusted temporarily the Community rules on oenological practices. [2] This decision, which was a follow-up to the 1983 exchange of letters between the Community and the United States on wine, should provide improved access for American wines to the Community market.

665. In the cereals sector, the Council authorized the Commission on 31 March to start negotiations with its main trading partners under Article XXVIII of the General Agreement with the aim of stabilizing imports into the Community of cereal substitutes, corn gluten feed being the product of greatest interest to American farmers and exporters. During these consultations [3] the Community tabled an offer of compensation as required under the General Agreement.

666. The 1977 agreement between the Community and the United States on fishing off the United States coasts was replaced, with effect from 14 October 1984, by a new agreement which is scheduled to remain in force until 1 July 1989. [4]

667. As a result of the adoption of the Foreign Sales Corporation Act, which entered into force on 18 July, some progress was made in 1984 towards replacing the Domestic International Sales Corporation (DISC) system, which is the subject of a long-standing dispute between the Community and the United States because of its incompatibility with GATT provisions. Although the new law contains some improvements on the previous legislation, there are still some provisions whose compatibility with GATT rules is uncertain, particularly the provision which provides for complete tax exemption for all taxes previously carried forward. The Community voiced its concern to the American Administration about these points and reserved its rights under the General Agreement.

Canada

668. As in 1983, [5] the Community's export opportunities on the Canadian market continued to be directly affected by a number of Canadian trade policy measures, such as the extension of the import quota arrangements for shoes,

---

[1] Bull. EC 3-1984, point 2.2.21.
[2] Bull. EC 3-1984, point 2.2.20; Bull. EC 6-1984, point 2.2.25.
[3] Bull. EC 3-1984, point 2.2.22; Bull. EC 4-1984, point 2.2.17; Bull. EC 6-1984, point 2.2.26.
[4] OJ L 272, 13.10.1984; Bull. EC 9-1984, point 2.1.102.
[5] Seventeenth General Report, point 664 *et seq.*

countervailing duties on tinned ham and galantine and the adoption of anti-dumping procedures.

669. Two major problems in Community/Canada relations had to be dealt with by procedures in the multilateral framework of GATT:[1]

(i) A panel looked into the level of the GATT tariff quota for newsprint granted duty-free access to the Community market.[2] In the light of the panel's recommendations, the two sides agreed that the Community would open a zero-duty quota of 650 000 tonnes for imports from non-member countries not entitled to such access under preferential agreement, and that 600 000 tonnes of this would be allocated to Canada. Should this quota be used up by 1 December each year certain further quantities may be allocated.

(ii) In addition, the Community invoked Article XXIII.1 of the General Agreement concerning the discriminatory practices of Canadian provincial liquor boards with regard to imported alcoholic beverages.[3]

670. A Business Cooperation Conference organized by the Commission in Toronto in November under the title 'New opportunities for Canada-EC Business in Manufacturing' gave a fresh boost to industrial cooperation between the Community and Canada.[4]

671. In 1982 the Community had proposed entering into negotiations with Canada with a view to updating and improving the nuclear cooperation agreement between Euratom and Canada[5] on specific points which the Community believed to be important. After four rounds of negotiations in 1983 and 1984, the two sides initialled in November the text of an exchange of letters amending the agreement which will be signed if and when the internal approval procedures have been completed.[6]

672. In December the Commission and the Canadian Government signed an agreement on medicine and public health research.[7]

---

[1] Bull. EC 6-1984, point 2.2.27.
[2] Seventeenth General Report, point 666; Bull. EC 12-1984.
[3] Seventeenth General Report, point 667.
[4] Bull. EC 11-1984, point 2.2.20.
[5] This agreement, which was signed in 1959, had already been amended twice, in 1978 and 1981.
[6] Bull. EC 11-1984, point 2.2.23.
[7] Bull. EC 12-1984.

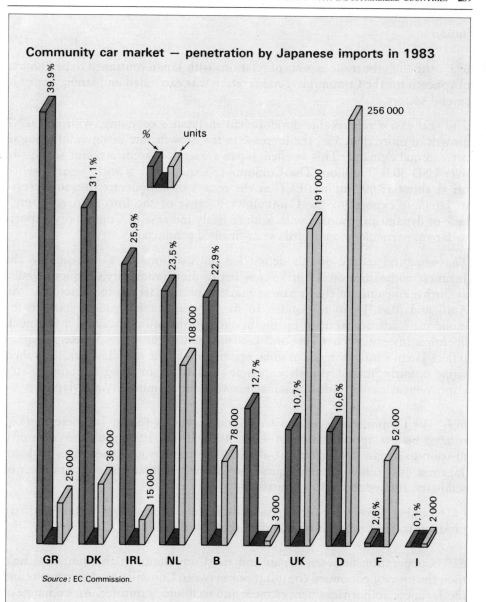

Community car market — penetration by Japanese imports in 1983

% | units

| GR | DK | IRL | NL | B | L | UK | D | F | I |

Source: EC Commission.

In 1983, 8 800 000 cars were sold in the Community. 766 000 of them (i.e. 8.6%) were Japanese. In the same year Japan imported only 33 000 cars from the Community, compared with total sales of 3 140 000. Community car manufacturers therefore held about 1% of the Japanese market.

Japan

673. Although the trade aspects of relations with Japan continued to be a source of concern for the Community, cooperation was expanded and strengthened in several sectors.

The year saw a remarkable development in Japan's economy, with real GNP growth of more than 5%, the increase in the growth rate being mainly due to net external demand. This swelled Japan's overall current account surplus to over USD 30 000 million. The Community's trade deficit with Japan levelled off at about 13 000 million ECU as the results of a moderate overall increase in Japanese exports to the Community because of the European economy's lack of dynamism, coupled with a more lively increase in Community exports to Japan, particularly as regards semi-finished products.

The structural nature of this deficit led the Commission to transmit to the Japanese authorities on 2 April a new list of the Community's requests aimed at further opening up the Japanese market, particularly in manifactures. [1] In April and May Japan responded to the requests of its trading partners by economic measures to open up the market, promote imports and investment, liberalize investment markets and internationalize the yen. [2] These measures reflect Japan's intention to continue opening up to the outside world, but their scope is fairly limited and they do not seem likely to bring any appreciable improvement in the trade imbalance between the Community and Japan.

674. The Commission's efforts to promote exports to the Japanese market, using a budget appropriation of 4 420 000 ECU for 1984, took the form of a mission to Japan by a group of about 30 young business executives to learn Japanese and follow training courses in Japanese companies, plus a number of seminars, studies and sectoral missions.

In December Japan gave further assurances that its exports of certain sensitive products to the Community would be restrained in 1985. [3]

675. Cooperation between Japan and the Community in the industrial field took the form of continued consultations between Commission departments and the Japanese authorities on investment and technology transfer. An exchange of letters on research and technology was signed in December. [3] Lastly, in the

---

[1] Bull. EC 4-1984, point 2.2.19.
[2] Bull. EC 5-1984, point 2.2.14.
[3] Bull. EC 12-1984.

area of development aid, two projects for joint co-financing seem to be ready for implementation.

676. There were two specific indications during the year of the mutual determination to strengthen links between the Commission and the Japanese authorities, namely the official visit to Japan paid by Mr Gaston Thorn from 9 to 12 May[1] and the first round-table meeting between members of the Japanese Government and the Commission on 15 May.[2] Mr Ortoli also went to Japan in June, and Mr Davignon in October and December.[3]

677. Two rounds of high level consultations were held in February and October.[4]

Australia

678. Ministerial consultations between the Community and Australia took place in Canberra in March.[5] The discussions covered agricultural policy, particularly trade in beef, sheepmeat and dairy products. In addition, the Commission representative, Mr Wilhelm Haferkamp, pointed to the concern in the Community about the difficulty of access for Community manufactures to the Australian market. He also expressed his concern about the initiation of investigations by Australia with a view to introducing anti-dumping measures and countervailing duties.

Following this meeting it was decided to organize regular meetings between specialists in the trade and marketing of Community and Australian agricultural products; the first meeting of this type was held in Brussels in June, the second in December. Similarly, it was decided to continue discussing difficulties of access on both sides for manufactured goods (especially for high-quality Community exports to Australia) and the possible effect of the operation of non-tariff barriers. It was further agreed to consider how business on both sides could be helped to cooperate more closely, possibly by means of joint ventures, and to set up a working party on commodities to examine the scope for complementarity.

---

[1] Bull. EC 5-1984, point 2.2.14.
[2] Bull. EC 5-1984, point 2.2.15.
[3] Bull. EC 7/8-1984, point 2.2.18; Bull. EC 10-1984, point 2.2.18; Bull. EC 12-1984.
[4] Bull. EC 2-1984, point 2.2.20; Bull. EC 10-1984, point 2.2.19.
[5] Bull. EC 3-1984, point 2.2.25.

Mr Ivor Richard, Member of the Commission with special responsibility for employment, social affairs and education, visited Australia in July for the opening of the Centre for European Studies at the University of Sydney.

New Zealand

679. On 2 May Mr Warren Cooper, New Zealand's Minister for Foreign Affairs and Minister for Overseas Trade, visited the Commission. In talks with Mr Wilhelm Haferkamp he conveyed the importance which New Zealand attaches to butter exports and its Government's concern regarding developments on the world butter market. [1]

680. Following the general elections on 14 July, these points were raised again when Mr M. K. Moore, the new Minister for Overseas Trade, visited the Commission in September. [2]

681. In July the Council decided to maintain, on a degressive basis, the arrangements for imports of New Zealand butter into the United Kingdom, [3] and to approve at the same time an exchange of letters with New Zealand on exports of sheepmeat to 'sensitive' areas (France and Ireland).

---

[1] Bull. EC 5-1984, point 2.2.16.
[2] Bull. EC 9-1984, point 2.2.21.
[3] OJ L 187, 14.7.1984; Bull. EC 7/8-1984, point 2.1.121.

Section 5

Relations with other countries and regions

Mediterranean countries

Overall Mediterranean policy

682. In connection with work since 1982 on an overall Mediterranean policy for the enlarged Community,[1] the Commission reported to the Council in March[2] on the exploratory talks it had had with Spain and Portugal and other Mediterranean countries regarding the problems which enlargement might pose for non-member countries and the prospects for the future development of relations in the area.

This report was accompanied by Commission proposals for maintaining and strengthening the preferential links between the Mediterranean countries and the Community of Twelve as regards their traditional trade and the development of cooperation in all spheres of mutual interest. The Council commenced examination of the proposals.

San Marino

683. A delegation from San Marino, lead by Mr Giordano Bruno Reffi, Secretary of State for Foreign and Political Affairs, visited the Commission on 19 July.[3] The talks with Mr Thorn, Mr Haferkamp, Mr Natali and Mr Giolitti centred on the memorandum sent by San Marino to the Commission in September 1983 on the development of its relations with the Community.

Turkey

684. The Community's relations with Turkey continued to be determined by the country's domestic political situation. The Commission stressed on many occasions, particularly on 23 January during the visit by Mr Vahit Halefoglu,

---

[1] Sixteenth General Report, points 674 and 675; Seventeenth General Report, point 678.
[2] Bull. EC 3-1984, point 2.2.28.
[3] Bull. EC 7/8-1984, point 2.2.22.

Turkey's Foreign Minister, the importance which it attaches to the restoration of full parliamentary democracy and respect for human rights. [1]

The Association Agreement continued to function normally, though there were no major developments and the Association Council did not meet. On 22 July a number of technical matters were discussed in a meeting of the Association Committee.

Cyprus

685. The second EEC-Cyprus Financial Protocol entered into force on 1 May. It provides for 44 million ECU of aid (28 million in EIB loans, 10 million in grants and 6 million in special loans) for the period up to 31 December 1988. [2] In May a joint delegation from the EIB and the Commission selected a number of projects (water supply, electricity and sewerage schemes) to which funds could be allocated.

As regards trade, a Commission delegation held exploratory talks with the Cypriot authorities in February with a view to future negotiations on setting up a customs union. [3] Pending completion of these negotiations, the Community and Cyprus applied the 1983 trade arrangements autonomously in 1984. [4] The arrangements were then extended into the first half of 1985. [5]

On 17 December a ministerial-level meeting of the EEC-Cyprus Association Council was held in Brussels. The discussions once again chiefly concerned setting up a customs union. [6]

686. The President of the Republic of Cyprus, Mr Spyros Kyprianou, had talks in January with Mr Thorn, Mr Haferkamp and Mr Natali. [7]

Malta

687. Pending negotiation to work out trade arrangements on a contractual basis, Malta and the Community applied the 1980 arrangements autonomously in 1984, [4] and they were also extended to cover the first six months of 1985. [5]

---

[1] Bull. EC 1-1984, point 2.2.22.
[2] OJ L 85, 28.3.1984; Bull. EC 3-1984, point 2.2.29.
[3] Bull. EC 2-1984, point 2.2.23.
[4] OJ L 366, 28.12.1983; OJ L 172, 30.6.1984.
[5] OJ L 335, 22.12.1984.
[6] Bull. EC 12-1984.
[7] Bull. EC 1-1984, point 2.2.23.

Yugoslavia

688. The year saw a strengthening of ties between the Community and Yugoslavia, with an increase and a more even balance in trade between them.

The second meeting of the Cooperation Council set up under the EEC-Yugoslavia Cooperation Agreement[1] took place in Luxembourg in June,[2] when the working of the Agreement's commercial and financial provisions was reviewed and a decision adopted concerning the implementation of industrial, agricultural, scientific and technical cooperation for 1984-85.

689. In the field of financial cooperation, Yugoslavia was accorded a loan of 66.3 million ECU for modernization of the trans-Yugoslav railway, using up the remainder of the 200 million ECU in loans from the EIB's own resources provided under the first Financial Protocol of 1980, which expires on 30 June 1985.[3] Exploratory talks took place in Belgrade in October with a view to negotiation on a second Financial Protocol.[4] A proposal for a protocol to provide EIB loans totalling 400 million ECU plus 80 million ECU from the Community budget was put to the Council in December.[5]

690. Also in October Yugoslavia received an additional loan of 60 million ECU from the EIB's own resources in order to finance the trans-Yugoslav highway and a tunnel through the Karawanken.[6]

691. A seminar on EEC-Yugoslav cooperation on the markets of developing countries was held in Bled.[7]

Maghreb (Algeria, Morocco, Tunisia), Mashreq (Egypt, Jordan, Lebanon, Syria) and Israel[8]

692. The Community's relations with the Maghreb and Mashreq countries and with Israel were dominated in 1984 by the prospect of its approaching enlargement, which further heightened the anxieties of its Mediterranean part-

---

[1] OJ L 41, 14.2.1983; Seventeenth General Report, points 686 and 687.
[2] Bull. EC 6-1984, point 2.2.33.
[3] Bull. EC 2-1984, points 2.2.25 and 2.4.36.
[4] Bull. EC 10-1984, point 2.2.24.
[5] Bull. EC 12-1984.
[6] Bull. EC 10-1984, point 2.2.25; Bull. EC 3-1984, point 2.1.174.
[7] Bull. EC 6-1984, point 2.2.34.
[8] With regard to the financial protocols between these countries and the Community, see point 745 of this Report; for Cooperation Council meetings, see point 751 of this Report.

ners, concerned as they were at the implication of enlargement for their cooperation agreements. The Commission's permanent contacts with these countries were intensified so as to provide a fuller picture of the likely problems after enlargement for the maintenance of their traditional exports to the Community and the furtherance of cooperation. [1]

693. During the year Mr Thorn visited Jordan [2] and Egypt. [3] He also had talks with Israel's Prime Minister and its Minister for Trade and Industry during their visits to Brussels. [4] Mr Pisani paid official visits to Tunisia [5] and Morocco. [6]

Euro-Arab Dialogue

694. Following a worthwhile discussion at the fifth meeting of the General Committee in Athens in December 1983, [7] further progress was made on the economic and technical sides of the Euro-Arab Dialogue. In the course of the year all the working committees except that on agriculture and rural development, and the *ad hoc* working party on technology transfer, met either in plenary session or at co-chairman and co-rapporteur level. There were also meetings of specialist working parties to discuss petrochemicals and refineries, basic infrastructure (Paris symposium on urban development entitled 'Deux civilisations face à la croissance urbaine'), scientific and technical cooperation (technical college) and culture—the last of these a follow-up to the Hamburg symposium. [8]

695. The *ad hoc* 'troika' group set up in November 1980 to prepare a Euro-Arab meeting at ministerial level [9] met on 12 and 13 November in Tunis to discuss the possibility of holding a sixth meeting of the General Committee in an Arab capital in 1985. [7] The group dealt primarily with the political side of the Dialogue, and agreed to hold another preparatory meeting wihin two months.

---

[1] Point 682 of this Report; Bull. EC 2-1984, points 2.2.27 and 2.2.28; Bull. EC 3-1984, point 2.2.31; Bull. EC 4-1984, point 2.2.23.
[2] Bull. EC 3-1984, point2.2.32.
[3] Bull. EC 3-1984, point 2.2.33.
[4] Bull. EC 1-1984, point 2.2.25; Bull. EC 2-1984, point 2.2.28.
[5] Bull. EC 3-1984, point 2.2.31.
[6] Bull. EC 5-1984, point 2.2.24.
[7] Seventeenth General Report, point 694.
[8] Bull. EC 4-1984, point 2.2.29.
[9] Fourteenth General Report, point 665.

Countries of the Gulf and the Arabian Peninsula

696. The Deputy Secretary-General of the Gulf Cooperation Council visited the Commission to discuss the two organizations' joint technical programme and other aspects of future inter-regional cooperation. [1]

In informal talks on 7 and 8 November in Bahrain, representatives of the Commission and the GCC explored the possibility of opening negotiations for a cooperation agreement between the two regions.

Yemen Arab Republic

697. A Cooperation Agreement between the Community and the Yemen Arab Republic was initialled in May [2] and signed on 9 October. [3] This is the Community's first agreement with a country in this region and results from an initiative taken by the Council in 1980. Due to run for five years, after which it will be renewable, the Agreement covers commercial, economic and development cooperation.

Asia

Association of South-East Asian Nations

698. The meeting between the Foreign Ministers of the Community and Asean which took place in Dublin on 15 and 16 November [4] confirmed the broad measure of agreement between the two groups on major political and economic issues. A protocol extending the EEC-Asean Cooperation Agreement to Brunei Darussalam (a member of Asean since January 1984) was signed. [5] The EEC-Asean Joint Cooperation Committee held its fifth meeting in Thailand on 17 and 18 December. [6]

---

[1] Bull. EC 4-1984, point 2.2.24; Seventeenth General Report, point 695.
[2] Bull. EC 5-1984, point 2.2.25.
[3] OJ C 258, 26.9.1984; Bull. EC 9-1984, point 2.2.23.
[4] Bull. EC 11-1984, point 2.2.28.
[5] Bull. EC 9-1984, point 2.2.24.
[6] Bull. EC 12-1984.

699. As part of EEC-Asean trade and economic cooperation arrangements, [1] three investment seminars were held in April, [2] and a group of European businessmen paid a trade visit to Bangkok, Singapore and Kuala Lumpur in December. [3]

700. Mr Thorn paid an official visit to Indonesia in May. [4]

India

701. The third meeting of the EEC-India Joint Commission, set up under the 1981 Agreement on commercial, economic and development cooperation, [5] was held in New Delhi on 5 and 7 May. [6] A programme for industrial cooperation for 1984 and of scientific and technical cooperation for 1984 and after was approved.

As part of this cooperation, a conference on technology transfer and investments was held in Berlin on 26 and 27 November. [7]

Pakistan

702. The eighth meeting of the EEC-Pakistan Joint Commission, set up under the 1976 Agreement, [8] was held in Islamabad on 25 and 26 February. [9] On 23 October the Council authorized the Commission to open negotiations with Pakistan with a view to the conclusion of a new agreement to cover commercial, economic and development cooperation;[10] these are to be held in January 1985.

In June the Pakistan Foreign Minister, Mr Sahabzada Yaqub Khan, was received by Mr Haferkamp.[11]

---

[1] Seventeenth General Report, point 700.
[2] Bull. EC 4-1984, point 2.2.25.
[3] Bull. EC 12-1984.
[4] Bull. EC 5-1984, point 2.2.28.
[5] OJ L 328, 16.11.1981.
[6] Bull. EC 5-1984, point 2.2.26.
[7] Bull. EC 11-1984, point 2.2.30.
[8] OJ L 168, 28.6.1976.
[9] Bull. EC 2-1984, point 2.2.29.
[10] Bull. EC 2-1984, point 2.2.30; Bull. EC 10-1984, point 2.2.28.
[11] Bull. EC 6-1984, point 2.2.35.

Bangladesh

703. The seventh session of the Joint Commission set up under the EEC-Bangladesh Commercial Cooperation Agreement[1] was held in Brussels on 16 and 17 July.[2]

Sri Lanka

704. The sixth session of the Joint Commission set up under the EEC-Sri Lanka Commercial Cooperation Agreement[3] took place in Brussels on 28 and 29 May.[4]

South Korea

705. Relations with South Korea were intensified during the year. In May Mr Thorn paid the first official visit by a Commission President to South Korea.[5]

The second session of annual high-level consultations between the Commission and Korea, as decided on in 1983, took place in Brussels on 3 and 4 July.[6] Preparations for this session had been made in the course of a visit to the Commission by the Korean Minister for Trade and Industry.[7]

Latin America

706. With a view to strengthening relations between the Community and Latin America, the Commission sent to the Council on 11 April a communication containing guidelines for action in various sectors;[8] specific proposals will be made in the light of discussions within the Council.

Bilateral meetings took place during the year with the government authorities of Bolivia,[9] Costa Rica,[10] Ecuador[11] and El Salvador.[12] Mr Thorn paid official

---

[1] OJ L 319, 19.11.1979.
[2] Bull. EC 7/8-1984, point 2.2.26.
[3] OJ L 247, 23.9.1975.
[4] Bull. EC 5-1984, point 2.2.27.
[5] Bull. EC 5-1984, point 2.2.30.
[6] Bull. EC 7/8-1984, points 2.2.24 and 2.2.25.
[7] Bull. EC 5-1984, point 2.2.31.
[8] Bull. EC 4-1984, point 1.3.1 *et seq.*
[9] Bull. EC 7/8-1984, point 2.2.28.
[10] Bull. EC 1-1984, point 2.2.27; Bull. EC 6-1984, point 2.2.37.
[11] Bull. EC 2-1984, point 2.2.31.
[12] Bull. EC 7/8-1984, point 2.2.27.

visits to Venezuela, Peru and Colombia towards the end of the year.[1] the EEC-Brazil and EEC-Mexico Joint Committees met in January[2] and December[3] respectively. Preparations continued with a view to setting up a Europe-Latin America Institute.[4]

Central America

707. In response to the wishes expressed by the Council in November 1983, which were based on an initiative by the Foreign Minister of the Federal Republic of Germany, the Commission sent to the Council in February a discussion paper on the scope for strengthening relations between the Community and Central America.

On an initiative by the President of Costa Rica, Mr Luis Alberto Monge, a conference was held in San José on 28 and 29 September,[5] attended by the Foreign Ministers of the five countries of the Central American Common Market and the Member States of the Community; the Commission was represented by Mr Pisani. Spain and Portugal, as prospective members of the Community, and the countries of the Contadora Group (Colombia, Mexico, Panama and Venezuela), which are trying to help the Central American States to a comprehensive regional agreement, were observers at the meeting, the aim of which was to obtain political solidarity and economic support from the Community for the countries of the region.

The meeting resulted in the establishment of a new political and economic dialogue, both between Europe and Central America and within the region itself. This structure could be placed on an institutional basis by the negotiation of a framework cooperation agreement. The Community undertook in San José to make a special effort, in the context of its present and future programmes of aid for developing countries, to promote the development and economic integration of the region.

Andean Group

708. With the endorsement of Parliament,[6] the Council approved in June[7] the Cooperation Agreement concluded between the Community and the Andean Group (Bolivia, Colombia, Ecuador, Peru and Venezuela).[8]

---

[1] Bull. EC 11-1984, point 2.2.31.
[2] Bull. EC 1-1984, point 2.2.26.
[3] Bull. EC 12-1984.
[4] Bull. EC 7/8-1984, point 2.2.29.
[5] Bull. EC 9-1984, point 1.3.1 et seq.
[6] OJ C 127, 14.5.1984.
[7] OJ L 135, 8.6.1984; Bull. EC 6-1984, point 2.2.36.
[8] Seventeenth General Report, point 708.

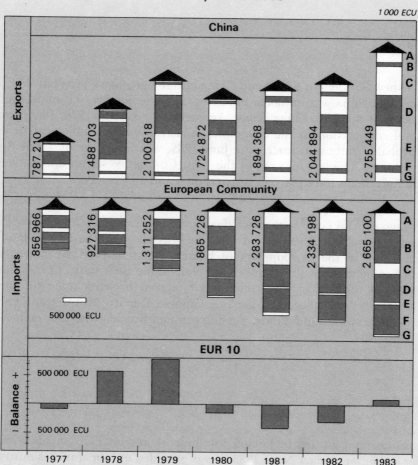

Community-China trade

1 000 ECU

A Food and live animals chiefly for food, beverages, tobacco
B Crude materials, inedible (except fuels), mineral fuels, lubricants, etc.
C Animal and vegetable oils, fats and waxes, chemical products
D Manufactured goods classified chiefly by raw material
E Machinery and transport equipment
F Miscellaneous manufactured articles
G Miscellaneous articles and transactions

There was a highly variable pattern of trade between the Community and the People's Republic of China between 1977 and 1983, surpluses and deficits alternating from year to year. The Community's main exports to China consists of manufactured goods, chiefly chemical products and transport equipment, and its imports are primarily raw materials and mass-market manufactures (mainly textiles). However, a certain increase, albeit irregular, is evident in the share of manufactured goods in China's exports.

State-trading countries

China

709. A new Trade and Economic Cooperation Agreement between the Community and China was initialled in Peking on 26 September. [1] It takes over the substance of the EEC-China Trade Agreement of 3 April 1978 [2] and extends bilateral cooperation to the economic, industrial and technological fields. It will probably enter into force on 1 June 1985, when the current Trade Agreement expires. The last meeting of the Joint Committee set up under the 1978 Trade Agreement took place in Brussels on 4 and 5 December. [3]

710. Two official visits took place during the year: in June the Chinese Prime Minister, Mr Zhao Ziyang, had talks in Brussels with the President of the Commission on the development of bilateral relations and on international issues; [4] in September and October Mr Haferkamp took part in Peking in the first session of high-level consultations, [5] agreed between the two sides in 1983. [6] On 4 December, Mr Jia She, Chinese Deputy Minister for Foreign Economic Relations and Trade, passing through Brussels, met Mr Haferkamp and Mr Narjes.

Poland

711. Humanitarian aid to Poland totalling 14 million ECU, made available under amending budget No 2/1983, [7] was provided in four tranches during the year. It was transmitted via Community non-governmental organizations for

---

[1] Bull. EC 7/8-1984, point 2.2.30; Bull. EC 9-1984, point 2.2.26.
[2] OJ L 123, 11.5.1978.
[3] Bull. EC 12-1984.
[4] Bull. EC 6-1984, point 1.7.1. *et seq.*
[5] Bull. EC 10-1984, point 2.2.30.
[6] Seventeenth General Report, point 712.
[7] OJ L 331, 28.11.1983; Seventeenth General Report, point 716; Bull. EC 10-1984, point 2.2.31.

distribution by the Church and other non-governmental agencies to the neediest sections of the population.

Romania

712. The EEC-Romania Joint Committee established under the Agreement of 28 July 1980 [1] held its fourth meeting in Bucharest on 8 and 9 November. [2] The Committee noted the considerable decline in Community exports to Romania in 1983, due largely to Romania's policy of improving its balance of trade and payments. The two sides expressed the hope that the slight increase in Community exports during the first half of the year would continue.

---

[1] OJ L 352, 29.12.1980.
[2] Bull. EC 11-1984, point 2.2.32.

Section 6

Development cooperation

North-South relations

713. Although the plan to reopen the North-South Dialogue in the form of global negotiations did not come any closer to realization in 1984, the problems of development and relations between industrialized and developing countries formed the subject of many meetings and much discussion in international forums, notably the United Nations General Assembly and the Economic and Social Council, the Bretton Woods institutions and Unctad.[1] Unido's Fourth General Conference in Vienna was one of the major events in this connection,[2] and North-South issues figured prominently in the Western Summit deliberations in London,[3] notably the debt problem; the debtor countries have also held a number of meetings on this subject.

The Dialogue has continued, then. The Community and the ACP countries have reached a new agreement to succeed the second Lomé Convention.[4] Generally speaking, the international community's attention has focused on Africa's problems, including the refugee question. There seems to be increasingly acute awareness of the need to reshape the world economy as a whole and of the various parties' responsibilities in this sphere, and also of the links between financial, monetary, trade and other problems.

There are still serious differences of opinion, however, concerning the solutions and the degree of multilateral cooperation needed, as demonstrated by the discussions concerning evaluation of the international development strategy.[5] The developing countries are of the opinion that if any progress is to be made, the system of economic relations must be reformed—especially its financial, monetary and trade aspects. In these difficult discussions the Community is endeavouring to see that a realistic, constructive spirit prevails, typified by an original development cooperation policy.

---

[1] Points 752, 757 and 769 of this Report.
[2] Point 76 of this Report.
[3] Point 118 of this Report.
[4] Point 714 of this Report.
[5] Point 754 of this Report.

Negotiations for a new ACP-EEC Convention

714. The new ACP-EEC Convention was signed in Lomé on 8 December by the Community, its 10 Member States and 65 African, Caribbean and Pacific States.[1] This represents the outcome of the negotiations begun in October 1983;[2] difficult at times, the negotiations continued through the year[3] and were concluded in Brussels in November.[4]

The negotiations were conducted by the Commission on behalf of the Community and by the Committee of Ambassadors on behalf of the ACP States.

As compared with the second,[5] the third Lomé Convention has been restructured. It clearly sets out the objectives and principles of ACP-EEC cooperation and contains many improvements and some major innovations which reflect the desire of the two sides to maintain and strengthen the special relationship they have enjoyed for a quarter of a century.

For the first time, explicit mention is made in the Convention of human rights and respect for human dignity. Attached to the Convention is a declaration which stresses the right of each individual, in his own country or in another country, to respect for his dignity and to protection under the law. The declaration also re-emphasizes the commitment by all the parties to oppose all forms of discrimination and to work towards stamping out apartheid.

In agricultural cooperation, more emphasis will be placed on the ACP States' food supply, with the Community agreeing to integrate its aid more closely into these States' own food strategies and to step up its supplies of agricultural products available in the Community. Improvements have also been introduced in the operation of the Technical Centre for Agricultural and Rural Cooperation.

---

[1] Bull. EC 12-1984. The ACP States which signed the Convention are: Antigua and Barbuda, Bahamas, Barbados, Belize, Benin, Botswana, Burkina Faso, Burundi, Cameroon, Cape Verde, Central African Republic, Chad, Comoros, Congo, Djibouti, Dominica, Equatorial Guinea, Ethiopia, Fiji, Gabon, Gambia, Ghana, Grenada, Guinea, Guinea-Bissau, Guyana, Ivory Coast, Jamaica, Kenya, Kiribati, Lesotho, Liberia, Madagascar, Malawi, Mali, Mauritania, Mauritius, Mozambique, Niger, Nigeria, Papua New Guinea, Rwanda, Saint Christopher and Nevis, Saint Lucia, Saint Vincent and the Grenadines, Samoa, Sao Tome and Principe, Senegal, Seychelles, Sierra Leone, Solomon Islands, Somalia, Sudan, Suriname, Swaziland, Tanzania, Togo, Tonga, Trinidad and Tobago, Tuvalu, Uganda, Vanuatu, Zaire, Zambia and Zimbabwe.
[2] Seventeenth General Report, point 738; Bull. EC 1-1984, point 2.2.29.
[3] Bull. EC 2-1984, points 2.2.32 and 2.2.33; Bull. EC 5-1984, point 2.2.39 *et seq.*; Bull. EC 6-1984, point 2.2.42 *et seq.*; see also Bull. EC 7/8-1984, point 2.2.37; Bull. EC 9-1984, points 2.2.27 to 2.2.29; Bull. EC 10-1984, point 2.2.34 *et seq.*
[4] Bull. EC 11-1984, point 1.1.1 *et seq.*
[5] Thirteenth General Report, point 509.

In the area of regional cooperation, the Community has agreed to provide aid for dealing with problems affecting two or more ACP States and requiring long-term solutions, such as natural disasters, endemic diseases, and more especially drought and desertification; it was decided that special attention would be focused on these problems.

In the case of financial and technical cooperation, the emphasis was placed on the Community assisting the ACP States' sectoral programmes, while at the same time maintaining its aid for projects in the ACP States. The Convention's financial resources have been increased considerably (by 60% in ECU) and this is evidence of the fact that, despite its own difficulties, the Community intends to continue its efforts in real terms. Specific funds have also been earmarked for contributions towards schemes to help refugees to integrate in their new country or in their country of origin.

TABLE 14

Funds available under the third Lomé Convention

million ECU

Sixth European Development Fund	
Subsidies	4 860
of which: projects and programmes	(4 360)
emergency aid/refugees	(290)
interest subsidies	(210)
Repayable aid	1 200
of which: special loans	(600)
venture capital	(600)
Stabex	925
Sysmin	415
Subtotal (A)	7 400
EIB own resources Subtotal (B)	1 100
Grand total (A) + (B)	8 500

In the sphere of commercial cooperation, the second Convention already granted almost completely free access to the Community market for goods from the ACP States. Under the new Convention, the Community has eased the rules on origin, offered better terms for imports of ACP rice and rum, and improved the procedure for examining ACP requests for preferential access for their agricultural produce. In addition, aid for ACP trade promotion has been extended to the services sector, notably tourism, and an ACP-EEC joint committee is to be set up to monitor and examine trends on the international commodity markets.

The system for the stabilization of export earnings from agricultural products (Stabex) has been extended and improved: three new products have been added to the list of those covered by the system, and the criteria determining eligibility for Stabex transfers have been eased for a number of ACP States. In addition, it has been agreed that the recipient States will provide more information on the use of the resources transferred, which will make the system more effective. Lastly, the amount of Stabex funds available has been increased to 925 million ECU.

Sysmin, the system for maintaining the mining industry as a going concern, has been revised and derogations have been introduced from the eligibility criteria on which the transfer of appropriations is based. In the light of experience gained with the second Lomé Convention, the system's management has been improved, and it will be open to a larger number of ACP States.

The new Convention contains specific provisions relating to shipping, fisheries and investment.

Cooperation in fisheries has been appreciably expanded. The Community will support efforts by the ACP countries to develop and conserve their fishery resources, and the new Convention also provides for the possibility of negotiating bilateral fishery agreements.

More attention has been paid to the question of investment than in Lomé II, with greater incentives for promoting and protecting Community investment in the ACP States, notably through a stable investment climate. It was agreed to carry out a number of studies, including one on the possibility of devising a joint ACP-EEC system of investment insurance.

The objectives of cooperation on energy and mining have been clarified, making it possible to step up the aid which the Community gives for assessing ACP resources and energy requirements, and adapting production infrastructure. The new Convention lays down aims for industrial cooperation based rather more on maintaining and rehabilitating what already exists. The role of the Centre for Industrial Development and how it is to operate have also been spelt out more precisely in order to make the Centre more effective.

Cultural and social cooperation is a completely new area in ACP-EEC relations; it emphasizes the importance of human resources, including women's contribution to the ACP States' economic and social development. Financial and technical cooperation will in future take greater account of cultural and social considerations, in order to preserve more fully the identity and cultural dignity of the local people. Provision is now also made for the situation of ACP migrant workers and students to be discussed within the bodies set up under the Convention.

As for environmental matters, the new Convention makes specific reference to the ecological aspect of development as it affects the objectives set and the main areas of cooperation, and also the procedures for implementing financial and technical assistance. [1]

The institutional set-up will remain largely the same, but with the guiding role of the ACP-EEC Council being reinforced. It has been decided to merge the Consultative Assembly and the Joint Committee into one body, the new Joint Assembly, so that parliamentarians can play a more effective role in the operation of the Convention. There will also be an improvement in the procedures for consulting representatives of the economic and social sectors in the ACP States and in the Member States.

Generalized preferences

715. On 18 December the Council adopted the various regulations and decisions concerning the opening of the Community's generalized tariff preferences for 1985, [2] the final year of the new scheme the structure of which was decided on by the Council in December 1980 for the period 1981-85. [3] The Commission had presented its proposals in July, [4] and Parliament and the Economic and Social Committee expressed their opinions in November and October respectively [5] and again in December. [6]

The number of beneficiary countries rose to 128 when Brunei Darussalam became independent, and Greenland, after its withdrawal from the Community, will benefit from the scheme as a dependent territory of Denmark once the Treaty changing its status enters into force.

---

[1] Bull. EC 10-1984, point 2.2.32 et seq.; Bull. EC 11-1984, point 2.2.34.
[2] OJ L 338, 27.12.1984; Bull. EC 11-1984, point 2.2.36; Bull. EC 12-1984.
[3] OJ L 354, 29.12.1984; Fourteenth General Report, point 579.
[4] OJ C 294, 5.11.1984; Bull. EC 7/8-1984, points 2.2.38 to 2.2.41.
[5] OJ C 337, 17.12.1984; OJ C 343, 24.12.1984; Bull. EC 10-1984, point 2.4.45.
[6] OJ C 12, 14.1.1985; Bull. EC 12-1984. These last opinions relate to the inclusion of Greenland (OJ C 316, 27.11.1984).

The preferential margin for some 35 agricultural products has been improved, three new products have been included. There are changes in the preferential duty on tobacco and the distribution between Member States of the five existing quotas.

For industrial manufactures and semimanufactures, the Community has made some slight changes to the list of sensitive products and to the management rules for a number of origins. Individual preferential amounts have been variously increased, while the offer for non-sensitive products has been increased by 10%.

The scheme remains unchanged in respect of ECSC products.

The ceilings for textiles covered by the Multifibre Arrangement have been raised by the same amount as last year in the light of trade between 1977 and 1981. In the case of the individual ceilings for products which do not come under the MFA, the 1984 amounts will continue to apply in 1985, with a few technical changes in the definition of categories.

716. In the course of the year, the Commission organized information seminars in the Philippines (Manila) and Malaysia (Kuala Lumpur) for the Asean countries,[1] Venezuela (Valencia, Caracas) for the Andean Pact countries,[2] and Mexico (Guadalajara, Monterrey, Mexico City). It also cooperated with the UNDP/Unctad project in arranging a regional seminar in Honduras (Tegucigalpa) for the Central American and Caribbean countries.

Commodities and world agreements

717. Levels of participation and capitalization reached were insufficient to allow the Common Fund for Commodities[3] to be set up in 1984, despite the appreciable improvement since last year and the steady increase in membership.

718. The fourth International Coffee Agreement, which came into force provisionally in 1983,[4] has had to cope with a shortage.[5] To hold prices to a level acceptable to consumers, the quota system has had to be bolstered by an

---

[1] Bull. EC 4-1984, point 2.2.33.
[2] Bull. EC 7/8-1984, point 2.2.42.
[3] Fourteenth General Report, point 610.
[4] Seventeenth General Report, point 732.
[5] Bull. EC 6-1984, point 2.2.47; Bull. EC 10-1984, point 2.2.40.

extra four allocations of a million sacks and the 1984/85 quota has been set at a considerably higher level than for the preceding coffee year.

719. Under the third International Cocoa Agreement, there was no need for intervention on the market to support prices (the price range is established in 1980 dollars); instead, cocoa prices rose in 1984 to a level higher than the lower intervention price set by the Agreement. The Community and its Member States formed part of the consensus in favour of extending the Agreement for a further year, i.e. until 30 September 1985, and are playing an active part in the negotiations for a fourth international agreement.

Two sessions of the negotiating conference have already taken place.[1] The second of them enabled great progress to be made in clarifying the positions of producers and consumers, especially as regards price mechanisms and further protective measures. The way thus seems to be open for the real negotiation of an effective stabilization agreement to be begun at the next session, which is due to begin on 18 February 1985.

720. On 29 June in New York the Community and its Member States signed the first International Tropical Timber Agreement,[2] which was negotiated in Geneva in 1983.[3] In September the Commission proposed to the Council that the agreement be finally approved, or at any rate applied provisionally by the Community as soon as it came into force.[4]

721. At the third session of the United Nations Conference for the negotiation of a new international sugar agreement, held in Geneva from 12 June to 5 July, the main parties (Australia, Brazil, the Community and Cuba) differed so widely in their assessment of the world market that it was not possible to conclude an agreement containing economic provisions.[5] An administrative agreement was nevertheless concluded and will enter into force on 1 January 1985. Acting on a Commission proposal made in October, the Council decided in December that the Community should sign and conclude this agreement.[6]

722. Under the International Wheat Agreement, the Community continued to play an active part on the International Wheat Council, whose 100th session was held in Ottawa in June,[7] and on the Food Aid Committee.

---

[1] Bull. EC 5-1984, point 2.2.46; Bull. EC 7/8-1984, points 2.2.43 and 2.2.44; Bull. EC 11-1984, point 2.2.37.
[2] Bull.EC 6-1984, point 2.2.45.
[3] Seventeenth General Report, point 737.
[4] Bull. EC 9-1984, point 2.2.29.
[5] Bull. EC 6-1984, point 2.2.48.
[6] Bull. EC 10-1984, point 2.2.39; Bull. EC 12-1984.
[7] Bull. EC 6-1984, point 2.2.46.

723. Pending the negotiation of a new international agreement, the International Olive Oil Council—in which the Community participates—decided to extend the existing Agreement, due to expire on 31 December 1984.

724. The International Agreement on Jute and Jute Products, which at present brings together 27 countries, including all the Member States of the Community, and the Community itself, entered into force provisionally on 9 January 1984. [1] With a view to its definitive entry into force, the Commissilon asked the Council in November to make provision for the Community and the Member States to conclude and ratify the Agreement.

During the year the Council and the Committee on Projects set up under the Agreement each held two sessions.

725. The Community and its Member States took part in the work of the International Natural Rubber Council and its committees, mainly concerning the management of a buffer stock of some 270 000 tonnes, which was accumulated over the period 1981-83 and helped considerably in stabilizing natural rubber prices on the international market. Since the 1979 Agreement is due to end in 1985, the Council is considering convening a conference to negotiate a second international agreement.

Hunger in the world

726. In 1984 the Community pursued its efforts to implement the 'plan of action to combat world hunger' adopted by the Council at the end of 1981. [2]

727. In June the Commission presented a report [3] to the Council on the implementation of the food strategy programme [4] and in October a full evaluation of progress and prospects in this sphere. The Council examined the report in November and confirmed the importance it attached to this initiative being continued and widened. [5]

In June the Council, having discussed in detail the guidelines for the campaigns with a specific theme, [6] stressed the importance of these operations designed to safeguard and improve natural production factors.

---

[1] Bull. EC 1-1984, points 2.2.30 and 2.2.31; Bull. EC 5-1984, point 2.2.47.
[2] Fifteenth General Report, point 659; Seventeenth General Report, points 720 and 721.
[3] Bull. EC 6-1984, point 2.2.49.
[4] Seventeenth General Report, point 720.
[5] Bull. EC 11-1984, point 2.2.42.
[6] Bull. EC 6-1984, point 2.2.50.

728. The special action programme against hunger in the world, decided on by the Community at the end of 1983 and allocated 50 million ECU, [1] was being implemented during the year.

729. Further operations were decided on by the Commission in November and December. [2] The programme, with a total appropriation of 5.8 million ECU, is largely made up of schemes to combat desert creep and erosion, to improve the use of water, and to contribute to the operation of grain marketing bodies and agricultural credit establishments, mainly in the least-developed countries.

730. In view of the grave situation caused by drought in many parts of Africa (especially Ethiopia and the Sahel), the Community set two emergency plans in motion in 1984. The first—in April—provided over 80 million ECU (23 million ECU being used as emergency aid and 60 million ECU as food aid in 1984). The second—approved in October—was for some 60 million ECU (of which 35 million ECU has already been used as emergency aid and 23.5 million ECU as food aid). [3]

At its meeting in Dublin on 4 December the European Council stressed the urgency of concerted international action to combat the famine in Africa, especially in the Sahel and in Ethiopia. It considered that the food aid and emergency aid to be supplied from the Community and its Member States, by the next harvest, should total 1.2 million tonnes of cereals.

Food aid

731. Under the procedures laid down in the framework Regulation of December 1982, [4] the Council decided on 7 May to grant the following aid to the developing countries for 1984: cereals: an initial instalment of 927 663 tonnes; a second instalment which may go up to 200 000 tonnes; milk powder: a maximum of 122 500 tonnes; butteroil: a maximum of 32 760 tonnes; sugar: a maximum of 13 500 tonnes; vegetable oil/olive oil: a maximum of 20 000 tonnes; other products; the equivalent of at most 147 000 tonnes of cereals. [5]

Under the same Regulation [5] the Commission then took a number of decisions:

---

[1] Seventeenth General Report, point 721.
[2] Bull. EC 12-1984.
[3] Bull. EC 10-1984, point 2.2.41; Bull. EC 11-1984, point 1.2.1 et seq.; Bull. EC 12-1984.
[4] OJ L 352, 14.12.1982; Sixteenth General Report, point 728.
[5] Bull. EC 5-1984, point 2.2.49.

(i) food aid allocations for non-governmental organizations, international
agencies (WFP, UNHCR, ICRC, etc.) and developing countries—in particular low-income countries with a food shortfall; [1]

(ii) emergency food aid allocations to certain countries, [2] mainly in East, West
and southern Africa and in Central America.

732. In September the Commission presented its proposals to the Council for
the 1985 food aid programme. [3]

733. On 19 June, after Parliament had delivered its opinion, [4] the Council
adopted a Regulation authorizing the implementation of alternative operations
in place of food-aid deliveries; where the food crop situation or the level of
stocks in a given country was such that it would be wasteful or harmful to
supply food aid, [5] financial aid could be given instead.

734. On 28 June, after Parliament had stated its views, [6] the Council adopted
the new Convention between the Community and the United Nations Relief
and Works Agency for Palestine Refugees. [7] This Convention, which will run
for three years, covers the provision of food aid and a cash contribution to an
education programme.

Emergency aid

735. During the year, emergency aid totalling some 64 million ECU was granted
for the ACP States and associated overseas countries and territories. This aid,
of a humanitarian nature, went primarily to the victims of the drought severely
affecting many African countries. In 1984 the Commission adopted decisions
for such emergency aid totalling 60 million ECU. An initial series between
January and October enabled foodstuffs, emergency transport, seeds and medical care worth more than 27 million ECU to be made available to these
countries.

As the situation deteriorated during the second half of the year in a number of
Sahel countries and in Ethiopia, the Commission adopted a second plan to

---

[1] Bull. EC 5-1984, point 2.2.51; Bull. EC 6-1984, point 2.2.53; Bull. EC 7/8-1984, point 2.2.46.
[2] Bull. EC 2-1984, point 2.2.40; Bull. EC 3-1984, point 2.2.42; Bull. EC 4-1984, point 2.2.36; Bull. EC
5-1984, point 2.2.50; Bull. EC 6-1984, point 2.2.5; Bull. EC 7/8-1984, point 2.2.47.
[3] Bull. EC 9-1984, point 2.2.30.
[4] OJ C 127, 14.5.1984.
[5] OJ L 165, 23.6.1984; Bull. EC 6-1984, point 2.2.54.
[6] OJ C 172, 2.7.1984.
[7] OJ L 188, 16.7.1984; Bull. EC 6-1984, point 2.2.51.

combat hunger on 31 October. [1] This provides for 35 million ECU's worth of emergency aid (immediate supply of foodstuffs, emergency transport, medical programmes, etc.), and covers the Sahel countries, [2] Sudan and a number of countries in southern Africa, though the main beneficiary is Ethiopia, with 18 million ECU. Total emergency aid to Ethiopia, where the situation is at present worse than anywhere else in Africa, amounts to 23 million ECU for 1984. Some 2.5 million ECU has also been allocated to finance programmes to help refugees from Ethiopia and Chad in a number of other countries, and others who have returned to Ethiopia.

In addition to these two plans, other emergency aid totalling about 4 700 000 ECU was granted for ACP countries and associated OCTs. This included aid to victims of cyclones in Swaziland (100 000 ECU), Madagascar (520 000 ECU) and Mayotte (270 000 ECU), and also aid to Mozambican refugees in Zimbabwe (1 800 000 ECU), displaced persons in Uganda (250 000 ECU) etc.

Operations totalling 7 950 000 ECU were launched to help disaster victims in other non-member or developing countries. The principal recipients of such aid were the victims of the drought and of Cyclone Domoina in Mozambique (4.6 million ECU); aid for drought victims also went to Morocco (500 000 ECU) and Brazil (500 000 ECU), and aid was also granted to the victims of the typhoons in the Philippines (500 000 ECU) and the floods in Cambodia (250 000 ECU).

Aid for displaced persons amounted to 1 600 000 ECU: Central America (800 000 ECU), Thailand (300 000 ECU), Angola (500 000 ECU).

Trade promotion

736. During the year, more emphasis was placed on regional programmes for the ACP States than on measures financed through national programmes. The aid was focused in particular on setting up ACP chambers of commerce, a joint ACP-EEC conference for businessmen in Hamburg and continuing support for the organizations set up to promote ACP trade (COLEACP, Fedeau, Aproma, export credit insurance). Encouraging results have been obtained by selected

---

[1] Bull. EC 10-1984, point 2.2.41; Bull. EC 11-1984, point 1.2.1 et seq.
[2] Mali (2 million ECU); Niger (3 million ECU); Burkina Faso (500 000 ECU); Senegal (1 million ECU); Mauritania (2 million ECU); Chad (3 million ECU); Sudan (1 million ECU). Some emergency aid, and the quantities of emergency food aid to be allocated to these countries, have yet to be determined.

countries which have taken part in specialized trade fairs and in trade missions. Increased attention has been paid to tourism as a factor of development.

Stabex

737. The Commission received 51 transfer applications in respect of 1983 under the export earnings stabilization system (Stabex) set up under the second Lomé Convention. Of these, 30 were rejected under the Convention rules and, following appraisal, 21 gave rise to transfers totalling 50 403 601 ECU.

The breakdown by recipient country is given in Table 15.

TABLE 15

ACP State	Product	Amount of transfer (ECU)
Ethiopia	Sesame seeds	3 150 900
Ethiopia	Cotton	1 665 021
Grenada	Cocoa beans	1 230 867
Guinea-Bissau	Sawn wood	267 121
Guinea-Bissau	Shrimps and prawns	710 289
Guinea-Bissau	Palm nuts	437 356
Madagascar	Raw sisal	1 461 636
Mali	Groundnut products	3 200 724
Sao Tome and Principe	Cocoa beans	3 397 335
Solomon Islands	Copra	1 463 298
Solomon Islands	Sawn wood	34 791
Sudan	Groundnuts	7 900 891
Swaziland	Cotton products	5 085 350
Rwanda	Leather	497 157
Tanzania	Cashew nuts and kernels	—
Tanzania	Raw sisal	—
Togo	Coffee	4 190 324
Togo	Cocoa	9 543 759
Tonga	Copra products	732 546
Tonga	Bananas	11 034
Tuvalu	Copra	7 384

The Commission has also received four transfer applications from one overseas territory and two ACP States still covered by the OCT allocation. None of these applications is admissible.

The financial resources available (97 897 637 ECU) are enough to cover the whole amount of transfers to be effected in respect of 1983.

ACP protocols

738. The Protocols on bananas and rum have been applied to the satisfaction of all the parties concerned. [1]

Under the Protocol on ACP sugar, the guaranteed prices for the 1984/85 delivery period were fixed at 44.34 ECU/100 kg for raw sugar and 54.68 ECU/100 kg for white sugar. As the body managing the Protocol, the Commission decided to reduce the agreed quantity for Trinidad and Tobago, following non-delivery for reasons not attributable to *force majeure*. The same quantity was temporarily reallocated. [2]

Mining cooperation

739. Contributions under Sysmin (system of mining cooperation) were approved for Guyana (white bauxite) and Rwanda (tin) with respect to 1982 and 1983, years when market conditions were depressed. [3] The aid will be made available as far as possible as part of co-financing arrangements (EIB, IBRD, IFC).

Energy cooperation

740. The implementation of financial and technical cooperation in the energy sector continued within the framework of the guidelines set out in the Lomé Convention, the main emphasis being on efforts to achieve energy self-sufficiency through the exploitation of the ACP States' own resources. The total volume of EDF operations (over 15 million ECU) fell sharply by comparison with 1983 (77 million ECU), but all the operations were concentrated on electrification schemes, particularly electrification in rural areas (80% of the sums allocated).

Industrial cooperation

741. Industrial cooperation (excluding mining and energy but including small business) absorbed some 25.4 million ECU during the year. This form of cooperation mainly concerns agro-industry (tea, abattoirs/refrigerated plant,

---

[1] OJ L 172, 30.6.1984.
[2] Bull. EC 11-1984, point 2.2.46.
[3] Bull. EC 9-1984, point 2.2.34; Bull. EC 10-1984, point 2.2.49.

walnut processing, textiles) and the building sector (cement works, marble extraction, quarrying). Small business operations consist mainly in opening credit lines and technical cooperation.

742. In addition, the EDF contributed 6.82 million ECU to the financing of the Centre for the Development of Industry in 1984. The Centre continued to improve its performance with a greater number of operations, more projects at the production stage and better use and administration of the budget.

Agricultural cooperation

743. Rural development continued to be one of the Community's priorities in development cooperation. In 1984 rural development projects and programmes totalling about 300 million ECU were approved; this amount represents some 25% of total Community development aid for projects.

In the ACP countries the Community intensified its efforts in fields such as integrated rural development, the development of cash crops, stock farming and fisheries. In accordance with the priorities set by the Community, new projects were approved to develop food crops, safeguard and improve natural resources and aid rural credit institutions.

In the non-associated developing countries the bulk of EEC aid went to the agricultural and rural sector.

Operations for a total of 58 million ECU were approved under the special programme to combat hunger in the world; most of them concerned the least-developed countries.

The Community also made considerable efforts to promote agricultural research in the Third World during the year, using the various cooperation instruments at its disposal.

Financial and technical cooperation

ACP States and OCTs

744. Implementation of the ACP States' indicative programmes continued satisfactorily; commitment of funds speeded up markedly, the level rising from 48%[1] to 66.2%. Some ACP States' indicative programmes had to be modified

---

[1] Seventeenth General Report, point 741.

to take account of the new priorities sent by their governments in the light of economic developments. [1]

TABLE 16

Lomé II financing decisions (EDF + EIB)[1] for ACP States, by sector, at 31 December 1984

	Commitments									
	1981[3]		1982[3]		1983[3]		1984[4]		Total[4,5]	
	million ECU	%	million ECU	%	million ECU	%	million ECU	%	million ECU	%
Development of production	312.2	45	690.6	63	383.7	43	416.0	54	1 802.5	52
Industrialization	237.6	34	329.9	30	219.3	25	225.0	29	1 011.8	29
of which: (i) energy	(86.7)	(12)	(84.7)	(8)	(116.1)	(13)	(76.2)	(10)	(363.7)	(10)
(ii) Sysmin			(95.0)	(9)			(3.0)	(. .)	(98.0)	(3)
Tourism	0.2	. .	5.6	1	11.6	1	0.8	. .	18.2	1
Rural production	74.4	11	355.1	32	152.8	17	190.2	25	772.5	22
Economic infrastructure, transport and communications	84.8	12	112.1	10	251.1	28	151.4	20	599.4	17
Social development	117.5	17	117.4	11	127.0	14	101.7	13	463.6	13
Education and training	22.2	3	65.3	6	77.3	9	55.1	7	219.9	6
Health	7.5	1	11.0	1	17.0	2	18.0	2	53.5	2
Water engineering, urban infrastructure and housing	87.8	13	41.1	4	32.7	3	28.6	4	190.2	5
Trade promotion	8.4	1	9.4	1	7.1	1	15.9	2	40.8	1
Emergency aid	24.5	4	19.1	2	12.7	1	32.8	4	89.1	3
Stabex[2]	138.0	20	142.8	13	103.2	12	50.4	6	434.4	13
Other	10.7	1	3.3	. .	7.6	1	6.1	1	27.7	1
Total	696.1	100	1 094.7	100	892.4	100	774.3	100	3 457.5	100

[1] For EIB operations, see the Bank's annual report.
[2] Does not include agreements with former OCTs which have acceded to the Convention but are still covered by the OCT allocation.
[3] Includes mid-year adjustments.
[4] Estimated.
[5] Includes 31.5 million ECU from Stabex resources committed in the form of development projects.

[1] These countries were: Comoros, Samoa, Niger, Rwanda, Ghana, Solomon Islands, Mauritius, Guinea, Jamaica and Liberia.

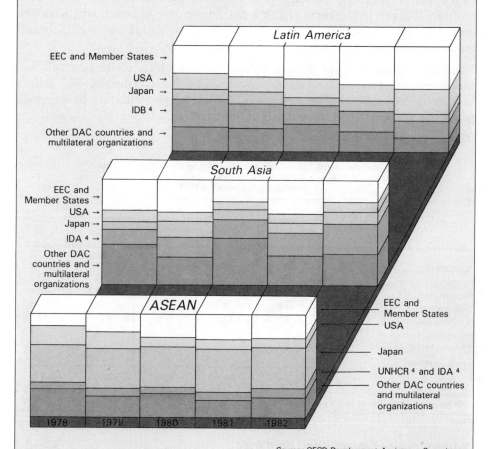

Official development assistance (bilateral and multilateral) for Latin America (20 countries), [1] the countries of South Asia [2] and Asean, [3] by the DAC (OECD) countries and multilateral organizations

Source: OECD Development Assistance Committee.

[1] Except Venezuela (not available).
[2] Indonesia, Malaysia, Philippines, Singapore, Thailand.
[3] Bangladesh, India, Nepal, Pakistan and Sri Lanka.
[4] IDB, UNHCR, IDA — see list of abbreviations.

Although the Community has less of a special relationship with these three groups of countries than with the ACP States, it is nevertheless the principal donor for South Asia and Latin America (except in 1978 for Latin America). The proportion of Community aid is still marginal compared with the financial aid provided by the Member States.

Southern and eastern Mediterranean countries

745. A large proportion of the total aid package available for the Maghreb and Mashreq countries and Israel for the period until 31 October 1986 under the respective second Financial Protocols [1] has already been committed. By 31 December financing decisions totalling 391.9 million ECU had been taken, 38.6% of the total aid package (1 015 million ECU). [1] Of this total, 226.5 million ECU was in the form of EIB loans. In the case of Israel, which receives only EIB loans, cooperation operations were also carried out with a limited amount of funding from the Community budget.

The Commission and the EIB also decided on projects to be financed with funds remaining from the various first protocols. Nevertheless, 47.7 million ECU of these funds, allocated to projects whose implementation poses special problems, still remained unused at 31 December.

TABLE 17

Commission and EIB financing decisions under the first and second
Financial Protocols for Maghreb and Mashreq countries and Israel: [1]
position at 31 December 1984

	Maghreb (million ECU)	Mashreq (million ECU)	Israel (million ECU)	Total	
				million ECU	%
Agriculture	54.6	59.0	—	113.6	11.2
Industry	71.9	218.5	50.0	340.4	33.6
Infrastructure	266.9	188.4	—	455.3	44.9
Training	38.8	20.4	—	59.2	5.9
Scientific cooperation	6.8	19.2	—	26.0	92.5
Industrial cooperation	4.1	4.1	—	8.2	0.8
Technical cooperation	4.7	3.9	—	8.6	0.9
Trade promotion	1.7	0,2	—	1.9	0.2
Total	449.5	513.7	50.0	1 013.2	100

[1] For EIB operations, see also the Bank's annual report.

Non-associated developing countries

746. Under the 1984 programme of aid for non-associated developing countries, the geographical allocation of the total budget of 218 million ECU, minus overheads, was 75% for Asia, 20% for Latin America and 5% for Africa.

[1] Seventeenth General Report, point 690.

In all, the programme should provide for some 28 projects directly benefiting 14 countries and two regional organizations. About 20 of the projects, representing 60% of the funds available for the 1984 programme, were approved in the course of the year. As in previous years, the main emphasis was on agricultural production in the broad sense and related projects in crop and livestock production, fisheries, forestry, etc. (research, crop protection and conservation).

747. The Commission transmitted the report on the implementation of the 1983 programme and guidelines for 1985 to the Council and Parliament in October. [1]

Relations with non-governmental organizations

748. A total of 35 million ECU was earmarked for development cooperation with non-governmental organizations in 1984. At 31 December 32 million ECU had been committed for co-financing 281 development projects in 79 countries in Africa, Asia and Latin America.

The NGOs, and the Commission, continued with substantially the same sectoral priorities, first place again going to integrated rural development projects followed by vocational training and health. Projects financed in countries on the least-developed list account for approximately 38% of the total Community aid. At the end of the year a total of 3 million ECU had been set aside for development education (i.e. operations aimed at making European public opinion more aware of development issues).

Regional cooperation

ACP States and OCTs

749. Total regional cooperation commitments under Lomé II (including operations financed from EIB-administered resources) stand at 64% of the total of 631.5 million ECU set aside for this purpose. This overall percentage conceals considerable regional variations. The Caribbean and Pacific subregions have the highest commitment rates thanks to their high degree of regional integration.

---

[1] BULL. EC 9-1984, points 2.2.36 and 2.2.37.

Institutions

ACP-EEC

750. The third ACP-EEC Lomé Convention was signed on 8 December.[1] The main areas of negotiation had been exhaustively discussed at ministerial meetings, including one in Fiji in May.[2]

The ACP-EEC Consultative Assembly held its ninth annual session in Luxembourg from 19 to 21 September following two preparatory meetings of the Joint Committee.[3] It adopted nine resolutions, one of which, based on the ACP-EEC Council's annual report, set out the latest guidelines for the final stage of the negotiations on the new Convention. Under the Assembly's aegis, a very well-attended meeting was held on 15 September for the purpose of consulting the economic and social sectors in the ACP States and the EEC; the subjects discussed were the Lomé III negotiations and industrial cooperation.[4]

On 5 March St Christopher and Nevis had acceded to the second Lomé Convention, thus becoming the 64th ACP State.[5]

Southern and eastern Mediterranean countries

751. The outlook for bilateral cooperation and the effects on mutual relations of the Community's future enlargement to include Spain and Portugal were the subjects aired at meetings of the EEC-Israel,[6] EEC-Egypt[7] and EEC-Jordan[8] Cooperation Councils and the EEC-Morocco Cooperation Committee.[9]

The meeting of the EEC-Israel Cooperation Council resulted in the conclusion of a third Additional Protocol to the 1975 Agreement. It comes into force on 1 January 1985 and one of its provisions is the postponement until 1 January 1989 of Israel's complete dismantling of tariffs on the Community's non-agricultural exports.

---

[1] Point 714 of this Report.
[2] Bull. EC 5-1984, points 2.2.39 and 2.2.58.
[3] Bull. EC 2-1984, point 2.2.48; Bull. EC 9-1984, point 2.2.39.
[4] Bull. EC 9-1984, point 2.2.40.
[5] Bull. EC 3-1984, point 2.2.51.
[6] Bull. EC 2-1984, point 2.2.27; EEC-Israel Agreement: OJ L 136, 28.5.1975.
[7] Bull. EC 4-1984, point 2.2.23; EEC-Egypt Agreement: OJ L 266, 28.9.1978.
[8] Bull. EC 10-1984, point 2.2.26; EEC-Jordan Agreement: OJ L 268, 29.9.1978.
[9] EEC-Morocco Agreement: OJ L 264, 27.9.1978.

Section 7

International organizations and conferences

United Nations

General Assembly

Thirty-ninth session

752. The 39th session of the United Nations General Assembly, which opened on 18 September, took place against the background of a recovering world economy and hope for an easing of the tension between the superpowers. [1] At the same time, the debates reflected the concern caused by the persistence, and in some cases the exacerbation, of the problems affecting much of the Third World and the tentative nature of the recovery. The President of the Council, Mr Barry, in presenting the Community's views, stressed that the benefits of the recovery should extend to the developing as well as the industrialized countries and that the problem of underemployment had to be tackled in the North and the South alike. The problems of the developing world, in particular, needed to be dealt with in an integrated way and over the longer term.

753. On the economic front, the serious situation in Africa profoundly influenced the work of the Assembly at a time when the Community was preparing to sign a new Convention with its ACP partners. [2] Of the many texts on the subject adopted by the Assembly, the most significant is the declaration on the critical economic situation in Africa. This constitutes a sort of policy manifesto expressing the international community's wish to assist the African continent to overcome its short-term and long-term problems.

The Assembly also adopted a series of guidelines on consumer protection, work on which had been in progress since 1981. The Community and the Member States played an active part in the preparation of a text which should be formally adopted in 1985. It was also decided, the United States dissenting, to

---

[1] Bull. EC 9-1984, points 2.2.41 and 3.4.1; Bull. EC 12-1984. The session was suspended on 18 December and will be resumed in 1985.
[2] Point 714 of this Report.

18th GEN. REP. EC

continue with the list of toxic products subject to national rules. There were also differences of opinion between the developing countries and certain developed countries about the financial burden of certain operations normally paid for through voluntary contributions. These mainly concerned industrialization and the resolutions charging this expenditure to the ordinary budget were adopted by majority votes.

The developing countries achieved the adoption by majority vote of a resolution asking the Secretary-General to consult governments and specialized agencies about the development of international cooperation in financing, monetary questions, debt and trade. This initiative, motivated by the considerations underlying the global negotiations, a matter which the Assembly again postponed without detailed discussion, was opposed by the majority of industrialized countries, which wish to restrict work on such questions to the institutions set up by the Bretton Woods agreements. As in 1983, there was no firm decision on the idea of an international monetary and financial conference for development. Finally, the Assembly was forced to take note of the breakdown in the work of the committee responsible for reviewing and appraising the International Development Strategy for the Third United Nations Development Decade. [1]

Economic and Social Council

754. The Economic and Social Council's two sessions were taken up with a complex of issues mostly relating to Third World development. The world recession and its effects and the problems of the developing countries, including their indebtedness, were dwelt on at length. The Community insisted that recovery in the North should be paralleled in the South and pleaded for increasing alignment of the economic policies of the major industrialized nations, since renewed efforts to assist development were required. The critical problems facing Africa were gone into very thoroughly. Although the debates confirmed that the gravity of these problems has been recognized, unanimity could not be reached when it came to advocating solutions, and discussion is to be continued in the General Assembly. The Community reminded the Council of its long-standing cooperation with the African countries under the EEC-ACP Conventions. Another issue which was referred to the General Assembly was the precise definition of the general principles that should underlie consumer protection. Nor did consultations on the application of the

---

[1] Point 754 of this Report.

International Development Strategy progress far beyond the position reached at the meeting of the committee of the UN General Assembly responsible for reviewing and appraising the strategy, which had met in New York in May. [1]

755. At its annual session in April the Economic Commission for Europe looked at many aspects of East-West relations, among them trade, energy and the environment. [2] The atmosphere of the session worsened after general statements by delegates from Eastern-bloc countries attempting to politicize the meeting. As a result, it did not prove possible to arrange a further meeting of ECE Governments' Senior Advisers on Energy. However, a fair number of proposals were accepted in the area of the environment and on the convening of an *ad hoc* group to study the ECE's working methods, particularly the role of the Sessional Committee. At the meeting of the Committee on the Development of Trade in December, [3] the Commission emphasized the considerable reduction in Community exports to the Soviet Union and the growing trade deficit with the Eastern-bloc countries as a whole.

Convention on the Law of the Sea

756. On 7 December the Community signed the Convention on the Law of the Sea, after eight Member States had decided to sign in their own name. [3]

The Convention is the first to be drawn up by the United Nations in which, in order to acknowledge the existence of the Community, it is expressly stipulated that it may be signed by international organizations to which its Member States have transferred powers. The Community will in future attend the meetings of the preparatory committee as a member instead of as an observer, as hitherto.

United Nations Conference on Trade and Development

757. Since the Belgrade Conference in June 1983, [4] Unctad has returned to its normal pattern of work and meetings, with the Community continuing to play an active part in them. One of these meetings, at which the Community tried hard to bring about a constructive result, concerned the mid-term review of the

---

[1] Bull. EC 5-1984, point 2.2.33.
[2] Bull. EC 4-1984, point 2.2.45.
[3] Bull. EC 12-1984.
[4] Seventeenth General Report, point 756.

International Development Strategy; [1] another was the conference to negotiate a new International Cocoa Agreement. [2]

758. The atmosphere in Unctad after the Belgrade Conference has been marked by a certain unease which came to the fore at the three meetings of the Trade and Development Board, Unctad's executive body. Progress in following up the carefully balanced agreements worked out in Belgrade was halting and slow, perhaps because of the frequently ambiguous nature of the agreements. However, a work programme on protectionism and structural adjustment was adopted.

759. Discussions continue on the possibility of holding a short session of the Trade and Development Board, at ministerial level, in 1985. As yet, however, the industrialized and the developing nations have not been able to agree either on an agenda or on whether such a session should be formal or informal.

760. Since the beginning of the year the industrialized countries have been giving serious thought to ways of improving Unctad's operation. The Community has been active in such discussions, which have dealt with both substantive and procedural aspects. There have been informal contacts to this end with Unctad's Secretary-General and a number of developing countries. The results of this hard thinking and of the Board's ministerial sessions will be a major factor in determining whether the present tension at Unctad will continue and perhaps intensify or whether it will give way to a more positive attitude.

United Nations Industrial Development Organization

761. The Fourth General Conference of Unido, held in Vienna from 2 to 20 August, was one of the main events in the North-South dialogue in 1984. [3] It was attended by more than 1 050 delegates, 78 of them ministers or their deputies, representing 139 countries or international organizations. Nine resolutions relating to the work of Unido and the international community in connection with support for Third World industrialization were adopted unanimously. Two other motions for resolutions did not fare so well and were referred to the UN General Assembly. Finally, an introductory text, dealing for

---

[1] Point 754 of this Report.
[2] Bull. EC 5-1984, point 2.2.46; Bull. EC 7/8-1984, point 2.2.43; Bull. 11-1984, point 2.2.37.
[3] Bull. EC 7/8-1984, point 2.2.31 et seq.

the most part with world economic problems, was adopted by 79 votes to 1 (the United States), with 12 abstentions.

762. During the debates, the Community made eight statements on economic matters, two of them in the general debate. In the two Conference committees, Community statements were made on world industrial restructuring and redeployment, mobilizing financial resources for industrial development, Africa's Industrial Development Decade, the industrialization of the least-developed countries and the development of scientific and technological capacities in the developing world.

763. The Community also attended the Industrial Development Board's session in Vienna in May and the Standing Committee's meeting there in November. It took part in two sets of consultation meetings: on the fertilizer industry and on leather and leather products.

United Nations Environment Programme

764. The Commission took part in the 12th session of the Governing Council of the United Nations Environment Programme in Nairobi in May.[1] Items on the agenda included the environment in the dialogue between industrialized and developing countries and measures to combat drought and desertification.

World Food Council

765. The main items on the agenda of the World Food Council's 10th ministerial meeting in Addis Ababa from 11 to 15 June were the progress made since the World Food Conference in 1974,[2] the food situation in Africa and measures to eradicate hunger in the world.[3] The Community described its initiatives with regard to the latter (food strategies and campaigns on specific themes); a plea was made by the Commission's representative that steps be taken to stabilize markets in agricultural products.

In the conclusions of the meeting, which in the main restated the importance of suitable food policies in developing countries, emphasis was placed on the need to replenish the International Fund for Agricultural Development.

---

[1] Bull. EC 5-1984, point 2.1.117.
[2] Eighth General Report, point 393.
[3] Bull. EC 6-1984, point 2.2.39.

Food and Agriculture Organization of the United Nations

766. The Community took part in various FAO activities during the year. Discussions focused on world food security, rural development, food aid and trade in agricultural products.

767. The Community attended the meetings of the Council and participated in the Intergovernmental Groups on Commodities and the Committee on Food Aid Policies and Programmes. It continues to participate in the global information and early warning system on food and agriculture and took part in the regional conference for Europe, one of the results of which was a resolution on the protection and conservation of Europe's forest resources.

United Nations Educational, Scientific and Cultural Organization

768. The Commission and Unesco began to put the finishing touches to their cooperation in the field of communication, which is to reflect both Unesco's latest work on an intergovernmental programme for the development of communications and the progress made in the Lomé III negotiations.

International Monetary Fund and World Bank

769. The International Monetary Fund and the World Bank held their annual meetings in Washington in September. Commission representatives took part in the proceedings and also attended meetings of the Interim Committee of the IMF's Board of Governors in April and September. [1]

International Atomic Energy Agency

770. The Commission and the IAEA held a number of meetings for in-depth discussions on the implementation of the cooperation agreement they have signed in sectors other than safeguards. At the IAEA's General Conference in Vienna in September, the Commission representative described industrial and economic aspects of nuclear energy in the Community.

---

[1] Points 127 to 129 of this Report.

General Agreement on Tariffs and Trade

771. Most of GATT's activities during the year consisted of implementing the work programme adopted at the ministerial meeting of the Contracting Parties in November 1982. [1] Thus, the Committee on Trade in Agricultural Products examined all measures affecting agricultural trade internationally, with a view to submitting conclusions and recommendations to the Contracting Parties. [2] The Group on Quantitative Restrictions and Other Non-tariff Measures completed its three-part work programme [3] and submitted its report to the session of the Contracting Parties in November; [4] the Committee on Tariff Concessions continued with the groundwork for the negotiations on a harmonized system of tariff nomenclature; a working party to look into the problems of non-ferrous metals and ores, forestry products and fish and fishery products was formed; [5] another working party looked at the GATT Secretariat's study on textiles and clothing in the world economy.

772. Informal discussions were held on international trade in services and the Community's study on the subject was lodged with the GATT Secretariat. The Community's implementation of Part IV of the General Agreement underwent searching scrutiny in October, [6] and the many positive aspects of the Community's commercial policy towards the developing countries were thrown into relief.

773. In other areas, such as safeguards, progress was less marked. Nevertheless, at the November session of the Contracting Parties, [7] intensive discussions led to the adoption of texts relating to fluctuations in exchange rates and their effects on trade and to the trade in counterfeit goods.

774. There was again a great deal of GATT work on the settlement of disputes. Several contentious issues were examined by panels, resulting in the adoption of reports on such subjects as the compatibility of the 'manufacturing clause' in US copyright legislation with GATT rules, the incorporation of VAT in government procurement contracts, Japanese restrictions on leather imports

---

[1] Sixteenth General Report, point 802.
[2] Bull. EC 11-1984, point 2.2.54.
[3] Bull. EC 3-1984, point 2.2.57; Bull. EC 5-1984, point 2.2.64; Bull. EC 6-1984, point 2.2.69; Bull. EC 9-1984, point 2.2.44; Bull. EC 10-1984, point 2.2.54.
[4] Bull. EC 11-1984, point 2.2.52.
[5] Bull. EC 6-1984, point 2.2.71.
[6] Bull. EC 10-1984, point 2.2.55.
[7] Bull. EC 11-1984, point 2.2.55.

and the reduction of the US import quota for Nicaraguan sugar. The panel that has examined the US complaint against the Community's preferential tariff treatment of citrus imports is due to complete its work shortly, while the conclusions reached by the one set up to look into the Canadian complaint about the Community's tariff quota on newsprint imports following the establishment of free-trade arrangements in this sector with the EFTA countries have been adopted by the GATT Council. Agreement was reached with Canada at the end of the year on the basis of the panel's recommendations.

775. Following the Commission's decision in October to take measures to dispose of butter outside the Community,[1] the GATT International Dairy Products Council, meeting in October and November,[2] adopted a statement encouraging the Community, and all parties to the International Dairy Arrangement, to follow a policy designed to reduce stocks and ease the pressure which they exert on the market.

776. Discussions on the timetable, objectives and contents of a possible new round of multilateral trade negotiations in GATT are proceeding.

777. The annual meeting of GATT Contracting Parties last November[3] concentrated on progress on work begun as a result of the 1982 ministerial meeting. It was agreed that an appropriate body within GATT would continue work on international trade in services. The Contracting Parties also set up a group of experts to study trade in counterfeit goods. As a result of the effects of exchange-rate fluctuations on international trade, the Contracting Parties also agreed to hold further discussions on the relationship between exchange-rate instability and international trade.

Organization for Economic Cooperation and Development

778. OECD has continued to provide the industrialized countries with a forum for reflection. As in the past, the Community made its contribution to this process, which focuses primarily on issues of economic policy and international trade, including the North-South facet of these matters.

---

[1] OJ L 279, 23.10.1984; Bull. EC 10-1984, point 2.1.99.
[2] Bull. EC 10-1984, point 2.1.99; Bull. EC 11-1984, point 2.1.99.
[3] Bull. EC 11-1984, point 2.2.52.

779. The Organization's major area of concern, as demonstrated during its Council meeting at ministerial level on 17 and 18 May,[1] is to ensure a stable economic environment, sustained growth and higher employment, with the essential underpinning of low inflation. An economic environment of this kind presupposes positive adjustment policies and improved labour market performance.

780. In the area of international trade, the members of the Organization restated their commitment to reducing trade barriers and distortions (a programme of work was agreed) and exchanged views on the importance of specific problems (trade in services and high-technology products) and the prospects for a new round of multilateral trade negotiations. Here, the Community referred to the need to ensure that the monetary and financial system operated more effectively.

Where the developing countries were concerned, Ministers noted that progress had been made in managing and containing the problem of international indebtedness but pointed to the need for financial support commensurate with requirements. The roles of both multilateral institutions and foreign direct investment were stressed.

Ministers also agreed to strengthen application of the 1976 Declaration on International Investment and Multinational Enterprises,[2] and they appointed a new OECD Secretary-General, Mr J.C. Paye.

781. Two ministerial-level conferences were held in February. The first dealt with employment matters, particularly in relation to new technologies,[3] and the second with the longer-term performance of the OECD economies[4] and with educational affairs.[5] In the same month, a high-level informal meeting examined the situation on the dairy-product and cereal markets.[6] The various committees (the Economic Policy Committee, the Trade Committee, the Committee for Agriculture and the Development Assistance Committee) devoted most of their time to filling in what Ministers had outlined.

---

[1] Bull. EC 5-1984, point 2.2.65.
[2] Tenth General Report, point 499.
[3] Bull. EC 2-1984, point 2.2.55.
[4] Bull. EC 2-1984, point 2.2.56.
[5] Bull. EC 11-1984, point 2.2.56.
[6] Bull. EC 2-1984, point 2.2.58.

International Energy Agency

782. The Commission played a particularly active role in the negotiations in the International Energy Agency leading to the agreement in July on the utilization of stocks in the event of oil supply disruption. This agreement marks an important step by the industrialized countries in their efforts to safeguard and stabilize their oil supplies. The Commission discussed with the Member States how this agreement could be put into practice.

Conference on Security and Cooperation in Europe

783. Three meetings were held in 1984 pursuant to the closing document of the Madrid meeting on the follow-up to the Conference on Security and Cooperation in Europe: the conference on confidence-building measures, security and disarmament in Europe which opened in Stockholm on 17 January,[1] a meeting of experts on the peaceful settlement of disputes held in Athens in March and April[2] and a seminar on economic, scientific and cultural cooperation in the Mediterranean held in Venice from 16 to 26 October.[3] On all three occasions, the Ten spoke with a single voice.

The Venice seminar was attended by the 35 States which took part in CSCE, by Egypt and Israel and by five international organizations (Unesco, ECE, UNEP, WHO and ITU). Participants took stock of progress on cooperation in the Mediterranean area since the last seminar of the same type, held in Valletta in 1979. In a final report, representatives of the States taking part in CSCE recommended that cooperation should be intensified, especially on issues such as the protection of the environment, transport, scientific research and culture.

Council of Europe

784. The Community's cooperation with the Council of Europe has grown steadily since it was admitted as an observer to certain Council of Europe bodies such as the Steering Committee on the Mass Media: joint action has been undertaken, particularly with regard to the fight against drug abuse, help for the handicapped and education. The Commission also played an active role

---

[1] Bull. EC 1-1984, point 2.4.1.
[2] Bull. EC 3-1984, point 2.4.4; Bull. EC 5-1984, point 2.4.4.
[3] Bull. EC 10-1984, point 2.2.59.

in the Conference of Research Ministers organized by the Council of Europe in Paris on 17 September. [1] The Community participated in further work on drafting a European convention on the protection of vertebrate animals used for experimental or other scientific purposes and a multilateral convention on mutual assistance between national tax authorities in combating international tax avoidance and evasion.

785. The annual discussions between the Commission's Secretary-General, Mr Emile Noël, and the Council of Europe Ministers' deputies took place in Strasbourg on 18 June. [2]

786. In May the Council of Europe's Parliamentary Assembly elected the organization's new Secretary-General, Mr Marcelino Oreja Aguirre, who commenced his five-year term of office on 1 October. [3]

At its autumn session (26 September to 4 October) the Parliamentary Assembly adopted a report on the future of European cooperation, recommending that a committee of eminent personalities, chaired by Mr Emilio Colombo, former Italian Foreign Minister, be set up to map out prospects for European cooperation beyond the present decade. [4] The Committee of Ministers approved this proposal at its 75th session on 21 and 22 November.

---

[1] Bull. EC 9-1984, point 2.1.117.
[2] Bull. EC 6-1984, point 2.2.74.
[3] Bull. EC 5-1984, point 2.2.67a.
[4] Bull. EC 10-1984, point 2.2.58.

Section 8

European political cooperation

787. The four major items on the political cooperation agenda for 1984 were East-West relations, the Middle East, Latin America and southern Africa.

788. On 27 March the Ten appealed to the Soviet Union to cooperate in progress towards genuine *détente* based on the faithful implementation of the Helsinki Final Act. [1] The European Council, at its 3 and 4 December meeting, welcomed the announcement that the United States and the USSR were to begin fresh negotiations on arms limitation agreements. [2] On 23 July the Ten welcomed the Polish Government's amnesty for political prisoners and detainees. [3] In response to a new Soviet offensive in Afghanistan, the Ten adopted a statement on 14 May again calling on the Soviet Union to withdraw its troops and settle the conflict by other means. [4]

789. The Ten appealed on 27 February, and again on 27 March, for a ceasefire in Lebanon and the withdrawal from the country of all foreign forces. [5] The European Council of 3 and 4 December voiced the hope that the negotiations already under way with United Nations participation would lead to Israel's complete withdrawal. [2] The Ten undertook, on 27 March, to support any constructive step towards a negotiated settlement in the Middle East. [6]

The European Council of 3 and 4 December considered that contacts aimed at bringing the parties to the negotiating table should be stepped up. [2]

790. On 27 February, and again at the December meeting of the European Council, the Ten also called for a peaceful solution to the Iran-Iraq conflict, [7] emphasizing the need to protect civilian populations and ensure freedom of navigation in the Gulf. They recorded their unqualified condemnation of any

---

[1] Point 783 of this Report; Bull. EC 3-1984, point 2.4.2.
[2] Bull. EC 12-1984.
[3] Bull. EC 7/8-1984, point 2.4.1.
[4] Bull. EC 5-1984, point 2.4.1.
[5] Bull. EC 2-1984, point 2.4.1; Bull. EC 3-1984, point 2.4.3.
[6] Bull. EC 3-1984, point 2.4.3.
[7] Bull. EC 2-1984, point 2.4.2; Bull. EC 12-1984.

use of chemical weapons in the conflict [1] and subsequently took measures to control exports of chemicals which might be supplied directly or indirectly to warring countries. The Council agreed that these measures would be taken on a coordinated basis and in consultation with the Commission, in accordance with Article 224 of the Treaty. [2]

791. On 27 March the Ten expressed their profound satisfaction at the restoration of democracy in Argentina. [1] On 9 April, 11 September and 12 November they deplored acts of repression by the Chilean authorities following demonstrations which provided the Chilean people with their only effective means of expressing their democratic aspirations. [3] On 26 November they expressed their concern at the situation in Bolivia. [4] On 27 March, and again at the December meeting of the European Council, they reaffirmed their support for peace and stability in Central America and for the efforts being made by the Contadora Group. [5] This support was demonstrated at the ministerial meeting held in San José, Costa Rica, on 28 and 29 September. [6]

792. On 27 February the Ten noted with satisfaction the agreement reached in Lusaka on military disengagement in southern Angola, and welcomed the accord between South Africa and Mozambique. [7] On 11 September they adopted a statement ascribing the recent violence in South Africa to the frustration of black South Africans at their deliberate exclusion from South Africa's political life and calling again for an end to apartheid. [8] On 20 November they adopted the fourth report on the application of the Community's code of conduct for companies with subsidiaries in South Africa. [9]

---

[1] Bull. EC 3-1984, point 2.4.3.
[2] Bull. EC 5-1984, point 2.4.2.
[3] Bull. EC 4-1984, point 2.4.1; Bull. EC 9-1984, point 2.4.2; Bull. EC 11-1984, point 2.4.1.
[4] Bull. EC 11-1984, point 2.4.5.
[5] Bull. EC 3-1984, point 2.4.3; Bull. EC 12-1984.
[6] Point 707 of this Report.
[7] Bull. EC 2-1984, point 2.4.3.
[8] Bull. EC 9-1984, point 2.4.1.
[9] Bull. EC 11-1984, points 2.4.2 and 3.4.1.

793. On 27 March the Ten again called upon the Turkish Government to withdraw its recognition of the self-styled 'Turkish Republic of Northern Cypus'. [1]

794. On 20 November the Ten adopted a joint policy statement on the consequences of the adoption by the 10 Member States of the London guidelines for the export of nuclear material, equipment and technology. [2]

795. On 11 September the Ten agreed on a set of measures to strengthen cooperation in the fight against international terrorism and the abuse of diplomatic immunity. [3]

---

[1] Bull. EC 3-1984, point 2.4.3.
[2] Bull. EC 11-1984, points 2.4.3 and 1.3.7.
[3] Bull. EC 9-1984, point 2.4.1.

Chapter IV

Community law

Section 1

General matters

Structure and powers

796. On 10 April the Court of Justice gave judgment in a second action by Luxembourg against the European Parliament concerning the places of work of Parliament and the staff assigned thereto. [1]

It will be remembered that Parliament, by resolution of 7 July 1981, while not calling in question the rights or duties of the governments of the Member States on the subject, decided to hold its part-sessions in Strasbourg, to organize the meetings of its committees and political groups as a general rule in Brussels, and to review the operation of its Secretariat and technical services to meet these requirements. [2] In February 1983, in *Luxembourg v Parliament I,* the Court held that the resolution did not infringe the decisions of the Member States and was not beyond the powers of Parliament. [3]

On 20 May 1983 Parliament adopted a resolution [4] on the consequences to be drawn from its earlier resolution; the new resolution provided for the staff of its Secretariat to be divided permanently between Strasbourg (part-sessions) and Brussels (committees), and instructed its Bureau and its Secretary-General to work out the necessary reorganization measures. On 10 June 1983 the Grand Duchy of Luxembourg commenced an action to have this resolution declared void.

---

[1] Case 108/83.
[2] OJ C 234, 14.9.1981.
[3] Case 230/81.
[4] OJ C 161, 20.6.1983.

The Court began by rejecting Parliament's submission that the action was inadmissible because the resolution merely represented a call to act addressed to its own staff with a view to giving a policy direction to any decisions they might take. The Court said that permanently to divide offices and staff between Strasbourg and Brussels was to take concrete measures and such measures were in the nature of decisions having effects in law.

On the substance, the Court recalled the Decision of the Member States adopted on 8 April 1965 on the provisional location of certain institutions and departments of the Communities (Article 4): 'The General Secretariat of the Assembly and its departments shall remain in Luxembourg'. [1] While its earlier judgment of 10 February 1983 had accepted that Parliament 'must be in a position to maintain ... outside the place where its Secretariat is established the infrastructure essential for ensuring that it may fulfil ... the tasks which are entrusted to it by the Treaties', it had nevertheless added that 'the transfers of staff must not exceed the limits mentioned above since any decision to transfer ... wholly or partially, *de jure* or *de facto*, would constitute a breach of Article 4' of the 1965 Decision. [2] The disputed resolution expressly provided that the staff of the Secretariat were to be based *permanently* in Brussels or Strasbourg, and that Luxembourg was merely to be 'dedicated to remaining the seat of the judicial and financial institutions'; the Court found that the limits clarified in the previous judgment had not been respected, and declared void the resolution of May 1983 on the ground that Parliament had exceeded its powers.

Judicial review and fulfilment by the Member States of their obligations

797. The number of letters of formal notice sent to the Member States under Article 169 rose once again in 1984, as it has regularly done in recent years, apart from the fall in 1983 (when there were fewer cases concerning transposition of directives). This year 454 procedures were initiated, compared with 289 in 1983 and 332 in 1982.

The number of reasoned opinions sent by the Commission followed the same trend: there were 148 in 1984, compared with only 83 in 1983 and 166 in 1982.

The number of cases brought before the Court of Justice remained much the same. In 1984 the Commission took Court actions against Member States in 54 cases, compared with 42 in 1983 and 46 in 1982.

---

[1] OJ 152, 13.7.1967.
[2] Grounds of judgment 54 and 55.

Sixteen cases were removed from the register of the Court during the year, the Member States involved having complied with Community legislation during judicial proceedings.

Of the 45 cases brought before the Court, 16 concerned the non-implementation or incorrect implementation of directives, and 19 concerned infringements of Article 30 of the EEC Treaty, which confirms the shift observed in the last few years: economic crisis increases protectionist temptation.

To take each country separately, the Commission brought proceedings before the Court against France on 14 occasions (2 concerning directives), against Italy on 12 (5 concerning directives), against Germany on 7 (4 concerning directives), against Greece on 4, against the United Kingdom on 4, against Ireland on 3 (2 concerning directives), against Belgium on 4 (3 concerning directives), against Luxembourg on 3 and the Netherlands on 2 (all concerning directives) and against Denmark on 1 occasion.

The Court delivered 17 judgments in cases brought under Article 169, censuring Member States for failure to apply Community law in 16 cases. It dismissed the Commission's action in one case, which concerned the import of Italian pasta into France.

There were no proceedings under Article 170 of the EEC Treaty.

Fuller information on the application of the rules of the Treaty by Member States will be given in the second annual report to Parliament on Commission monitoring of the application of Community law.

Section 2

Interpretation and application
of the substantive rules of Community law

Free movement of goods and customs union

798. In its judgment in *Duphar BV v The Netherlands State*, [1] the Court again had occasion to rule on the compatibility with Community law of certain national measures designed to combat rising social security costs.

The Court acknowledged that certain expensive medicinal preparations may be excluded under a compulsory national sickness insurance scheme on condition that the determination of the preparations excluded did not involve any discrimination regarding the origin of the products and was carried out on the basis of objective and verifiable criteria. The Court also confirmed that Article 36 of the EEC Treaty cannot be relied upon to justify a measure intended to achieve a budgetary objective.

799. In its judgment in *Criminal proceedings against Karl Prantl*, [2] the Court interpreted Article 30 of the Treaty as meaning that national legislation permitting a certain shape of bottle to be used only by certain national producers, when the use of that shape or a similar shape of bottle is consistent with a fair and traditional practice in another Member State, constitutes a measure having an effect equivalent to a quantitative restriction on imports. This judgment means that Germany cannot prohibit the importation of Italian wines traditionally sold in bottles resembling the *Bocksbeutel* bottle, which in Germany is reserved for Franconian wine.

800. The Court ruled, for the first time, on the interpretation of 'public security' within the meaning of Article 36 of the EEC Treaty. [3] It held that a Member State which is almost totally dependent on imports for its supplies of petroleum products may rely on grounds of public security for the purpose of requiring importers to cover a certain proportion of their needs by purchases from a refinery situated in its territory. This ruling is, however, subject to a number

---

[1] Case 238/82; see also Case 181/82 *Roussel Laboratoria v The Netherlands*.
[2] Case 16/83.
[3] Case 72/83 *Campus Oil Limited v Minister for Industry and Energy and Others*.

of conditions: that the production of the refinery cannot be freely disposed of even at competitive prices, and that the quantities of petroleum products covered must not exceed the minimum supply requirements without which the public security of the State concerned would be affected or the level of production necessary to keep the refinery's production capacity available in the event of a crisis and to enable it to continue to refine at all times the crude oil for the supply of which the State has entered into long-term contracts.

801. The Court once again reaffirmed its *Cassis de Dijon* rulings by finding that a Member State is not permitted to limit the importation of confectionery products containing more than a certain proportion of animal gelatine, lawfully manufactured and marketed in other Member States. [1]

802. In *Kohl v Ringelhan*[2] the Court held that Article 30 of the EEC Treaty prevented the application of the legislation on unfair competition in an importing Member State, which it was argued prohibited the use of a distinctive symbol lawfully used in the Member State of export. The ruling was grounded essentially on the finding that the legislation did not apply without distinction to domestic and imported products, as such a prohibition would be based on the possibility that the public might be misled as to the domestic or foreign origin of the goods; there were no other factors in the case with would demonstrate the existence of unfair competition. The Court also held that the words 'public policy' in Article 36 did not include considerations of consumer protection.

803. In infringement proceedings against Greece the Court interpreted the scope of Article 38 of the Act of Accession, which provides that the payments for imports which must be made in cash are to be reduced by instalments.[3] The Court accepted the Commission's view that the cash requirement had to be lowered equally for all individual transactions, and not merely over the whole volume of imports as the Greek authorities had maintained.

804. A judgment on the tariff classification of sports shoes is interesting in that it held that where an article consists of different materials the material which gives it its essential character must be determined by qualitative tests, and not merely by quantitative tests such as value, percentage, etc.[4] This interpretation

---

[1] Case 51/83 *Commission v Italy;* Bull. EC 10-1984, point 2.4.21.
[2] Case 177/83 *Theodor Kohl KG v Ringelhan & Rennett SA and Ringelhan Einrichtungs GmbH.*
[3] Case 58/83 *Commission v Greece.*
[4] Case 298/82 *Gustav Schickendanz KG v Oberfinanzdirektion Frankfurt am Main.*

represents an extension of Rule 3 of the general rules for the interpretation of the nomenclature of the Common Customs Tariff.

805. In *Fioravanti v Amministrazione delle Finanze dello Stato*,[1] the Court for the first time interpreted Article 36 of the Community transit Regulation. It held that when as a result of an offence or irregularity committed in the course of a Community transit operation the duties or other charges which are chargeable are not collected, recovery is to be effected by the Member State where the offence or irregularity was committed, even if the offence or irregularity does not give rise to a customs debt.

Competition

806. In *Ford of Europe Inc. and Ford Werke AG v Commission*[2] the Court declared void the Commission Decision of 18 August 1982 imposing interim measures on Ford. The basis of the Court's decision was that interim measures, since they are based on Article 3 of Regulation No 17/62, 'must come within the framework of the final decision which may be adopted by virtue of Article 3'. Since, in its final decision, the Commission could not have ordered Ford to resume supplies of right-hand-drive cars, concerned as it was with the question of the exemptability of Ford's German dealer agreement, the Commission had therefore exceeded its competence in doing so by way of interim measures.

807. The decision in *Compagnie royale asturienne des mines*[3] is of interest in view of the Court's findings that changing a company's formal identity is ineffective as a means of avoiding the obligations imposed by Article 85; that it is irrelevant for purposes of the applicability of Article 85 which party to an agreement wishes the restrictive clause to be inserted, or whether there is a common intention when the agreement is concluded; and that a mutual supply agreement between producers (in the event of a shortfall in production) is unlawful.

808. In *Hydrotherm*[4] the Court, giving preliminary rulings on questions referred by the Bundesgerichtshof, clarified certain provisions of Regulation No 67/67 on block exemptions. The issues discussed in the case are, however,

---

[1] Case 99/83.
[2] Joined Cases 228 and 229/82.
[3] Joined Cases 29 and 30/83: 1. *Compagnie royale asturienne des mines*; 2. *Rheinzink GmbH v Commission*.
[4] Case 170/83 *Hydrotherm Geratebau GmbH v Compact*.

also important for the interpretation of Regulation No 1983/83, [1] which has now replaced Regulation No 67/67.

Article 1(1) of Regulation No 67/67, provides that Article 85(1) of the Treaty does not apply to agreements to which only two undertakings are party. The Court ruled that, in the context of competition law, the term 'undertaking' must be understood to mean an economic entity. Although such an entity could, legally, consist of several legal or natural persons, for the purposes of the agreement it would constitute one party only. This is a logical extension of the Court's earlier case law. Secondly, the Court ruled that Regulation No 67/67 may also be applied where the commitments contracted extend not only to a defined part of the territory of the common market but also to countries outside the Community.

Article 3(b)(1) of the Regulation stipulates that the exemption under Article 1(1) is not to apply where the contracting parties exercise industrial property rights so as to make it difficult for intermediaries or consumers to obtain the goods to which the contract relates from other parts of the common market. The Court ruled that the exemption does not apply if the actual terms of the contract, or the way it is executed by the parties, show that the parties intend to use or are in fact using industrial property rights in such a way as to prevent or impede parallel imports.

The Court held, however, that the absence of a contractual clause which would make abuse of industrial property rights impossible is not in itself a sufficient reason to exclude the agreement from the application of Regulation No 67/67.

809. In a Decision adopted pursuant to Article 93(2) of the Treaty on 22 July 1982, the Commission took the view that aid in the form of grants and loans given by Belgium to a firm in the paper industry was compatible with the common market, because it was granted towards an investment programme intended to restructure the firm, but that an injection of capital by the public authorities, whose main effect was to rescue the firm from a difficult financial situation, constituted aid incompatible with Article 92. The Commission therefore asked the Belgian Government to take the measures necessary to ensure that the aid held incompatible did not continue to distort competition in the future.

Giving judgment on an application by the firm concerned pursuant to Article 173 [2] the Court accepted that the acquisition of a capital holding by the public

---

[1]   OJ L 173, 30.6.1983.
[2]   Case 323/82 *Intermills SA v Commission*.

authorities could constitute State aid incompatible with the common market. Whether they took the form of loans or of holdings, State aids were caught by the ban in Article 92 once the criteria it laid down were met. But the Court nevertheless annulled the Commission's decision because of contradictions it contained and because the Commission had not properly explained why the restructuring operation, which was both industrial and financial in scope, called for such a clear-cut distinction between the effect of the aid granted in the form of favourable loans and the effect of the acquisition of a holding.

810. Federal Republic of Germany v Commission[1] establishes the absolute nature of the requirement (resulting from Article 93(3) of the EEC Treaty) that the Commission open the procedure envisaged by Article 93(2) once it establishes that there are serious doubts about the compatibility with the common market of a proposed scheme of State aids. The Commission's failure to do so in this case resulted in the Court's annulment of the Commission's Decision of 18 November 1981 authorizing a restructuring scheme for the Belgian textile industry.

Free movement of persons, social provisions and movement of capital

811. On 31 January the Court delivered a very important judgment in response to two references for a preliminary ruling made by the Genoa District Court.[2] The cases concerned a dispute between two Italian residents, Graziana Luisi and Giuseppe Carbone, and the Ministry of the Treasury following the exportation of foreign currency far in excess of the maximum permitted per person and per year under Italian exchange legislation (at the material time—1974/ 75—LIT 500 000). Heavy fines corresponding to the difference between the amounts exported and the amounts permitted were imposed on both residents. They informed the national court hearing the action for a declaration of nullity of the measures imposing the fines that they had used the foreign currency in question for the purposes of tourism and medical treatment in the Federal Republic of Germany and France. They pleaded that the restrictions imposed by the Italian exchange control legislation were incompatible with Community law, notably with Article 106 of the EEC Treaty.

---

[1] Case 84/82.
[2] Joined Cases 286/82 *Luisi v Ministero del Tesoro* and 26/83 *Carbone v Ministero del Tesoro*.

The outstanding feature of the judgment delivered by the Court of Justice is that, for the first time, the Court explicitly acknowledges that freedom to provide services within the meaning of Article 59 of the Treaty includes the freedom for persons to visit another Member State in order to receive a service there without being subject to any restrictions whatever.

Once the major obstacle of interpreting Article 59 was overcome, the Court had no difficulty in finding that, by virtue of Article 106(1) of the Treaty, transfers of money made by recipients of services such as tourists, persons receiving medical treatment and persons travelling for the purpose of education or business are automatically liberalized from the end of the transitional period in the same way as the services to which they relate.

Such transfers constitute payments for services and not movements of capital (which are still subject to restrictions), [1] even where they are effected by means of the physical transfer of banknotes.

The Court was careful to point out that, in so far as it might be used by unauthorized movements of capital, the liberalization of payments relating to trade in services remains subject to the power of the Member States to impose controls on the nature and reality of transactions.

Such controls must, however, be neither disproportionate nor arbitrary in the sense that they may not have the effect of limiting payments and transfers in connection with the provision of services to a specific amount for each transaction or for a given period, or of rendering illusory the freedoms recognized by the Treaty or of subjecting the exercise thereof to the discretion of the administrative authorities.

812. In *Prodest Sarl v Caisse primaire d'assurance maladie de Paris* [2] the question arose whether an employee of Belgian nationality working for a temporary employment undertaking whose registered office was situated in France could retain affiliation to the French social security scheme during a period of employment spent in a non-member country. It had been held in a previous judgment [3] that the principle of non-discrimination based on nationality, in regard to the free movement of workers, applies to all legal relationships which can be located within the territory of the Community by reason either of the place where they are entered into or the place where they take effect. In

---

[1] As the Court held in Case 203/80 *Casati* [1981] ECR 2595, Article 67 of the EEC Treaty is not directly applicable.
[2] Case 237/83.
[3] Case 36/74 *Walrave v Union Cycliste Internationale* [1974] ECR 1405.

line with that ruling, the Court held that temporary work outside the Community cannot exclude application of the principle of non-discrimination where the employment relationship maintains a sufficiently close connection with Community territory, this being so in the case in point (work undertaken outside the Community for a Community undertaking). Accordingly, for the purpose of applying the national rules of the Member State in which the undertaking is established regarding retention of affiliation to the social security scheme of the Member State during the temporary secondment of workers to a non-member country, where such workers are nationals of another Member State they must be afforded the same treatment as that which they would enjoy if they were nationals of the Member State in question.

813. In *Castelli v Office national des pensions pour travailleurs salariés* [1] the question was the compatibility with Community law of the Belgian legislation whereby, to secure entitlement to the guaranteed income for old persons, a person not of Belgian nationality must be a national of a country with which Belgium has concluded a reciprocal agreement. Reference was made to settled case law [2] whereby equality of treatment between workers who are a Member State's own nationals and workers who are nationals of another Member State, notably in regard to social advantages, [3] is also intended to prevent discrimination against dependent relatives in the ascending line of such workers. After restating its well-established definition of social advantage, [4] the Court held that that definition included the income guaranteed to old persons under the law of a Member State and that the grant of that social advantage to the dependent relatives in the ascending line of a migrant worker could not be conditional on the existence of a reciprocal agreement between the Member State in question and the Member State of which such relative is a national.

814. On 12 July the Court delivered a very important judgment on freedom of establishment. [5] The case was referred by the French Court of Cassation, which was hearing an action between the Ordre des Avocats au Barreau de Paris and Mr O. Klopp, a member of the Düsseldorf Bar. The latter, who had all the French academic qualifications required to practise in France, had applied to

---

[1] Case 261/83.
[2] Case 32/75 *Cristini and Others v Société nationale des chermins de fer français* [1975] ECR 1085; Case 63/76 *Inzirillo v Caisse d'allocations familiales de l'arrondissement de Lyon* [1976] ECR 2057.
[3] Article 7(2) of Regulation No 1612/68 of 15 October 1968 on freedom of movement for workers within the Community (OJ L 257, 19.10.1968).
[4] e.g. Case 207/78 *Ministère public v Even and Office national des pensions pour travailleurs salariés (ONPTS)*; Case 65/81 *Reina v Landeskreditbank Baden-Wurttemberg* [1982] ECR 33.
[5] Case 107/83 *Ordre des Avocats au Barreau de Paris v O. Klopp.*

be registered with the Paris Bar, while retaining his residence and his chambers in Düsseldorf. The Paris Bar Council had rejected his application on the ground that under French law a lawyer may establish his chambers in only one area. The Paris Court of Appeal had annulled the Bar Council's decision as being contrary to Community law. The Court of Cassation, with which the Paris Bar Council had lodged an appeal, requested the Court of Justice to give a preliminary ruling under Article 177 of the EEC Treaty on 'whether, in the absence of any directive of the Council of the European Communities on the coordination of provisions governing access to the profession of advocate and the practice of that profession, the requirement that an advocate who is a national of a first Member State and who wishes to practise the profession of advocate simultaneously in a second Member State maintains chambers in one place only, a requirement which is imposed by the legislation of the country in which he wishes to establish himself which is intended to ensure the proper administration of justice and compliance with professional ethics in that country, constitutes a restriction which is incompatible with the freedom of establishment guaranteed by Article 52 of the Treaty of Rome'. The Court of Justice considered that the right of establishment carries with it the right to establish and maintain, in compliance with the rules of professional conduct, more than one centre of activity. Its reply to the question submitted by the French Court of Cassation is that 'even in the absence of any directive coordinating national provisions governing access to, and the exercise of, the legal profession, Article 52 et seq. of the EEC Treaty prevents the competent authorities of a Member State from denying, in accordance with their national legislation and the rules of professional conduct which are in force in that State, to a national of another Member State the right to enter and to exercise the legal profession solely on the ground that he simultaneously maintains chambers in another Member State'.

Equal treatment for men and women

815. In *Razzouk and Beydoun v Commission* the Court held that Article 79 of the Staff Regulations of Officials of the European Communities, which distinguishes between widows and widowers for purposes of survivor's pension entitlement, is inapplicable; in the view of the Court this difference breaches the principle of equal treatment between the sexes, which, the judgment confirms, forms part of those fundamental rights of which the Court has a duty to ensure the observance. [1]

---

[1] Joined Cases 75 and 117/82.

816. The judgments in *Von Colson and Kamann*[1] and *Harz v Deutsche Tradax*[2] are important to the interpretation of the equal treatment Directive of 1976[3] on the question of the nature and gravity of the sanctions provided for by national law where the principle of equal treatment is not respected.

The Court held that national legislatures have a measure of discretion here; but said that sanctions must be effective, and cannot be purely nominal. The courts referring the questions had also asked whether an individual could rely on the Directive in order to obtain specific compensation; the Court said no, as the Directive did not include any unconditional and sufficiently precise obligation to that effect.

817. In *Hofmann v Barmer Ersatzkasse*[4] the Court held that national rules restricting to the mother entitlement to additional leave, following maternity leave, until the child reaches the age of six months, during which leave the person concerned continues to receive her net pay from the State, subject to a ceiling, is not incompatible with the abovementioned Directive.[3] The Directive was not intended to deal with matters of family organization or to change the sharing of responsibilities between man and woman. Reference was made to the provisions of the Directive permitting Member States to maintain or introduce provisions intended to protect women in regard to pregnancy and motherhood, such protection covering not only a woman's medical condition following her confinement but also the special relationships between a woman and her child (which are liable to be perturbed by the excessive burden imposed on a working mother).

Accordingly, leave of that kind may be lawfully reserved to mothers, to the exclusion of any other person, having regard to the fact that only the mother can be subject to undesirable pressures to resume her work prematurely. Lastly, the Court held that Directive 76/207/EEC does not impose on Member States the requirement that they shall, as an alternative, allow such leave to be granted to the father, even where the parents assent thereto.

Common agricultural policy and fisheries

818. In *St Nikolaus Brennerei* the Court ruled that Article 46 of the EEC Treaty may be applicable even after the expiry of the transitional period.[5] It held that a countervailing charge (fixed by a Commission regulation) on imports of

---

[1] Case 14/83 *Von Colson and Kamann v Land Nordrhein-Westfalen*.
[2] Case 79/83.
[3] Council Directive 76/207/EEC (OJ L 39, 14.2.1976).
[4] Case 184/83.
[5] Case 337/82 *St Nikolaus Brennerei v HZA Krefeld*.

French ethyl alcohol of agricultural origin into four other Member States (Belgium, Netherlands, Luxembourg and the Federal Republic of Germany) cannot be challenged simply because the regulation introducing it is based on Article 46. That article may therefore be applied after the expiry of the transitional period, but only to products not yet subject to a common organization of the market.

819. In its judgment in *Jongeneel Kaas* the Court examined the distinction between Community powers and the residual powers of the Member States in the fields covered by a common organization of the market (in the case in point, the market in milk products). [1] The Community may exercise exclusive powers only where Community rules cover the matter in question. In the absence of Community rules, the Member States retain the power to adopt rules themselves, provided they are compatible with the common organization of the market concerned. In the absence of Community rules on cheese, a Member State may unilaterally adopt, for the purpose of promoting sales of cheese and cheese products, rules concerning the quality of cheeses produced on its territory, including a ban on producing cheeses other than those exhaustively listed. Under certain conditions a Member State may also adopt, in respect of domestic products, rules on the mandatory use of names, signs or control documents, provided that no distinction is made according to whether the cheese is intended for the domestic market or for export. Cheese producers may be required to belong to a supervisory agency provided that the objectives of the agency are consistent with Community law and that the marketing, resale, import, export or sale for export of cheese products are not exclusively reserved to persons belonging to the agency.

820. The judgment delivered in Joined Cases 47 and 48/83 is along much the same lines. [2] In contrast to the Regulation on milk, the Regulation on the common organization of the market in poultrymeat (2777/75) expressly provides for Community powers, [3] but no specific measures had been adopted in exercise of those powers.

The Court held that, in a situation characterized by the absence of implementing measures provided for by Regulation No 2777/75, national provisions laying down marketing and quality standards for slaughtered poultry, which must be observed upon penalty of disciplinary sanctions, are compatible with that

---

[1] Case 237/82 *Jongeneel Kaas BV and Others v State of the Netherlands and Stichting Centraal Orgaan Zuivelcontrole.*
[2] *Pluimveeslachterij Midden Nederland BV and Pluimveeslachterij Van Miert.*
[3] OJ L 282, 1.11.1975.

Regulation provided they are in keeping with the aim of the common organization of the market and applied in a way which does not restrict the importation of poultrymeat lawfully produced and marketed in accordance with the marketing and quality standards in force in the other Member States.

821. In *Unifrex v Commission and Council* [1] the applicant sought compensation for the loss it claimed to have sustained because the Commission had frozen MCAs on exports of cereals to Italy. Commission Regulation No 801/81 maintained MCAs at the same level as before the devaluation of the Italian lira on 23 March 1981. [2] The Commission contended that the decision to freeze MCAs was justified by the need to avoid increasing or introducing MCAs pending a decision modifying the representative rates, which was at that time imminent and was in fact taken on 31 March when the agricultural prices for 1981/82 were fixed. The Court accepted this view.

822. In *Wünsche* the Court applied the principle that the power to take a far-reaching measure implies the power to take a less far-reaching one. [3] Commission Regulation No 3429/80 adopted protective measures against preserved cultivated mushrooms from the People's Republic of China. [4] Rather than simply suspending imports, it required payment of an 'additional amount' on import. The Court refused to strike down the Regulation holding that Council Regulation No 521/77 [5] empowered the Commission to require such an additional amount as a protective measure; that Regulation makes provision for measures more restrictive than the requirement of an additional amount, although it does not explicitly refer to the possibility of a requirement of this kind.

823. In *Melkunie* [6] the Court accepted that national legislation prohibiting the marketing of goods lawfully produced and marketed in the country of exportation on the ground that they do not meet the microbiological requirements laid down in the Member State of importation constitutes a measure having an effect equivalent to a quantitative restriction within the meaning of Article 30 of the EEC Treaty. But it accepted that national legislation which does not allow active coliform bacteria to be present in a pasteurized milk product, and is aimed at excluding the presence in such a product, at the time of its

---

[1] Case 281/82.
[2] OJ L 82, 28.3.1981.
[3] Case 345/82 *Wünsche Handelsgesellschaft v Federal Republic of Germany*.
[4] OJ L 358, 31.12.1980.
[5] OJ L 73, 21.3.1977.
[6] Case 97/83 *Criminal proceedings against CMC Melkunie BV, now called Melkunie Holland BV*.

consumption, of a number of non-pathogenic micro-organisms which may present a risk to the health of the most sensitive consumers, and to that end fixes the maximum number of such micro-organisms permissible on the date of sale of the product, taking into account the extent to which it will deteriorate between its sale and consumption, complies with the requirements of Article 36 of the EEC Treaty.

824. In *Agricola Commerciale Olio and Others and Savma v Commission,* the Court annulled two Commission regulations; the first repealed a previous regulation calling for tenders for the purchase of substantial quantities of olive oil, and the second offered the same olive oil to the same tenderers who had previously been awarded them by drawing lots, but at higher prices. The Court did not accept the economic argument put forward by the Commission in justification of its decision, which had followed an unforeseeable movement in price levels and was intended to avoid serious disturbance on the olive-oil market as a result of the concentration of large quantities, at prices which were in reality absurdly low, in the hands of a very small number of operators. [1]

In *Biovilac v Commission* [2] the Court rejected an application by a Belgian firm manufacturing feedingstuffs for piglets and poultry, which was suffering damage as a result of the sale at very low prices of milk powder held in intervention stocks. The Court considered that these special measures, which the Commission had taken to clear surpluses, were justified. While it accepted the principle that the Commission might be liable for compensation for lawful acts on its part, the Court concluded that in the case before it the loss suffered was a commercial risk inherent in the activities of an industrial and commercial undertaking, as the legislation governing the market in milk products contained provisions allowing special measures.

825. In *R. v Kent Kirk,* [3] at the time of the contested acts, the United Kingdom was not permitted under Community law, in reliance on measures to conserve fishery resources, to restrict the access of vessels of the other Member States to its coastal zone. By virtue of the principle of the non-retroactivity of measures of a penal nature, the retroactivity of Council Regulation No 170/83 [4] could not validate, *ex post facto,* the contested measure.

---

[1] Joined Cases 232/81 and 264/81.
[2] Case 59/83.
[3] Case 63/83.
[4] OJ L 24, 27.1.1983.

Transport

826. The decision given in *Paterson v Weddel*[1] provided an important clarification of an exemption in Council Regulation (EEC) No 543/69 of 25 March 1969 on the harmonization of certain social legislation relating to road transport,[2] which has effect also in relation to Council Regulation (EEC) No 1463/70 of 20 July 1970 on the introduction of recording equipment in road transport.[3] The Court held that the expression 'transport of animal carcases and waste not intended for human consumption' employed in Article 14a(2)(c) of the former regulation envisaged carcases which were not intended for human consumption and waste which was not intended for oral human consumption. The exempted operations envisaged were limited to cases where the exempted products alone were carried. The decision will assist in ensuring a more uniform application of the Regulations by Member States.

827. In reply to a number of questions submitted by the House of Lords on the interpretation of Article 14a(3a) of Council Regulation (EEC) No 543/69 on the harmonization of certain social legislation relating to road transport,[2] the Court gave an interpretation of the meaning of one of the national transport operations (use of specialized vehicles...for door-to-door selling), for which Member States may, subject to authorization by the Commission, grant exemptions from the requirement of that Regulation and Council Regulation (EEC) No 1463/70 on the introduction of recording equipment in road transport.[4] The decision of the Court gives useful guidance to enforcement authorities and courts of the Member States, which were showing some divergence of practice in interpreting the provision.[3]

Convention of 27 September 1968 on Jurisdiction and the Enforcement of Judgments in Civil and Commercial Matters

828. During 1984 the Convention of Accession of 9 October 1978, by which Denmark, Ireland and the United Kingdom accede to the Judgments Convention, was ratified by France, the Federal Republic of Germany and Luxembourg.

---

[1] Case 90/83 *Michael Paterson and Others v W. Weddel & Co. Ltd and Others.*
[2] OJ L 77, 29.3.1969.
[3] OJ L 164, 27.7.1970.
[4] Case 133/83 *R. v Thomas Scott & Sons Bakers Ltd and Brian Rimmer.*

France also ratified the Convention of Accession of 25 October 1982, by which Greece likewise accedes.

829. In *Tilly Russ v Nova and Goeminne Hout* [1] the Court partly modified its earlier interpretation of Article 17, on the question of choice of jurisdiction agreements concluded orally and 'evidenced in writing'. In *Segoura v Bonakdorian*, in 1976, [2] the Court had held that 'the requirements of the first paragraph of Article 17 ... as to form are satisfied only if the vendor's confirmation in writing accompanied by notification of the general conditions of sale has been accepted in writing by the purchaser'; so that the written confirmation of an oral agreement had to be bilateral. In the new judgment, however, the Court finds a choice of jurisdiction clause printed on a bill of lading to be valid even though the bill of lading was signed only by the party wishing to invoke the clause, so that there was no bilateral written confirmation.

830. In *Zelger v Salinitri* [3] the Court held that the requirements for proceedings to become definitively pending are to be determined in accordance with the national law of each of the courts concerned, and that the court before which those requirements are first fulfilled is the court 'first seised'.

Commercial policy

831. In *Allied Corporation and Others v Commission* the Court held that producers and exporters in a non-member country may in certain circumstances have the right to challenge the validity of a Community regulation imposing an anti-dumping duty on goods exported by them to the Community. [4] The Court said that they have this right if they are identified in the acts adopted by the Commission or the Council, or if they were involved in the anti-dumping investigations. The Court had already ruled that a complainant may challenge the Commission's rejection of an anti-dumping complaint. [5]

832. In *STS v Commission* the Court dismissed as inadmissible the action brought against the Commission by a firm which had unsuccessfully tendered

---

[1] Case 71/83.
[2] Case 25/76 [1976] ECR 1851.
[3] Case 129/83.
[4] Joined Cases 239 and 275/82 *Allied Corporation, Michel Levy-Morelle, Transcontinental Fertilizer Company and Kaiser Aluminum and Chemical Corporation v Commission.*
[5] Case 191/82 EEC *Seedcrushers' and Oil Processors' Federation (Fediol) v Commission.*

for the award of a contract financed by the EDF.[1] Interpreting the rules contained in the second Lomé Convention, the Court held that the action taken by the Commission, in regard to the procedure for the award of contracts qualifying for EDF aid, is intended solely to ascertain whether or not the conditions for Community financing are satisfied. It cannot, therefore, call in question the principle whereby the contracts in question remain national contracts which only the ACP States have the responsibility of preparing, negotiating and concluding. Tendering firms accordingly enter into legal relations only with the ACP State responsible for the contract and they are not party to the relationships that exist between the Commission and the ACP States in regard to the matter. In this judgment the Court reaffirmed the fundamental philosophy underlying the cooperation established under the Lomé Convention between the Community and the ACP States, which is based on rigorous separation of their respective powers and responsibilities both as between the parties and in relation to third parties.

833. In a case referred to the Court for a preliminary ruling under Article 41 of the ECSC Treaty, the question arose whether the Federal Republic of Germany could continue to collect, in 1978, a differential duty on coal originating in a non-member country, previously released for free circulation in another Member State.[2] The Court left it in no doubt that the principle of freedom of movement laid down in Article 4 of the ECSC Treaty also extends to products originating in non-member countries which are released for free circulation in the Member States, exactly as applies in the case of the EEC Treaty; in the grounds of the judgment, it emphasized that the ECSC, in view of its structure, is close to being a customs union. It accordingly held that the Recommendations of the High Authority adopted between 1959 and 1963 on the basis of Article 74 of the ECSC Treaty still serve as a legal basis for authorizing Germany to collect the duty.

ECSC

834. As part of the arrangements for handling the crisis on the steel market the Commission in December 1983 adopted a Decision introducing a system of production certificates and accompanying documents in the steel industry with a view to establishing reliable statistics.[3] Under the current quota rules

---

[1] Case 126/83.
[2] Case 36/78 *Mabanaft GmbH v HZA Emmerich*.
[3] Decision No 3713/83/ECSC (OJ L 373, 31.12.1983).

drawn up in January, [1] the Commission inserted a new Article 15B, which authorizes Member States to complain to the Commission if they find that deliveries have been altered to a significant extent compared with traditional deliveries, and empowers the Commission to reduce the delivery quota of the undertaking in question to correct the imbalance in traditional deliveries. The European Independent Steelworks Association asked the Court to suspend both measures, arguing that the Commission had thus implemented a policy of freezing the flow of traditional trade between Member States. [2]

835. The Court dismissed the first application, finding that a measure relating merely to statistics and documentation was not likely to be prejudicial to the applicants' interests. It likewise dismissed the application in the second case, but only after taking note of the undertaking given by the Commission that Article 15B would be applied only where alterations in traditional deliveries were due to infringements of Community law and that, in the case of infringements of the Community rules on prices, competition or aids, it would apply first and foremost the sanctions laid down for such infringements.

836. In its judgment in *Walzstahl and Thyssen v Commission* the Court for the first time annulled one of the substantive rules adopted by the Commission in the context of the system of quotas provided in Article 58. [3] The Commission had, on the basis of the powers which the general decision establishing the quota system vested in it in certain cases, made changes to the system in order to bring about a general increase in the quotas for a whole group of undertakings. The Court held that the system was based on the application of uniform abatement rates for all undertakings, and that the changes in question could therefore be made only in accordance with the procedure laid down in Article 58 (consultations with the ECSC Consultative Committee and assent of the Council).

837. In separate actions [4] the Usinor company and its subsidiary Alpa challenged the lawfulness of the fundamental rules in the quota system [5] which deem a subsidiary and its parent company to form a single undertaking for purposes of the fixing and adaptation of quotas. The Court dismissed the applications, and found that the Commission had not exceeded the discretion

---

[1] Decision No 234/84/ECSC (OJ L 29, 1.2.1984).
[2] Joined Cases 37/84R and 45/84R.
[3] Joined Cases 140 and 221/82 and 146 and 226/82.
[4] Case 103/83 *Usinor v Commission* and Case 151/83 *Alpa v Commission*.
[5] Articles 2(4) and 14 of Decision No 1696/82/ECSC (OJ L 191, 1.7.1982).

conferred on it by Article 58 of the ECSC Treaty by deciding for practical reasons to allocate quotas to the firm which directs the activities of the group. The provision did not conflict with the definition of an undertaking given in Article 80 of the Treaty, as each individual undertaking retained its power to take legal proceedings in cases concerning it. The Court also held that it was legitimate for the Commission to distinguish betwen firms on the basis of size for purposes of the adaptation of quotas, as small businesses could have more difficulty in surviving the crisis than firms producing in several sectors.

838. In a number of judgments[1] relating to fines for exceeding quotas, the Court reaffirmed that proceedings instituted for the annulment of a fine could not call into question either an earlier individual decision fixing quotas which had gone unchallenged, or the provisions of a general decision not constituting the basis for the contested decision imposing the fine. It also held for the first time that the Commission may impose on an undertaking which exceeds both its production quota and its delivery quota two fines to be calculated separately, and that in so doing it does not impose a dual penalty.[2]

839. In another case dealing with fines for exceeding quotas,[3] the Court said it would serve no purpose to consider whether letters which the firm had written represented requests for the adjustment of its quotas or requests made pursuant to Article 35 of the ECSC Treaty, as the applicant had in any case failed to bring actions before the Court to challenge the implied decisions of refusal within the one-month time limit laid down by the third paragraph of Article 35. The fact that a firm was in serious financial difficulties did not justify reducing the fine; if this principle were to be accepted the production quota system would be seriously compromised.

840. In Case 8/83 *Bertoli v Commission* the Court upheld the principles followed by the Commission in applying Article 60 of the ECSC Treaty, for the infringement of which the Commission had imposed a fine; but the Court nevertheless substantially reduced the fine, holding that special circumstances of the case justified a reduction on grounds of equity.

---

[1] Case 2/83 *Alfer SA v Commission;* Case 76/83 *Usines Gustave Boël v Commission;* Case 10/83 *Metalgoi v Commission;* Case 348/82 *Industrie Riunite Odolesi SpA v Commission.*
[2] Case 270/82 *Estel NV v Commission.*
[3] Case 81/83 *Busseni v Commission.*

841. In Case 9/83 *Eisen und Metall v Commission* the applicant had asked the Court to annul a decision fining it under Article 15 of Commission Decision No 1836/81/ECSC on the obligation of distributive undertakings to publish price lists and conditions of sale and on prohibited practices in the steel trade, [1] or, in the alternative, to reduce the fine. The fine was the first one imposed pursuant to that Decision. The Court rejected all the applicant's submissions, but reduced the fine by half on the ground that in the case of an infringement by a dealer, the reduced influence which he can exercise on the market situation is a circumstance mitigating the gravity of the infringement.

---

[1] OJ L 184, 4.7.1981.

Section 3

Information on the development of Community law

842. At the end of the year, Celex, the computerized documentation system for Community law, contained almost 68 000 documents capable of being interrogated. Input of the full text of legislative instruments continued, and by the end of the year two thirds of the planned coverage had been reached.

843. Celex is linked to the national telecommunications networks through the Belgian DCS network and is accessible to the public through the Euris host. The subscribers, who are scattered throughout 16 European countries, include government departments, semi-public bodies, parliaments, law offices, industrial and commercial concerns and university research and teaching establishments. During 1984 the number of outside connections to Celex and the consultation time increased considerably.

844. The system now also covers Commission proposals pending on 1 January 1984 or transmitted to the Council since then. The technical link between Celex and the internal documentation systems which will allow national implementing measures to be included as well is now almost complete.

845. The *Directory of Community legislation* is compiled with the help of the Celex system and revised annually; the Directory was updated on 12 July, and this fifth edition was published in November in the seven Community languages (earlier editions were published with the title *Register of current Community legal instruments*).

The year in brief [1]

January

10 January

General election in Denmark.

17 January

Parliament passes resolution on the situation of women in Europe.

Bull. EC 1-1984, point 2.4.7

Commission sends Council proposal for recommendation on fire protection in hotels.

Point 138 of this Report

18 January

New Council President, Mr Cheysson, presents Parliament with programme for France's six-month term in Council chair.

Bull. EC 1-1984, point 3.4.1

23 January

Council adopts resolution on promotion of employment for young people.

Bull. EC 1-1984, point 2.1.40

31 January

Council adopts 1984 fisheries TACs and quotas for Community waters.

Point 461 of this Report

---

[1] This chronological summary does not claim to be exhaustive. For further details, see the passages of this Report and the Bulletin cited in the margin.

Commission decides to extend system of monitoring and production quotas for certain steel products until 31 December 1985.

Point 187
of this Report

February

1 February

Commission sends Council communication on technological change and social adjustment.

Point 280
of this Report

14 February

Parliament passes resolution on draft Treaty establishing European Union.

Point 1
of this Report

Commission sends Council, Parliament and Economic and Social Committee communication on unfair clauses in contracts concluded with consumers.

Point 400
of this Report

15 February

Mr Thorn presents 1983 General Report on the Activities of the Communities and Commission's programme for 1984 to Parliament.

Bull. EC 2-1984,
point 1.5.1 et seq.

21 February

Council expresses concern over mounting demands for protectionist measures in United States.

Point 660
of this Report

28 February

Council adopts Decision on European strategic programme for R&D in information technology (Esprit).

Point 195
of this Report

March

5 March

Saint Christopher and Nevis accedes to second ACP-EEC Convention (64th ACP State).

Bull. EC 3-1984,
point 2.2.51

Commission sends Council communication summarizing first five years of monetary cooperation.

Point 122
of this Report

12 March

Council signs agreement on future relations between Greenland and Community.

Point 7
of this Report

19 and 20 March

European Council in Brussels.

Point 20
of this Report

20 March

Commission sends Council communication on progress towards development of Community air transport policy.

Point 499
of this Report

30 March

Commission sends Council report and proposals on implementation of Mediterranean policy for enlarged Community.

Point 682
of this Report

April

9 April

Meeting between Community and EFTA ministers.

Point 652
of this Report

Inauguration of JET at Culham.

Point 560
of this Report

10 April

Council adopts resolution on Community policy on tourism.

Point 138
of this Report

Representatives of Governments of Member States sign Convention of Accession of Hellenic Republic to Rome Convention on the Law applicable to Contractual Obligations.

Point 152
of this Report

Council adopts eighth company law Directive (qualifications of persons authorized to audit company accounts).

Point 147
of this Report

11 April

Commission sends Council communication on guidelines for strengthening relations between Community and Latin America.

Point 706
of this Report

12 April

Parliament passes resolutions on political, economic and trade relations between Community and United States and relations on steel.

Bull. EC 4-1984,
point 2.4.7

May

11 May

Commission sends Council proposal for Decision adopting Community research action programme in the field of biotechnology (1985-89).

Point 199
of this Report

15 May

Council adopts resolution on computerization of administrative procedures in intra-Community trade.

Point 183
of this Report

23 May

Commission sends Council communication on telecommunications.

Point 196
of this Report

24 May

Commission sends Council communication on European Community and Africa.

Bull. EC 5-1984,
point 2.2.34

June

5 June

Chinese Premier, Mr Zhao Ziyang, visits Commission.

Point 710
of this Report

6 June

Commission sends Council proposals for two Directives on lead content of petrol and motor-vehicle emissions.

Point 367
of this Report

7 June

Council and Representatives of Governments of Member States meeting within the Council adopt resolution on easing of checks on persons at Community's internal frontiers.

Point 137
of this Report

Council adopts resolution on contribution of local employment initiatives to combating unemployment.

Point 278
of this Report

7 to 9 June

Western Economic Summit in London.

Point 118
of this Report

14 and 17 June

Second direct elections to European Parliament.

Point 11
of this Report

17 June

General election in Luxembourg.

19 June

Council adopts Regulations on reform of Regional Fund.

Point 344
of this Report

25 and 26 June

European Council at Fontainebleau.

Point 20
of this Report

28 June

Commission sends Council green paper on establishment of common market for broadcasting, especially by satellite and cable.

Point 136
of this Report

July

9 July

Commission sends Council amendments to May 1983 proposal on own resources system.

Point 80
of this Report

13 July

Franco-German Agreement on gradual abolition of border checks signed at Saarbrücken.

Bull. EC 7/8-1984,
point 3.5.1

24 July

Election of Mr Pierre Pflimlin as new President of Parliament and election of Vice-Presidents.

Point 13
of this Report

Representatives of Governments of Member States adopt three resolutions on measures to combat audio-visual piracy, the rational distribution of films through all the audio-visual media, and measures to ensure that audio-visual programmes of European origin are given an appropriate place.

Point 597
of this Report

26 July

New Council President, Mr Peter Barry, presents Parliament with programme for Ireland's six-month term in Council chair.

Bull. EC 7/8-1984,
point 3.4.1

28 July

Dr Garret FitzGerald, Council President, announces agreement of Member States to appointment of Mr Jacques Delors as Commission President from January 1985.

Point 25
of this Report

August

2 August

IBM undertakes to change its business practices in Community; Commission accordingly suspends action for infringement of competition rules.

Point 219
of this Report

September

10 September

Council adopts Directive relating to approximation of laws, regulations and administrative provisions of Member States concerning misleading advertising.

Point 399
of this Report

15 September

Council adopts Regulation changing value of unit of account used by European Monetary Cooperation Fund.

Point 123
of this Report

17 September

Council adopts Regulation on strengthening of common commercial policy with regard in particular to protection against illicit commercial practices.

Point 620
of this Report

Council adopts 15 Directives on removal of technical barriers to trade in different industrial sectors.

Point 143
of this Report

18 September

Commission sends Council communication on cooperation at Community level on health-related problems.

Bull. EC 9-1984,
point 1.2.1 *et seq.*

24 September

Commission sends Council communication on a people's Europe.

Point 137
of this Report

26 September

Commercial and economic cooperation agreement initialled by China and Community.

Point 709
of this Report

28 and 29 September

Conference at San José, Costa Rica, between Community and Member States, Portugal, Spain, Central American countries and Contadora Group.

Point 707
of this Report

October

9 October

Cooperation Agreement between Community and Yemen Arab Republic signed in Brussels.

Point 697
of this Report

24 October

Dr FitzGerald, Council President, Mr Soares, Portuguese Prime Minister, and Mr Natali, Commission Vice-President, sign joint statement in Dublin acknowledging irreversibility of process of Portugal's integration into Community.

Point 609
of this Report

25 October

President of Parliament declares 1984 supplementary budget finally adopted.

Point 61
of this Report

26 October

Mr François-Xavier Ortoli, Commission President from 1973 to 1977 and Vice-President from 1977 to 1984, resigns on taking up another appointment.

Point 24
of this Report

30 October

Commission announces emergency aid plan for Ethiopia and certain Sahel countries affected by serious famine.

Point 730
of this Report

November

6 November

Council adopts resolution on environmental dimension in Community's development policy.

Bull. EC 11-1984, point 2.2.34

8 November

Council decides to speed up Tokyo Round tariff reductions.

Point 651 of this Report

12 November

Council adopts two recommendations — on implementation of harmonization in telecommunications, and on first phase of opening up access to public telecommunications contracts.

Point 196 of this Report

14 November

Parliament refuses for first time to grant discharge to Commission for implementation of 1982 budget.

Point 83 of this Report

Commission sends Council amendment to its proposal for a Decision adopting new provisions relating to Chapter VI of Euratom Treaty (supply of nuclear materials for peaceful purposes)

Point 529 of this Report

20 November

The Ten, meeting within political cooperation adopt declaration of common policy on consequences of 10 Member States of Community adopting London guidelines for export of nuclear material, equipment and technology.

Point 794 of this Report

29 November

Commission sends Council and Parliament communication on Community action to combat international tax evasion and avoidance.

Point 267 of this Report

December

3 and 4 December

Dublin European Council.

Point 20
of this Report

4 December

Council adopts conclusions on measures required to ensure effective implementation of conclusions of European Council on budgetary discipline and on cooperation with Commission and Parliament in respect of budgetary discipline.

Point 82
of this Report

Representatives of Governments of Member States appoint Members of Commission for term beginning 6 January 1985 and ending 5 January 1989; Mr Jacques Delors appointed President (6 January 1985 to 5 January 1987).

Point 25
of this Report

6 December

Council adopts Directive on supervision and control of transfrontier shipment of hazardous wastes.

Point 378
of this Report

8 December

Third ACP-EEC Convention signed in Lomé.

Point 714
of this Report

13 December

Parliament rejects draft general budget for 1985.

Point 76
of this Report

18 December

Council and Ministers for Culture adopt resolution on increased use of European Social Fund to assist cultural workers.

Point 598
of this Report

19 December

Council adopts resolution on long-term unemployment.

Point 279
of this Report

Annexes

Annex to Chapter II — Section 2

Directives and proposals concerning the removal of technical barriers to tade in industrial products

I — Directives adopted by the Council

Reference	Subject	Date adopted	OJ No and page ref.	OJ date
84/424/EEC	Permissible sound level and exhaust system of motor vehicles (amendment of Directive 70/157/EEC)	3.9.1984	L 238/31	6.9.1984
84/525/EEC	Seamless, steel gas cylinders	17.9.1984	L 300/1	19.11.1984
84/526/EEC	Seamless, unalloyed aluminium and aluminium alloy gas cylinders	17.9.1984	L 300/20	19.11.1984
84/527/EEC	Welded unalloyed steel gas cylinders	17.9.1984	L 300/48	19.11.1984
84/528/EEC	Common provisions for lifting and mechanical handling appliances	17.9.1984	L 300/72	19.11.1984
84/529/EEC	Electrically operated lifts	17.9.1984	L 300/86	19.11.1984
84/530/EEC	Common provisions for appliances using gaseous fuels, safety and control devices for these appliances and methods of surveillance of them	17.9.1984	L 300/95	19.11.1984
84/531/EEC	Appliances using gaseous fuels for instantaneous production of hot water for sanitary purposes	17.9.1984	L 300/106	19.11.1984
84/532/EEC	Common provisions for construction plant and equipment	17.9.1984	L 300/111	19.11.1984
84/533/EEC	Permissible sound power level of compressors	17.9.1984	L 300/123	19.11.1984
84/534/EEC	Permissible sound power level of tower cranes	17.9.1984	L 300/130	19.11.1984

84/535/EEC	Permissible sound power level of welding generators	17.9.1984	L 300/142	19.11.1984
84/536/EEC	Permissible sound power level of power generators	17.9.1984	L 300/149	19.11.1984
84/537/EEC	Permissible sound power level of powered hand-held concrete-breakers and picks	17.9.1984	L 300/156	19.11.1984
84/538/EEC	Permissible sound power level of lawnmowers	17.9.1984	L 300/171	19.11.1984
84/539/EEC	Electro-medical equipment used in human or veterinary medicine	17.9.1984	L 300/179	19.11.1984

II — Directives adopted by the Commission

Reference	Subject	Date adopted	OJ No and page ref.	OJ date
84/8/EEC	Installation of lighting and light-signalling devices on motor vehicles and their trailers (adaptation to technical progress of Council Directive 76/756/EEC)	14.12.1983	L 9/24	12.1.1984
84/47/EEC	Electrical equipment for use in potentially explosive atmospheres employing certain types of protection (adaptation to technical progress of Council Directive 79/196/EEC)	16.1.1984	L 31/19	2.2.1984
84/291/EEC	Classification, packaging, and labelling of dangerous preparations (pesticides) (adaptation of Council Directive 78/631/EEC)	18.4.1984	L 144/1	30.5.1984
84/372/EEC	Permissible sound level and exhaust system of motor vehicles (adaptation to technical progress of Council Directive 70/157/EEC)	3.7.1984	L 196/47	26.7.1984
84/414/EEC	Clinical mercury-in-glass maximum-reading thermometers (adaptation to technical progress of Council Directive 76/764/EEC)	18.7.1984	L 228/25	25.8.1984
84/415/EEC	Cosmetic products (adaptation to technical progress of Annexes II, III, IV, V and VI to Council Directive 76/768/EEC)	18.7.1984	L 228/31	25.8.1984
84/449/EEC	Classification, packaging, and labelling of dangerous substances (adaptation to technical progress for the sixth time of Council Directive 67/548/EEC)	25.4.1984	L 251/1	19.9.1984

III — *Proposals transmitted to the Council which have not yet been adopted*

Reference	Subject	Date transmitted	OJ No and page ref.	OJ date
COM/84/513	Restrictions on the marketing and use of certain dangerous substances and preparations (second PCB/PCT Directive)	3.10.1984	—	—
COM/84/400	Roll-over protection structures incorporating two pillars and mounted in front of the driver's seat on narrow-track wheeled agricultural or forestry tractors	16.11.1984	—	—
COM/84/438	Permissible sound level and exhaust system of motorcycles (amendment of Council Directive 78/1015/EEC)	6.9.1984	—	—
COM/84/226	Lead content of petrol	6.6.1984	C 178/5	6.7.1984
COM/84/226	Establishment of limit values for 1995 (motor-vehicle pollutant emissions) (amendment of Council Directive 70/220/EEC)	6.6.1984	C 178/9	6.7.1984
COM/84/564	Establishment of limit values for 1995 (motor-vehicle pollutant emissions) (amendment of proposal COM(84)226)	25.10.1984	C 318/6	29.11.1984
COM/83/772	Ranges of nominal quantities and capacities permitted for prepackaged products (amendment of Council Directive 80/232/EEC)	12.1.1984	C 18/7	25.1.1984

Annex to Chapter IV

Activities of the Court in figures

TABLE 1

Cases analysed by subject-matter[1]

Situation at 31 December 1984

	ECSC				EEC									Euratom	Privileges and immunities	Proceedings by staff of institutions	Total
	Scrap compensation	Transport	Competition	Other[2]	Free movement of goods and customs union	Right of establishment and freedom to supply services	Taxation	Competition	Social security and free movement of workers	Agriculture	Transport	Article 220 Conventions	Other[3]				
Actions brought	167	35	64 (1)	169 (34)	462 (68)	66 (10)	118 (17)	282 (21)	285 (26)	783 (47)	29 (5)	50 (7)	120 (28)	12 (7)	8	2 088 (41)	4 738 (312)
Cases not resulting in a judgment	25	6	22	51 (18)	72 (7)	12 (3)	11 (1)	27 (2)	21 (2)	57 (3)	4 (1)	2	28 (7)	1	1	745 (74)	1 085 (118)
Cases decided	142	29	41	81 (22)	296 (27)	36 (5)	78 (12)	223 (16)	223 (17)	648 (42)	20 (3)	41 (5)	70 (10)	3	7	645 (61)	2 583 (220)
Cases pending	—	—	1	37	94	18	29	32	41	78	5	7	22	8	—	698	1 070

Tables 1, 2 and 3 were compiled in part from the Synopsis of the work of the Court of Justice of the European Communities in 1984.
The figures in brackets represent the cases dealt with by the Court in 1984.
[1] Cases concerning more than one subject are classified under the most important heading.
[2] Levies, investment declarations, tax charges, miners' bonuses, production quotas.
[3] Contentious proceedings, Staff Regulations, Community terminology, Lomé Convention, short-term economic policy, commercial policy, relations between Community law and national law and environment.

TABLE 2

Cases analysed by type (EEC Treaty)[1]
Situation at 31 December 1984

	Art. 169, 93 and 171	Art. 170	Art. 173				Art. 175	Art. 177			Art. 181	Art. 215	Protocols to Art. 220 Conventions	Grand total[2]
			By governments	By individuals	By Community institutions	Total		Validity	Interpretation	Total				
Actions brought	310	2	54	8	312	374	29	189	1 060	1 249	7	203	50	2 224
Cases not resulting in a judgment	91	1	8	3	38	49	3	4	60	64	—	30	3	241
Cases decided	140	1	35	5	230	270	22	161	879	1 040	1	137	40	1 651
In favour of applicant[3]	127	1	10	2	62	74	1				1	15	—	219
Dismissed on the merits[4]	13	—	24	3	114	141	3				—	105	—	262
Rejected as inadmissible	—	—	1	—	54	55	18				—	17	—	90
Cases pending	79	—	11	—	44	55	4	24	121	145	6	36	7	332

1 Excluding proceedings by staff and cases concerning the interpretation of the Protocol on Privileges and Immunities and of the Staff Regulations (see Table 1).
2 Totals may be smaller than the sum of individual items because some cases are based on more than one Treaty article.
3 In respect of at least one of the applicant's main claims.
4 This also covers proceedings rejected partly as inadmissible and partly on the merits.

TABLE 3

Cases analysed by type (ECSC and Euratom Treaties)[1]
Situation at 31 December 1984

| | Number of proceedings instituted | | | | | | | | | Total | |
| | By governments | | By Community institutions | | By natural or legal persons | | Art. 41 ECSC Questions of validity | Art. 150 Euratom Questions of interpretation | Art. 153 Euratom | | |
	ECSC	Euratom	ECSC	Euratom	ECSC	Euratom				ECSC	Euratom
Actions brought	23	—	1	1	409	9	3	3	2	436	15
Cases not resulting in a judgment	9	—	—	—	95	—	—	—	1	104	1
Cases decided	13	—	—	1	277	1	2	3	1	292	6
In favour of applicant[2]	5	—	—	1	55	1	—	—	1	60	2
Dismissed on the merits[3]	8	—	—	—	168	—	—	—	—	176	1
Rejected as inadmissible	—	—	—	—	54	—	—	—	—	54	—
Cases pending	1	—	1	—	37	8	1	—	—	40	8

[1] Excluding proceedings by staff and cases concerning the interpretation of the Protocol on Privileges and Immunities and of the Staff Regulations (see Table 1).
[2] In respect of at least one of the applicant's main claims.
[3] This also covers proceedings rejected partly as inadmissible and partly on the merits.

Directory of the institutions and other bodies

Secretariat of the European Parliament [1]

Secretary-General	H.J. Opitz
Office of the Secretary-General	L. Mormino
Office of the President	E. Vinci
	P. Fontaine

Directorate-General I

Sessional and General Services

Director-General	E. Vinci
Directorates	
A. Members' general affairs	G. Bokanowski
B. Publications and distribution	H. Rømer
C. Translation	J. Hargreaves (acting)

Directorate-General II

Committees and Interparliamentary Delegations

Director-General	F. Pasetti-Bombardella
Deputy Director-General	R. Bruch
Directors	A. Ducci
	S. Guccione
	M. Michel
	A. Van Nuffel

---

[1] Commission translation of French version supplied by Parliament.

Directorate-General III

Information and Public Relations

Director-General   P. COLLOWALD [1]

Directorates
   Operational sectors   A. FERRAGNI
   Geographical sectors   G. NAETS

Directorate-General IV

Administration, Personnel and Finance

Director-General   K.H. NEUNREITHER
Deputy Director-General   G. VAN DEN BERGE (acting)

Directorates
A. General administration   J. FEIDT
B. Personnel and social affairs   M. SCHMIDT
                                                 (D. QUEMENER (acting))
C. Finance and informatics   M. CHAMIER
D. Interpreting   F. PRETE [2]

Directorate-General V

Research and Documentation

Director-General   M. PALMER [1]

Directorates
A. Institutional affairs and Legal Service   K. PÖHLE
B. Economic affairs and external relations   F. ROY

Adviser on Human Rights   J. TAYLOR [2]

---

[1] From 1 December 1984.
[2] From 1 January 1985.

General Secretariat of the Council

Secretary-General   N. ERSBØLL

Directorate of Private Office   P. SKYTTE CHRISTOFFERSEN

Legal Department

Director-General
Jurisconsult of the Council   H.J. GLAESNER

Deputy Directors-General   J.L. DEWOST
D. GORDON-SMITH

Directors   R. FORNASIER
H.J. LAMBERS
A. SACCHETTINI (acting)

Directorate-General A

Administration and Personnel — Operations and Organization — Information, Publications, Documentation

Translation Department

Director-General   U. WEINSTOCK

Directorates
I.   Administration and personnel   P. GUEBEN
II.   Operations and organization   J.J. FABBRI
III. Information, publications, documentation   R.POURVOYEUR

Translation Department   W. MOTTE

Directorate-General B

Agriculture and Fisheries

Director-General   L. FRICCHIONE

Directorates
I.   Agriculture policy (including international matters), organization of the markets in agricultural products and approximation of laws   F. DUHOUX

II. Agri-monetary, financial and budgetary questions; agricultural and forestry structures; national aids; research; fisheries (including external relations)   H.I. DUCK

Directorate-General C

Domestic Market, Industrial Policy, Approximation of Laws, Right of Establishment and Services, Company Law, Intellectual Property

Director-General — E.H. A CAMPO

Directorates

I. Free movement of goods; customs union; rules on competition; industrial policy (iron and steel industry, new technologies etc.) and approximation of laws — ...

II. Right of establishment and services; company law; public contracts; banks and insurance; stock exchange legislation; intellectual property; approximation of civil and commercial law; intra-Community agreements — V. SCORDAMAGLIA

Directorate-General D

Research Policy — Energy Policy — Transport, Environment and Consumer Protection

Director-General — D.M. NELIGAN

Directorates
I. Research policy — P. SIEBEN
II. Energy policy — A. CORET
III. Transport — H. SCHMIDT-OHLENDORF

Directorate-General E

External Relations and Development

Director-General — A. DUBOIS

Directorates
I. Commercial policy; non-European industrialized countries; State-trading countries; North-South Dialogue — F. BJØRNEKAER

II. Development: ACP/OCT/FOD; non-associated developing countries; Development Council — D. VIGNES

III. Accession negotiations; Western Europe;
Mediterranean; Latin America; Asia   E. CHIOCCIOLI
Office for liaison with the European Office
of the United Nations; GATT (Geneva)   K.D. JAGSTAIDT

Directorate-General F

Relations with Parliament and the Economic and Social Committee — Institutional Affairs — Budget and Staff Regulations

Director-General   W. NICOLL

Directorates
I. Relations with Parliament, the Economic and
Social Committee and with other European
organizations and movements   M. YEATS
II. Budget and Financial Regulations; accounts;
ACPT; Staff Regulations   J. LENTZ

Directorate-General G

Economic, Financial and Social Affairs

Director-General   G. LESORT

Directorates
I. Social and regional policies; education   J. CONTARGYRIS
II. Economic and financial affairs; export credits
and tax harmonization   W. PINI

The Commission

Secretariat-General

Secretary-General	E. Noël
Deputy Secretary-General	H.G. Krenzler

Directors
with special responsibility for the Registry — R. Gachot
with special responsibility for relations with the Council — A. Marchini-Camia
with special responsibility for relations with Parliament and the Economic and Social Committee — J. Peters
Inspector of delegations; with special responsibility for coordination of the General Report and Other Periodical Reports Unit, the Inspection, Planning and Organization Unit and the In-house Information and In-service Traineeships Unit — H. Beck

Legal Service

Director-General	C.D. Ehlermann
Deputy Director-General	G. Olmi
Principal Legal Advisers	D. Allen
	R. Baeyens
	R.C. Beraud
	G. Close
	J.P. Delahousse
	H. Etienne
	C. Maestripieri
	B. Paulin
	A. Toledano-Laredo
	B. Van Der Esch
	E. Zimmermann

Joint Interpreting and Conferences Service

Director-General	R. Van Hoof

Statistical Office

Director-General	S. Ronchetti (acting)

Directorates
A. Processing and dissemination of statistical information — J. Nols

B. General economic statistics — P. Erba
C. External trade, ACP, non-member countries and transport statistics — S. Ronchetti
D. Energy and industrial statistics — P. Nanopoulos
E. Demographic and social statistics and agricultural statistics — D. Harris

Customs Union Service

Director-General — F. Klein

Directorates
A. Tariff questions — H. Chumas
B. Customs legislation — A. Hazeloop

Directorate-General I

External Relations

Director-General — L. Fielding

Deputy Directors-General
with special responsibility for Directorates C and D — J. Loeff
with special responsibility for Directorates A and E — P. Luyten
with special responsibility for Directorates B, F and G — G. Giola
Head of the Delegation for Enlargement — I. Nielsen

Directorates
A. GATT, OECD, commercial questions with respect to agriculture, fisheries, services and high technology and relations with South Africa — R. Abbott
B. Relations with North America, Australia, New Zealand, Japan; external relations in the research, science and nuclear energy fields — R. Phan van Phi
C. Relations with the developing countries in Latin America and Asia (except the Far East); relations with international organizations, including United Nations economic agencies other than Unctad; coordination with the Directorate-General for Development; generalized tariff preferences; external relations in the field of energy (other than nuclear energy) — E. Volpi
D. General questions and instruments of external economic policy — H.F. Beseler

E. Negotiation and management of textile agreements; trade in industrial products   J.P. LENG

F. Relations with northern, central and southern European countries   E. RHEIN

G. Relations with State-trading countries
   Chief Adviser, Special Representative for the Conference on Security and Cooperation in Europe   L. KAWAN

H. Delegation for Enlargement; accession negotiations and bilateral relations
   Head of Delegation   I. NIELSEN

Directorate-General II

Economic and Financial Affairs

Director-General   M. RUSSO

Deputy Directors-General
   with special responsibility for coordination of Directorates A and B   ...
   with special responsibility for coordination of Directorates C and D   H. MATTHES
Secretary of the Monetary Committee and the Economic Policy Committee   A. KEES
Economic Adviser   E. HOLM

Directorates
A. National economies   P. VAN DEN BEMPT
B. Economic structure and Community intervention   G. RAVASIO
C. Macroeconomic analyses and policies   M. EMERSON
D. Monetary matters   J.P. MINGASSON

Directorate-General III

Internal Market and Industrial Affairs

Director-General   F. BRAUN

Deputy Directors-General
   with special responsibility for Directorates A and D   P. CECCHINI
   with special responsibility for Directorates C and E   A.A. VAN RHIJN

Directorates
A. Industrial affairs I   T. GARVEY
C. Industrial affairs III and distributive trades   D. VERDIANI

D. Approximation of laws, freedom of establishment and freedom to provide services ... I. SCHWARTZ

E. Steel ... J. FAURE
Policy and relations with industry
Chief Adviser ... H. KUTSCHER

F. Industrial restructuring, non-member countries and raw materials ... R. MÖHLER

Information Technology and Telecommunications Task Force

Director-General ... M. CARPENTIER

Directorates
A. Information technology—Esprit ... J.M. CADIOU
B. Telecommunications ... T. SCHURINGA

Directorate-General IV

Competition

Director-General ... M. CASPARI

Deputy Director-General ... J.L. CADIEUX

Directorates
A. General competition policy ... J.L. CADIEUX
B. Restrictive practices and abuse of dominant positions I ... J.E. FERRY
C. Restrictive practices and abuse of dominant positions II ... G. ROCCA
D. Coordination of competition decisions ... A. PAPPALARDO
E. State aids ... R. SUNNEN

Directorate-General V

Employment, Social Affairs and Education

Director-General ... J. DEGIMBE

Director (with special responsibility for medium-term social policy planning ... ...

Directorates
A. Employment ... P. GOMMERS
B. Living and working conditions and welfare ... N. SCANDAMIS
C. Education, vocational training and youth policy ... H.C. JONES

D. European Social Fund
   Chief Advisers

W. Stabenow
E. Toffanin
E. Fitzgibbon

E. Health and safety

A.E. Bennett

Directorate-General VI

Agriculture

Director-General

C. Villain

Deputy Directors-General
   with special responsibility for Directorates C.
   D and E

P. Pooley

   with special responsibility for Directorates F
   and G

A. Pizzuti

   with special responsibility for Directorate H

H. von Verschuer

Chief Adviser attached to Deputy Director-General with special responsibility for Directorates F and G

J. Scully

Directorates
A. General matters
B. Agricultural legislation
C. Organization of markets in crop products
D. Organization of markets in livestock products
E. Organization of markets in specialized crops
F. Agricultural structure and forestry
G. European Agricultural Guidance and Guarantee Fund
H. International affairs relating to agriculture

A. Ries
M. Barthelemy
T.L.W. Windle
T. O'Dwyer
C. Driesprong
R. Craps

H.H. Wächter
M. Marcussen
F. Milano

Directorate-General VII

Transport

Director-General

J.R. Steele

Directorates
A. General programming; international and institutional relations; air and maritime transport

J. Erdmenger

B. Inland transport markets; transport and energy

R. Papaioannou

C. Infrastructures; transport technology; State intervention

D. Vincent

Directorate-General VIII

Development

Director-General	D. Frisch

Deputy Directors-General
  with special responsibility for coordinating Directorates A and E and the Non-governmental Organizations Department — M. Foley
  with special responsibility for coordinating Directorates B, C and D, the General Planning Questions and Finance Committees Unit and the Technical Specialists' Groups for Agriculture Sector Projects and Infrastructure (I and II) — M. Hauswirth

Directorates
A. Development activities — F.J. Van Hoek
B. West and Central Africa — E. Wirsing
C. East and southern Africa; the Indian Ocean — G. Livi
D. The southern and eastern Mediterranean; the Caribbean and Pacific; aid to non-associated developing countries — C. Cornelli
E. Finance — A. Auclert

Directorate-General IX

Personnel and Administration

Director-General — J.C. Morel
Deputy Director-General — R. Hay

Directorates
A. Personnel — G. Valsesia
B. Administration — A. Pratley
C. Translation — ...
D. Personnel and administration in Luxembourg and general services — I. Dubois
E. Informatics — W. De Backer
F. Coordination and resources — E. Brackeniers

Directorate-General X

Information

Director-General — F. Froschmaier

Directorates
A. Information to Member States, applicant
   countries, ACP and non-member countries
   and priority milieux   P. SOUBESTRE
B. Methods and media   M. PICCAROLO

Spokesman's group

Spokesman   M. SANTARELLI

Directorate-General XI

Environment, Consumer Protection and Nuclear Safety

Director-General   A. ANDREOPOULOS

Directorates
A. Protection and improvement of the environ-
   ment   A.J. FAIRCLOUGH
B. Protection and promotion of consumer inter-
   ests   J.P. SHEEHAN

Directorate-General XII

Science, Research and Development

Director-General   P. FASELLA

Deputy Directors-General
   with special responsibility for Directorates C
   to G   D. DAVIES
   Director-General of the JRC   J.A. DINKESPILER

Directorates
A. Scientific and technical coordination, cooper-
   ation with non-member countries, and COST   J.P. CONTZEN
B. Means of action   R. GEROLD
C. Technological research   H. TENT
D. Nuclear research and development   S. FINZI
E. Alternative energy sources, energy conser-
   vation and energy R&D strategy   A. STRUB
F. Biology, radiation protection and medical
   research   F. VAN HOECK
G. Environment, raw materials and materials
   technology   P. BOURDEAU

Fusion programme — D. Palumbo

JET project — H.O. Wüster

Joint Research Centre

Director-General — J.A. Dinkespiler

Programmes Director — H. Helms

Establishment Directors

Ispra — G.R. Bishop

Geel — W. Muller

Karlsruhe — R. Lindner

Petten — E.D. Hondros

Directorate-General XIII

Information Market and Innovation

Director-General — R. Appleyard

Directorates

A. New technologies — H. Burgard

B. Information management — C. Jansen van Roosendaal

Directorate-General XIV

Fisheries

Director-General — E. Gallagher

Director (with special responsibility for coordination) — R. Simonnet

Directorates

A. Markets and international questions - South — R. Simonnet

B. Internal resources and international questions - North — J. Pearson

C. Structures, legislation, aids and national measures — E. Pino

Directorate-General XV

Financial Institutions and Taxation

Director-General — O.B. Henriksen

Directorates

A. Financial institutions — G. Imbert

B. Taxation — R. Goergen

Directorate-General XVI

Regional policy

Director-General	P. MATHIJSEN

Directorates
A. Regional development policies — G. RENCKI
B. Development and conversion operations — R. SOLIMA

Task force for the coordination of structural
financial instruments
Chief Adviser — ...

Directorate-General XVII

Energy

Director-General	C. AUDLAND
Deputy Director-General	M. CARPENTIER

Directorates
A. Energy policy, analyses and forecasts, and
   contracts — C. JONES
B. Coal — K. REICHERT
C. Oil and natural gas — G. BRONDEL
D. Nuclear energy — F. CACCIA DOMINIONI
E. Energy saving and alternative energy sources,
   electricity and heat — M. DAVIS
F. Euratom safeguards — W. GMELIN

Directorate-General XVIII

Credits and Investments

Director-General	E. CIOFFI

Directorates
A. Borrowings and administration of funds — A. VAN GOETHEM
B. Investments and loans — O. HAHN

Directorate-General XIX

Budgets

Director-General	D. Strasser

Directorates
A. Financial intervention appropriations and administrative expenditure — H. Andresen
B. Financing of the budget — L. Duck
C. General affairs and relations with Parliament and the Court of Auditors — F. De Koster
D. Accounting and finance — A.S. Mastrantonis

Directorate-General XX

Financial Control

Director-General (Financial Controller) — C. Facini

Directorates
A. Questions of principle. Control of operating, research and cooperation expenditure (Deputy Financial Controller) — J. Lemmens
B. Control of revenue and expenditure under EAGGF and the Social and Regional Funds — L. De Moor

Euratom Supply Agency

Director-General — G. von Klitzing

Security Office

Director — T. Noyon

Office for Official Publications

Director — W. Verheyden

External Delegations

(a) *In non-member countries*

Australia (Canberra) — K.O. Barlebo Larsen
Canada (Ottawa) — D. Hammer
India (New Delhi)
(HQ of the Delegation for South Asia) — M. Macioti
Japan (Tokyo) — L.J. Brinkhorst

Thailand (Bangkok)
(HQ of the Delegation for South-East Asia)   J. HANSEN
United States (Washington)   SIR ROY DENMAN
Venezuela (Caracas)
(HQ of the Delegation for Latin America)   L. BOSELLI
Yugoslavia (Belgrade)   A. MAES

(b) *To international organizations*

GATT (Geneva)   P. TRAN VAN THINH
UN (New York)   M. HARDY
OECD (Paris)   P. DUCHATEAU
IAEA (Vienna)   M. GOPPEL

Court of Justice [1]

Registrar	P. HEIM
Assistant Registrar	J. VAN HOEY
	SCHILTHOUWER POMPE
Directorates	
Documentation and library	S. NERI
Translation	M. KOEGLER

---

[1] Commission translation of French version supplied by the Court.

Court of Auditors [1]

1. President's Office	P. KEEMER S. BOSMAN F. DE FILIPPIS V. GINSBURG J.A. STOLL

Secretariat, staffing and administration, budget and accounts

External relations (other institutions, national audit bodies and public relations)

Court's work programme and working methods, professional training, studies, technical preparation of annual and special reports

2. European Development Fund	P. EVERARD
3. Own resources	A. WOODWARD
4. Research and investment, energy, industry and external bodies (including those in receipt of grants)	K. FUELSTER
5. European Social Fund and related expenditure, EAGGF Guidance Section (other than regional measures), fisheries	W. HEDDERICH P. KOTZONIS
6. Borrowing and lending, ECSC, general accounts, accounting principles	P. BLOCMAN H. IBSEN
7. Cooperation with developing and non-member countries (excluding European Development Fund)	T. JAMES
8. European Regional Development Fund and EAGGF Guidance Section (regional operations)	G. CARNEROLI
9. EAGGF Guarantee Section	J. BELLE R. BONDURRI E. O'FEARCHAIN
10. Staff and operating expenditure, including Publications Office and Information Offices	G. COGET A. WIENRICH

---

[1] Commission translation of French version supplied by the Court.

Economic and Social Committee

Secretary-General, Registrar, Press, Information
and Publications, Studies and Documentation   R. Louet

Director-General of the General Directorate for
Administration, Translation and General Affairs   P. Pixius

Personnel Director   C.A.F. d'Ansembourg

Directorates
A. Secretariats of the sections for:
    Economic and financial questions
    Social questions
    Protection of the environment, public health
    and consumer affairs   O. Kuby
B. Secretariats of the sections for:
    Regional development
    Industry, commerce, crafts and services
    Transport and communications   D. McLaughlin
C. Secretariats of the sections for:
    Energy and nuclear questions
    Agriculture
    External relations   A. Graziosi

Economic and Social Committee

List of abbreviations

ACP	African, Caribbean and Pacific countries party to the Lomé Convention
Asean	Association of South East Asian Nations
Badea	Arab Bank for Economic Development in Africa
Brite	Basic research in industrial technologies for Europe
CAD	Computer-aided design
Caddia	Cooperation in automation of data and documentation for imports/exports and agriculture
CCITT	Consultative Committee on Innovation and Technology Transfer
CCT	Common Customs Tariff
CGC	Management and Coordination Advisory Committee (Comité consultatif en matière de gestion et de coordination)
Codest	Committee for the European Development of Science and Technology
Comext	Data base of external trade statistics
COST	European Cooperation on Scientific and Technical Research
Crest	Scientific and Technical Research Committee
Cronos	Data base of macroeconomic time series
CSCE	Conference on Security and Cooperation in Europe
DAC	Development Assistance Committee (OECD)
EAGGF	European Agricultural Guidance and Guarantee Fund
ECE	Economic Commission for Europe (UN)
EDF	European Development Fund
EFTA	European Free Trade Association

EIB	European Investment Bank
EMS	European Monetary System
ERDF	European Regional Development Fund
Esprit	European strategic programme for research and development in information technology
Euronet-Diane	Direct information access network for Europe
EVCA	European Venture Capital Association
FADN	EEC Farm Accountancy Data Network
FAO	Food and Agriculture Organization of the United Nations
FAST	Forecasting and assessment in the field of science and technology
GATT	General Agreement on Tariffs and Trade (UN)
GSP	Generalized system of preferences
IAEA	International Atomic Energy Agency (UN)
IBRD	International Bank for Reconstruction and Development (World Bank) (UN)
IDA	International Development Association (UN)
IDB	Inter-American Development Bank
IEA	International Energy Agency (OECD)
IMF	International Monetary Fund (UN)
Insis	Community interinstitutional integrated services information system
Irdac	Industrial Research and Development Advisory Committee
JET	Joint European Torus
JRC	Joint Research Centre
MCA	Monetary compensatory amount
MFA	Multifibre Arrangement (Arrangement regarding International Trade in Textiles)
NCI	New Community Instrument
NEA	Nuclear Energy Agency (OECD)
NET	Next European Torus
NGO	Non-governmental organization

Nimexe	Nomenclature of goods for the external trade statistics of the Community and statistics of trade between Member States
OCTs	Overseas countries and territories
OECD	Organization for Economic Cooperation and Development
SADCC	Southern African Development Coordination Conference
Sedoc	European system for the international clearing of vacancies and applications for employment
SELA	Latin American Economic System (Sistema Económico Latinoamericano)
Siena	Système intérimaire d'exploitation de la Nimexe automatisé (a data base of external and intra-Community trade based on Nimexe)
Stabex	System for the stabilization of ACP and OCT export earnings
Sysmin	Special financing facility for ACP and OCT mining products
TAC	Total allowable catch
UN	United Nations
Unctad	United Nations Conference on Trade and Development
UNEP	United Nations Environment Programme
Unesco	United Nations Educational, Scientific and Cultural Organization
UNHCR	United Nations High Commissioner for Refugees
Unido	United Nations Industrial Development Organization
UNRWA	United Nations Relief and Works Agency for Palestine Refugees in the Near East
WFC	World Food Council (UN)

Publications cited in this Report

General Report on the Activities of the European Communities
   (abbr: General Report), published annually by the Commission

— *the Agricultural Situation in the Community*
   (Published in conjunction with the General Report
   (abbr: Agricultural Report), published annually

— *Report on Social Developments*
   (Published in conjunction with the General Report)
   (abbr: Social Report), published annually

— *Report on Competition Policy*
   (Published in conjunction with the General Report)
   (abbr: Competition Report), published annually)

Bulletin of the European Communities
   (abbr: Bull. EC), published monthly by the Commission

Supplement to the Bulletin of the European Communities
   (abbr: Supplement...—Bull. EC), published at irregular intervals by the Commission
4/78 Approval of persons responsible for auditing of company accounts. Proposal for an Eighth Directive

5/80 New trade-mark system for the Community

2/81 The European automobile industry—Commission statement

1/82 A new Community action programme on the promotion of equal opportunities for women, 1982-85

3/82 The institutional system of the Community—Restoring the balance

4/82 A Community policy on tourism

4/83 Adjustment of the common agricultural policy

1/84 Unfair terms in contracts concluded with consumers

Official Journal of the European Communities
   Legislation series (abbr: OJ L)
   Information and notices series (abbr: OJ C)

Reports of Cases before the Court
   (abbr: ECR), published by the Court of Justice in annual series, parts appearing at irregular intervals throughout the year

All the above publications are printed and distributed through the Office for Official Publications of the European Communities, L-2985 Luxembourg

Annual Report of the European Investment Bank
   published and distributed by the EIB,
   100, boulevard Konrad Adenauer L-2950 Luxembourg

European Communities—Commission

Eighteenth General Report on the Activities of the European Communities—1984

Luxembourg: Office for Official Publications of the European Communities

1985—372 pp., 9 figs.—16.2 × 22.9 cm

DA, DE, GR, EN, FR, IT, NL

ISBN 92-825-4858-9

Catalogue number: CB-41-84-814-EN-C

Price (excluding VAT) in Luxembourg:

ECU 5.56   BFR 250   IRL 4.10   UKL 3.40   USD 4.50

The General Report on the Activities of the European Communities is published annually by the Commission as required by Article 18 of the Treaty of 8 April 1965 establishing a Single Council and a Single Commission of the European Communities.

The Report is presented to the European Parliament and provides a general picture of Community activities over the past year.